THIERRY HENRY

Philippe Auclair has been *France Football*'s and RMC Radio's UK correspondent for over a decade, and is a prolific freelance journalist on both sides of the Channel. In 2009 he wrote the critically acclaimed and prize-winning *Cantona: The Rebel Who Would Be King*. He is also a regular contributor to *The Blizzard* and *Champions* magazine, and a bestselling author in his native France. He lives in London.

By the same author

Cantona: The Rebel Who Would Be King

PHILIPPE AUCLAIR

THIERRY HENRY

LONELY AT THE TOP: A BIOGRAPHY

MACMILLAN

First published 2012 by Macmillan,
an imprint of Pan Macmillan, a division of Macmillan Publishers Limited
Pan Macmillan, 20 New Wharf Road, London N1 9RR
Basingstoke and Oxford
Associated companies throughout the world
www.panmacmillan.com

ISBN 978-0-230-74839-2 HB
ISBN 978-0-230-75799-8 TPB

Picture credits: Pages 1, 227 and 245 © Getty Images;
11, 29, 47, 73, 121, 161, 185 and 263 © Offside Sports Photography Ltd;
83 © Popperfoto/Getty Images; 139, 205, 281 and 331 © AFP/Getty Images;
295, © Guibbaud Christophe/ABACA/Press Association Images.

9 8 7 6 5 4 3 2

A CIP catalogue record for this book is available from
the British Library.

Typeset by Ellipsis Digital Limited, Glasgow
Printed and bound by CPI Group (UK) Ltd, Croydon CR0 4YY

Visit **www.panmacmillan.com** to read more about all our books
and to buy them. You will also find features, author interviews and
news of any author events, and you can sign up for e-newsletters
so that you're always first to hear about our new releases.

To Stewart, Nick and Amy

Contents

I've been around the world
Had my pick of any girl
You'd think I'd be happy
But I'm not
Ev'rybody knows my name
But it's just a crazy game
Oh, it's lonely at the top

(Randy Newman, 'Lonely at the Top', 1970, 1975)

'When you look at his record, the greatest striker ever. The Michael Jordan of football. He took the ball in the middle of the park, passed everybody and scored a goal when he wanted. The biggest talent ever, maybe, in football. He had everything you dream to have in a football player. Highly intelligent, analyses very quickly, great pace, great power, great jump. He only used 50 per cent of his jumping power. He could have been a tremendous header of the ball. He didn't fancy it too much. Still, he managed to be the best goalscorer ever [for Arsenal]. In the modern game, what he did is just . . . amazing.'

(Arsène Wenger, 2007)

Preface

It was late in the summer of 2005. I was waiting for George Best, somewhat anxiously, in the office of his agent, Phil Hughes, just off the North End Road, a short walk away from the pubs where the 1968 European Footballer of the Year had spent the best part of the last twenty years downing pints of neat vodka and umpteen bottles of Pinot Grigio. Best was to be a guest of honour at my magazine *France Football*'s forthcoming celebration of the *Ballon d'Or*'s fiftieth anniversary. His own trophy had long been sold to a collector, and the cash raised by the sale frittered away on booze, birds and failed business ventures. My task was not to prise anecdotes from him, tragi-comic stories which hundreds of others had already been told and which were at some points in his life the only things he could sell to survive. On 2 December, I was to accompany the footballer whose photograph had been pinned above my boarding-school bed to Paris, where a replica of the golden ball would be presented to him in the presence of most of its other recipients. I had been granted the privilege of arranging the details of that trip.

The man who finally stepped out of the taxi (late, naturally) looked frail but still exuded the charm that had seduced so many, men and women alike. He was also chatty, witty, engaging in a way that came as a wonderful surprise to someone accustomed to the aloofness of today's 'star' footballers. There was no way one could have known that the interview he granted me – for free – would be his very last. You may have seen some of the pictures we took that day: Best, unshaven, his greying hair unkempt, clad in a black leather jacket, his back resting against a rust-coloured brick wall. They're not easily forgotten.

A couple of weeks later, Best's exhausted body finally broke down, and a heart-rending death vigil began in front of of the Cromwell Hospital. George would never make it to Paris. The replica of his *Ballon d'Or* was passed on to Manchester United FC instead, where it is now exhibited in the club's museum. The engraved invitation I was to pass on to him lies unread in a sealed envelope, a mournful memento of the most poignant afternoon in my career as a journalist.

Thierry Henry's life followed a course that is so markedly different from George Best's that you might wonder why I choose to begin a book about Henry there, on that afternoon in West London. I do so because of what Best said as we were about to part: 'I don't recognize myself in the players I see today,' he told me (I'm quoting from memory, as my tape-machine had been switched off already). 'There's only one who excites me, and that is Thierry Henry. He's not just a great footballer, he's a showman, an entertainer.'

These words have come back to me time and again over the past couple of years. It should have been easy to write about a footballer whom I had seen and spoken to regularly throughout his stay at Arsenal – the club I've supported since 1979 – a footballer who had contributed so much to the Gunners and to my national team. But I found that the more I learnt about Henry, the more I talked to people who had known him far better than I had, the less I felt drawn to him in the way I had been drawn to George Best – or Liam Brady. My awe at the scale of Henry's accomplishments hadn't waned, but I soon realized that I was falling out of love with the prodigious striker who had made me forget all press-box etiquette and leap out of my seat, screaming, when he scored *that* goal against Real Madrid at the Bernabéu in 2006. What was happening was the exact opposite of what I had experienced whilst researching my biography of Éric Cantona, when I had fallen under the spell of a player whose outbursts of violence and pompous pronouncements had often repelled me previously. It had been clear then that, despite his sulphurous reputation, which he had done everything in his power to cultivate, Cantona was ultimately a man who had been truly loved, and had been – in his own bizarre, paradoxical and sometimes unjustifiable way – worthy of being loved that much.

That much was clear: writing this book would be a much more

arduous task than recounting Éric's life and career had been. In that case, I had started from the assumption (a modus operandi, if not an absolute truth) that a biographer should assume the role of an explorer whose duty was to question the maps that have been drawn before him. These maps – profiles, interviews, essays, earlier biographies – presented a tormented, even chaotic, landscape in Cantona's case, full of accidental breaks and faultlines placed there almost at random. It certainly made for an interesting journey.

But Thierry? If you'll forgive the image, whilst previous accounts of Éric's life could be compared to a messy (but tasty) *millefeuille* of contradictory opinions, there was very little to bite into as far as Henry was concerned, even if his collated interviews ran to thousands of pages. Only one account of his career has been published so far, in 2005: Oliver Derbyshire's optimistically subtitled *Thierry Henry: The Amazing Life of the Greatest Footballer on Earth*. In an age when footballers who've yet to reach their twenty-first birthday put their names to ghosted autobiographies, this absence of books about Henry struck me as very odd indeed – and revelatory, too, of his puzzling image and status within the game. If he were indeed 'the greatest footballer on earth', why had no one bothered to scratch the veneer of the glossy picture he had presented to us for so long? And why were men who had routinely been described as his 'friends' proving so reluctant to praise him unequivocally when I spoke to them? Why was there always an element of reserve in their appreciation?

I had fond memories of the man myself, but the further I delved into his past, the more these memories appeared to lose their relevance. It's not that I dug up previously unknown scandals in his quasi-perfect ascent to the top of his profession. Up to the infamous 'Hand of Gaul' incident that might well, in the longer term, define him in the collective psyche – far more than the titles and honours he's coveted and collected so assiduously – Henry's career had been almost devoid of public controversy. I wrote the following piece shortly before France faced Ireland in Paris to decide which of these two teams would play in the 2010 World Cup:

Footballers often live on in the game's folk history through the iconisation of a single moment in their careers, regardless of how much or how little that moment captures of their individual brilliance. Marco Tardelli is better remembered for his celebration of Italy's second goal in the 1982 World Cup final than for the goal itself. Éric Cantona will forever launch himself in the crowd at Selhurst Park, and Ferenc Puskas juggle the ball like a cheeky schoolboy in the centre circle of Wembley, whilst Diego Maradona punches the ball past Peter Shilton ad infinitum, his mesmerising run through the English defence – almost – reduced to a sideshow in that particular melodrama. Charlie George still lies on his back on the Highbury pitch. Pelé has already offered the ball to Carlos Alberto and strolls on, casting a casual glance to his right: the slowness of his pace tells us more about his art, and his mastery of it, than any of the 1,281 goals he scored himself.

Of Thierry Henry, however, there is no such image. He may have been called 'the greatest striker in the world' by his mentor Arsène Wenger, beaten all manner of records – and records which carry genuine significance – collected every single major trophy that domestic and international football has to offer, ravished huge crowds with a game that is simultaneously spectacular, explosive and graceful – but the truth is that the 'icon' of Arsenal FC and 'legend' of Les Bleus has yet to provide one of these 'moments' which, for some obscure but compelling reason, elevate a great player beyond simply how 'good' he was.

Like many devotees of Arsenal, I was surprised that the club's fans had voted Henry their 'greatest of all time'. My vote would have gone to Dennis Bergkamp, who had the unique gift of slowing down time on the field of play, and, one night at St James' Park, fashioned a goal of such bewildering beauty that, no matter how often you saw it, it lost none of its miraculous quality – just like the closing stanza of Larkin's 'Whitsun Weddings' never fails to hit its target, whether it is the first time you read it, or the hundredth. Even Thierry's astonishing pick-up, pivot and volley against Manchester United appeared locked in the two dimensions of TV replays, when lesser footballers had taken us beyond these bounds.

Then Thierry used his left hand, twice. His moment had finally arrived.[*]
And I had to start this foreword all over again.

---

[*] It cannot be a coincidence that the only book devoted to Henry in France is *La Main noire de Thierry H.*, the work of a hitherto unknown French novelist, Hervé Colin, who published it in early 2011.

It was a moment of injustice: injustice towards a fine, superbly organized and combative Irish side for whom qualification would have been a fair reward, but injustice, too, towards a magnificent player whose previous on-field behaviour had been almost blameless, and who was vilified to such an extravagant degree that he found himself turned into a figure of hate, even in his own country, for a 'crime' he had the courage to confess almost immediately after he had committed it. I devote a whole chapter to this 'defining moment' in Thierry's career and, anyway, this is not the place to dwell upon it. I'll just say that on that evening I had been invited to take part in a discussion of the 'scandal' on a popular radio programme, and that I was surprised by how difficult I found it to control my anger. It had been the most shameful night in the history of French football, I said. Not you, Thierry, please, not you. The next morning, Henry Winter opened his *Daily Telegraph* column using almost exactly the same words. 'Say it ain't so, Joe.' But it was.

I then realized that there was no contradiction between these events and what I had written before they happened. My own reluctance to elevate Henry to a status comparable to that of Bergkamp told its own story: Thierry was not an easy footballer to feel genuine affection for, regardless of how much you admired, even revered him. He was not an artist in Éric Cantona's mould. He had shown touches of genius, but seemed impervious to the inner torment that defined his countryman, for better or for worse. There was something unremittingly *efficient* about his prowess. He was a record-breaker who felt a genuine passion for his craft, and an admirable ambition to write (or rather, kick) him-self into the history books. A Roger Federer rather than an Ilie Nastase, a Don Bradman rather than an Archie Jackson, except that the summits which Federer and Bradman ascended ultimately receded before him: Thierry never truly reached the horizon, which, for us spectators, is the same thing as going beyond it. He never scored in a World Cup, a Champions League, a Euro or even an FA Cup final. He still won all these trophies, but he didn't seem to 'own' them, somehow.

There was his demeanour, too, which he himself has called 'arro-gance', familiar to anyone who's ever heard NBA stars being interviewed, or who has engaged in conversation with the children of the French *banlieues*, where what would be construed as rudeness in more polite circles is first and foremost a mechanism of self-protection, a telling sign of apprehension. Then the pendulum would swing the other way: I would feel compelled to talk about another Thierry, whom Robert Pirès described with one word, *adorable*, and whom I had seen on more than one occasion. Others would use different adjectives. Among those I heard were *manipulative, machiavellian, selfish, calculating*, and I would think: hold on – what allows you to speak of him with such hostility? One of my overriding memories of that 'selfish' man was Thierry coming out of the players' tunnel, long after the final whistle, when there were only a couple of rain-sodden journalists left by the touchline at Highbury, cursing under their breath, 'The bastards have all gone.' The superstar emerged and apologized for having kept us waiting. 'Sorry, guys,' he said, 'you must be freezing, what bloody awful weather.' (Wrong – no 'bloody' – I never heard Thierry curse, not once.) Then *Titi* spoke, at length, eloquently, as always when it was football we talked about – no footballer loves football more deeply than he does, none that I've come across anyway. We had our story after all. We all loved Thierry then.

I am not a friend of his, however, and could never have become one. I was always taken aback by his reluctance to open up and show a modicum of trust to outsiders; he could give it, I am sure of that, but to earn that confidence, you had – as a journalist – to accept his word as final and repay it with an almost slavish kind of loyalty that I couldn't accept. Whereas a Cantona often struck privileged relationships with people who had stood up to him, it was obvious that this was not the way to Thierry's heart. He craved assent and praise as no other footballer I have come across did. A few sycophants placed themselves in his trail, but they ultimately found themselves meandering behind, as there was no harsher critic of Henry – as a player – than Henry himself. No fool he.

I had already written over 120,000 words of this book when I finally accepted that I would be unable to complete it in the form I had initially chosen. This form – a chronological account, augmented by ancillary essays – had served me well when Cantona had been my subject, but I soon felt that I was drowning in a flood of minutiae and losing track of my original purpose – losing track of Henry himself. The devil is in the detail, certainly; but only if that detail has a synecdochic quality. Otherwise, one finds oneself as disorientated as Orson Welles's character in the last reel of *The Lady from Shanghai*, when he's looking for Rita Hayworth in a gallery of mirrors. The denouement can only occur when a bullet shatters the glass.

To carry on with this simile: a biographer holds a mirror to his subject, not necessarily the most flattering one. Through trial and error, he'll adjust the light, in the knowledge that what will eventually show will belong to the realm of verisimilitude rather than truth. But what else can we aspire to? In the case of Éric Cantona, this mirror was regularly smashed to smithereens, as grappling with such a tempestuous personality was sometimes akin to holding water in a sieve. I had to pick up the pieces of that mirror and reassemble them as best I could. But the more fragmented the image, the more complete it looked to me. Thierry Henry posed a different problem. That word, 'posed', actually gives that particular game away, as, almost all the way throughout writing this account of his life, I felt as if I were dealing with a series of 'poses': Thierry's public persona was as smooth as the surface of the mirror I endeavoured to present to him. No matter how many pebbles I threw in that placid pool, the ripples soon faded away. A sign that he belonged to another age, perhaps, when every hint of rugosity in a footballer's character had to be carefully planed to a glass-like shell by the hands of paranoid media consultants, press officers and image-makers anxious to protect a precious commodity. Cantona, a master at milking the public's perception of, and fascination with, his extravagances, never truly lost his essential humanity, even when he exploited it for personal gain. Henry, as loquacious and knowledgeable an interlocutor as you could wish for among modern-day footballers, hardly engaged the heart in a similar fashion.

To start with, there were no 'stories' to tell, not of the kind that lead you to warm to their main protagonist, when he's seen laughing at his own failings. Henry's career path was remarkably linear from a very young age, especially for a young man driven by what he called his 'anger', and could be compared to that of a very bright student whose natural position is at the very top of every class he's in, enters

Oxbridge and continues his progress almost unchecked. He has often been referred to as 'a graduate from the Clairefontaine academy', and, for once, the word 'graduate' seemed apt when applied to a footballer. Talent, personal dedication and superb schooling played their part in his progress – but luck? None, unless you call luck the happy coincidence that Thierry emerged precisely at the moment when France's youth programme was taking wing. From then on: Monaco, the prelude; Juventus, the mistimed rehearsal; Arsenal, the symphony; Barcelona, the soap opera; and finally New York, the coda in search of a forgotten tune – the tune I have tried to transcribe, whose first notes were written by a man other than himself: his father.

1

'I wouldn't have wanted to grow up anywhere else.'
Back at Les Ulis, 1996.

IN THE NAME OF THE FATHER

*'Who do I owe, and for what? I don't think about the word "owe".
I owe something to my dad, yes, who put me on this planet.'*
(Thierry Henry, April 2006)

The name of Robert Camelot is all but forgotten today, a
footnote in the history of twentieth-century modernist architecture.
Like so many young men of his generation, he wished to build a better
world over the ruins left by the First World War. His country had to
turn its back on that awful butchery, and in order to do that, the mud
would be covered in concrete. Driven by the noblest of motives, supported by authorities trying to keep up with the pace of industrialization,
Camelot (irony can be found everywhere, even in a family name) set
out to turn the featureless expanses that surrounded major French cities
into high-density 'urban projects' – the vast high-rise developments that,
today, house millions of Frenchmen whose lives are lived away from the
gaze of most of their countrymen, unless trouble flares up, as it regularly
does: the *banlieues*.

Les Ulis, where Thierry Henry was born and grew up, was one of
those grotesque creations, one of Camelot's last. At the time the first
tower blocks were erected in the Vale of Chevreuse, in the early 1960s,
France was experiencing an unprecedented economic boom, and it was
hoped that this hitherto ignored suburb of southern Paris, so unimpor-
tant that it didn't even have its own train station (it still hasn't), would
become a hub for two of the country's most successful and symbolically
charged industries: IT and nuclear power. Companies like Hewlett-

Packard moved into a purpose-built 'technology centre'; the Nuclear Energy Commission had preceded them by ten years, choosing the nearby town of Saclay as its headquarters; but as the first residents of Les Ulis took possession of their new homes – in May 1968 of all times, when France was convulsed by a social upheaval that was aimed precisely at the 'values' that had driven Camelot's paymasters – a number of the just-finished flats were still without running water. Les Ulis didn't even have a town council: the local authority was established in the year of Thierry's birth, 1977, as was the football club he would register with as a six-year-old, CO Les Ulis. The white-collar, middle-class workers the planners had tried to attract were quick to realize that they had been sold a pipe dream; as soon as they woke up, and it was very soon, they moved out to more genteel environments, leaving behind them empty tower blocks. Less-fortunate occupiers were sucked into this vacuum. In a matter of years, Les Ulis turned from social utopia to a *zone sensible,* literally 'sensitive zone', a euphemism that should fool no one. In 2010, 40 per cent of its population paid no income tax whatsoever: they were no richer when Thierry's life began.

The population of Les Ulis was young, very young. Thierry's parents, Tony and Maryse, were in their early twenties when they settled there and, like many of their new neighbours, they hadn't been born in *la métropole.* They were French citizens, certainly, but, because of the colour of their skin, were also indistinguishable from the 'guest workers' who had been called in their millions from the former colonies of northern and western Africa to work in factories and construction sites, thousands of whom had settled in Les Ulis. Tony hailed from La Désirade, a tiny island off the eastern coast of Guadeloupe, whose inhabitants have a reputation for fierceness of temper and independence of mind; Maryse, who already had a son from a previous relationship, Willy,* was born in Martinique, a gentler environment, where the descendants of slaves and their owners, whilst not making peace, had come to live in greater

---

* Thierry and Willy have always referred to each other as 'brothers', not 'half-brothers'. A third brother, Dimitry (whose existence many acquaintances of Thierry's seem to be unaware of), was born much later; the age difference explains why he is a quasi-invisible character in his elder's story.

harmony. Tony would later insist on how much playing a World Cup in South Africa meant to his son, whom he called 'an African'. This was a *Guadeloupéen* speaking. Thierry, however, used subtly different words on one of the few occasions when he spoke publicly of his West Indian roots: 'A man looks to find himself, and when I was trying to form myself, despite being born in Les Ulis, I didn't forget that my parents came from Martinique and Guadeloupe. I knew the music, the culture, the food; my parents spoke to me in Creole. One always looks for one's roots, and when I travel there I find peace. When I go [there] I feel naked. Nobody looks at me. When we won the World Cup with France I went to Guadeloupe. There were celebrations, but the look on people's faces is different. It's normal. The day I arrived there was a meal, we played the bongos, everyone came to my house to sing – but the next day it was all over. [There] I go out barefoot in shorts, on a Vespa. It's paradise.'

A paradise that has become more remote for Thierry as the years have gone by, however. He hasn't visited his father's island (where he still has numerous relatives*) since 2005, three years before he confided the above, something for which he has expressed regret – and which, according to a friend of Tony's who is also one of mine, has much to do with the loosening of the relationship between Thierry and the man who has been his constant advocate and harshest critic for so many years. The son hasn't forgotten the debt he owes the father, and still supports him: Tony lives rent-free in a comfortable flat that his son purchased in Pointe-à-Pitre and, at least until recently, received frequent invitations to watch his son play for *Les Bleus*, Arsenal and Barcelona. But a point came in Thierry's career when he had to shake off the influence of his well-meaning, devoted, but also overbearing father. I'll come back to that pivotal decision, taken when he left Monaco for Juventus in 1999. All that needs to be said at this point is that it must have caused Thierry a great deal of pain and exacerbated the feeling of loneliness that had been a longstanding companion of his since

---

* It is to these relatives that the message he unveiled – 'For the West Indies' – after scoring in Arsenal's 3-1 win over Manchester United on 25 November 2001 was addressed.

childhood, and especially since the age of eleven, when his half-brother Willy was called up to do his military service, and he found himself 'an only child', with his mother Maryse for sole company.

But Tony and Maryse were still together when the young family moved to a new two-bedroom flat in 1977, a few months before Thierry was born on 17 August. Its windows overlooked the Avenue de Saintonge, near the western border of the city, a short walk away from the two football pitches of the Jean-Marc Salinier Stadium. They would stay there until Tony and Maryse separated in 1985. The name chosen by urban planners for Thierry's *quartier* was misleading, to say the least, almost cruel in its delusionary overtones: 'Les Bosquets' means 'the copses'. Trees were and are scarce in the area – a few mournful specimens dotted in a ring of concrete, when I was last there. The architects had dreamt of a city where cars would only be used to drive to the workplace or the local Carrefour hypermarket. In order to fulfil that dream, they linked the housing estates by a network of pedestrian bridges and underground passages which almost immediately turned into a haven for skateboard fanatics, graffiti artists and small-time drug dealers – and a no-go zone for the rest of the population.

Les Ulis wasn't quite the 'urban hell' later described by some profile-writers, however. 'Growing up, it didn't feel poor at the time,' Thierry recalled in 2007. 'It was all I knew.' 'Complicated, but not a slum' was another of his descriptions for the suburb he grew up in; he said on numerous occasions that, 'should [he] be given the choice, [he would] wish to grow up in the *cité* again'. It's worth noting that, more often than not, his home town was spared the eruptions of violence that have sporadically shaken the Parisian *banlieues* and encircled the capital with a necklace of burning cars for the last three decades at least. For one thing, the colour of one's skin didn't matter. 'In Les Ulis, everyone came from everywhere,' Thierry explained. 'France, Spain, Africa – so I didn't notice any racism.' It's only when he 'started to move out of [my] neighbourhood that I noticed that people would give me funny looks, like "What are you doing here?"'; but these were isolated incidents, which mostly occurred when he played with French youth teams in 'the middle of nowhere', as he put it, in small provincial towns where darker faces were hardly ever seen. By his own account, it is only in April 2001, when he heard the awful monkey grunts which greeted him and his black Arsenal teammates at Valencia's Mestalla Stadium (an experience which he relived two years later, in the same arena) that Thierry became truly aware of how the racist disease had infected large swathes of the football world. He had 'to do something' – and he did, in a very Henry-esque way.

In December 2004, Thierry called on the support of his sponsor Nike to launch the *Stand Up, Speak Up* campaign, which proved spectacularly successful with the public, at least in terms of the number of black-and-white interlocked wristbands sold. Six million of these bracelets quickly found a buyer, generating a £6 million profit that was channelled to the Belgian Roi Baudouin charitable fund, then split between 238 projects over the next three years. Two months later, Sepp Blatter – wearing one of the wristbands for the first and last time in his never-ending presidency – announced that Henry had been appointed a 'FIFA fair-play ambassador for the fight against racism'. Then, in 2007, Thierry teamed up with couturier Tommy Hilfiger to start the One 4 All foundation (his Arsenal number, fourteen, trans-lated by merchandisers), 'designing' and modelling a collection of preppy garments to raise cash for a variety of football-related projects. It is easy, and sometimes proper, to be cynical about operations of this kind, and at least one of Henry's fellow footballers – Manchester United's right-back Gary Neville – voiced concerns about Nike's involvement in the *Stand Up, Speak Up* campaign, which he feared 'cheapened' the project, as the sportswear giant was, in his eyes, pri-marily using it as a promotional tool. What cannot be doubted is that Thierry himself genuinely believed they could make a difference. It would be easy to see this as an example of modern celebrity hubris – Bono saving the world, Gwyneth Paltrow converting the planet to natural childbirth and vegetarianism – and forget how awful it must have been for a black Frenchman to hear the abuse spat out by foot-ball crowds, especially when this kind of behaviour was almost unheard of in his native country. Thierry later recounted how shocked he had been when one of his primary school teachers brought an English

book into the classroom, the cover of which featured a famous photograph of John Barnes kicking away a banana that had been thrown
at him from the stands. 'I didn't know that sport could tolerate such
things,' he said, 'and that a great player like Barnes could be treated
like that. It is at that moment that I became aware of the problem.'
Maybe that is also one of the reasons why Thierry could call the bleak
tower blocks of Les Ulis a 'paradise' without irony: at least one very
modern evil was kept at the gates of that *cité*.

He often reminded journalists that, contrary to legend, he 'had the
chance to have a good education, good parents and some good facilities
around me, somewhere where you could play football and basketball'.
Especially football, which Thierry and his friends, many of whom had
first got to know his half-brother Willy and were older than he was,
played not on one of the council's fields, but on whichever improvised
surface could pass as a pitch. A bedroom would do, that of his cousin
Gérard Grandadam for example, the child of Maryse's sister. Two-a-side,
shoes off, Gérard (eight years Henry's elder) and his brother Daniel in
one 'team', Willy and Thierry in the other. The aim was to kick a tennis
ball at the space between a window and the bedroom door, closed of
course, so that Gérard's mother, who was also Titi's godmother, couldn't
hear them play. At other times they would head for the city's outdoor
handball court, where as many knees were grazed on the tarmac as goals
were scored. 'Thierry was already playing up front,' Grandadam recalled,
'and our opponents, from the *quartier des Amonts*, weren't soft with
him.' This said, they always lost, with Thierry inevitably being their
main tormentor.

Other games would see the children assemble on a concrete esplanade bordered by four incongruous fir trees, very close to the Henrys'
flat. There, teams of up to fifteen players would assemble after school
hours, challenging each other to *parties-pizzas*, thus named because
the losers were expected to treat the opposing side to a cheap feast at
the local Italian restaurant. No jumpers for goalposts – more often
than not a couple of supermarket trolleys which had been dumped
on the pavement. And there, standing or, rather, jumping up and

down, shouting and gesticulating, was the ever-present Tony, a man who, according to our mutual West Indian friend, 'knew everyone in the *cité*', especially those good-for-nothings that Willy and, especially, Thierry should avoid.

Many years later, in a suite of the Landmark Hotel, one of his favourite London haunts, Tony's now-famous son told me and some of my *France Football* colleagues how, taking his newborn in his arms, Tony had announced that 'one day, Thierry [would] play for France'. I've never forgotten the expression of incredulity in Thierry's eyes when he told us this tale of family folklore. Tony would often repeat this prophecy throughout Titi's progress from street footballer to Clairefontaine scholar, much to the annoyance of those around him, including, once, a police motorcyclist who stopped him for speeding, and to whom he exclaimed: 'Don't you know who I am? I am Thierry Henry's father!' Thierry was thirteen at the time.

Stories like these are legion. One of Henry's first coaches told me: 'Once, at the Parc des Princes, when Thierry was still very young, Tony addressed somebody to say: "You see that kid next to me [*his son*]? Remember his name. One day, he'll be a pro, and he'll play for France." You had to have some nerve to say that in the middle of a crowd at the Parc!' But the belief Tony had in his son's destiny as an international footballer was absolute, as everyone I've talked to has testified, whether they approved of his obsessiveness or not. Unless one is willing to accept that Tony had powers of second sight, it showed a fierce determination to shape his son's life according to his own plans. It was all about foot-ball – playing it, and watching it. One of Thierry's earliest memories is of his father's joy when Marius Trésor scored the second goal for *Les Bleus* in their heart-stopping World Cup semi-final against West Ger-many on 8 July 1982 in Seville – when Thierry had yet to reach his fifth birthday. Trésor, whom Tony idolized and called '*le monument*', was born in Guadeloupe, of course. Unsurprisingly, it was Trésor's team, Bordeaux, for which Thierry felt the keenest attraction even if, later, after Tony and Maryse had separated, father and son would go to PSG's Parc des Princes or to Colombes. Colombes, formerly France's unofficial national stadium, was now home to the newly founded Racing Paris

Matra, which was attempting to redraw the power map of French foot-ball with imported stars such as the German winger Pierre Littbarski and the Uruguayan 'magician' Enzo Francescoli, who also happened to be the childhood hero of one Zinedine Zidane. At the summit of Thierry's own Olympus was another player, however: Milan's supreme striker Marco van Basten, whose style the ten-year-old Henry strove to replicate – with some success – and whose shirt number, twelve, he adopted when he became a French international. As Tony recalled: 'the way he hit the ball was based [on van Basten's method]. Today, he does it exactly as he did it when he was a boy.' Speaking of shirt numbers, a quick aside: it is not to celebrate another Dutchman (Johan Cruyff, of course) that Thierry picked fourteen at Arsenal. The truth is far more prosaic. 'I was in the locker-room, and they gave it to me. It went well, so I kept it.'

To turn Titi (a nickname his father gave Thierry when he was still a toddler) into Thierry Henry was the mission Tony assigned himself from the very beginning, and not even his divorce from Maryse could change that. Woe betide anyone who might doubt him or set obstacles, real or imagined, in his way; at which point it must be stressed than this one-man crusade was ultimately proven a success. Tony might not have been able to predict the future, but he undoubtedly did everything in his power to make sure it would be as close to what he had hoped as possible.

Titi's father had been a decent footballer himself, playing – in defence – with the seniors of Les Ulis and Marcoussis, and once harboured the dream of turning professional himself, a dream he quickly projected on to his son with all the considerable strength of his own thwarted ambi-tions. It has also been said that one of Thierry's uncles had been a French champion hurdler at 400 metres, though I haven't managed to find any tangible record of this. Thierry, however, showed no sign of such ath-leticism in his early youth. He was blessed with natural speed, but his health was precarious. 'He was very fragile,' Tony recalled in 1998. 'He was born with "duck feet". He kept getting very bad colds and, because of that, had to avoid sweating too much when he played football.' Thierry's condition was so severe that he had to pay regular visits to the

Saint-Vincent-de-Paul hospital to undergo tests that made his father sick with worry, to the point that he stopped attending these appointments with his son. Willy took over, Willy, the guardian angel of these first years, who was instructed to keep a watchful eye over the younger Thierry. 'I always had a towel with me,' he said, 'to wipe away the sweat, so that our parents wouldn't know he had played.'

If Tony is to be believed, the frail child was eventually cured of his condition on one of his regular visits to the West Indies, where holidays were spent alternatively in La Désirade or Fort-de-France. There, his father recalled, Thierry was nursed with 'a kind of tea that his grandmother made with a herb called *mallomé,* which gives out a special milk when you cut it'. The effect was instantaneous: 'since then, he's never caught a cold'. Maybe he had learnt to be a bit more careful as well. Jean-Claude Giordanella, one of Henry's first coaches, remembers the coughing fits of the slightly built boy he looked after at CO Les Ulis (of which he is now the vice-chairman), but offers a different explanation. 'Thierry wasn't an outstanding athlete,' he told me. 'He was very quick – because he weighed nothing! – but, physically, he wasn't that strong. A shoulder charge, he was down. It's true that he kept getting colds, but it was partly down to him. He wouldn't shower after the games, he didn't get changed, he sweated, he got caught in a draught or in the rain, *et voilà!*'

Fortunately, Willy was there, Willy 'who dressed Titi from head to toe, put his boots on, laced them up, and took his brother home after every game', as Giordanella recalls it. Poor Willy, guardian angel and scapegoat. 'We had to be careful,' he said. 'Once, I was chatting with a girlfriend on the esplanade, and Thierry had gone off to play. My father came down and asked: "Where is the little darling?" He wasn't there any more, and I was given a right dressing-down. I had no problem finding Titi – he was on another football pitch.' Tony was appalled by the behaviour of some of the youths who drifted around the estates, many of whom paid regular visits to the police station and, later, jail. Protectiveness drove him as much as vicarious ambition. He wanted to make sure that neither Willy nor Thierry could be led down the self-destructive path that was so easy to follow in Les Ulis. Let's be clear: he was not one of these abusive parents that you come across far too often in the world of sport,* but he didn't always stop at a verbal reprimand, and Willy was almost always the target. 'I took the hits,' he said without bitterness; which doesn't mean that Thierry himself escaped the paternal wrath. On one occasion, feeling rather pleased with himself after scoring six goals, he had to endure a tirade about the crosses and the chances he had missed; much later, however, he could say: 'I am who I am thanks to my father. I saw very hard things in my childhood but, fortunately, I had parents that were very straight. I couldn't understand why my friends could go out at night. I could see them from the window. It frustrated me. While they were having fun outside I was asking my mother why I couldn't go out. It hurt a lot. Almost all of my friends from that time are now in prison. It wasn't easy to get out of that life. If you're a father you have to be hard in a suburb like that.'

As Willy puts it: 'My dad pushed him. [Thierry] had no choice: he had to succeed. He told me: "I've had enough, dad gives me a bollocking even when I've been good."' The young Thierry genuinely wanted to please his father, however, even if football was not uppermost in his mind to begin with. 'I started playing thanks to my dad,' he recalled much later. 'Every child wants to do something for their father . . . I was only trying to make him happy. He took me to the ground, and I could see that when I played he was more happy than me.' Because Thierry *was* good, almost too good for his half-brother's taste, not that this 'half' ever mattered to either of them. 'He never wanted to play in my team [*Willy played in goal*], as I kept having a go at him: he never let go of the ball.'

It says a lot about Willy's affable character that, when he could have felt envy and rancour towards his sibling, he fully accepted his supporting role in Thierry's upbringing and ascent. The bond between the two youngsters strengthened into unshakeable trust. 'With him,' Thierry confided to *Onze* magazine in 1997, 'it goes beyond sport. I love to be with him, because we rarely speak about football – ten minutes about

---

* One of these, the father of a well-known French footballer, forced his son to run all the way from the stadium to his home when he'd failed to score, driving at a snail's pace behind the boy, lights flashing, honking his horn, shouting insults through the car's window.

the game when I come home, then it's over. We talk about the stupid things we did when we were kids. With my dad, he can't help it, we always come back to football.' Once he had become an outstanding footballer, Thierry relied on Willy to serve as a conduit between himself and a world from which he grew increasingly remote, whilst wishing to exert ever more control on how it interracted with him. To gain access to Titi, who changed his mobile phone number with maddening frequency, one called the jovial, gregarious Willy, who would pass on the message. Friends, journalists, former teammates would ring the elder 'brother' to ask for tickets, jerseys or an interview. They still do.

Willy, however, wasn't and is not an 'adviser' in the mould of Nicolas Anelka's notorious brothers Claude and Didier. Thierry rewarded him for his help, made sure his brother was all right, but Willy, despite Thierry's generosity, never sought personal benefit. He still drives trains on the Paris Métro ('Nothing to do with football,' he said, 'except that we sometimes take passengers to [the Stade de France in] Saint-Denis'). Willy didn't have to ask: the two brothers shared, as they always had.

Their son was only eight years old when Tony and Maryse separated and seems to have taken this upheaval in his stride; in fact, when he later referred to his parents' divorce, it was to insist that it didn't have as great an emotional impact on him as outsiders might have thought, and there is no reason to believe he said this to hide a deeper scar. Those who knew the couple were not surprised by the break-up of the relationship. One of their friends described Tony and Maryse to me as 'chalk and cheese', adding that the biggest surprise had been that they had been together at all, such was the contrast between their personalities. Parental duties were divided with a minimum of fuss, in a way that suited everyone. Tony went off on his own, to turn up whenever and wherever there was football to be played, no one being quite sure of what he was up to between his appearances on the touchline; Maryse later moved to the nearby city of Orsay, where her employers – the local university, for whom she worked as a receptionist – had provided her with a flat on the campus. There she looked after her son from day to day, instilling in him a sense of discipline and a respect for 'good manners' that would serve Thierry well in the years to come. Those who've known Maryse invariably describe her as 'discreet', 'softly spoken' and even 'shy', but she must also have been a woman of great strength of character to raise her two sons as she did, providing them with a simple but comfortable enough existence in an unforgiving environment. Hers was a home run on strict rules: Thierry couldn't pin posters of his favourite footballers above his bed, as it would have damaged Maryse's wallpaper; at the age of eighteen, Willy still had to abide by her rigidly enforced curfew (no coming home after midnight, even on a Saturday night). If Tony was the spur that drove Thierry throughout the first decade of his footballing life, Maryse was the rock on which he could count at all times, the one person who did more than anyone else to shape his attitude towards the outside world: distant, sometimes, if not withdrawn, but also unfailingly polite and respectful in his dealings with strangers. As for football? That was Tony's remit, and Tony's alone.

The young Maradona was filmed juggling a ball in the centre circle of the Boca Juniors pitch; but there are no images of Thierry Henry wowing a crowd at the Parc des Princes at the same tender age, only a few amateur VHS tapes showing him celebrating a goal in front of a smattering of spectators. He was much better than any of his teammates (and opponents) – anyone could see that, even if the players around him were more strongly built and older than he was. By 1989, approaching his twelfth birthday, Thierry had spent six years at CO Les Ulis under the aegis of Claude Chezelle, who, whilst he recognized the exceptional ability of the youngster, wasn't entirely convinced that he had all the qualities required to fulfil Tony's ambitious plans. 'Lots of [players] at that age are really good,' he recalled in 2006, 'but many give up along the way. In Thierry's case, his father was there to guide him; he came with him to every single match at the club. Tony was someone who liked things done properly, he never let him slack off.' Tony felt the minuscule *banlieusard* club was holding back his son back, and that he would have to move on to a bigger team if he were to exploit his gift. Willy too was convinced that his half-brother had in him 'the potential to turn professional', and Giordanella agreed with them – up to a point.

'Thierry was gifted,' he told me, 'but no one could have guessed what would happen. He was also very selfish. It was all for him. He never gave the ball to anyone else. Thank God there weren't any bonuses for the goals you scored – he would have gobbled up the whole lot. That's why a number of his teammates didn't like him very much. It was all about him. He took the ball, and ran away with it. And when he wasn't given the ball . . . I wouldn't say he cried, but he wasn't happy.' Unless Tony was there, Tony who had no time for sulkers and divas. Nevertheless, 'towards the end, the team played for him and him only. He was so much above the others.'

At the time – the very end of the 1980s – French professional clubs had yet to set up the far-reaching scouting networks which are taken for granted today. They relied on hearsay, private recommendations and informal relationships, which is not to say they were necessarily less effective in detecting young talents. They got there in the end, as Monaco finally did with Thierry, but not before he had carried on his apprenticeship in clubs which were far below the prestigious ASM in the country's footballing pyramid. Tony might have believed that his son had it in him to make it to the very top of the game, but didn't go knocking on Paris Saint-Germain's door to request a trial. Nor did he choose Henry's next club, US Palaiseau. In fact, Thierry got there more by accident than design, when Jean-Marie Panza, the coach in charge of the club's thirteen- to fifteen-years-olds, was told of 'a good little player at Les Ulis' by one of his closest friends, Christian Fuoco. Panza, though not a scout himself, was always on the lookout for a player who might strengthen a particular position and had numerous contacts in the area, which he had mostly made by following his own son Mathieu each and every weekend. Fuoco – who died a few years ago – then introduced him to Tony Henry; fortunately, the two men struck up an instant friendship, and Panza didn't have to wait long to be convinced of the eleven-year-old footballer's potential. Some time in 1988, Les Ulis came across Palaiseau in a minor seven-a-side tournament; Palaiseau won 6–5 – and all five of Les Ulis' goals had been scored by Titi. 'His qualities were already eye-catching,' he told me, 'speed, placement, finishing. A year later, he had joined us – not because I had poached him, but because Christian [Fuoco] and Tony requested it, as many people did anyway: we were well known for the high standard of our youth teams. Without detracting from the qualities of Les Ulis, Palaiseau represented a big step up for Thierry, and it wasn't long before other people were alerted to his talent.' In the meantime, USP could provide an ideal base for his development. Orsay, where Thierry now lived with Maryse and Willy, was less than five miles away from his new club. He nevertheless had to be ferried between home, school and training ground, a task that was taken on by Tony and Panza on an almost daily basis, and for which they could expect no other reward at the time than the fulfilment of the child's promise.

As Panza puts it, 'Thierry doesn't owe his career to his father, if you're talking about his intrinsic qualities as a player. But he owes his career to Tony in other ways. I won't go into details, but the father made huge sacrifices for the son.' These included Tony quitting a regular job to devote himself fully to his son's progress. Money was so tight that there was sometimes none left to fill the tank of Tony's car and drive Titi to the training ground. It had to be found, somehow. This hardship was the price Tony had chosen to pay to fulfil his mission: to make a great footballer out of Thierry. 'He took him to training,' Panza told me, 'he picked him up at school, he did everything so that Thierry would have the best possible conditions to be a footballer. Within his means – which were very modest – Tony did his utmost to help him realize his ambition.' Saying 'his', Panza meant 'Thierry's', but he might as well have alluded to his father, not that Thierry was reluctant to comply with Tony's demands. 'Titi was totally committed to football, despite his young age,' Panza says. 'And Palaiseau was right for him, inasmuch as we were committed to our youngsters as well. We organized training camps, tournaments; we played teams like Nantes and Angers. This kid lived football, 100 per cent, which doesn't mean he lagged behind at school . . . It's clear that his parents had instilled a very strong sense of respect and discipline in him. And he was lucky enough to be surrounded by people who were passionate about the game.'

Panza, who now trains the young 'keepers of Ligue 1 club Montpellier, was not alone in recognizing that Thierry possessed a very special talent. Not only was he blindingly fast, his tactical awareness was already well developed, and his movement on the pitch caught the eye as readily as his composure in front of goal. In his first – and only – season with Palaiseau, Henry scored on fifty-five occasions, enabling his club to win both regional League and Cup with ease. Not for the last time in his career, Thierry was also fortunate in that his own progress was matched by that of several of his teammates. A number of these later became professionals, one of them, Jonathan Zébina, having a fine career with Cagliari, AS Roma, Juventus and Brescia in Italy's Serie A. Fittingly, Henry would be on the pitch when the defender earned his solitary cap for France against Sweden in February 2005. A measure of Palaiseau's strength in depth was that, out of sixteen registered players in Thierry's age group, all but three were selected to represent their *département* (the Essonne) in the 1989 inter-regional competition. The local 'giant', PSG, who had a virtual monopoly over the whole of the Parisian *banlieue*, took notice and tried to sign Panza's own son Mathieu, to no avail. 'There was no need for that,' Jean-Marie says. 'The kids were training three times a week and played at weekends. They knew and liked each other. There was no need to send them to a big club's academy.'

Palaiseau, however, soon became too small for Thierry or, more to the point, for his father. Panza euphemistically speaks of Tony's 'big personal investment' in his son's progress and of an 'unusual environ-ment'. On one occasion, to the great embarrassment of his son, Tony staged a one-man pitch invasion to protest against a refereeing decision. Aside from this incident, which was bad enough in itself, some members of the club's directorate (and a number of parents whose sons played alongside Thierry) couldn't countenance the behaviour of Henry's entourage and felt that its involvement with the team's affairs was having a detrimental effect on the group as a whole. 'Why did Thierry not play?' they would be asked by Titi's protectors. 'Why wasn't the ball passed to him?' Listening to Panza, I couldn't help but think of what Robin van Persie would later say of the player from whom he had sought – and got – advice as soon as he arrived at Arsenal, in the late spring of 2004. 'Thierry could be very demanding,' the Dutchman recalled. 'He could never understand why a player would give him a bad pass and he would give them that look. You know the one I mean.' I don't think it is too far-fetched to guess where, or rather from whom, Thierry had learnt that particular look.

It had become obvious that, as far as Tony was concerned, Palaiseau represented a springboard for the prodigy and little else, which the club couldn't possibly accept. Sadly, but inevitably, the Henrys – and the Panzas, fathers and sons – were shown the door. No blame could be placed on Thierry himself, who was having fun banging in the goals while his father glowed with pride on the touchline. Another club, Viry-Châtillon, was all too happy to welcome him – and those who followed his every step. As Panza recalls, 'I'd told Palaiseau, "There's no way I can stay if you don't want to keep a kid like that, whatever his environment may be." So I joined Viry, with Thierry and my son Mathieu. Think of that what you want! One thing I can assure you of is that money never came into it.'

2

'What's my mark?' Relaxing at Clairefontaine, 1997.

ONE OF THE CHOSEN FEW

Again, it was a logical step forward, which had only been precipitated by the degradation of Tony's relationship with Palaiseau. Thierry Plet, the head coach of Viry's under-15s and under-16s, already was a good friend of Panza and had been told enough about Titi to welcome him with open arms, as did his club as a whole. Crucially, whilst both Palaiseau and Viry played in the same regional division at Henry's age level, only the latter took part in national tournaments. As a result, youngsters – from Les Ulis as well – would often hop from club to club to club in order to get their first taste of proper competition, Viry being the logical destination in their progress. Panza, who never sought and never got financial reward for his work, only wished the best for his 'kids'. As Plet puts it, 'If one of them had the potential to play in the national league, he wouldn't try to keep him, contrary to what many others do, who only think about their team being the best in their area.'

In fact, Panza had alerted Plet some time before the rift with Palaiseau made Thierry's early departure inevitable, and Plet himself had already seen with his own eyes what the 'very slim, lithe figure' was capable of on a football pitch, when a friendly between the two neighbouring sides was organized on a small pitch next to Viry's main stadium. He remembers a teenager who 'wasn't bigger than the others in terms of bulk; taller, though. But I wasn't on the lookout for a player. Thierry still had two years to go before he could play with me. He scored a few goals that afternoon, but I didn't think too much about him. You have no idea what a thirteen-year-old will be like two years later. You can't tell how growth will have an impact on their mobility and their coordination. What's more, Jean-Marie told me his parents had divorced, which made things even more complicated. His mother Maryse couldn't take him to Viry. So JM [Panza] said, "OK, I'll add my son Mathieu – he knew I rated him – and I'll take care of transport as well.'"

All went smoothly for a year or so. Thierry's father was busy elsewhere, it seems, though no one exactly remembers at what. Maryse, who feared seeing her son get injured, never attended his games, then as well as later. Incredible as it may sound, and even though she visited Titi regularly once he had gone to England, then Spain, Maryse never saw him in the flesh in a Monaco, Arsenal, Barcelona or France shirt. Football was a dialogue conducted exclusively between men in his family, which is why it is Panza, not Maryse, who stepped in to fill the void left by Tony's temporary exit from the scene, partly driven by the fear that Thierry could fail at Viry, drift back to a smaller club and disappear, as happened to so many young men of his generation. In 1998, at the instigation of *France Football*, the newly crowned world champion paid a rare visit to the town of his birth, which he had left for good less than ten years previously. It didn't take long for him to come across some of the friends he had challenged to *parties-pizza*: young black and Arab men named Anderson, Idrissa, Mourad, Ali, inhabitants of a world that had been Henry's in another life, but one that, by now, could as well have been someone else's. The talk drifted to those who had almost made it, like Ahmed El Awad, who had got himself a contract in Belgium, or Cyril Ebouki, who was trialling with AS Cannes. These were the lucky ones. Most had retreated into an obcure existence in the *cités*. Some had fallen into petty criminality and ended up in jail. Thierry might have left Les Ulis behind – to the point that the artificial pitch which bears his name there, paid for by one of his sponsors' charities, still awaits its official inauguration, the dedicatee having been unable to find the time to do it in person – but he never forgot how easily he too could have been sucked into that downward spiral. Talent mattered less than luck, it seemed.

Thierry had both, and it wasn't long before other, more powerful figures heard about the super-quick centre-forward who was scoring so freely for Viry's under-15 team – and this when he was a year younger than all those played around him, and when his coach was reluctant to 'burn' him out against physically stronger opponents. Plet's caution was not to everyone's taste, however; certainly not to Tony's, when Thierry's father finally reappeared on the touchline, as forceful and voluble as ever. Plet was torn between his desire to see Thierry blossom as quickly as possible, his inclination to protect him and the need to field a competitive team in which a bulkier, if less talented, centre-forward could sometimes prove of more use than the slightly built West Indian teenager. Tony would have none of it. Thierry was the best, Thierry had to play. And to those who asked why the father was so damn sure that his son really was the best, Tony could now reply: of course he is – he's just been accepted at the Institut National du Football of Clairefontaine. What he didn't add, not yet anyway, was that one of the top clubs in the country – AS Monaco – were hot on his son's trail, and that he knew it. The situation got out of hand in a matter of weeks. In this instance, circumstances rather than personalities precipitated what could be described as a 'tug-of-war' for the youngster's future. Choices had to be made, and quickly. The first one could easily be agreed on by all parties: Thierry had to make the most of his chance at Clairefontaine.

The academy in which the rest of the world would later see one of the foundations of France's rise to the very top of the international game hadn't acquired its prestigious reputation yet. It was still a full-scale experiment, rather than the finely tuned production line it would soon become; and when it is said, as is so often the case, that Henry (and Nicolas Anelka and Louis Saha and so many others) were 'products' of the French Football Federation's (FFF) *École Normale Supérieure de football*, it could also be argued that the exceptional quality of the school's intake in its first two years, which also included future internationals Jérôme Rothen and William Gallas, was one of the main reasons why the project took wing. Yes, Clairefontaine made Henry, up to a point. But the opposite is also true to an extent, just as the debt owed by Thierry to Arsène Wenger is shared by his mentor as well.

The institution had been functioning for barely three years when Thierry sat its entrance exam in the spring of 1991. Lucky Titi: until then, twelve- to fifteen-year-old apprentices were excluded from the recruitment process. Lucky Clairefontaine: this change of policy would totally transform a structure which fitted well enough in the organizational skeleton of French football, but with not much flesh attached to its bones. The arrival of youngsters who were – as extensive research had demonstrated – at an age where receptivity to coaching is at its highest, and motricity at the most crucial stage of its development, gave a new focus to the project. The DTN (National Technical Directorate) had long known that French football suffered from a 'skills vacuum' in youth football which clubs were not necessarily inclined to fill, as their priority was not to *teach* football but to *train* footballers. These two visions are not mutually exclusive, of course, but a policy which aims to produce results for a collective entity will not concern itself with the individual as a Clarefontaine could. The new academy would never be an employer; it aimed to complement the work done by the clubs, not to be a substitute for it.

The way it went about its business was typically French; it stuck to the principle of selective meritocracy which had driven the country's education system since the reign of Napoleon I, when most of the *grandes écoles* were created or acquired the pre-eminence they've preserved to this day. Just as prospective top civil servants were and still are picked from the École Nationale d'Administration, the French footballers of the future could now be fast-tracked to their own elite school. Christian Damiano, Claudio Ranieri's assistant at Monaco at the time of writing, after helping Gérard Houllier at Liverpool and Jean Tigana at Fulham, was a key member of Clairefontaine's technical staff from the academy's inception. Listening to him, it was clear that this was a top-driven initiative, built on the pyramidal system so beloved of French administrators. 'At the head is the National Technical Director,' he explained. 'He is assisted by seven or eight national coaches, of which I was one; then you have the regional technical advisers, who themselves supervise the work of the coaches based in the *départements*. The coaches – at district level – make recommendations which are passed on to the upper echelons of the hierarchy. They put forward the names of the best young players they've seen in their small clubs; these are be invited to sit the entrance exam – there is and was no question of someone, anyone, making an unsolicited application.' However fortuitously, Thierry's emergence was timed to perfection.

The laborious selection process entailed a series of physical and technical tests, followed by a trial game, a process which was repeated at every level of the pyramid from January onwards. A shortlist of thirty to forty players was eventually drawn up in every *département*, covering the whole of the Paris region (the main reservoir of talent in quantitative terms, hitherto left more or less untapped due to the lack of top-level clubs in the area) and neighbouring Normandy. These youngsters were then invited to go to Clairefontaine, where, from April to June, they were submitted to further tests, ever more narrowing the size of the funnel. By then, the FFF's inspectors and examiners had reduced a field of over 50,000 potential candidates to a final group of just twenty-two. Is it that surprising that those who were successful felt that they were part of a 'chosen few'? It was a heady notion for a thirteen-year-old like Henry, as it was for each of his new teammates. He derived great pride from his success, as he had every right to, and perhaps, back at Viry, showed it too eagerly for some who were less talented or had been less fortunate. Thierry soon found out that his remarkably swift and smooth progress inspired envy and jealousy as well as admiration among the players with whom he had trained and performed almost every day to that point. But no one could tell how far the 'chosen few' would go. The more select the company they had to keep, the more competitive, the crueller the environment would be, as Thierry reminded the scholars of his old club AS Monaco when he paid them a surprise visit before the 2009 European Supercup. 'That's the toughest thing in football,' he told the starstruck teenagers, who were probably expecting quite a different message from the Barcelona striker. 'Only one of you guys will make it as a pro. Maybe. When you arrive in an academy, you think you've made it. But you've achieved nothing yet. Nothing at all.'

Henry was right. It is too often forgotten how exceedingly small the proportion of promising footballers who 'make it' is in the final analysis. Have a look at the line-ups of teams who have taken part in any given international under-17 or even under-20 tournament and you'll see that, in most cases, even among the victors, more than half of these obviously gifted footballers had lapsed into obscurity or quit football altogether within a few seasons. To survive in that greenhouse required strength and wits, as well as the capacity to walk alone in a crowd, but faster than anyone else. Christian Damiano is quick to point out that 'we made sure that they wouldn't be more than ninety minutes away from their homes', but these ninety minutes might as well have been light years.

The teenagers who had been plucked from the cosy environment of their families and their provincial clubs had to build self-defence mechanisms from the outset, which partly explains why the graduates of this elite academy, Thierry most certainly included, often found it almost impossible to drop their guard once they had become professionals. They would only trust those who had grown up alongside them, and whom they had seen growing. This wariness is the price Henry, like so many others, had to pay for the privilege of being singled out as an exceptional talent when still a boy, transplanted into a hyper-competitive environment for which no child can be prepared. Outwardly relaxed, always willing to 'take the mickey' (*chambrer*, as the French say, which happens to be a word quite revealingly related to *chambrée* – 'dormitory'), and a bit of a lad by his own admission, Titi learnt how to protect what little privacy was granted to him by the Clairefontaine régime, which had more than a whiff of the barracks about it.

Its pupils spent weekdays in the château. This was not some fairy-tale labyrinth of ivy-clad turrets and mysterious corridors. Clairefontaine, like hundreds of other aristocratic and grand bourgeois estates which have been put to good use by the Republic, is – to my eyes at least – a fairly undistinguished pile of bricks, divided into offices, sleeping quarters and communal areas: a boarding-school, in short, and not one of the more exclusive kind. Life within the château's walls had the harsh predictability you could expect from such an establishment. Up at 7 a.m., the boarders filed up to the classrooms an hour later, studied, lunched, resumed studying until 3.30 p.m., and were only given a one-hour break before a team of three dedicated coaches worked on their football skills for ninety minutes. It is only from 6 p.m. onwards that they could truly play with the ball as children do. And all this they did in almost complete isolation from the world they had just left behind. It must have been hard for Thierry; but it was even harder for his father, who tried ever-more desperate means to keep hold of his son's development. Clairefontaine is set in a 56-hectare domaine within the Rambouillet forest and can only be accessed after clearing a number of security checks. Even allowing for a more relaxed attitude in the early 1990s, establishing contact with Titi required an almost comical degree of ducking and diving to avoid detection. Damiano remembers how Tony 'used to hide behind trees' to catch a glimpse of Thierry, and how he would phone the academy's staff every single day to pass on advice to his son. But it wasn't all comedy. Damiano soon grew infuriated by Tony's constant shadowing of Thierry, and Thierry himself, who had quickly forged a relationship with his coach, started to see his father's role in a new, not necessarily flattering light. The Clairefontaine regime suited the young Henry in many respects. For five days a week, at least, there was relief from the constant pressure Tony had put him under, and the chance to experience guidance of a more benign nature. Damiano and his assistants were no less demanding than Tony had been in their own way; but what they pursued was technical excellence for the sake of it, not 'success' in the competitive sense. Not as paradoxically as it sounds, one of the reasons why Thierry and Christian bonded so early was that the coach didn't display favouritism towards any of his charges, including the West Indian teenager who had shot up to 5 feet 7 inches and stood out, literally, head and shoulders over his teammates. Titi was 'the tall number nine in a red bib' who scored goal after goal, as Christian took great care not to single out one or the other of his charges by calling them by their first names; not to start with, anyway, for he rapidly grew very fond of Thierry, whom he describes as 'very mature, but very sensitive too, and someone who, under the surface, was very docile, eager to succeed and to listen to those who could help him'. 'If Thierry Henry went so high, so quickly, it is thanks to Clairefontaine. It was there that he was given the technical tools that would enable him to impose himself at the top level. He seized that chance. He could give the impression of being a little nonchalant, but was highly intelligent – and a very hard worker.'

A hard worker at school too, it seems, where Henry's academic results improved enough for him to be considered a suitable candidate for the *baccalauréat* (his remarkable progression in football meant that he had no time to prepare for the exam in the end). They needed to. 'I was a *bandit* [tearaway] in the classroom' was the way a twenty-year-old Thierry described a slightly younger self. 'I wasn't even asking myself the question whether there was homework to be done or not. But I had to knuckle down [at Clairefontaine], so that I could stay there.' Damiano was there to make sure that Titi learnt that particular lesson. 'Titi saw me as a tutor and had complete trust in me,' Christian says. Not so Tony. 'His father had a type of behaviour that could not be excused at his age . . . It was not just a lack of humility, it was a lack of respect towards others. He talked a lot, sometimes nonsense.' Damiano goes much further: 'Thierry suffered a great deal because of it. I asked Tony to stay away: I wanted to work in peace.'

Ah, peace. But not at weekends, when Henry went back to Viry – and Tony. His second season there was a disaster; not in terms of performances, as he was, again, his team's top goalscorer, but of how the relationship between the three men who mattered most in his foot-ball education at the time was damaged beyond repair. His father, who felt his influence diminishing with every single day Thierry spent at Clairefontaine, tried to reassert it when he was reunited with his son and took it very badly indeed when Plet decided to leave Titi out of his line-up, which he did on a number of occasions. Damiano himself struggled to understand how his star pupil could be left out and didn't shy from saying so, eventually encouraging him to leave Viry as soon as he could. Plet himself was nonplussed. Much as he loved Thierry, as a human being and as a footballer, he hadn't been entrusted with the development of a single player, but with the success of a team that wasn't quite good enough to accommodate a striker who considered any kind of defending a task best left to others. 'The first year,' Plet recalls, 'when he was training with our fifteen-year-olds, he was excellent: he was sur-rounded by very, very good players who could supply him with great service and he scored a lot of goals. But he didn't like physical contact, he didn't head the ball. He wasn't yet the athlete we now know; in fact, compared to some of the others, he was slightly built.' Plet believed he was protecting a special talent. Others were convinced he was holding him back. Thierry himself, pulled this way, then that, couldn't under-stand what was taking place. How could he, when he was only fourteen? 'When Tony reappeared, in the second year,' Plet says, 'there was a 180-degree turn in Titi's behaviour. He became sullen, remote. I was on my guard to start with, because of what I had been told about Tony.

But he is also someone who is very sociable, who'll sit next to you on the team bus and tell you great stories. He could be lovely on the way to the game, and awful on the way back, because we'd lost, or Thierry hadn't started . . . There were no half-measures. And when you manage a group of footballers, there comes a point when, regardless of the kid's qualities, you can't play with one player instead of eleven.'

The 'kid' and his former coach met by chance many years later in Antibes, where they happened to have lunch in the same restaurant. It was Henry, by then the star of Arsenal's attack, who came up to Plet, tapped him on the shoulder and, unprompted, told him: 'We didn't have a strong team at Viry. And when you're fourteen, it's difficult to understand that your dad is doing you harm.'

I asked Plet to repeat that sentence, and he did, word for word.

'He'd gone from teacher's pet to a player who didn't play every game,' he went on. 'And I wasn't around to explain things to him day to day. Not having Thierry at training meant that we couldn't manage him properly. He became more remote and more aggressive when we spoke to him. We could see he had trouble listening to us; he was so self-centred that he found it difficult to accept what we had to tell him about himself. I fancy Tony must have been behind that, saying things like: "You're better than the others, you should be playing, it's not normal," etc. The break-up occurred after a game in Nevers. I'll never forget it. He'd been injured and he was coming back after a month's absence. I put him on from the start: I knew we could win that game, and Thierry could make a difference, despite being one year younger than the others. We'd see how long he could last. These games consisted of two halves of forty minutes. On the hour, I see that he's gone, physically, and I take him off. Tony crosses the pitch, incensed, to demand an explanation. In his mind, Thierry was the best, full stop. It was all about him. The idea that football was a collective game didn't mean a thing to him. And that day, something gave. Between Tony and the other parents. And I'm confronted with this dilemma: either I lose Thierry, or I lose a number of other players.'

Plet kept the 'other players'. In the summer of 1992, Thierry moved to FC Versailles, the destination of choice for Clairefontaine scholars, where, alongside Rothen and Gallas, he reached the semi-finals of the national under-15 championships, scoring over fifty goals in the process. One of those games stuck in Rothen's mind, a quarter-final against PSG, no less, which the Parisian club led 2-0 at the interval. Then, in the second half, he remembers: 'I provided three assists, but it was Thierry who scored the two goals that enabled us to qualify. He was already well ahead of anybody else.' So much so that, in the two years he spent at Clairefontaine, Henry scored a barely believable seventy-seven goals in twenty-six games for his various teams in all competitions. FC Versailles didn't make it to the final: well, Thierry was injured. This quite extraordinary group of players was just as successful on the rare occasions they lined up for INF Clairefontaine – rare, as competition per se was anathema to its coaches. The academy team played half a dozen times a year at the most, but when they did, they invariably swept the opposition away. In October 1991, Guy Roux, the manager of Auxerre, whose reputation for nurturing young talent was unrivalled in the country, saw his side overwhelmed 6-0 and complained to Damiano afterwards: 'I'll never play against you again! Your boys are too strong!' Which was true: towards the end of that year, they also took part in a short international tournament, winning their three matches 8-1, 9-1 and 5-0. One of their opponents had been the *primavera* of AC Milan. Try telling those players they should stay on the bench when they rejoined their modest clubs at the weekend.

The regret is still perceptible in Plet's voice when he says: 'I think of Thierry racing down the left flank to score with an angled shot on the other side – a Titi trademark. Well, he was already doing that with us, he didn't learn that at Arsenal! I kept a video of a game against Bourges for a long time – he did that twice in the match, when he was a year younger than anyone else in his team. You could sense that he had more talent than the others'. Plet wasn't the only one to feel that. A fourth man stepped into the picture – or a fifth, as Jean-Marie Panza was still ferrying Titi diligently to weekend games: Arnold Catalano, one of Monaco's chief scouts.

Catalano, who was in his thirty-sixth year at the *Monégasque* club when I spoke to him, seemingly knew everybody in French football, including Jean-Marie Panza, who had alerted him to Thierry's talent when the twelve-year-old was still at Palaiseau. It didn't hurt that this club enjoyed a close relationship with ASM, which gave Panza the opportunity to spend a week each year in the Principality at the club's invitation. Catalano heeded the tip, had the player regularly watched by ASM scouts like Pierre Tournier, but waited another two years before first watching Henry in person, on the occasion of a friendly played for Clairefontaine in Orléans. Thierry naturally scored a few goals, 'without breaking sweat'. One week later, Catalano had made his mind up, even though the player he was supposed to monitor that day was not Henry, but Djamel Belmadi, the future Algerian international who later wore the colours of Manchester City and Southampton. Appearing for Viry against Sucy-en-Brie in the Championnat de Paris, Henry netted all of his team's goals in a 6-0 victory, again 'without breaking sweat'. No trial was needed. 'We signed him very quickly after that,' Catalano told me. 'It was a very easy deal to make; his dad, his mum, Titi himself – they all liked the idea of his playing for Monaco.' The deal was not quite as straightforward as that, in truth. Thierry had to complete his two-year cycle at Clairefontaine before he could rejoin ASM, and the agreement was kept secret by Tony until, sitting alongside Plet in the Viry team bus, produced a non-solicitation contract with Monaco, apparently unsigned. 'I knew that a few clubs were sniffing around [Thierry],' Plet recalls. 'Tony asked me: "What do you think?" "Well, it's a basic contract," I told him. "But don't rush it." In my mind, Monaco was a club where there was good coaching for the youngsters, but where the transition from the youth team to the professional squad was difficult. Thierry would play earlier if he went to a team that had less money to spend – or so I thought. But Tony told me: "Don't worry, it's signed already." "What? Why did you ask me my opinion?" "Because I like you, and because I wanted you to know." He wasn't easy to manage. He wasn't a bad guy, just one of these parents who tend to crowd the place out. In terms of how he put his belief in Thierry across, let's say that Tony wasn't a lacemaker. Not the subtlest.'

No money had changed hands. Monaco guaranteed that Thierry's parents could visit him in the principality at the club's expense, and that was that. In any case, the player was still too young to sign professional forms: his sixteenth birthday was still three months away. That

ASM was one of France's richest clubs made no difference; Henry would only earn the modest stipend of a *stagiaire* (literally, 'intern'), not much more than pocket money in fact, until he had convinced his new club that he deserved a chance in the first-team squad. In fairness, few thought that he could fail. By the time Henry started a new life by the Mediterranean, he had had his first taste of international football, scoring three goals in four games for France's under-15s; four more (in eight) had followed with the under-16s in 1993–4. It was a logical progression for the star pupil of Clairefontaine, whom the observers of the FFF could hardly ignore when he trained and played five days a week right under their noses. But what was startling about this progression was how smooth it had been, Titi rising to each new level without a hitch, adapting to the new demands made of him at every turn, indeed positively thriving on them. Talent alone couldn't explain this, as there were still a number of rough edges to his game, which, at this stage, relied far more on pace and movement than on more refined skills; Nicolas Anelka, who soon followed in his steps at Clairefontaine, was by all accounts a far more accomplished footballer in terms of technique at the same age. Those who lauded Henry as a highly 'technical' player in his heyday at Arsenal often saw his virtuosity as a God-given gift; my own view is that to overlook the sheer amount of work, the constant rehearsal of skills (which didn't come easily to a player who admitted to a certain laziness in his temperament) that took Henry to the very top of the game is to diminish his achievements. The former Brazilian professional Francisco Filho, one of the coaches who looked after him at Clairefontaine, has said: 'His nature was to work hard, constantly, always try to improve himself.' But what is perhaps even more remarkable is that the first thing Thierry had to work on was, precisely, his 'nature'. Filho himself had no inkling that the fourteen-year-old he was taking through training routines day after day was truly special.

Thierry certainly possessed a natural ability to run with the ball at barely believable speed, but he didn't have the natural balance and astonishing ball control that made Dennis Bergkamp a first among near-equals at the Arsenal. And later, when defenders had come to fear Henry more than any other forward in the Premier League, there were times when the mere mortal, not the 'Invincible' could be glimpsed in the number fourteen shirt. Balls would bounce at awkward angles from his shinpads; passes he customarily trapped with barely any effort flew into touch; free-kick after free-kick cleared the bar by several yards. You understood, then, that there would always be an element of rawness to his game.

On one hand, you couldn't quite apply to Thierry the equivocal compliment I once heard a colleague pay Frank Lampard – that all the Englishman knew of football was what could be taught, and learnt. Henry could be visited by genius. On the other, it is not – not just – the extravagance of his gifts that took him so high. It can be argued that there was a stage in his career, from 2002 to 2004, when Henry had a legitimate claim to be considered the world's best player. Many thought that he would have been a more deserving recipient of the 2006 *Ballon d'Or*, a trophy he craved so much, and the only significant one that escaped him in the end, than Italy's captain, Fabio Cannavaro. Throughout those glorious years, there isn't a club in the world that wouldn't have paid a fortune for him (and they tried: £50 million offers from Real Madrid and Barcelona were pushed aside by David Dein in 2006), not one team into which he wouldn't have walked. But even then, at the peak of his powers, was he the greatest? I doubt it, when Zinedine Zidane was still walking out onto the pitch of the Bernabéu; or Bergkamp, indeed, onto that of Highbury. That distinction between 'best' and 'greatest' (and the realization that the football world would never quite equate the two superlatives in his own case) is far from gratuitous when Henry's progress is scrutinized; I would go as far as to say that it haunted him, and that, his love of statistics notwithstanding, nothing spurred him on more in his unremitting pursuit of records. The more lists he topped, the closer he got to football's pantheon; or the furthest, if you will, as it became clear that, whatever he might achieve, he hadn't been touched by the kind of grace that made a Best or a Yashin stand out – and cannot be quantified. What should matter at this point in the narrative of Thierry's life, on the cusp of a professional career at AS Monaco, is that no one was more acutely aware of his limitations than he was. But he was also conscious of the one weapon that distinguished him: pace. 'I used to love it,' he told Amy Lawrence in the spring of 2004. 'When you are the quickest at school, you are always looked up to [*what would be called 'respect' in the Parisian ban-lieue*]. You feel good, king of the class! People always wanted to be in my team. I was aware of that really young.'

The very clear idea Thierry had of his own worth could make him come across as excessively 'proud', even to those who loved him most. As Panza told me (and remember he was talking about a teenager whose voice had just broken): 'Thierry exuded a sense of certainty about himself. He never came across as someone who could be overcome by what was happening around him. He forged his own character. He learnt to choose his friends, to be in control.' But this pride was always mixed with humility, and I would say that the ambivalence towards Thierry that is so noticeable in so many of those who have got near to him is in no small way related to which of these two qualities asserted itself over the other, with an unpredictability that was from very early on one of the very few predictable aspects of his temperament.

I remember how, in the spring of 2003, I think, I was heading for the exit of Arsenal's London Colney training ground and found myself walking alongside Thierry. It was one of those days when the sun plays hide-and-seek behind the clouds, when the wind seems incapable of making up its mind, calm and soothing one minute, bone-chilling the next, drops of rain falling out of a blue sky. I always felt strangely ill at ease in Henry's company at the time; I couldn't 'read' him, even though (or because?) he had always been remarkably polite towards me, whilst making sure there was a safe distance between the footballer and his twice-weekly chronicler. It's true that I came to football journalism very late, compared with most of my French colleagues, many of whom had been groomed from their early twenties onwards, if not earlier, to develop 'special relationships' with future stars of the game. *L'Équipe* and *France Football*, by far the most prestigious publications of their kind in my country (though others became more influential as time went by, the daily *Le Parisien* and the Sunday paper *Le Journal du dimanche*, for example), would identify up-and-coming writers who would then be assigned the task of following national youth teams or particularly promising academies. The idea was that, later on, once the cream had risen to the top, they would have their lips on the rim of the cup to lap it up. A millionaire footballer is far likelier to trust – and talk to – someone roughly of his own age group who had taken the trouble to report on minor under-17 tournaments than an older reporter such as myself. So I ventured some small talk, using the English expression 'four seasons in a day', which he repeated in a dreamy tone which I have never forgotten. I then felt, with absolute certainty, that there were an infinite number of seasons in Henry's calendar, not that you could predict exactly when they would arrive. His mood could change from one moment to the next even more swiftly than the crazy skies above us, and I am now reminded of G. K. Chesterton's essay 'The Glory of Grey': 'in a real sense there is no weather at all anywhere but in England'. Elsewhere, they have a climate; as most people do; but Thierry was definitely a weather-man. Perhaps it is not too fanciful to say that that is one of the reasons why he loved and loves England so much. 'The rain is a footballer's friend,' he once told me. Forget the gloves, the stockings and, much later, the snood rolled up to the bridge of his nose: I never heard him complain about cold February nights north of Manchester. If the ball zipped across the grass, so much the better. He rejoiced in multiplicity. But then, he was a many-sided man, which could be infuriating to others. Some things, however, wouldn't change.

This should be admired, unreservedly: what set him apart was not just his physique, it was his capacity to look at and analyse his own performance, fed by a passion for the game that was remarkable in one so young, and which he would retain until the twilight of his career. The teenage Thierry also possessed the intelligence to understand how vital it was for him to seek advice. Those who offered it to him knew they would be listened to and could be assured of Thierry's gratitude. Take the case of Jean-Marie Panza. When Pascal Blot interviewed Henry for *L'Équipe Magazine* shortly before the 2002 World Cup, the superstar was not afraid to cite the unknown 'JM' as one of the pivotal figures in his life, alongside Arsène Wenger and Jean Tigana. Until very recently, he made sure always to pass on his mobile number (which, as you know, he changed at increasingly shorter intervals as his career blossomed) to his former coach. When in Paris, he would sometimes call on the man who found a bed for him at weekends and served as a chauffeur when Tony was unable to play that role. Henry sometimes disappeared from Panza's life, notably after the 1998 World Cup, only to pop up again out of the blue, as when he called him just before the 2006 Champions League final. Panza's phone rang. 'Jean-Marie, it's Titi. All set for the game?' 'What do you mean?' 'We're playing the final in Paris, and you're coming – everything's arranged.' And Thierry really meant 'everything' – Panza's trip and hotel room had been paid for as well. The portrait of Henry I'm attempting to paint is not coloured by flattery, and there will be moments when you will find it difficult to feel sympathy for him (as I did); but this is something we should keep in mind: at the heart of Thierry's character, and 'heart' is the word, is an unfailing memory, and the deep-seated sense of loyalty that goes with it. Heaven knows it was to be tested at Monaco.

3

Artist on the left, audience missing.

THE MAN WHO BROKE THE RANKS AT MONTE CARLO

The club Thierry had joined was an oddity in French football. In truth, many wondered if the Association Sportive de Monaco Football Club was French at all. Others had their doubts over its status as a proper 'club'. The principality of Monaco, with its minuscule population of just over 30,000 inhabitants, 84 per cent of whom are wealthy foreigners, and a territory so exiguous that the new Louis II Stadium had to be built on land reclaimed from the Mediterranean, owed its survival to the political cunning of its rulers since the late thirteenth century, the Grimaldi family. AS Monaco's ascent from the amateur leagues to the French First Division, which it joined in 1953, more or less coincided with the accession to the throne of the football-loving prince Rainier III, who turned *Le Rocher* ('The Rock') from a quaint Ruritania-by-the-sea favoured by smugglers and dubious transalpine types to a must-see, must-be-seen-there destination for the international jet-set. Rainier wished to shake his fiefdom from its age-old slumber in the sun. He possessed the drive and the intelligence to pursue this aim; he also had the looks and the luck to achieve it. He fell in love with the ravishing Hollywood star Grace Kelly, and when he married her in 1956 their wedding attracted reporters, photographers and film crews from the world over; one day of pomp and circumstance was enough to transform the tiny state known only by stamp- and coin-collectors into a genuine global power – in terms of media exposure and attractiveness to tax exiles.

Rainier had other tools at his disposal: the documentaries of Jacques Cousteau, who was based in Monaco and whose films were partly financed by the wealth of the House of Grimaldi, the synthetic glamour of the famous casino, a world-renowned ballet company – and the football club, whose famous strip, a diagonally divided red-and-white, was redesigned by Princess Grace in person. ASM had one overwhelming advantage over its adversaries in the old First Division: as Monaco players paid close to no income tax at all, their net wages were significantly superior to those offered by clubs who commanded five or ten times the meagre popular support of the *Monégasques*, if 'popular' is the right word. This understandably rankled with a number of people within French football, indeed with most of the French population. Many wished that General de Gaulle had carried on his threat to 'send the tanks into Monaco' in 1962, when a temporary blockade was set up at the border of the tax haven. But he hadn't, and, thirty-one years later, when Arnold Catalano introduced Thierry Henry to his first professional club, ASM players still brought home some of the most generous salaries in French football, more than enough money to compensate for the strange experience of kicking a ball on a bumpy pitch in front of a couple of thousand spectators.

The lack of atmosphere in the Louis II Stadium didn't seem to have much of an impact on their performances, however. By the time Thierry first unpacked his kit at the training ground of La Turbie (located on French territory, as there wasn't enough space in the principality itself) in the summer of 1993, Monaco had won eleven major trophies since their first, a 4-2 victory over Saint-Étienne in the 1960 French Cup final. What's more, following the arrival of a hitherto unknown Alsatian coach called Arsène Wenger in 1987, Monaco had started to pull their weight in European competitions as well, something they had previously failed to do. A place in the semi-finals of the 1990 European Cup Winners' Cup was followed two years later by qualification for the final of the same tournament, which the *Monégasques* all but let Werder Bremen win. Three days earlier, eighteen dead bodies had been laid out on the pitch of Bastia's Furiani Stadium, the victims of the collapse of a hastily erected stand. More than a decade later, Wenger still blanched at the recollection of this tragedy. 'We never played that day,' he told me. 'We simply couldn't. It's as if the game never really started.'

One of the teams who had played in Corsica on that dreadful night – 5 May 1992 – was Olympique de Marseille, then the all-conquering plaything of the millionaire businessman and politician Bernard Tapie, the man Éric Cantona called 'a devil' and against whom Wenger fought a personal crusade almost entirely on his own, a battle that was to shape his character for the rest of his life. OM had won all four League titles between 1989 and 1992, amidst constant rumours of bribery, false accounting and drug-taking, about which the Monaco manager was then the only major figure to speak openly. Wenger would be vindicated in 1993, when the police found the equivalent of £25,000 in cash hidden in the home of the parents of a Valenciennes player, Christophe Robert, one of three 'VA' footballers who had been approached by Marseille and asked to 'take it easy' in a League game prior to OM's Champions League final against Milan. Within one year of the scandal becoming public, OM had been demoted to the Second Division and stripped of its 1993 championship title, Tapie had lost his licence (he would receive a jail sentence in November 1995), and Monaco seemed ideally placed to exploit the turmoil that had engulfed the Stade Vélodrome. Henry had joined a genuine contender for domestic and international honours, not that there were indications that he would have a significant impact as rapidly as he did.

To start with, and as expected, he joined *les 17 nationaux,* the teenagers who represented Monaco in the under-17s national league; but what was not expected was that he should skip over the next logical step in his development – the grim environment of ASM's 'B' team, where youngsters hardened off their game in the company of older pros who were not quite good or fit enough to be in the first team. In fact, Henry hardly ever lined up with the reserves, as Wenger gave him his full debut within less than two years of his arrival. In that, too, Thierry was exceptional. 'He was already very mature,' Catalano recalls. 'He never caused a problem; there were no personality clashes, no shenanigans. He trained, he scored hatfuls of goals, he helped his team win, as simple as that.' More than anything, Thierry knew what he wanted, and what he had to do to get it. Clairefontaine had toughened him up, but only to a degree. There is a world of difference between a pupil whose primary objective is the pursuit of excellence for its own sake and an apprentice who is put to the test by a prospective employer, hoping to be offered a job in the end; the same difference, as it happens, that there is in the French educational system between an exam and a *concours*, a word that translates quite appropriately as 'competition'. Henry's intelligence, which was remarked upon by every man to have coached him, extended far beyond his understanding of football, his quick wit and a remarkable ear for foreign languages. It was an emotional intelligence as well. He immediately sensed that 'if it wasn't me who succeeded', as he recalled on an impromptu visit to his old academy in 2009, 'it'd be somebody else'. 'And that's the most difficult thing in football. We have to play together, and succeed together, because if the team doesn't win, nobody will make the grade. If there's a ball to give, and it means someone else will score, not you, you must give it – even if it means that you'll be less visible as a result. We have to try to live as a community. No jealousy . . . but that's not easy at that age, when people start taking the mickey, when you think about girls, when you think you're somebody else. If you don't go to bed early, someone else will. If you don't do your work, someone else will do it for you. I sometimes meet guys from the old days, who tell me, "Hey, you've been lucky." But I wasn't lucky. I worked.'

Thierry did everything quickly: running, thinking, especially growing up. Maybe he remembered what Catalano, who had seen so many 'young Zidanes' fall by the wayside through lack of focus and dedication, had told him in the presence of Tony at the very beginning of his stay at Monaco. 'You – if you don't succeed, you'll have only one person to blame: yourself, because you won't have worked hard enough.'

This is not to say that Henry was a Stakhanovist *à la* David Beckham, first to arrive at the training ground, last to leave it. Monaco, where, as he put it in 1997, 'if you haven't got any money, you don't exist', offered many distractions which he wasn't always inclined to ignore. He was, then as later, remarkably reticent to spend much time or effort on improving his heading, which remained shockingly poor for an athlete of his build and flexibility. Thierry had to fight, not always with success, a natural inclination to laziness to which he often confessed with a half-smile that implied 'don't take me too seriously when I say that'. This contrived self-deprecation will be familiar to all those who've met him, a psychological tic which Gilles Grimandi, his teammate at Arsenal and Monaco for a decade, described to me as 'false inverted modesty'.

But Henry already had a clear idea of the qualities that made him stand out, and these he would work and work to sharpen on the academy pitch. As Gilles told me, 'he had a real talent for analysing his own performances, he'd go over them time and again – "I should have done this, I shouldn't have done that" – and he knew a lot about the other players, whether this one was quick or not, which side you should take them on. Later, he loved playing against Italian defenders like Alessandro Nesta. He knew all about them, he knew that they couldn't live with him in terms of speed.' Bear in mind that Grimandi was talking about the 'kid' he saw for the first time in 1993, not the majestic record-breaker of the twenty-first century.

I remember chatting to Thierry in September 2005, shortly after he had scored the superb goal, perhaps the most important of his international career, that gave France a 1-0 victory over Ireland in Dublin (no, not *that* one) and meant that *Les Bleus* had all but qualified for the 2006 World Cup. 'I want to dedicate it to Claude Puel,' he said. Puel, the future manager of Lyon, had looked after the young Thierry as a fitness trainer and coach after seventeen seasons spent playing for ASM. 'He'd put the cones on the pitch and make me go through the same series of exercises over and over again, finishing with that shot in the opposite corner. That goal against the Irish was made in Monaco.'

Listening to those who witnessed close-up his rise from scholar to first-teamer within less than two years, I was struck by how much of what they were saying of the teenager could be applied to the mature footballer – and grown man – of the Arsenal and Barcelona years, as if he had already emerged fully formed from the mould, only needing a brief period of exposure to the outside world to harden into a well-defined and unchanging, if often elusive, shape. Catalano, for example, was infuriated by Thierry's reluctance to shoot at goal, preferring to 'pass the ball into the net', a complaint I've certainly heard a few times at Highbury and elsewhere. He was 'effortless', surely one of the most misguided epithets in the sporting vocabulary; he could produce astounding bursts of pace 'without cramping up and hitting the wall', he 'never seemed to be in any pain', he was 'languid', 'graceful', a prodigious scorer of goals, for sure, but one who lacked the instinct of his soon-to-be teammate David Trezeguet: Thierry thought outside the box, the six-yard box, that is. He was unquestionably individualistic, but his affinity with and love for the game itself were so acute, so deep-rooted, that he could bend the collective dimension of football to his own purpose – to succeed, to win, to be the best. Call it a blessing or a curse, there's no escaping how far this led him.

In temperament too, the Titi of Monaco didn't appear to differ markedly from the Henry of Arsenal, if Grimandi's reminiscence of his first impression isn't too coloured by what he saw afterwards. Had Henry always been thus? Or can it be that, suddenly transplanted into a super-ficially more glamorous, but far more unforgiving, environment, he had to piece together another self to survive? Charming, funny, easy-going, generous – Thierry could be all these things. '*Adorable*', as Robert Pirès summed him up, remembering how Henry had taken him under his wing when he arrived at Arsenal, cooking 'delicious' pasta for the new-comer in his Hampstead home, even offering to let him stay there until Bobby had found a flat of his own. But there seemed to be an element of calculation in everything he did, as if he were watching himself as much as he was keeping an eye on others, making 'moves' as a chess player does, trying to think two or three steps ahead, learning new combinations along the way. 'He already had this "attitude" when he arrived at Monaco – but only with people who were the same age,' Gilles told me. 'He respected those who were above him, but, gradually, as his status changed, as he got older, he accepted less and less from fewer and fewer people. He was clever. He was quite shy to start with, so that people would accept him.' Once they had done so, Thierry could move on, to other aims, to other people. This 'respect', to use the lingo of the *banlieue*, is not the most attractive of characteristics, but one shouldn't forget it is a tool for survival first, for domination second. Thierry was on his own, far, far away from his friends and family; he was pulled forward by two ambitions that weren't necessarily comple-mentary: his and his father's. Tony couldn't afford to live on the riviera, not yet anyway, but remained the judge to whom Thierry was ultimately accountable – at least for the moment.

I must point out that not everyone shared Grimandi's misgivings. Éric Di Meco, a European Cup winner with Marseille in 1993, had joined ASM immediately after the *Marseillais* had been demoted to the

Second Division and soon assumed the role of elder brother for many of Monaco's youngsters. What struck him immediately, coming as he did from a team composed almost exclusively of seasoned internationals, was that 'these guys were very different from us. They wouldn't play cards or have a drink downstairs. No – if you wanted to be with them, and have some sort of a relationship, you had to go to their room and spend the evening in front of a television screen. Video games were starting to become popular. I remember many evenings spent with Thierry and the other *minots* playing Sega Rally. They'd wipe the floor with me, and they'd take the mickey out of me. I didn't mind; in fact, I quite liked it.' Despite the age difference (a full fourteen years separated the two men) Di Meco grew very fond of the teenager; he could also see that 'he was hungry to learn; he was very, very ambitious; and he'd get there', an opinion shared by another of Titi's seniors at the club, Laurent Banide, who helped his father Gérard run the academy at the time and recalls a 'polite, kind, courteous, likeable young man', who 'made himself available for others', 'felt good, smiled, looked happy' and had 'absolutely no problem adapting to Monaco'. What Laurent, who became Monaco's manager in January 2011, if only for a short while, remembers most, apart from Thierry's trademark run, 'moving down the left, then opening the foot to shoot with the inside of his boot', is his passion for basketball, which they practised after working out in the gym with other youngsters such as Philippe Christanval, a future French international, and Sylvain Legwinski, later of Fulham and Ipswich. Henry had long been an NBA fan, of course. But whereas Didier Drogba, another aficionado of that sport, practised it to build up his upper-body strength and learn how to barge defenders and defend the ball with his back to goal, what Henry brought into his own game from watching his idol Michael Jordan were the polar opposites of showmanship: on the one hand a taste for the spectacular, on the other a puzzling desire to mask his emotions when he had scored a goal. Look at Jordan's stone-faced expression after dunking a ball in the hoop; then look at Henry finding the net, even at the beginning of his career. It is pure mimicry. It was also a persona he had adopted at an age when it should be about fun and nothing else. With Henry, self-awareness was often indistinguish-able from self-consciousness, as is bound to happen when you feel yourself to be alone. It was also exacerbated by a merciless, almost masochistic self-critical streak in his character, which prevented him from immersing himself totally in the sheer joy of playing. 'I'm the first to have a real go at myself when I'm not doing well,' he told L'Équipe TV in 2005. 'When I make a mistake and you see a closed expression on my face, [it is because] I am talking to myself.' I would add: becoming his own father for a second, chastising the son who's missed an open goal.

He could clown around, of course, but did he ever drop his guard completely? It is a subject which I'll come back to, and often, as I have talked to dozens of people who are routinely described as 'friends' of Thierry's, but who all seemed to express their 'friendship' with a measure of diffidence. Gilles Grimandi, who, by the way, has no reason to hold a grudge against his former teammate, told me that he didn't believe that Henry had a single true friend in football. Elsewhere, perhaps – but not in the world he has inhabited ever since he moved to Monaco. He is not unique in this, of course. A number of footballers have hated their everyday environment with a passion and, more often than not, what they hated the most was the impossibility of trusting anyone who was part of that suffocating microcosm. They found themselves cut off as a result; Vikash Dhorasoo is a striking example of that. But Thierry never *hated* the world of football. He seemed at ease with it, at least outwardly. It could be that his drive to succeed was so fierce, and his success so prompt and so remarkable, that he experienced a caesura familiar to some of the greatest achievers in the world of sport (I am thinking of Don Bradman in this instance), whereby the act of giving without any ulterior motive becomes a near-impossibility, as the giver knows all too well the price he may pay for his generosity. And don't let's forget how young Thierry was when he completed the transition from scholar to professional. Arsène Wenger first picked him on 31 August 1994, for a League game against OGC Nice, when Henry had only just celebrated his seventeenth birthday. Little more than a year previously, he was still turning out for FC Versaille in a regional league; he now found himself in the midst of far more experienced footballers, many of whom were established internationals old enough to be his father. It can't have been easy. '[Life in] a football academy is war,' he told *Sport* magazine in 2008. 'Everybody thinks it's rosy. But we're [a group of] twenty-four mates, and there's only one of us who will make it. I reckon that it's the same thing that happens to others when they finish their studies. People come to shake hands, wishing each other good luck, but they're just waiting for you to fall on your face. And that's the same thing in football, but worse, because you have to play together. When you're fifteen, it's a jungle out there.'

It shouldn't be assumed that Wenger had seen in Thierry something that no one else had noticed before him. To start with, a succession of injuries had forced the manager's hand to an extent, as his main striker, the Brazilian Sonny Anderson, whom Henry idolized, found himself bereft of attacking partners. The youngster Wenger gambled on ahead of more seasoned reserve-team players had scored over thirty goals in his first season with the *17 nationaux*, plus ten in eleven games for the French under-17s. It wasn't a question of if, but when Thierry should be tested at senior level. It is often implied that, in bringing his former protégé to Highbury, Wenger was rekindling a relationship that had been forged in France five years previously. This isn't entirely accurate. Wenger had the courage and the foresight to turn to a seventeen-year-old in an hour of need, but what he did with Thierry couldn't be compared with the way David Moyes entrusted, then protected, an even younger Wayne Rooney at Everton, for example, or Wenger himself nurtured Cesc Fàbregas or Jack Wilshere at Arsenal. For one thing, the Alsatian coach wasn't given the time to do this. Monaco had shown worrying signs of weakness from the very beginning of the season, and selecting Henry wasn't just about gauging what the future could hold for him, but also addressing more pressing problems. What the game against Nice showed was that Thierry was not a solution, not yet anyway. When he left the field in the sixty-fourth minute, his team was trailing 0-2 to the Niçois, in a fixture that had drawn a crowd of over 10,000 spectators, at least half of whom were supporters of the neighbouring club: that's the price you pay when you play for ASM.

 The next game brought another defeat, 0-1 away to Le Havre, in which Henry came on as a substitute for the last half-hour and didn't provide much more in the way of attacking thrust than on his debut at the Louis II Stadium. Weakened by injuries, undermined by internal quarrels that partly explain why Wenger's dismissal came so quickly, and in such a brutal fashion, Monaco found themselves three points away from the relegation zone after seven games. The manager, who had refused a firm offer from Bayern Munich in the summer in the hope he would be given a free hand in rebuilding Monaco, was sacked only a few hours after the club's chief executive had called him 'a monument of ASM'. The decision – and especially the manner in which it was carried out – shocked French football. Gérard Houllier, who was approached to fill the vacant position, turned it down without a second thought. Not everyone was as principled as Houllier, it's true. Crafty guns for hire such as Raymond Goethals and Bora Milutinović let it be known that they could be interested in a spell on the *Rocher*. The club decided to deal with the mess they had created in-house, however, and picked a duo of former ASM players, Jean Petit and Jean-Luc Ettori, who kept their temporary position until February 1995, when another insider, Gérard Banide, was installed in the manager's seat for the rest of the season. Thierry himself receded into the background, as Petit, Ettori and Banide understandably played the experience card in what was at first a fight for survival, then a steady climb towards the top third of the table. But if Henry only played another six games in that campaign, all of them coming on as a substitute, he also, for the first time, caught the attention of the general public, and spectacularly so, when he scored a brace in the demolition of RC Lens on 28 April 1995. A head injury sustained by Mickaël Madar in the twenty-second minute prompted Banide to turn to his young striker, who, combining beautifully with Youri Djorkaeff, all but humiliated his future – and ephemeral – Arsenal teammate Guillaume Warmuz, who fished six balls out of the back of his net that day. The first of Thierry's two goals was a thing of beauty, the equal of any he would score afterwards in terms of technique, intelligence – and cheek.

Djorkaeff had seen his young teammate racing towards goal and spotted the opportunity to play him in one-on-one with the 'keeper; his pass was slightly overhit, however, and Warmuz surged from his line, confident he could reach the ball before the onrushing Henry. But Thierry was far too quick and stole it from under the 'keeper's gloves. There was still much to be done. First, dribble past Warmuz – but this Henry could only do by heading away from the goal and, driven by his momentum, ending up outside the penalty area. Out there on the eighteen-yard line, he lifted his head to see defenders retreating frantically towards their unprotected net. The angle was so narrow that it seemed Henry had no choice but cross a hopeful ball towards a teammate. But Thierry had other ideas. Taking what felt like an eternity to make up his mind, he curled a powerful right-footed shot into the 'cobweb', as the French call it, just underneath the intersection of the bar and the far post. It was a staggering goal, worthy of inclusion in the shortlist for goal of the season; what made it so memorable was not just the perfection of its execution, but its impudence, too, and the simple fact that Henry had found the answer to an apparently unsolvable question. Much later, I asked Arsène Wenger what exactly made Thierry 'great' in his eyes, and he said: 'Football at the highest level confronts players with an infinity of possibilities, from which they must choose one within a fraction of a second. A great player like Thierry will almost always find the only solution, which, watching from the touchline, you often didn't know existed.'

That goal, Henry's first as a professional, was undoubtedly 'great' as Wenger understood that adjective; and, if scoring it didn't instantly turn Thierry into a 'great' player, it certainly made a number of observers, for whom he had only been a name on the team-sheet of French youth games until then, sit up and take notice of his prodigious potential. *France Football*'s reporter at that game spoke of 'a revelation' and gave Henry a maximum rating of five out of five. That game also marked another first for the youngster, who couldn't disguise his delight at being sought out by a number of journalists at the final whistle. Media training was – happy days! – still a thing of the future in 1995, but the most demanding communications officer would have been delighted with the few interviews that were published in the wake of the Lens match. 'I first must thank my teammates and also Mickaël Madar, of whom I'm thinking now. I scored thanks to them,' Thierry said, and said again. He could 'do' humility without making it sound *too* forced, even if his tongue must have been firmly in his cheek when, questioned by a TV journalist, he answered: 'I hope to play in a Second Division club, and, if I manage a few good games, impress a First Division club. You never know. What I want is to succeed . . . [it doesn't matter] if I succeed at

Lille, or Saint-Étienne. What I want is to play for a First Division club. That's what I've wanted to do since I was a kid.' This was quite a remarkable statement of non-ambition from a footballer who had been on the books of one of France's biggest clubs for close to three years already and had also scored a brace for the French juniors against England in September 1994, prompting France's National Technical Director Gérard Houllier to say: 'He has the capacity to beat defenders, he's very good with the ball at his feet. He's also got great potential in terms of power, which he can use to go past opponents. He's a striker of the future. When he has got his finishing right, he'll be very close to the top level.' Hardly Second Division material, then.

Watching again the short clip of that interview, however, the thing that struck me the most were not Thierry's words, but his accent. Those familiar with the polished tone he adopted at Arsenal would be struck by how *banlieusard* he sounded then, his overstressed *r*s as revelatory of his origins as the dropped 'aitches of Estuary English, a far cry from the 'cool', sophisticated, cosmopolitan metrosexual that would prove such a hit with British advertisers. He also looked slightly ungainly in front of the camera. Perhaps he was too self-conscious; or simply too young. The dreadlocks he had grown in homage to Ruud Gullit, whose autograph was the most cherished in his collection, looked more like a not-too-successful imitation of Frank Rijkaard's and gave him an appearance of awkwardness that was at odds with the self-confidence he showed elsewhere, now that he had taken the first step towards the first-team squad. Di Meco told me how Thierry loved jokes, especially if they were at someone else's expense. Nutmegging the 'hard men' in training, for example. 'If I see a guy with open legs, I do it, I can't help it, I feel obliged to do it,' he admitted later on, long after Éric Di Meco had been a victim of his trickery and made him pay for it with a heavy tackle. This taste for 'banter' and 'mickey-taking' never left him. Whilst at Juventus, he organized 'nutmegging competitions' with another fairly tough egg, Edgar Davids, who, fortunately for Henry, saw the funny side of it and responded by trying nutmegs of his own. One thing is certain: those who lived and worked alongside the seventeen-year-old knew that the 'real' Thierry Henry was far more self-assured than the image he wanted to present to the rest of the world. He hadn't 'arrived' yet: despite his brace of goals against Lens, which were shown repeateadly on French national television, Banide didn't give him a place in Monaco's starting eleven until the very last day of the season, a 0-2 defeat at Metz, when ASM was already assured of sixth place and a spot in the next season's UEFA Cup. It had been quite a remarkable turnaround for the *Monégasque* club since it had cast Wenger aside at the start of the autumn, but not quite as remarkable as what the next two years held in store for the teenage winger who had only played a walk-on part in their renewal, and a fairly inconsequential one at that. For that, Henry would have to thank a new manager, Jean Tigana, not that thanks were what Tigana got from his protégé. For Thierry was a *protégé* in the original sense – not a teacher's pet, but someone who is *protected*, handled with care, sympathy and firmness. Henry got all three from Tigana, went along with the prudent approach of his coach at first, flourished, then came very close to throwing it all away through youthful pride and impatience, egged on by the unscrupulous 'friends' and advisers who flocked to his side as soon as it became clear that his was an exceptional and potentially very lucrative talent. It is to his then manager's immense credit that Thierry was ultimately saved from self-destruction. This part of Henry's career has largely been forgotten in France and is barely known about elsewhere. It is not just because of this that I choose to devote a significantly large part of this book to this episode, however, but because, without understanding the turmoil which threatened to engulf the 'rising star of French football' (a liberally used expression at the time), it would be almost impossible to understand the future king of Arsenal, the *galáctico*-turned-outcast of Barcelona and the showman of American Major League Soccer.

To anyone who followed or supported France in the mid-1980s (and those who followed that glorious French team tended to support it, regardless of their nationality), Jean Tigana will always remain one of the cardinal points of the famed 'magical quartet' (*le carré magique*), together with his then Bordeaux teammate Alain Giresse, Luis Fernandez and, of course, Michel Platini, which gave my country its first major title in international football – the 1984 European Championships – and could, maybe should, have put a star on the jersey of Les Bleus before Henry finished his team's top goalscorer at the 1998 World Cup. Seville 1982,

Guadalajara 1986: talk to any Frenchman about those legendary games against West Germany (lost, so cruelly) and Brazil (won in a penalty shoot-out, after a grandiose exhibition of attacking football by both sides); their throats will tighten, their eyes will mist over. It is no exaggeration to say that no other national team in history, save, maybe, the Yugoslavians who were denied a place by civil war in the 1992 European Championships, possessed as talented and well-balanced a midfield as France did then. Jean Tigana was its tireless dynamo, the fighter whose run on the right flank – in the 119th minute, for goodness sake – allowed Platini to crucify Portugal in the semi-finals of Euro 1984. A magnificent footballer who deserved far more than his fifty-two caps, Tigana immediately made his mark as a manager when, having retired in 1991, he took Olympique Lyonnais to second place in the 1994–5 championship behind an exceptional FC Nantes, before being offered a one-year rolling contract by Monaco. 'Jeannot', as he is almost universally referred to, is not quite as easy-going as his nickname would suggest. To be blunt, 'Jeannot' is a grump of the first order, and if one were to lapse into stereotypes, he would be closer to a strong, silent Yorkshireman than to the easy-going, voluble West African he's supposed to be. He was also the perfect mentor at the the perfect time for Thierry. Tigana never courted popularity with anyone, journalists and players included. He was and is tough, uncompromising, abrupt, sometimes, but rarely without reason; he was and is a fine judge of footballers too and, in the case of Thierry, knew he had to wave a stick, and use it sometimes, while so many others were dangling carrots in front of the teenager.

The 1995–6 season was one of transition for player, manager and club alike. ASM's progress in Europe was cut short by Tony Yeboah, the outstanding player in an otherwise average Leeds United team, Monaco suffering a humiliating 0-3 defeat at home in the first leg of their first-round tie, all three goals scored by the Ghanaian striker, with substitute Henry very much a bystander. There could be no way back from such a drubbing. In the French championship, where Henry contributed three goals and five assists in eighteen appearances, a superb second half of the season pushed ASM up to third place, securing a place in the UEFA Cup again, with Brazilian forward Sonny Anderson providing twenty-one goals in thirty-four League matches. As these statistics show, Henry had by no means established himself as a first-choice attacker in Tigana's starting eleven. Monaco, who had lost the wonderfully inventive Djorkaeff to PSG in the summer, was in the process of rebuilding itself, with some difficulty, around established match-winners such as Anderson and the brilliant Belgian playmaker Enzo Scifo, who endured a rare barren spell in the first third of the campaign. Recruits such as Fabien Barthez, who had just been signed from OM, had to be bedded in. Risking unproven talents such as Thierry would have been suicidal when Tigana's priority was to bring purpose and organization to a group of players known for their volatility and who were rumoured to be split into a number of cliques. Keep in mind that Henry was still thought of as 'one to watch' (closely, mind you) and that many at the club held the view that twenty-one-year-old left-back Manuel Dos Santos was a better prospect than his teenage partner in the longer term. Thierry's name hadn't even been mentioned – not once – in the long preview that *France Football* had devoted to Tigana's Monaco before the start of that season, and his inclusion on the left wing of the team that opened its account with a 3-1 defeat of Rennes on the championship's opening day raised a few eyebrows. He was not so much an unknown quantity as an unknown, full stop. The manager might have kept Henry in his starting line-up a while longer, had the player not been forced to leave the field through injury in the following League game, a 2-1 victory at OGC Nice; it is far more likely, however, that, just as would often turn out to be the case, he would have played him as a *joker*, a late substitute whose pace could unsettle tiring opponents.

Tigana saw 4-3-3 as the default formation of his ASM, with Madar and Ikpeba flanking the redoubtable Sonny Anderson, ahead of a good-looking midfield trio composed of Emmanuel Petit, Enzo Scifo and Ali Benarbia. The Dane Dan Petersen and the Liberian Christopher Wreh, yet another Monaco player who would wear an Arsenal shirt, provided alternative attacking options for Tigana, who never excluded Henry from his group, but preferred to use him sparingly: twenty minutes here, half an hour there, as on 29 August, the day a nineteen-year-old Patrick Vieira was made captain of AS Cannes. Thierry scored his first goal of the campaign against Lille that day. In 'crunch' games such as the visit to PSG, where Thierry only came off the bench in the eightieth minute, Tigana mostly relied on his young winger as a last or last-but-one resort when

ASM seemed to have run out of solutions. Henry's presence on the pitch barely exceeded a full hour from mid-September to mid-October, and the winger had to wait until the twelfth round of the championship to feature in the starting line-up again, when he scored his second of the season against Montpellier. Another start, against Cannes (Vieira had joined Milan by then), another substitution, another spell on the touch-line – and so it went on until the end of that season, be it in the League or in the French Cup, in which Monaco reached the quarter-finals.

That is not to say that Tigana was less aware of his player's qualities than any of the coaches who called on Thierry whenever the French under-17s or under-18s played an international match. In fact, Tigana was one of the first to see in Henry a genuine candidate for a place in France's squad for the 1998 World Cup; not that he told his player that this was the case. That was not Jeannot's style. Far more important to him was to hone that special talent, patiently, steadily, and if he had to leave him on the sidelines to avoid burn-out, so be it. In Tigana's eyes, as incomprehensible as it may be to twenty-first-century readers who are accustomed to hear coaches raging against the demands of the UEFA- and FIFA-imposed international calendar, Monaco's interests ultimately came second to those of the national team he had served so magnificently as a player, and to which he contributed so much as a manager, with close to no public recognition.

Thierry didn't protest much to start with. He too was bedding himself in. One of the ways in which he did so was by cultivating Anderson's friendship, constantly seeking his company, mimicking his mannerisms, such as rolling his socks above the knee, a habit he took to England, Spain and America. He admired the Brazilian's ability in front of goal, which would eventually earn the striker a record-breaking transfer to Barcelona in 1997. You may think that Henry was merely serving his own interest by placing himself in his elder's wake, a remora attached to the flank of the local big fish: Anderson was assured of a place in Tigana's starting eleven, when Titi clearly wasn't close to one himself yet. Or you may show more indulgence and contend that he behaved like any other starstruck teenager would have done. To me, he was doing both, without necessarily knowing it. It is too often assumed that players have a clear 'career plan' when, in fact, they only have a set of remarkably similar ambitions, which is not quite the same thing. I have asked this question to a number of footballers: 'When did you realize you'd made it?' Hardly any could provide a conclusive answer; more to the point, none of them had asked this question to themselves in those terms. Their progress had been a succession of transitions, accidental or not, of which they had hardly been aware when they were taking place. So it goes for most of us. Chances are seized or spurned; all we can do is strive to ensure they come our way, and this is exactly what Thierry did. The bond he formed with Anderson certainly contributed to his development, both on and off the pitch. To hold the view, which I've heard aired more than once, that this was part of a machiavellian plot to gain an advantage over players who competed for a spot on the wing, such as the Nigerian Victor Ikpeba, seems far-fetched and mean-spirited to me.

What's more, Thierry had already 'made it' in another respect – not with ASM, but with the French under-18s, where he played alongside many other former Clairefontaine scholars. By the end of the 1995–6 season, he had already clocked up thirty-six games for France's youth teams, scoring twenty-three goals, an outstanding return for a player who could not be called a natural finisher. Even better was to come at the 1996 UEFA European Under-18 Championship, which was played over a single week in July in France and, through a quirk that no one could quite understand, Luxembourg, perhaps the only host nation not to have taken part in a tournament it was staging, as UEFA insisted they went through a preliminary round, which ended their involvement, as might be expected. France, by contrast, buoyed by home advantage, went all the way and secured their second win in that competition thirteen years after their first success.* The French had never sent out such a strong group of juniors, and it is unlikely that they will ever do so again. This isn't the first or the last time that we have or will come across their names: William Gallas, Nicolas Anelka, David Trezeguet, Thierry Henry, most of them Clairefontaine graduates, the young guns in Aimé Jacquet's and

---

* A third European title had been won in 1949 at the expense of the Netherlands, but the tournament was not staged by UEFA at the time, and is generally excluded by statisticians for that reason.

Roger Lemerre's 'commando' that would take France to an undisputed place at the very top of the world game in the next few years. It should be stressed that this exceptional collection of talents might not have quite attained such heights if it hadn't been looked after by an equally exceptional technical staff. At its head was Gérard Houllier, who, following *Les Bleus*' traumatic failure to qualify for the 1994 World Cup, when only one point was required from their last two home games – one of them against Israel – moved down from a similar position with the senior team. Gérard had two outstanding assistants in Jacques Crevoisier and Christian Damiano, both of them key members of the Clarefontaine set-up. Only in France, I think, and only then, when the 1998 World Cup was uppermost in everyone's mind, could it have been possible to assemble such a well-qualified coaching team for juniors. One can only wish that far-sightedness of that kind could have survived the complacencies engendered by the ensuing success.

Gérard, who had been mindlessly pilloried in the press for the 1994 debacle, felt fortunate to rekindle his love for football in the company of this group of youngsters, who were quite unlike any who had preceded them at this age level. To start with, a number of them were the sons of first-generation 'immigrants' of Afro-Caribbean origin who had been raised in the high-rise estates now encircling most of France's biggest cities. In that respect, Thierry was just one of many. What they brought with them was a certain *insouciance,* a love of fun, but also the kind of mental toughness that is required to be your own man (whatever your age may be) in the harsh environment of the *banlieue* – or the football academy. This was also very much a transitional generation, one that hadn't relinquished the values of hard work and respect towards its elders which are far less in evidence today; and if you think these are merely the gripes of a cantankerous middle-aged writer, please consult any coach charged with Henry's heirs in 2012, then read this again. Thierry himself, who has had his brushes with a Nasri or two towards the end of his career, would be the first to concur.

Be that as it may, Houllier developed an affectionate relationship with his *lads*, who paid him back in kind. Thierry in particular took to the former English teacher; no doubt, he must have compared Tigana's somewhat distant and unforgiving management style with Gérard's live-and-let-live approach ('He knows that we're young, that we need a laugh, even to be allowed to go crazy sometimes'). What's more, Houllier cemented Henry's position within the team as soon as he had a chance to do so. 'I made him captain for his very first game with me for the under-18s, against Germany, in the autumn of 1995,' Gérard told me. 'He played centre-forward [for the juniors, if not ASM, as we've seen] at the time, until, in the autumn, we came across this young boy who couldn't speak French, and whom we'd heard of through Luis Fernandez, Paris Saint-Germain's manager at the time.' The young boy's name was David Trezeguet, a name that was familiar to Houllier. 'At the time David was born,' he recalled, 'when I was at Noeux-les-Mines, I'd played against his father Jorge, a pro with FC Rouen. We could pick him for France! David wasn't eighteen yet when I first selected him, in the autumn of the same year – he scored two and made two when we beat the Czechs 6-2. After such a debut, that was that. Thierry moved to the left.' Again.

Trezeguet had by then become one of Henry's teammates at Monaco, after Paris Saint-Germain had failed to navigate the paperwork required for his registration. Luis Fernandez, in a gesture he might have regretted later on, was so incensed by the incompetence of his own club's administrators that he recommended the youth to his fellow former *Bleu* and close friend Jean Tigana. In 'Lucho's' eyes, France could not afford such a talent to be wasted. His intuition and his generosity would be richly rewarded, after a fashion: Trezeguet heaped misery on PSG throughout the five seasons he spent in the principality, but the French team inherited one of the deadliest finishers in world football, who would otherwise have beaten a retreat to his father's country, Argentina, where he had learnt his football at CA Platense as a child and a teenager after his family moved back to Buenos Aires. Fernandez, born in the Spanish city of Tarifa, and Tigana, born in Bamako, then the capital of French Sudan, which became Mali after decolonization, had demonstrated a patriotism that should tell you all you need to know to understand how, well before the *black-blanc-beur* rainbow team of 1998, *Les Bleus* had been a force for integration in France. Similarly, if I may be forgiven for getting ahead of myself for a second, when Aimé Jacquet asked for the support of French club coaches in the season preceding that glorious tournament, Jean Tigana did not hesitate to alter his team's shape to suit the wishes of the national team manager. Lilian Thuram was moved to the right flank of his defence, whilst Henry, rotating with Trezeguet, was given the best possible chance to approach the World Cup in peak condition, and this at a time when neither youngster's place in the final squad was secure. *O tempora, o mores*, indeed. But let's go back to Gérard.

'There are many types of captain – people who shout a lot, organizers like Didier Deschamps, and those I'd call "technical leaders". Juninho [Pernambucano] was one for me at Lyon, and so was Thierry with the under-18s. He's not a natural talker, someone who feels at ease addressing a room full of people; but the thing he's very good at is putting his arm around a young teammate's shoulders and explaining to him in detail a particular aspect of the game, the "technical-tactical" side of things. Of all the players I've come across, none loves and understands football better than Thierry. "Carra" [Jamie Carragher] eats and breathes football, but even he is not as voracious as Titi. Mention a game between Le Mans and Guingamp, and the likelihood is that he'll not only have watched it, but he'll also be able to name every single player on the field and recall every incident in the match.'*

One of his teammates at the 1996 European Junior Championships later confided – anonymously – that '[Henry] didn't lead us with his voice. He wasn't a "boss", as people understand the word,' and one of France's specialist coaches, the former Bordeaux 'keeper Philippe Bergeroo, also expressed reservations about Thierry's ability to lead: 'A

---

* Thierry, when he arrived at Arsenal in 1999, took his first lodgings at Sopwell House, the luxurious hotel situated close to the club's training ground, where new signings were routinely billetted until a permanent home has been found for them. His first request was to have two giant television screens installed in his room, so he could follow – you've guessed it – two games simultaneously. In the same vein, this is how Gilles Grimandi recalls a quiz held for the Arsenal staff: 'We were asked to name the twenty players who had played in all three major championships: Spain, Italy and England. Arsène Wenger – who is in a category of his own in that respect – named nineteen. And Thierry? Eighteen! The next best only got eleven or twelve.'

striker must be selfish, and that doesn't suit a captain. Has he got the type of personality required from someone who can rally the troops?' These doubts would linger for a very long time, and will have a special resonance for Arsenal supporters; but no one expressed them when France beat Spain 1-0 on 30 July 1996, with Thierry scoring in the twenty-sixth minute, one of only two occasions on which he found the target in a final, the other being the winning goal in the 2003 Confederations Cup, a statistic his critics have never allowed him to forget. The goal that gave France the trophy at the tiny Stade Léo-Lagrange in Besançon, and thereby guaranteed them automatic qualification for the 1997 under-20 FIFA World Cup, was not a thing of beauty – an awkward bounce off his knee rather than a true strike of the ball – but was in keeping with France's performances throughout the tournament. They had been efficient, but lacked the flair you would have expected from such an assemblage of talents. In the short group phase that preceded the final, Houllier's team had notched two wins by a solitary goal, against Hungary and Portugal, followed by a lacklustre draw with Belgium. Henry, the figurehead, the wearer of the armband, the star in the making, hadn't been France's best performer, even if this competition did wonders for his profile with the general public. Trezeguet was the author of four of his side's five goals; he should have walked away with the plaudits, but didn't.*

Ah, Trezeguet. Depending on whom you listen to, Titi and David were like brothers, or the worst of enemies; or both. The official line, or headline, as seen above a *Journal du Dimanche* (*JDD*) joint interview a few months after the 1998 triumph, read: 'forever friends'. Titi had seen David, who was only two months younger than he, unpack his bags at Monaco late in the summer of 1995, barely able to say *oui* or *non*. He immediately took a shine to the shy Argentinian and did everything in his power to make him feel at home in his new, bewildering surroundings. He also admired the footballer he trained with every day

---

* France retained their title in the 1997 tournament, which was held in Iceland. Thierry had by then moved to the Espoirs (under-21s), and only one player played in both tournaments: Nicolas Anelka. Louis Saha scored a 'golden goal' against Portugal in the final to ensure victory.

of the week: Trezeguet was already the archetypal 'fox in the box',* a centre-forward who possessed an uncanny gift to 'smell' goals and unerringly found the position where the ball would sit to be hit, skewed, volleyed, headed, bundled into the net. David was a born goalscorer, like Pippo Inzaghi, Hugo Sanchez or Gerd Müller, the owner of skills that Thierry knew he could try to learn, but would never master to the same supreme degree, when intelligence becomes indistinguishable from instinct. I well remember a fascinating conversation I had with Henry at Highbury after Trezeguet had broken yet another record with Juventus; I was expecting a salute to the faraway friend, but what I got was something different altogether. Thierry proceeded to analyse how David had created the chance leading to his goal, shuffling feet like a madison dancer to describe how his friend had launched not one, not two, but *three* runs in quick succession within the eighteen-yard box, darting from post to post to create the space needed to beat the 'keeper, waiting, goodness knows how, for the ball to land precisely where it needed in order for him to prod it beyond the 'keeper's reach. Of all the memories I keep of Thierry, this is one of the most precious. I rang my desk to tell them: Titi just said the most wonderful things to me and . . . what

---

* Now is as good a moment to tell you how I believe that this expression first appeared in football speak, as both Thierry and I have a joint claim to authorship. This was on 12 May 2001, at the Millennium Stadium in Cardiff, the day Michael Owen facilitated an improbable 2-1 victory over Arsenal in the FA Cup final. The scrum of reporters in the improvised mixed zone (a concrete tunnel leading to the players' car park) was such that the *Evening Standard* football correspondent Steve Stammers and I decided to position ourselves towards the exit, in the hope that the large French-speaking contingent present in both teams would stop in this quieter area when they heard themselves addressed in their native language. Thierry did, at length. He was visibly incensed. Arsenal had all but crushed Liverpool but had only converted one of their many chances through lack of sharpness in the eighteen-yard box. What they lacked, Henry told us, was 'un renard de surface'. Steve wasn't familiar with this turn of phrase and turned towards me: 'What was that?' Without thinking, I replied: 'Thierry believes that what they need is a fox in the box,' which happens to be a literal, if rhyming, translation of the original French. 'Don't repeat that to anyone!' Steve interjected. The *Evening Standard* had its back-page headline, and soccerese another cliché in the making, not that I had the faintest idea of this at the time.

was it exactly? My transcript read like an autopsy report, and we binned it. What was so beautiful, indeed so moving, was Thierry's excitement, his sense of wonder at what David had done and which he, the showman who ruled Arsenal, could never do. This, to me, was the real Henry, the football lover, in the proper sense: the man who loved football unconditionally and could lose himself in that love so fully that all ideas of competition made no sense any more.

But Trezeguet *was* a competitor, and a competitor of the most dangerous kind. Should he succeed at Monaco, or with the juniors, or, sooner rather than later, with the senior team, he would be an obstacle to Thierry's progress. Things were tough enough with Ikpeba, Madar and Petersen at ASM. France, who had performed honourably at the 1996 Euros, missing out on a place in the final on penalties against the Czech Republic, primarily relied on a 4-3-2-1 system in which the two playmakers behind the sole striker (a role for which Trezeguet was far better suited than Henry) had to be Djorkaeff and Zidane, now that Éric Cantona had chosen to take himself out of Aimé Jacquet's equation. In an ideal world, Thierry would have seen himself operating in tandem with David at the tip of a 4-4-2 system, or perhaps as a wide man in a 4-3-3 set-up, but Jacquet would never sanction this. In any case, the idea that the national manager could pick more than one teenager in his World Cup squad of twenty-two players appeared fanciful at the time, especially as Henry, Trezeguet – and Anelka – had yet to appear for the under-21 side and could not even command a regular starting place at their clubs. Thierry himself did his utmost to defuse the potential tensions between Trezeguet and himself. A willing and articulate interviewee, Henry stressed how he, who had taken on the role of a school prefect in youth teams ever since he had been called up to represent his country, was no more than a first among equals, who had only been singled out because he had played a few games in the top division of the *championnat* and the others had not. Reading the numerous interviews he gave at the time, when he was still only eighteen years old, I can't help but notice how they are almost interchangeable with those he granted when he had become the most potent symbol of Arsenal's ascent to the summit of English football. He comes across as confident yet humble, is quick to praise others, generous to his coaches, wags a finger at those who belittle the collective nature of the game – he is pitch perfect. And you wonder – what about Trezeguet? Did you fear him, Thierry? Contrast the answers they gave to the *JDD* reporter who asked them: 'Were there moments [during the 1998 World Cup] when you felt sorry for each other?' Trezeguet replied: 'When Thierry got injured against Paraguay. I really believed the World Cup was over for him at this moment.' Henry said: 'I didn't ask myself questions about David, even when he was on the bench. I didn't have time to think about it. When you're focused on the title, you can't ask yourself who's playing instead of whom.'

The dynamics of their relationship was a talking point within French football throughout the years both forwards spent together in the national team. It was suggested that Thierry was using his growing influence to undermine the position of his 'friend' – not directly, of course, but, for example, by advocating changes to the game plan and the tactical organization of the team that could only harm David's chances to shine as he did, so magnificently, with Juve in Serie A. This constant stream of innuendo caused Henry a great deal of pain; I often heard him complain bitterly about the 'people' (a word that carried so much disdain in his voice) who were sniping at him from behind their writing desks, letting their readers guess, often without great subtlety, that he, Thierry, was jealous of his teammate at Monaco. 'But no one rates David more highly than I do!' he exclaimed. 'I *know* we can play together – haven't we done it often enough?' But his protestations fell on deaf ears. The more he expressed his affection and admiration for Trezeguet, the more it was assumed that he did so to hide his resentment. It is true that Thierry's appraisal of a fellow player could change quite dramatically whether he was on or off the record – not that he was the only footballer to be guilty of this duplicity. I have in mind the case of a well-known Premier League defender whom Henry always professed to have great respect for in public, but whom he savaged with relish in less guarded moments. Now, if he could use double-talk in X's case, why would it be otherwise with Trezeguet? As for me, I believe it *was* different; but what hurt Thierry so much is that very few have shared my opinion, and that he was powerless to make them change their minds. The innocence of those blessed days with the juniors had long faded away. It is true that, then, there was only one star, and his name was Thierry Henry.

Monaco wasn't always that much fun.

THE BETRAYAL

Twelve months later, by the end of the 1996–7 season, two months away from his twentieth birthday, Thierry had already achieved more than any other French player of his generation. *France Football*'s newly elected Young Player of the Year had won a European title with France's under-21s; become a national champion and reached the semi-finals of the UEFA Cup with Monaco; and been called up by Aimé Jacquet to train with the national squad, which everyone expected him to join on a full-time basis in the near future. But he very nearly threw it all away by getting embroiled in a scandal that could have cost him far more than a fine, though the price he paid was in many ways far bigger than that. Several months later, he reflected: 'In one year, I've seen everything, and aged ten years.' He also re-evaluated his relationship with the man he feared, loved and admired more than any other, and the conclusion he came to must have hurt him tremendously. Thierry would end up having no choice but to loosen the tie that had bound father and son ever since Tony first asked the six-year-old Titi to take penalties against him on a concrete pitch.

To think that it had all started so promisingly, when Thierry, the captain of the under-21 European champions, rejoined Jean Tigana's group after a short holiday. Éric Di Meco has not forgotten how Henry scorched the pitch in his first game of the season, which was Monaco's third, a 2-0 victory at AS Cannes' La Boca Stadium on 28 August: 'It was so hot. I was knackered – I'd just come back from the Euros in England. I was getting on thirty-five, running at two miles an hour. Thierry was more like 2,000 miles an hour. But we played on the same flank that day, and I loved it. That afternoon, he worked so fucking hard.' That performance set the tone for the next five months, and Tigana soon had no choice but to give start after start to the striker whom the headline writers of *L'Équipe* now routinely called 'the diamond' or 'the phenomenon' and the Stade Louis II announcer 'Titi' Henry. This mix of hyperbole and familiarity was the surest sign that Thierry had 'arrived' for good. The goals came, some of them spectacular, like the opener he struck against Strasbourg on 13 November, and which a French television presenter introduced as 'a stroke of genius'. One month earlier, he had opened his account in European football, coming off the bench – a rarer and rarer occurrence – to contribute one of his side's four goals in a spectacular defeat of Borussia Mönchengladbach that made qualifying for the third round of the UEFA Cup a formality. He had also played a major part in brushing aside KS Hutnik Kraków in the previous round. Thierry was walking on water, feeding Sonny Anderson from the left wing when he was not on the scoresheet himself; as for ASM, which had been strengthened by the arrival of Scottish playmaker John Collins from Celtic, a League title seemed to be a near-formality from the autumn onwards. Tigana's team was moving ahead at an unmatchable pace, scoring an average of close to two goals per game, enjoying a burst of national popularity such at it had never known before, not even when Arsène Wenger had been in charge. They were that good; and so was Thierry, the sole member of the French Junior European Championship-winning side whose face was recognized in the stands when that team was introduced to the crowd at the Parc des Princes shortly before the A team beat Turkey 4-0 on 9 October. How far could he go? Jean Tigana remained cautious, telling reporters that it was not unknown for very young players to go through a purple patch, then fall away as soon as their euphoria had been checked by an injury, a suspension or an indifferent performance. One of the youth-team coaches – Paul Piétri – went as far as saying that, compared to the now-forgotten Strasbourg striker David Zitelli, Henry wasn't much to shout about. Henry had his fan club, of course, of which Raymond Domenech, the manager of the French under-21s, was one of the most vocal members. After all, hadn't he selected Thierry for a friendly against Norway as soon as he would become eligible for the *Espoirs*? 'If he carries on like this,' Domenech prophesied, 'I am convinced that he has the potential to be a candidate for the next World Cup!', one of the rare instances when *Raymond-la-science* was proved right in his predictions. But high in Monaco's hierarchy, chairman Jean-Louis Campora and his fellow board members felt increasingly uneasy as the media fought harder and harder for a piece of the 'prodigy'. What worried them the most was that Thierry revelled in the attention, volunteered interviews, talked out of turn and got drunk on this first sip of fame, expecting nothing but unconditional compliments. They could also see that a growing number of hangers-on had wormed their way into the player's entourage. Most of them were, to be brutally frank, starfuckers. Most of them, but not all. Some were not after glory, but money. It wasn't just France that had woken up to the emergence of an exceptional talent.

The story of how Thierry Henry was led to believe he could and would join Real Madrid in 1996 has never been told in detail outside of France. Even there, the very complexity of the affair precluded it from being given the exposure that it merited. Too many parties were involved, none of whom trusted the other, with some justification. Too many people lied. Lost in a sea of sycophants, cheats and exploiters, the teenage Thierry was made to realize that there was no one he could trust but himself. I've heard some of his critics argue that what happened was the first manifestation of a manipulative character. They're mistaken. They saw the Titi of 1996 in the light of the Henry of the 2010 World Cup. What can be said is that the Henry of 2010 would probably have been a very different man, had it not been for what happened fourteen years earlier.

According to contemporary reports in the French press, *L'Équipe* and *France Football* in particular, which followed the saga in great detail from day one, it all started with one Michel Basilevic, or Vasiljevic, and a few other spellings beside, who called himself a 'recruiting adviser to a number of clubs' but didn't hold the then compulsory FIFA agent's licence. What Basilevic, or Vasiljevic, did have was good looks, charm, imagination and contacts. Of Croatian roots, but educated in the West and mostly active in Spain, he had made a name for himself over a decade earlier, when he had taken over the management of Johan Cruyff's

affairs with catastrophic results for the player, whose ruin was so complete that he had to come out of retirement and join Los Angeles Aztecs
to rebuild his fortune. I regret not having the space to recount the whole
sorry business, which involved investments in pig-farming, accounts in
Switzerland and multiple accusations of betrayal, blackmail and skuldug-
gery and petered out in threats of lawsuits which – to the best of my
knowledge – never reached court. What matters is that Basilevic survived
with his career (but not his reputation) intact.

Seventeen years later, in October 1996, attending an informal meeting
with Real Madrid executives, the same Basilevic heard them lamenting
the lack of a left-sided player who could bolster their attack. Henry's
name popped up. It was to be expected, as Thierry was already one of
the most talked-about youngsters in European football and had started
the French domestic season in superb form, scoring six goals before the
autumn set in. The 'businessman', as he also described himself, asked
for and received a mandate from the Spanish club: his mission was to
establish contact with their target. But, if accounts of the meeting which
were published in France after FIFA brought the matter to a close are
to be believed, it is not the player whom Basilevic got in touch with
– it was Tony, whom he met in the palatial Hôtel Crillon on the 29th
of that month. Real's chairman, Lorenzo Sanz, and the club's chief legal
officer, Juan Antonio Samper, were also present to discuss a five- or
six-year contract for Thierry, which would earn the player the equivalent
of £60,000 – after tax – per month, plus a signing-on fee of £800,000.
It is understandable that Tony's head might be turned by sums as colossal
as these, which far exceeded the salaries paid by French clubs at the
time; there was also the prospect of seeing Titi in the legendary *merengue*
jersey, the first Frenchman to wear it since Raymond Kopa.

According to Basilevic, Thierry's father assured the Real delegation
that his son's contract with Monaco would expire eight months later,
on 30 June 1997, which was untrue: the agreement ran until 30 June
1998. Thierry himself apparently had no idea of what was being said
about his future: as the meeting in Paris ended, he was hundreds of
miles away, preparing to play a UEFA Cup game against Borussia
Mönchengladbach at the Stade Louis II. Almost immediately after
leaving the Crillon, however, Samper and Basilevic boarded a plane to

Nice and from there drove on to Monaco, where Thierry was informed that Real Madrid were interested in securing his services. Thierry, stunned, phoned his father on the spot, who advised him to stay put and promise nothing. What Thierry didn't know was that, two days after the first discussion had taken place in Paris, Tony had been spotted in Barcelona. Shortly afterwards, extraordinarily, while watching an Italian football programme in his flat, Thierry thought he had recognized his father in a stand at San Siro. What could this all mean? He decided to keep his own counsel from then on.

By mid-November, Basilevic was convinced that he had got his man and asked Samper to join him at the Hôtel Abela in Monte Carlo. The starstruck Thierry signed a pre-contract agreement on the spot, receiving £15,000 in cash (for which he had to sign an IOU, and with which it is said he bought his teammate Victor Ikpeba's 4x4). By that time, according to those who saw him train and play every day, Thierry had 'lost it'. He headed back to Paris for Christmas, having disconnected his mobile phone. In the meantime, Real's lawyers were putting the finishing touch to a proper contract, and, by January, Basilevic had finally informed Tony – against Thierry's wishes – that the deal was done. All hell broke loose. This is how Gilles Grimandi described the scene. 'The whole Real Madrid thing was crazy,' he told me. 'His dad was crying in the hall, Thierry was crying upstairs. I wondered what on earth could be going on. The deal was done. It really destroyed him at the time, and it caused huge problems in his relationship with his father.' Was Tony the villain of the piece, then? Grimandi didn't think so. 'His father is not a bad guy,' he said, 'but he didn't understand the system. This brought him to the brink with his son, which is a real pity. It changed everything in their relationship. And it changed Thierry, not necessarily for the better.'

Monaco at last understood why their striker had seemed so agitated during the few weeks that preceded the traditional winter break. ASM chairman Jean-Louis Campora was understandably beside himself with fury. In October, hadn't Sanz expressly stated in an exchange of letters between the two clubs that Real Madrid would not seek to approach any Monaco player during the season? Campora tore into Henry's entourage. 'There are plenty of people who try to destabilize young players and their parents,' he said, 'promising them the Moon and God knows what. These people behave like scavengers who jump on anything that moves.' Real was stung and produced its evidence: a contract dated 12 January, signed by the player in person, which was swiftly passed on to the Spanish League, then to the Spanish FA. 12 January, really? Strange. On that day, Thierry was playing a League Cup game in Le Mans, a long way away from Madrid. How could Thierry's signature appear on the contract?

Real had also instructed a non-registered agent to act on their behalf. Never mind: they flatly denied that they had even been in touch with Basilevic, when all evidence pointed to the contrary. Thierry, in the meantime, following his father's recommendation, extended his current contract with ASM by two-and-a-half years, thereby deepening the hole others had dug for him. Unfortunately, he hadn't moved an inch; in fact, he was back at square one, stuck in and with Monaco. Thierry – and his football – went to pieces. Jean Tigana tried to protect him, giving him time and space to recover a modicum of peace of mind; Henry played a mere three minutes between 25 January and 4 March. On the eve of an under-21 friendly against the Netherlands, towards the end of February 1997, he tore into Tigana. 'I don't understand,' he said. 'The coach doesn't give me any explanation. And when I hear that I've got plenty of time ahead of me, it drives me crazy. I don't have the time. I'm not saying it's bad to be protected, but if you're good, you play, right?' But his ordeal was not over, far from it. Yielding – for the last time in his life – to his father's instructions, he agreed to take on the FIFA-registered Alain Migliaccio as his agent for the next two years, the French press reporting that Tony had received a substantial sum to facilitate the agreement – something, it should be emphasized, that was and is common practice in football, and broke no law or regulation. That was on 2 March. Two days later, a letter arrived on Migliaccio's desk: Thierry was terminating his contract with him! He had a very good reason to do so. Since 20 February, he had agreed to be represented by another FIFA-registered agent, the former French international Jean-François Larios. Migliaccio – who had also worked for Éric Cantona, had been sucked into Olympique de Marseille's murky financial deals during the Bernard Tapie era and would later team up with Zinedine

Zidane – instantly referred the case to FIFA, arguing that Henry's agreement with Larios was invalid, and that his own should stand.

It took months to unravel this unholy mess. As late as July 1997, Samper was adamant that 'Thierry Henry had signed this contract [the one dated 12 January] in person, within the legal six-month limit before the expiry of his previous contract [with AS Monaco]' in the presence of 'several most qualified [*sic*] witnesses'. The FIFA investigators were less impressed. In early September 1997, Real was fined the equivalent of £80,000 for illegal approach of a contracted player and use of an unregistered agent. Basilevic disappeared for a while, to resurface in 2002, when his name was linked to the financial wrongdoings that brought German club Kaiserslautern to the brink of bankrupcy. Nothing more has been heard from him since. All things considered, Thierry escaped lightly, since, had the agreement with Real Madrid been validated, he would have been found guilty of both breach of contract and the use of an unregistered agent and liable to pay a far larger sum to the wronged club than the fine that ended in FIFA's charitable funds. In the end, the £40,000 he had to pay was little more than a firm rap on the knuckles. Monaco's support had proved crucial in earning him the relative leniency of FIFA's disciplinary commission. To inflict the heaviest punishment possible on the player (a two-year ban) would have been contrary to the interests of the club he was contracted to, when Monaco were the only party to have behaved properly throughout the whole affair. Commendably, he also took it on himself to compensate Migliaccio out of his own pocket, when the mistakes he had undoubtedly made could have been blamed on others – Tony to start with.

Henry might have felt betrayed by the man he trusted the most; but he also knew that his father, foolish as he may have been, had not sought to enrich himself at the expense of his son. Blinded by the prospect of seeing Thierry join one of Europe's biggest clubs, with all the rewards this entailed, Tony was foolish enough to believe he could outsmart a system he knew almost nothing about. Basilevic and the others couldn't have hoped for an easier prey. Tony, the most naive of conspirators, was chewed up and spat out by men vastly more experienced than he was. Thierry was no longer the schoolboy who could accept that grown-ups should decide what to do with him, as when

Tony had conducted negotiations with AS Monaco three years earlier. He never failed to acknowledge the huge debt he owed his father; so often, and so fulsomely, in fact, that I'm tempted to think these tributes were also a form of long-drawn-out apology, almost penance for what he had had to do to become himself, that is 'killing the father', which he did for good when he wrong-footed everyone, Tony and agents included, by opting for Juventus in 1999.

I have no right to pass judgement on the rights and wrongs of a relationship in which power unavoidably shifted from one to the other as Thierry grew older, and which, given the personalities it involved, was bound to be defined for good – crystallized – by a crisis. What I am certain of, however, is that it shaped the Henry who would emerge in the years to come. It hardened him. It made him look at others wondering if they too were only interested in what they could gain from his friendship and his trust. There had long been a calculating streak in Thierry's character, which had been noticed by some of his *Monégasque* teammates almost as soon as the teenager was asked to join the professional squad. 'Thierry hadn't got the friends who could tell him: "You're wrong, don't do that,"' Gilles Grimandi told me. 'Manu [Petit] could do it, because of his status. Only one other person could stand up to him and win: Lilian Thuram. Lilian would go to him and say: "Don't do that, kid." And Thierry would listen. Because Lilian is a fantastic guy, and because he'd had a prodigious career.' At times, though, Thierry could and did seek advice from his elders. Di Meco remembers how the teenager asked him questions 'not just about the game, but about football as an environment. Thierry had been caught in that episode with Real Madrid. He was a kid. A kid lost in this milieu.' But Di Meco was an exception, and his advice had been called on too late anyway.

Thierry was a quick learner. The superstar who, later in his career, would always show genuine pleasure when coming across former teammates and coaches, and even journalists who had last talked to him a long time beforehand, possessed just as sharp, if not a sharper, memory for those who had wronged him in the past. Grimandi believes that the Real affair was 'the source of so many problems for Thierry in his life'. When I asked him to single out which of these 'problems' had had the greatest bearing on Thierry's development, he answered: 'His refusal to hear certain things. It's the same for everyone: we don't accept contra-diction from many people; but if there is one person you should accept contradiction from, it's your father.' But could Thierry do it any longer if he wished to be his own man? As he said himself in a 2004 interview with *Paris Match*, 'I am quite cold with people I don't know, because I took some hits that taught me to be cautious.' When pressed by the magazine's reporter to reveal what these 'hits' (*claques*) had been, Thierry batted back the question with the most evasive of answers and swiftly moved on to the doubts many people had about him in the run-up to the 1998 World Cup. I am convinced that what he really had in mind were events that had happened a year and a half before that tournament.

5

Joy, and nothing but.

THE MIRACLE OF 12 JULY

The sad affair of Thierry's botched transfer to Real Madrid didn't reach its denouement until the autumn of 1997, as we have seen. Nevertheless, some order had been restored to his professional life by then, mostly thanks to JeanTigana's assured handling of the situation. When Monaco had come very close to putting Thierry on the transfer list in May 1997, Tigana had done all he could to dissuade his board from doing so. That is not to say that Henry felt more grateful towards the manager who had frozen him out of the team towards the end of the winter, when the player, egged on by his entourage, believed he had earned the right to take part in every game in Monaco's schedule. His passage through purgatory had been short-lived, however, and, whilst not quite a guaranteed starter in ASM's line-up, he made a significant contribution to the club's superb League campaign, finishing with ten goals and thirteen assists in forty-eight appearances in all competitions – often from the bench: the best return of his Monaco career. This constituted remarkable progress for the nineteen-year-old Henry, whose status had changed from leader of a new generation of French footballers – that was already clear before the 1996 under-18 Europeans – to contender for a place in Aimé Jacquet's 'A' team for the 1998 World Cup. As years went by, Thierry grew to understand that Tigana had played a key role in his development, a role which his pride prevented him from acknowledging unreservedly at the time. 'There were quite a few clashes between the two of them,' Di Méco recalls, 'but Thierry had to check himself, as he had to have the coach on his side to further his career, to become an international, for example. They needed each other, and that made things much easier.' But this was a marriage of convenience, not a love-match, which could only last as long as the interests of both parties coincided; and they did – for the moment.

Tigana had been exasperated by the praise lavished on Henry by his courtiers, and wasn't alone in noting an excessive eagerness, on Thierry's part, to accept that praise. Raymond Domenech, who had called the player to the under-23 national side before his twentieth birthday, asked the media to 'leave the kid alone'. 'There are players who've proved far more than he has,' he said. 'Don't turn him into a star before his time!' Quite naturally, and quite rightly, Tigana had taken the view that to further the cause of both his club and his player, he must counterbalance the enthusiasm of supporters and pressmen alike, in the way he used him on the pitch as well as in the words he employed when discussing the youngster's future with reporters. When a microphone was placed in front of him, Thierry claimed that he understood that Tigana had his welfare in mind and explained that he still had to 'make a little space for himself' at Monaco, not that everyone accepted these regular displays of humility at face value. 'I've thought long and hard (*gambergé*),' he told *France Football* in April 1997, reflecting on the turbulence that had engulfed him over the past eight months. 'The coach takes the decisions, and even if a player wants to be on the field, there's nothing to comment upon. I must relativize things . . . I've been called on [to play] quite often this year. I'm part of the squad and I rather have a thought for my mate Dos Santos who was often on the pitch last year and who isn't playing any more today. It's very difficult for him. So I shouldn't complain.'

I'm sure that you will feel, as I do, that these remarks – particularly the reference to Dos Santos's problems – do not come across as well as Henry would have wished them to. They sound rehearsed, unconvincing, far too polite in fact, remembering that 'polite' is a cousin of that equivocal word 'policy', in English. Not that Thierry was lying – far from it. He did not complain. He turned up for training on time and did what was asked of him. John Collins remembers how Titi and Trezeguet never moaned when they were asked to carry the equipment of the senior pros, as ASM's kit-man, who was well into his seventies, couldn't do it himself any more. There were no half-hearted performances, no sulking fits when the touchline official indicated that Thierry had to let another player take his place on the field. Henry was intelligent enough to silence his misgivings and concentrate on what lay ahead: captaining the French side at the 1997 FIFA under-20 World Cup in Malaysia. In that environment, at least, he was assured of the leading role – though he must have been disappointed to miss out on the Tournoi de France, which was held almost simultaneously, and one of Aimé Jacquet's key dress rehearsals for the World Cup proper.

Thierry's France travelled to Kuala Lumpur as one of the favourites for the tournament. A quick look at the squad was enough to unders-tand why: players like Willy Sagnol, Mickaël Landreau and Philippe Christanval, all of whom would become full internationals and wear the respective colours of Bayern Munich, PSG and Barcelona, had been added to the core of the 1996 under-19 European champions. France's group was not the strongest, despite the presence of Brazil, and their 3-0 defeat at the hands of the *auriverde* in their opening game could be interpreted as a logical retribution for Gérard Houllier's rashness. Naming Henry, Trezeguet and Anelka in his starting eleven was at best the gamble of an arch-optimist. Reminiscing about this game in 2010, Gérard could not suppress a naughty chuckle. 'I'm the only coach to have ever put Titi, David and Nico in the same team,' he told me, 'and it's only fair to say that our full-backs had quite a lot of work to do.' Then as later, none of that trio had a reputation for tracking back, despite Henry's protestations that he understood the need to *mouiller le maillot* (literally 'wet the jersey'). But the sweat that drenched their shirts had more to do with the fiendishly humid, numbingly hot atmos-phere of Malaysia than with the forwards' sense of self-sacrifice. Anelka, the youngest of the three, was used only as a substitute from then onwards.

Henry and his teammates had a far easier task against a desperately weak Korean side, which would ship no fewer than ten goals against the Brazilians later in the same competition. Within ten minutes, France had raced to a 3-0 lead – a brace by Henry, a strike by Trezeguet. Only wayward finishing and an understandable desire to preserve some energy in the stifling tropical heat explain why the final scoreline was a rather modest 4-2, which was repeated against South Africa on 22 June. This time, it was Trezeguet who found the net twice, Henry once. Mexico were then beaten – just – in the round of sixteen, Peter Luccin scoring in the ninetieth minute, only for France to fail in a penalty shoot-out against a determined Uruguayan side whose players have since all receded into minor-league football and obscurity. Thierry was not at his best, missing two good chances to put France ahead, and was subbed in the seventy-second minute, shortly after the eventual Player of the Tournament, Nicolás Olivera, had cancelled out Trezeguet's opener. Anelka, not for the last time of his career, fluffed his spot-kick, and France exited the youth World Cup far earlier than most had predicted.

France's collective failure was also a personal setback for Henry, who had come to expect laudatory accounts of his performances every time he turned up for one of the national youth teams. Whereas Trezeguet, then a relative unknown, saw his stock rise thanks to five well-taken goals and the consistency of his performances, a number of questions were asked of his skipper's anonymity in the pivotal games of the competition. Tiredness alone could not explain why he had failed to live up to his reputation as a 'game changer'. Thierry had hoped that the under-20 World Cup would provide him with a springboard; it turned out to be a reminder that his development was not yet complete. After giving Thierry starts in the first two League games of the 1997–8 campaign, in which the winger looked more like a player approaching the end of an exhausting season than one who was beginning a new one afresh, Tigana decided to get back to the formula that had served Monaco so well in the previous year: Thierry would feature regularly, but more often than not from the substitutes' bench, and this despite Monaco selling their striker Sonny Anderson in the summer to FC Barcelona for a then colossal £12.5 million. Victor Ikpeba, the reigning African Footballer of the Year, remained Tigana's preferred option in attack, and Thierry sometimes struggled to contain his frustration, on one hand appearing to endorse his coach's caution, on the other coming up with statements that were undisguised challenges to Tigana's authority, and veiled threats to seek a transfer ('I'll talk about my future when I start games for Monaco. Right now [in late September 1997], everything's blurred, I can't see anything'). The twenty-year-old even had the cheek to call on his manager to purchase another centre-forward and adopt a 4-3-3 formation in which he, Thierry, and Ikpeba could each 'own' their respective wing. Funny, this. Didn't Monaco already have Thierry's best friend David Trezeguet at their disposal? What of 'the Wizard', the Chadian Japhet N'Doram, who had just been bought from FC Nantes?

In any case, Tigana had more pressing matters to attend to. Monaco hadn't just lost Anderson. Enzo Scifo had gone back to his first professional club, Anderlecht. Arsène Wenger, who had put an end to a two-year exile in Japan by becoming the first-ever Frenchman to coach an English club, had taken both Emmanuel Petit and Gilles Grimandi to Arsenal, much to Thierry's envy. (Thierry is said to have pestered Gilles at the training ground when his move to the Gunners became a certainty, half-jokingly imploring his elder to take him along, as playing for the north London club had been a dream of his.) The dependable Patrick Blondeau had left for England as well, where he failed to impose himself at Sheffield Wednesday. It is a testimony to Tigana's management skills that, despite being deprived of five key players for whom no like-for-like replacement had been found, his Monaco side performed far better than expected, both at home – where ASM occupied top spot in the League at Christmas and finished a highly creditable third – and especially in Europe, as Manchester United fans are unlikely to have forgotten.

It might be, as Gilles Grimandi told me, that 'Henry had already become too big for the club', inasmuch as everyone saw in him a superstar in the making, who was bound to be snapped up by one of Europe's most powerful clubs. It might also be that Anderson's departure had unsettled him far more than he let it show in the numerous interviews he was still granting to anyone with a tape recorder and a notebook at hand, it seems. Thierry perhaps overplayed it a fraction when he claimed that he and the Brazilian striker were 'inseparable'; but there had been a genuine complicity – and affection – between the two men, who sought each other's company on the training ground, teaming up in every exercise thrown at them by the coaching staff, including one-on-one challenges ('I never took the ball off him,' Henry recalled). Their understanding also shone on the pitch, with Anderson very much the senior partner in this association. 'I knew him *par cœur* (by heart),' Henry said, and on this occasion, the heart was speaking.

Be that as it may, Henry's progress had been checked. The 1998

World Cup? No chance. 'Those who do not start games for their club won't be selected,' he said in the first days of the autumn. When asked who would be Jacquet's centre-forward, he instantly replied: 'Florian Maurice'. Maurice, the 'next Jean-Pierre Papin', had started the campaign well for his new club, PSG, and had already been picked by Aimé Jacquet for a walk-on part in a friendly against Mexico in 1996. To think that, little under a year later, Thierry's father Tony would burst into tears when his son raised the World Cup trophy.

It is unlikely that Thierry would have been at the Stade de France on 12 July 1998 if he had been judged on his performances in the *championnat* alone. Europe smiled on him, fortunately. Tigana obviously considered that his winger's game was better suited to the Champions League than to the rougher environment of the French championship; and it didn't hurt that Thierry missed out on Monaco's first outing in the UEFA tournament through suspension. ASM were sunk in Lisbon, where Sporting scored three times without reply. By contrast, with Henry restored to the line-up, Monaco swatted Bayer Leverkusen 4-0 on 1 October 1997. Thierry opened the scoring and finished with a double, giving the kind of performance that made it difficult to understand how his manager could possibly do without him in the future. And – at least in Europe – Tigana didn't. Henry played his part in each of the seven games that followed, scoring seven goals over the whole campaign, a Champions League record for a French player, including a very late equalizer against Bayer in December that ensured that Monaco topped their group.

Just as importantly, Thierry's terrific display against the German vice-champions had been timed to perfection, as Aimé Jacquet was about to announce his squad for a friendly against South Africa. The manager of *Les Bleus*, who was keen to test as many players as possible in any case, didn't surprise anyone when he picked Henry to start that game on 11 October. As debuts go, however, Thierry's left a lot to be desired, and the score awarded him by *L'Équipe* (five out of ten) erred on the side of generosity, judging by the comments that accompanied this modest evaluation. 'We had to wait a full hour to see him finally use his strengths . . . he didn't give enough decent balls . . . he lacked boldness . . . he didn't fulfil our expectations', etc., etc. In 2004, looking back on this first acquaintance with international football, this is how the now-'Invincible' of Arsenal judged his younger self: 'At the beginning with *Les Bleus*, I was afraid of doing something wrong. For my first cap, I did not play with any freedom, I feared losing the ball. Jacquet had picked me so that I could offer something extra up front – but I kept passing the ball backwards. I was nineteen. I was in awe of Desailly and the others.'

Thierry had fluffed his lines, badly, and found himself cast to the periphery of the national team. That first cap could even be considered a step backwards, at it showed that the youngster was not yet fit for national service: Aimé Jacquet didn't call on him once in the six months that followed. It was all the more galling for Henry that his great friend David Trezeguet had now superseded him in the pecking order and missed making the squad in only one of the six games France played during that period – and then through injury. 'I was super-happy [*sic*] for David,' Thierry later confessed, 'but I was hurt, too. It's frustrating to see your mate move ahead of you, and not to be with him.' Henry's absence could not be explained by a tactical switch either. On the contrary, at this stage, Jacquet often deployed a 4-3-3 formation in which a place for Thierry could be found far more readily, at least in theory, than in the 4-3-2-1 that had been seen at the 1996 European Championships. Nor was Henry's anxiety lessened by the emergence of Nicolas Anelka, who had taken full advantage of an injury to Ian Wright to establish himself as Arsenal's main striker and made his international debut on 22 April 1998 in a goalless draw with Sweden. Doubt set in. 'I'm asking myself more and more questions,' Henry confided in the spring of 1998. He dared not tell Tigana how much he was hampered by an ankle injury that had hindered him since the beginning of the year, the severity of which was known only to his closest friends. He had no time for convalescing when a place in Monaco's starting eleven was still beyond his grasp, or so he believed, when a proper rest was perhaps what he needed the most. For four years on the trot, as soon as the domestic season was over, he had joined a succession of youth teams to represent his country in friendlies or international tournaments. In March 1998, shortly before Monaco stunned Manchester United at Old Trafford thanks to a Trezeguet rocket, the fastest goal in the Champions League,* Thierry had confided to his half-brother Willy that he felt unable 'to put one foot in front of the other'. His father Tony added that 'he'd been cooked in every sauce for the past five years', which wasn't much of an exaggeration. Henry hadn't enjoyed a proper break from football during that period, an exhausting pattern that would continue until the end of his international career. France would not host another World Cup until his playing days were over. In all probability, missing out on the 1998 tournament meant squandering an opportunity that hadn't been presented to a Kopa or a Platini – and Thierry knew that Jacquet couldn't possibly gamble on including too many juniors in his final squad. One, without a doubt; two, perhaps; three, certainly not. He also knew that the endearingly old-fashioned 'Mémé' was irritated by the amount of attention Henry was receiving in the media, complaining about 'gossiping', which everyone interpreted as a direct criticism of Thierry's remarkable availability to reporters. 'I don't read papers,' he said. Yeah, right. Then, as later, his sensitivity to criticism was only matched by his desire to be praised and would shape the personality of the serial record-breaker to the extent that, for us journalists, it would come to define him as a human being. Allow me to tell you why, and how, for which I must leave the Thierry of 1998 for a moment.

The scene takes place in the 1970s. The veteran journalist has a piece of advice for his young Fleet Street colleague. He takes out a notebook and opens it with a flourish. 'As long as you've got these, you'll never go hungry.' 'These' meant: the phone numbers of what were not yet routinely called 'football stars', a collection which the hack had assembled over a number of years pottering about in freezing car parks and rain-sodden grounds. What's more, they were home phone numbers,

---

* I cannot resist adding a footnote at this point. Arsène Wenger watched the 1-1 draw that took his old club to the semis at the expense of his new rival in his Totteridge home and proceeded to celebrate it in a way far remote from his image as an austere teetotaller. Arriving at the Arsenal training ground the morning after the night before, he gently whispered to his captain Tony Adams: 'Please don't talk too loudly – my head feels a bit sore,' or words to that effect.

pure gold, not the base metal of mobile numbers that the luckiest of pressmen trade with circumspection these days, knowing full well that, in a month or two, whoever rings them will get a dead tone. Modern-day footballers don't cover their tracks – they erase them. Henry was quite good at that.

Most British journalists agree that a sea-change took place during the 1990 World Cup, when tabloids went in for the kill and dispatched news reporters, known in the trade as 'rotters', to follow Bobby Robson's England team in Italy. Their sole *raison d'être* was to collect 'stories', preferably of the scandalous kind; hooligans were also a pet subject. *All Played Out*, Pete Davies's superb account of life within the England camp during the tournament, paints a ghastly picture of what the 'rotters' were up to and of the complete breakdown of trust between footballers and writers to which their dirt-digging led. Football had entered the showbiz age in the least dignified way possible, not so much a white shirt hanging outside a drunk's tuxedo as fake Calvin Klein pants showing above a pair of sullied blue jeans. It is often said that the creation of the Premier League (Brian Glanville's 'greed-is-good' League) in 1992, which coincided with Sky Sports acquiring the broadcasting rights for the competition, was the tipping point, the decisive moment at which football ceased to be 'the working man's game' and instead became 'global entertainment'. In truth, the worm was already struggling to wriggle out of the fruit by then and emerged as an unappetizing insect two years later in America, where the World Cup organizers came up with the concept of the 'mixed zone', which has now become one of the last points of contact between footballers and the overwhelming majority of those who write about them. The word 'contact' should be taken with a rather large pinch of salt as well; more often than not, as I and my colleagues know from bitter experience, this 'contact' is reduced to a vague acknowledgement, a hand gesture (not always of the politest kind) and, at best, a brief exchange between a gaggle of grateful reporters and someone who would rather be somewhere else and makes little effort to conceal his boredom.

It is to Thierry's great credit that he, a genuine 'star' of the game, didn't feel it was beneath him to offer quotes to the expectant pack of writers who had procured the magical pass to the 'mixed zone'; moreover, what he gave us – and, through us, what he gave to football fans every-where – was generally worth quoting. He could read and describe a game as well as any analyst; he could do both better than most, in fact, as he possessed – and nurtured – a gift which is exceedingly rare among players: that of being simultaneously within and without the flow of a match, to act whilst observing, and vice-versa. Thierry was the very opposite of Flaubert's Fabrice in *L'Éducation Sentimentale,* who is tossed this way and that in the slaughter of Waterloo, a pebble rocked by the rushing waves, uncomprehending and helpless. Arsène Wenger's defini-tion of a 'great player' as one who could, among a million answers to the same question, choose the right one precisely when it was most needed, applied to Henry more than any other Arsenal player of his era, bar the supreme master of space and time, Dennis Bergkamp – the teammate whom Thierry himself most revered. Even when Thierry, his touch deserting him for once, failed to translate his mastery of a game's ebb and flow into a telling pass or an attempt at goal, you could still perceive how his run, his attempted flick, his use of this, rather than that, part of his boot all stemmed from an exceptional ability to inhabit the present and to mould it. In his case, it was not so much a matter of 'reading' a game as of 'reading' and 'writing' it concurrently, an abi-lity that distinguishes the true elite of footballers from the merely talented. Henry – and that is even rarer among sportsmen – could also verbalize his own perception of a game with ease and fluency, in English as in French, which made him, in the words of the *Mirror*'s Martin Lipton, 'an interview waiting to happen'. No one could doubt that here was an exceptionally intelligent young man, whose modest academic accomplishment could be explained, as we have seen, by the fact that, as he had been earmarked for a football career from a very young age by his mentors as well as by his family – and himself – formal studies would be a distraction.

Henry was not one to underestimate his talent to explain the subtler points of a game. The fiercely competitive streak that is such a major constituent of his personality could sometimes lead him to remind his interlocutors that he, Thierry, knew best, in an uncompromising, not to say brutal, manner. I remember how, early in his Arsenal career, I expressed my surprise to have seen Ray Parlour (whom nobody would compare to Garrincha) adopt an advanced position on the right wing for long periods of a particular game and ventured that the traditional 4-4-2 of the Gunners had often looked more like a skewed 4-3-3. The look Thierry directed at me made my blood freeze instantly. 'My friend,' it said, 'you've got absolutely no idea what you're talking about.' Then his face relaxed into a pleasant smile, and he embarked on a quite superb explanation of why Arsenal had slightly altered their shape on that occasion. He had guessed – rightly – that the awkward way in which I had expressed my opinion stemmed from being in his presence and not (or not just) from my ignorance of the game; I had only recently become a football journalist and still found it difficult not to be starstruck in the presence of a World Cup winner. He had felt my embarrassment, too, and how hurt I had been by his first reaction; and when I left Highbury that night, I was in no doubt that the proud, prickly footballer was also capable of genuine kindness. Nevertheless, as Robert Pirès told me, 'If Titi has a defect, it is that, if you have a discussion with him, only one person is ever going to be right, and it won't be you.'

In any case, British journalists were so grateful to speak to such a willing interviewee that they would simply let the tape roll and keep their reservations to themselves if they had any. A consequence of his unfailing availability, whether he had won or lost, was that, in the words of a colleague then working for a tabloid, 'we gave him an easy ride'. Henry's almost complete absence from the front pages of newspapers for which the private lives of footballers provide a never-ending supply of scandalous gossip, either true or unfounded, was primarily due to his leading a lifestyle that Arsène Wenger never failed to commend. 'One thing about Thierry,' he told me (and quite a few others), 'is that, when it's 10.30 in the evening, I know where he is.' That is: in his north London home, probably watching a game of football, or about to go to bed having cooked himself a fine, calorie-conscious dinner. Having said that, Henry wasn't quite the monk described by his manager. I saw him tuck into club sandwiches and double portions of french fries on more than one occasion. His social circle included a number of celebrities – such as Sharleen Spiteri, the lead singer of the band Texas, whom he met shortly after his arrival in London – and he wasn't averse to the odd night on the tiles himself. The difference is that the newspapers didn't tail him on these occasions, or wonder who the 'mystery brunette' might be that he had been spotted with in one of the capital's posher restaurants or night-clubs. He gave enough – more than enough – for the newshounds to feel that there was no need to take more than he willingly offered. It simply wasn't worth it, and Thierry's privacy was scrupulously respected, up to the very end of his stay in England. A number of rumours had circulated in the press rooms about the state of his marriage months before his entourage was shocked to learn that Claire Merry and he were to divorce; but nothing filtered out until their separation was made public. Henry being Henry, there was an element of self-protection and, indeed, manipulation involved. He was clever enough to understand that the best way to shelter himself from unwanted intrusions in his private life was to accommodate the demands of the media when he was called to do so; what's more, he did it with a good deal of grace, even at times when no one would have begrudged him making a swift exit from a football ground.

Of course, it wasn't always a love-in. It couldn't be with a young man whose skin could be pricked with the lightest of rebukes and seemed only to accept criticism when he provided it himself. Once, at a charity auction organized for the benefit of Patrick Vieira's Diambars foundation (at which Henry, to gasps from the audience, theatrically bid £10,000 for one of Spiteri's guitars), Thierry spoke to me for nearly half an hour about a piece he had read that morning in the *Daily Mirror*; I had seen it and, whilst it could have been more flattering in its appraisal of Henry's performance, I hadn't thought that it was a hatchet job either. Thierry, however, was still smarting, and none of my sympathetic comments and reassurances – expressed in sentences that I never had a chance to finish – had the least effect on his diatribe. He would make the same point over and over again, only stopping to ask: 'Don't you agree?'; and by the time I had said, 'Yes, but . . .', the verbal torrent had resumed, flowing as wildly as before. Why did he have to do this? I wondered. We were not friends – at best two men who didn't mind being brought into contact with one another by their professional obligations. I had never aspired to enter Thierry's tight/jealously guarded circle of trusted pressmen. Still, he had chosen me to vent his anger to (and there was real anger in his eyes and his voice as he spoke), in the middle of a glitzy reception, surrounded with A-listers in Ozwald Boateng suits and Vivienne Westwood evening gowns. But he hadn't chosen me, naturally; I just happened to be there, a journalist, that is: a cipher in the media game, another interchangeable version of the man who had had the audacity to question his greatness in the morning paper.

Later, on another occasion (in the autumn of 2003, I believe), I was not a 'version', but the very man himself. Quite late one evening, my mobile rang ('number withheld').

'Philippe Auclair?'

'Yes?'

'This is Thierry Henry.'

' . . .'

'Thierry Henry. Apologies for calling so late. I hope I'm not disturbing you.' (Not only was I not expecting that call, but I couldn't quite understand why Thierry, whose voice I had finally recognized, was speaking in English.) 'I wanted to talk about that piece of yours about me in *France Football*.'

Ha – yes. Thierry was referring to a couple of grumpy paragraphs I had written about his performance in Arsenal's last game, in which, shall we say, he had not been at his best. I hadn't shied from the fact that Henry had been distinctly sparing in his efforts, and had suggested – as respectfully as I could – that he hadn't quite earned the right to chide his teammates that night, as he had done on several occasions, striking a variety of familiar poses (hands on hips, eyes turned up to the heavens, head shaking this way and that) that hadn't escaped those playing around him, or those watching him from the stands. To go back to what had finally become a conversation of sorts – Thierry did the talking, I the listening – not once did he raise his voice or depart from the most exacting courtesy, whilst making perfectly clear that I had written tripe, being unaware (as I was) that he was carrying an injury at the time and would have sat the game out if it hadn't been for the good of his team. The next time we met, he didn't even mention this rather unusual exchange. This in itself was revealing: Thierry hadn't aimed to understand why I had written the words that infuriated him so; and at no point had I felt that he had attempted to 'connect' with me as a human being, as he would have if he had screamed abuse at me. He cared a great deal, to be sure. But about what?

I once had a similar experience with Gérard Houllier, at a time when I hardly knew the then manager of Liverpool. All I had done was to echo the barbs that had been aimed at him by the British press after a series of poor results. Unfortunately, some brutal late-night editing had transformed what was essentially a 'what the papers say' kind of piece into an unpleasant attack on a man I had no right to speak of in such terms, as I discovered to my horror when the magazine finally landed on my doorstep. Gérard called me three times in twenty-four hours – once, from a plane that was about to take off to Eastern Europe – making absolutely sure that I understood how hurt he had been; and understand I did. The difference with Thierry is that this unfortunate incident led Gérard and me to become much closer to each other, once we had accepted that it had been just that – an accident. By the time we had had our third chat, Gérard had passed me not just his mobile number, but also his home number, and our relationship quickly grew to resemble something like friendship. Such a thing couldn't happen with Thierry Henry. 'Number witheld' said it all.

It was hard to reconcile the sweet, generous Thierry who had stood talking to us at Highbury, barely protected from the rain by an umbrella-wielding press officer, with the increasingly aloof Henry I had to deal with on a weekly basis later in his career. The carapace had hardened with the passage of years, as you would expect when every word he now said was amplified to a ridiculous degree, as if he were talking in capital letters, each sentence punctuated by an exclamation mark. Then I remembered what older French reporters had told me – how, for example, the teenage Thierry would walk up to the Monaco press box of his own accord, to pass on his new mobile number to local journalists. He loved to see his name in print and hardly missed a piece that had been written about him; if he had, no doubt his father Tony would have got hold of it anyway. There was nothing unusual in that: most players care a great deal about what's said of them in the press and are voracious readers, especially in France, where copies of *L'Équipe* and *France Football* are to be found in every dressing-room, and where particular attention is given to the evaluation of individual performances. I would go as far as to say that some journalistic careers have been affected by how high or how low a reporter marked so-and-so's performance; especially how high. The consistent award of flattering sevens and eights out of ten to footballers who didn't deserve such high ratings on the night (and knew it) has long been a sure means to get an extra five minutes of quality time with the footballers in question after the next match.

I am far from the only journalist to have received one of Thierry's slaps on the wrist. When I related Henry's late-evening call to a Parisian colleague, his first comment had been 'Welcome to the club.' Oliver Holt of the *Daily Mirror* has told how – on the eve of the 2006 Champions League final – Thierry had spent twenty minutes chastising him for having mistaken the council estate he grew up in with another in a preview piece; one example among so many others. An amateur psychologist would perhaps explain this hypersensitivity as a direct consequence of the willingness of his father to simultaneously praise (in public) and chastise (mostly in private) his son for his performances, which he ultimately found unbearable. What is certain is that at the heart of this superb player lay a feeling of insecurity that he often found it impossible to disguise, and which he tried to assuage by trying to exercise an ever-growing measure of control over what he said and what was said about him. He battled against it by writing himself into the history books with a single-mindedness, a ferociousness, even, unequalled among his contemporaries, as honours are, to him, incontrovertible proofs of success; and statistics, of which he's so fond and for which he has a remarkable memory, provide him with a pedestal from which he could tell the rest of the world: I'm right, you are always wrong. Those who were willing to concur with him could, with some luck, and provided they wrote for a publication that carried enough clout, join the 'inner circle' I've alluded to, and about which I should add a word or two, as it is they who wrote a great part of Thierry's golden legend. Likewise, some of those who, much to their chagrin and despite their best efforts, were not asked to sit at the master's table or were told to leave it contributed much to darken the player's reputation out of sheer spite and resentment, with scant regard for their target's outstanding achievements.

It is not necessary to name names. Those within the business of quote-hunting and 'exclusives' know them already, and to those without, they don't matter. Each paper has at least a couple of these privileged reporters on its staff; some of them are groomed from a very young age, sent out to follow youth teams in international competitions, in the hope they'll sympathize with players whom it'll be indispensible to develop a close working relationship with later on in their careers. The first time I engaged in small talk with one of them, I felt like a concert-goer who had crossed the path of a record company executive wearing an invisible 'access all areas' badge around his neck. What puzzled me most was why a Henry would seek their company. These guys were shallow, opportunistic and lazy in anything but the pursuit of their own ambitions. One was even known to fabricate interviews to spare himself the trouble of a phone call, something with which the fictitious inter-viewees assented.

Their fallacious intimacy with the players is a source of great jealousy among their peers, a very powerful, but also very dangerous, weapon to use in their climb to the top of their profession. And yet the day always comes when the footballers who feed them their daily bread retire from the game, and ex-players aren't worth much on the market. One of the most pathetic sights I ever came across in my career was that of a younger journalist who aspired to become a big swinging dick himself, to the extent that he would go on holidays to some destination he couldn't afford in order to cross the path of a player he had heard owned a few flats there. He knew which brand of car every single member of club X was driving at the time, down to their tyre specifi-cations. He hung out in clubs and restaurants where footballers were said to enjoy their downtime, spending a fortune to let it be known to his colleagues that he had had a chat with so-and-so's latest girlfriend. He failed in his enterprise, as he was too transparent himself: he tried too hard; he had never managed to shake off that measure of innocence that, as he had almost forgotten, had led him to fall in love with the game of football in the first place and fantasize that, one day, he would tread the same earth as his heroes. But these heroes, who had been surrounded by agents, groupies and starfuckers ever since they signed their first professional contract, had developed a sure instinct to replace what nobody had cared to teach them: how to recognize someone you could trust. In Thierry's case, that instinct wasn't far from paranoia. But there was innocence, too; and part of Henry's greatness is that he never completely lost touch with it.

Yes, he had his messengers, his mouthpieces, who published interviews in which self-deprecation and self-aggrandizement could often be read in the same sentence, depending on which side of the fence the reader sat, as when he constantly minimized his own contribution to his team's success. Words that would have been interpreted as refreshingly modest could be interpreted as contrived, insincere even, when Thierry used them. By highlighting how good the others had been, wasn't he also reminding the world that, if they had been that good, he must have been exceptional? In that respect, the regal Henry of 2006 was not that different from the deeply insecure Henry of early 1998. He shouldn't shoulder too much of the blame for that, as he was also kind and generous. Yes, no one was quicker to single out a teammate for compliments than Henry, just as no striker was quicker to acknowledge the player who had created a goalscoring opportunity for him. But he did it in such a way that it was difficult not to ask oneself: why did he say that? Did he really mean it? On 17 October 2008, the night he broke France's goalscoring record, beating the Lithuanian 'keeper twice to eclipse the great Michel Platini's forty-one goals for the national side, the French skipper praised his young teammate Jeremy Toulalan as if he had been the only man on the pitch. It was just as ridiculous a performance as when, in November 2004, he had spoken of José-Antonio Reyes in glowing terms to *L'Équipe*, when almost everyone else, a number of teammates included, had come to the conclusion that he regarded the young, homesick Spaniard as little more than a talented nuisance.

What is remarkable is that the messengers and the mouthpieces never got the better of Thierry Henry: they missed out on what he really had to offer. Away from their fawning company, Thierry was the most eloquent of interviewees. All you had to do was to let him talk about his sport. And when he talked about the game he knew so well, you were compelled to listen, warming up to his child-like enthusiasm for football. I mean 'child-like' as the highest of compliments. Child's play is joyful and serious; a child knows something we have forgotten, and which Thierry remembered better than most. To him, truth was shaped like a football, a football with which he wanted to play with for ever.

Jacquet took what must have seemed an eternity, to Thierry and quite a few other hopefuls, to finalize the squad that would take part in the World Cup. In late March, only a few days before the friendly against Sweden, for which Anelka and Trezeguet made the cut at the expense of Henry, the national manager, for whom 'the World Cup [had] already started', asked no fewer than thirty-seven players to join him at Claire-fontaine, where they underwent physical and medical tests. According to Youri Djorkaeff, Thierry was 'shaking like a leaf at the idea of not going to the World Cup – he didn't think Jacquet would select him'. In truth, Jacquet himself hadn't come to any conclusion yet. 'I have a central core of players,' he confided to the same Djorkaeff, who was certainly part of it, shortly after *Les Bleus'* unconvincing 0-0 draw in Solna. 'I want to be 100 per cent sure, especially when it comes to *mentalité*,' a word that means 'strength of character' as well as 'attitude' in French.

Slowly, though, Henry got back to something resembling form at the moment when it mattered most, scoring a fine goal in Monaco's ultimately meaningless 3-2 victory over Zidane's Juventus in the semi-finals of the Champions League, on 15 April 1998. Juve, inspired by an Alessandro Del Piero hat-trick, had whipped ASM 4-1 in the first leg. Claude Puel, to whom Thierry owes so much, had spent close to two months in the winter working with the injured winger at the train-ing ground of La Turbie when his troublesome ankle (a chipped bone was the cause of the pain) prevented him from playing for Tigana on a regular basis. Tigana himself – unbeknown to his player – quietly promoted Henry's cause in his frequent chats with Jacquet. So did Raymond Domenech, who was convinced that Thierry could be France's not-so-secret weapon at the forthcoming World Cup. An often tearful Henry spent hours on the phone with members of his family, with Tony in particular, trying to make sense of his inner turmoil, desperately seeking reassurances, which his father was happy to provide in spite of the upheaval in their relationship following the Real Madrid affair.

Overcoming the reservations he harboured against Tigana, Thierry swallowed his pride and sought his elder's advice, which the manager was willing to give.

Henry had no choice. The undisputed leader of a 'new' generation of French players, most of whom were black, nearly every single one of them raised in the *banlieues*, was still just a boy when he joined the pros of ASM on the training ground, older players having little in common with apparently carefree upstarts like himself. There would come a day when Thierry himself would seem remote from twenty-somethings such as Samir Nasri and Hatem Ben Arfa, and when it would become clear that many of his principles were not that different from those of an earlier generation: his insistence on the value of hard work, his courtesy towards others, his love of the game for the game's sake, his relative indifference to money and aversion of the celebrity circus. The French he spoke in the company of friends and teammates of his own age, punctuated with cool street-speak and the *verlan* slang beloved of Parisian and Marseillais rappers, though not an affectation or an attempt to mask his true self, was a façade nonetheless, whose many windows he sometimes opened, and through which you could see a very different man, in some ways slightly old-fashioned in fact. Take these words, which must have surprised his questioner from *L'Équipe Magazine*, when he asked a twenty-four-year-old Thierry what kind of a father he hoped he would be.

I'll be very strict as far as education is concerned. I'll try to pass on what is good about life – not to believe that you're entitled to everything, just like that – and respect. Above all. And politeness. I haven't opened a dictionary for a while, but I wonder if that word, 'respect', is still in it. There's no respect any more. When I see an old lady who finds it hard to lift her shopping bags, I go and help her. If I get into a supermarket, and there are 200,000 people there, I'll hold the door of the person behind me . . . Respect, respect, respect.

Thierry bestrode two ages of football, belonged to them both and to none as well: if you began by looking at the 4x4 SUV and the designer headphones, here was a precursor of the 'bling' generation; but you could also say that, among the game's twenty-first-century superstars, he was one of the last to go through a footballer's traditional apprenticeship, scraping muddy boots and carrying nets, cones and balls to the training pitch – and a bit of a grumpy old man before his time as well. What happened in those last two years at Monaco is that those two worlds collided. He was pushed ahead at extraordinary speed by his sheer talent and his dedication to the game. He was also held back by his naivety and his clumsy attempts to control an environment in which there were far craftier manipulators than himself. The injury he suffered in the winter of 1997–8 sparked the crisis, but was not its underlying cause. There would be other dark moments in Thierry's life and career, but few as dark as these, and it is to his great credit that he found the resources to fight his way back into contention, both with Monaco and with *Les Bleus*, when he had been very close to losing all hope himself. 'Everything's happened to me over the last two years,' he said when he had won that battle. 'I experienced both extremes – the revelation, the fall. I knew what I was worth on a football pitch, and I wasn't proving that worth. I know that I'm not as bad as it's been said, but also not as good as some have written for a while.'

Happily, the good outweighed the bad as far as Jacquet was concerned. On 5 May 1998, the national manager crossed out nine names of his original list of thirty-seven, with Claude Makelele and Sylvain Legwinski among the victims. Thierry had survived the first cull; but so had Nicolas Anelka, on his way to doing the Double with Arsenal, and David Trezeguet, the scourge of Manchester United in the Champions League, who had scored eighteen goals in twenty-seven League games for Monaco. To many in France, this smacked of indecision on Jacquet's part. Why wait to release the final list of twenty-two, the only one that mattered? The national team's first game was only thirty-eight days away. 'Will we play with thirteen players?' was the sarcastic question put by *L'Équipe*, for whom nice-but-dim 'Mémé', the bespectacled former factory worker, couldn't be 'the man the situation demands'. Conflict had long been simmering between the 'dukes' of the French daily, who liked to think of themselves as kingmakers – Gérard Ejnès and Jérôme Bureau among others – and Jacquet, who publicly deplored the influence of a 'nauseating' press (whilst cultivating the favours of the national TV broadcaster TF1, which did nothing to ease the tension with the rest of the media) and went as far as saying he would gladly punch Ejnès if he were given a chance. Full-blown war ensued. The manager wanted a country united behind his 'commando' unit. The Parisian newspaper refused to enter what it considered a 'collaboration' (a word that is heavier with signification in France than in any other country) with the supposed gravedigger of French football, as Jacquet, a disciple of the arch-romantic Reims and Saint-Étienne coach Albert Batteux, nonetheless favoured a primarily defensive approach which negated the natural qualities of *Les Bleus*, and was an insult to the traditions of the gold standard team, that of the two Michels, Platini and Hidalgo, the enchanters of 1978–86. It was an ugly fight, the scars of which have yet to heal completely in 2012. Jacquet used the animosity of the press to create the siege mentality that he thought essential to achieve his objective; the press responded by switching from robust criticism – France hadn't been that convincing since Euro 1996 – to character assassination. The seeds had been sown a few years before. As early as 1995, Ejnès had come up with that headline: 'Mourir d'Aimé' – 'to die of love', but also 'Death by Aimé [Jacquet]'. Witty, but oh so cruel; cruel, but nothing compared with the barrage of invective the manager had to endure in the last few weeks leading up to the World Cup. The extraordinary scenes that would be witnessed on 12 July were beyond the imagination of the most fervent optimists until very late in the tournament, something which should be kept in mind when that victory is interpreted as that of a united nation, a moment of redemption and self-discovery. It wasn't, not as the propagandists of the *blacks-blancs-beurs* wanted us to believe, until the old wounds were reopened in South Africa in 2010, with Thierry very much at the centre of things this time.

Entrenched in Clairefontaine, denied almost all access to the outside world apart from smuggled copies of *L'Équipe* and *France Football* which were read with anything from hilarity to fury, the players tried, not too successfully, to steady themselves for Jacquet's final decision. The coach didn't want for advice, A pleading B's cause, C agitating for D and so on, which might explain why it took him a full two weeks to reach a verdict. Those who lived through the last few days leading to the publication of the *liste des 22*, which was leaked to *Le Parisien* (another snub directed at *L'Équipe*, of course, even if both papers were part of the same group), remember it as a comedy of sorts: anxious players shuffling through the corridors of the château at all times of the day and night, some of them sick with worry, others affecting not to care. Thierry was very much among the former. He couldn't sleep. He barely dared to speak to the senior members of the squad. He would find himself sitting next to the great Zidane at meals, but couldn't utter a word, awed by the presence of the legend in the making, paralysed by his own fear.

Then, on the evening of Friday 21 May, Jacquet made his way to six bedrooms – those of the players he had decided would not take part in the World Cup. Ibrahim Ba, Martin Djetou, Pierre Laigle, Sabri Lamouchi, Lionel Letizi and Nicolas Anelka were the ones who heard the fateful knock on the door. The impact this had on their international careers can be gauged by the fact that, taken together, the first five of these outcasts only collected a further six caps from this date onwards, all of them in friendlies. Would young Titi have become Thierry Henry if he had been one of them? As for Anelka, that most enigmatic of footballers, it is beyond doubt that the manner in which his manager broke him the news deeply affected his relationship with the national team. Jacquet made it sound as if, all things considered, to have made the twenty-eight and trained with the seniors had been a 'bonus' for the striker, who should thank his lucky stars and walk out with gratitude in his heart. But Anelka, who had finished the season like a rocket with Arsenal, was understandably furious. He wasn't the only one to think a great injustice had been done. Christophe Dugarry hadn't had the best of seasons with Barcelona (no goals in seven League games) or Marseille, whom he had joined in December 1997 (one in nine), but 'Duga' was in, whereas 'Nico' was out. Jacquet remembered the skilful, inventive player who hadn't disappointed at the 1996 Euro; others remembered that Dugarry happened to be one of Zinedine Zidane's best friends, with whom he co-owned a restaurant in Bordeaux. France '98 wasn't quite – not yet – the happy family later depicted in a fly-on-the-wall documentary that was a huge success in France, *Les Yeux dans les Bleus*; but Thierry was part of it, to his huge relief – and to the surprise of many, Henry included. 'Last week,' he said, 'Philippe Léonard [his teammate at Monaco] called me to say that he hadn't been included in the twenty-two for Belgium. And I thought: three months ago, he was an automatic choice in the starting line-up, whereas I wasn't on any list myself. Football moves quickly. The wheel keeps turning.' Thierry contacted Anelka repeatedly, tried to get in touch with 'Ibou' Ba as well, overjoyed with his own selection, genuinely disappointed for the friends who had fallen by the wayside, whose company he had sought during those never-ending weeks of waiting at Clairefontaine. But what concern he had for them swiftly receded into the background. Thanks in no small part to the support of advocates such as Tigana, Domenech and Houllier, Thierry had been given a chance to leave behind two years of doubt, uncertainty and pain and seized that chance superbly.

France immediately travelled to Morocco for a short friendly tournament, where, to use Jacquet's words, Henry 'imposed himself', despite statistics that highlighted the rawness of his talent at international level: he received the ball on thirty-three occasions in the 153 minutes he was on the pitch against Belgium (1-0) and Morocco (2-2), and lost it to an opponent on twenty-two. Thierry hadn't scored, Thierry hadn't provided an assist, but Jacquet had been struck by his willingness to take risks and 'take on ('*provoquer*') defenders – to the extent that some members of the Belgian squad had told France's goalkeeper, Fabien Barthez: 'This guy's an aeroplane. He's impossible to stop. He's going to do some damage at the World Cup.' In fact, the 4-3-3 formation and the personnel Jacquet used in the win over Belgium were exactly those he deployed in France's inaugural World Cup game against South Africa on 12 June. Henry was now positioned on the right side of an attacking trident, not the most natural of positions for a centre-forward who had been moved to the left wing first by Gérard Houllier, then by Jean Tigana; but the spring had uncoiled for good. No longer hampered by his ankle injury, no longer fretting at the prospect of being ignored by Jacquet, no longer wondering why he wasn't starting games with Monaco – safe at last – Henry showed the enterprise and the quickness of thought and limb that had marked him out as a special talent ever since he had left Les Ulis. 'Henry belongs to that category of players whose potential is so impressive,' Jacquet said in his typically convoluted and unfelicitous French. 'Let us respect what he can do.' These were unlikely words in the mouth of a coach who valued discipline above all other footballing virtues, which convinced many of his listeners that Thierry was bound to start against South Africa in Marseilles, less than two weeks away.

Henry himself sounded like John Fogerty, needle stuck in that same groove: 'big wheel keep on turnin', a phrase he used in interview after interview, and heaven knows there were plenty of them. The cockiness was back. 'Every job deserves a salary,' he said. 'It didn't happen by chance.' I've never forgotten how he answered the question 'What is your wildest wish?' 'I know it's not possible,' he answered, 'but I've always dreamt of jumping from the top of a building to see what it was like to be dead.'

Maybe 'cocky' isn't the word I was looking for.

Jacquet had one last chance to test his players before deciding on the eleven that would face South Africa on 12 June, and it was widely expected that the line-up of the France team fielded against Finland in Helsinki six days beforehand would give a reliable indication of the personnel and the tactics that would be used at the World Cup. Henry, fresh from his eye-catching performances in Morocco, must have been disappointed to find out that he wasn't thought to be worth bringing off the bench on this occasion. The French won an uneventful game 1-0 thanks to a cool finish by substitute David Trezeguet, while Thierry watched Djorkaeff and Dugarry occupying the flanks in his stead. What couldn't be guessed at the time was that Jacquet's paramount concern was to establish a settled back-line, and that he intended to shuffle the pack upfront, depending on the nature of the opposition. 'Keeper Bar-thez was protected by a formidable back-four composed of Lilian Thuram, Laurent Blanc, Marcel Desailly and Bizente Lizarazu, with captain Didier Deschamps marshalling a tight two- or three-man defensive screen in midfield. Djorkaeff and Zidane provided the creative thrust, sometimes supported by a 'false winger', who could be any one of four players: Robert Pirès, slight of build but deceptively quick and gifted with exceptional ball control and acuity of vision; Bernard Diomède, a dependable journeyman who could never be accused of shying from hard work; Dugarry, who understood Zidane's game better than anyone else; and Henry.

His absence from the team that beat Finland led some to believe that Thierry had been chosen as one of the twenty-two *pour encourager les autres*, to keep the Guivarc'hs and Dugarrys on their toes. They were wrong. Jacquet's plan was more subtle and more tactically astute than his critics guessed. Other teams were lucky enough to be able to rely on proven goalscorers: Brazil had Ronaldo, Italy Christian Vieri, England Alan Shearer, the Netherlands Patrick Kluivert. France had Stéphane Guivarc'h, the League's Golden Boot with Auxerre in the two seasons leading to the World Cup – but whose international record read: played nine, scored one. Jacquet's idea, which analysts such as Jonathan Wilson have singled out as one of the decisive factors in France's eventual success, was to exploit the twenty-seven-year-old striker's stupendous work-rate to (this time, literally) 'defend from the front'. Guivarc'h, who famously played four games in the tournament without scoring once, took on the thankless task of harrying the opposition's defenders, devoting his considerable energy to breaking up their rhythm, which meant he had hardly any left when a chance came his way. The ridicule that was heaped on him afterwards must rank as one of the most inane manifestations of football idiocy ever. Ask Blanc, Deschamps, Thuram about Guivarc'h's contribution to their triumph. They will all praise his selfless sacrifice and their manager's far-sightedness. So would Thierry.

Henry learnt from Jacquet himself that he would be playing in France's opening World Cup match. 'People were wondering what I was I was doing there,' Thierry recalled in 2010. 'On the eve of the game [against South Africa], the coach [Aimé Jacquet] came to see me and told me I'd be in the starting eleven. He said: "This way, you'll sleep well!" . . . Yeah, right . . . I called my father. It was something unbelievable – but, at the same time, I had the devil-may-care attitude that is associated with youth. I was telling myself: "Tomorrow, I'll set the pitch on fire!" When you're twenty years old, you think you're Superman. You're not Superman, but you think you are. I wasn't thinking about what was being said: that we were rubbish, that we wouldn't go past the first round.' And on the day? 'On the day? Forgive the expression – but I felt fucking proud. When I talk about it now, I still have shivers down my spine.' Eyes closed, he sang the 'Marseillaise' with a fervour unmatched by any of his teammates.

The game itself, against a South African team that was taking part in its first-ever World Cup, was not as fluent a victory as the 3-0 score-line would suggest and failed to convince Jacquet's numerous critics that they would soon have to revise their judgement on the potential of these *Bleus*. Positioned on the right flank of a three-pronged forward line, Henry brought spark and directness to France's attacks without quite 'burning the pitch', as he had dreamt he would do, until very late in the game, when he surged down the right flank in the second minute of added time to score the first of his fifty-one goals for France – or so decided FIFA's equivalent of the 'dubious goals committee' after a deliberation process that lasted long into the night. Until then, it had been Dugarry's show, for the best and the worst of reasons. A comically poor piece of control turned the Marseilles crowd against him, affecting the player to such an extent that he wished he had been taken off the pitch there and then. But Dugarry it was who opened the scoring with a header from his friend Zinedine's corner-kick and then gave Djorkaeff the opportunity to strike a shot which defender Pierre Issa, who didn't have the best of evenings, deflected into his own net. It was again Dugarry who hit the corner-kick that led to Henry's goal, the 1,600th to be scored in the history of the World Cup proper. Issa had helped the ball on the way before it had crossed the line, when it seemed he still had time to push it out to safety; but the initial shot, a lovely dink over the onrushing Vonk, had been on target, and FIFA ruled in favour of Thierry. Up in the stands of the Stade Vélodrome, Tony Henry celebrated his son's strike with so much enthusiasm that he suffered (or so he told reporters) a fracture of the leg. 'I didn't feel a thing,' he said, showing an impressive gash on his calf.

Six days later, whatever pain Tony must still have felt was well and truly forgotten when his son went one better at the Stade de France, scoring the first of his six braces for the national team in a 4-0 demolition of Saudi Arabia which ensured the hosts' presence in the last sixteen of the competition. Watching this game again, I couldn't but feel how we tend to reconstruct what we witness on a football field from disparate elements, most of them accidental, and project them onto a fictional, if not fictitious, frame; we must find logic and reason where often there is only chaos. The Saudis, who looked as if they were heading for a stinging defeat when their defender Mohammed Al-Khwaili was sent off for a flying tackle on Lizarazu in the thirteenth minute, had the best chance of a very open first half-hour, only for Sami Al-Jaber to lose his balance after winning a fifty-fifty challenge with Fabien Barthez. Dugarry then pulled a thigh muscle and had to be replaced by David Trezeguet. France dominated but kept slicing their shots, misplacing the last pass, Jacquet looking ever more agitated on the touchline – until Henry capped a glorious move between Lizarazu and Zidane by surging at the far post and finding the net from six yards. He never scored 'big' goals in 'big' games, did he? Typical of Thierry: he barely acknowledged the crowd's joy, as all the hard work had been done by someone else, whereas a huge smile split his face when Trezeguet, exploiting a fumble by the Saudi 'keeper, doubled France's lead. The ten men of Saudi Arabia gamely tried to respond, but only ended up being overrun by fitter, more skilful athletes. Even Zidane's late sending-off for a nasty stamp on Saudi skipper Fuad Amin didn't affect France's superiority, a fact which was forgotten in the post-mortem that followed. Their talisman's absence hadn't deprived *Les Bleus* of their zest; quite the opposite, in fact. This time, Henry had well and truly 'set the pitch on fire', racing onto a long Barthez clearance to score his second goal, the last of his three at this World Cup, which he celebrated this time, with his now-familiar *toreador* pose by the corner flag. But much better was to follow, even if his name disappeared from the scoresheets from then on.

The trauma felt at Zidane's loss had a strange effect on the way the French public and analysts (of every hue) viewed France's progress after their 4-0 win over Saudi Arabia. It was described as 'laboured', 'painful' and 'lucky' almost until Emmanuel Petit's goal made sure Brazil couldn't come back in the final. So much was hoped, so much was expected from the 'genius' Zidane that his absence prevented a majority of people from savouring the most satisfying French win of the tournament so far, when a team featuring a number of reserves beat a full-strength Danish eleven 2-1 in Lyons on 24 June; and this, when the Denmark of Peter Schmeichel and the Laudrup brothers were by no means assured of qualifying for the last sixteen and needed a positive result. Henry was – until the seventy-first minute – one of the players Jacquet had decided to rest, alongside Deschamps, Blanc, Lizarazu and Thuram. Odd, isn't it, that being left out of a team could mean that you were now truly part of it; but so it was for Henry, who was given another proof of it when Jacquet trusted him from the start in France's awkward 1-0 win over Paraguay in their first match of the knock-out phase. The 38,000 spectators seated in Lens's vibrant Félix Bollaert Stadium had to wait until the 114th minute to see Laurent Blanc volley the winner past José Luis Chilavert – the first 'golden goal' to be scored in a World Cup tournament. Thierry had struck a post before that, but, in the main, had also struggled to find space behind a tightly organized and aggressive Paraguayan back-line, and it wasn't a surprise to see Robert Pirès take his place shortly after an hour of cat-and-mouse football had been played.

Whether it was because of Henry's indifferent performance, Zidane's return from suspension or, what is more likely, the nature of France's opponent in the quarter-finals, Jacquet chose to revert to his trusted 4-3-2-1 for the game against Italy. Seeing Karembeu, Deschamps and Petit lined up in midfield, with Djorkaeff and Zidane the sole creators to face a team that boasted one of the finest back-fours in the competition, a close tactical battle could be expected; it was anything but, however. Both Pagliuca and Barthez – who made one of the finest, and bravest, saves of his career in a one-on-one with the tournament's then most prolific striker, Christian Vieri – had to intervene far more often than anyone could have predicted. Perhaps mindful of his team's tiredness after it had played nearly two hours of football in the previous round, wishing to avoid another one or two periods of extra-time, Jacquet gambled and brought on his young guns Henry and Trezeguet in the sixty-fifth minute. But Italy held on, despite the French displaying remarkable levels of fitness to dominate the game until the final whistle. There was no 'golden goal' this time, but a penalty shoot-out, which, at the very end, provided one of the most memorable images of that World Cup. Lizarazu, his teeth clenched, his eyes betraying the huge effort he was summoning to beat his fear, had already seen his spot-kick saved by Pagliuca. Advantage Italy – but only for a matter of seconds, as Barthez dived to his right to parry Albertini's shot. Whose turn was it to place the ball on the spot? Marcel Desailly had engaged in a comical argument with Didier Deschamps in the centre circle, which had Henry bent double in hilarity. Deschamps pretended he had cramp, Desailly was beside himself at the thought of missing the target; and it was left to a couple of twenty-year-olds to save the two Serie A veterans from further public embarrassment. The Monaco friends, Trezeguet first, Henry second, had volunteered for duty and they dispatched their penalties with authority. 'I was telling myself that this was the moment I had always dreamt of, but when everything could go wrong,' Thierry remembered twelve years later. 'To reassure myself, I told myself that Aimé Jacquet trusted me, that I wasn't an imposter.' Tony was there, of course, sitting next to Arnold Catalano, who remembers Thierry's father hiding under his seat when it was his son's turn to advance towards Pagliuca's goal. 'I thought he was about to die,' Arnold says.

But France were not in the semi-finals just yet, as Costacurta and Vieri beat Barthez. At this point in time, the youngsters who had dared to walk up to the D and take a shot at Gianluca Pagliuca, who had done what men who were older than them had not dared to do, looked like kids again. Thierry hid behind David as Laurent Blanc took an eternity to place the ball on the spot, flattening imaginary blades of grass with his palm. A camera caught their anxiety – and, more importantly, their innocence. Football remained a game, after all. It is a picture that I, and millions of other French supporters, will never forget.

Then Di Biagio's shot rebounded off the bar.

Mayhem erupted on the field, in the stands, then in the French dressing-room. Lilian Thuram, one of five French *calcio* players to have started that quarter-final, led his teammates into a noisy chorus of 'Ils sont où, les Italiens?' – 'Where are they, the Italians?' Out, of course; whereas France had qualified for its fourth World Cup semi-final in history. The previous three, as no one needed reminding, had all been lost: to Brazil in 1958, to Germany in 1982 and 1986, the last two in circumstances that still smarted. The Franco-Italian rivalry hadn't yet reached the intensity it now assumes, and you could even argue that the match played at the Stade de France on 3 July 1998 marked the birth of an 'international derby' which is rivalled in ferocity only by matches between the Netherlands and Germany or England and Argen-

tina, and which was to be re-enacted in thrilling fashion in the 2000
Euro and 2006 World Cup finals, with Henry a prime actor on all three
occasions. To beat Italy (even if, strictly speaking, that match didn't
produce a winner) was bound to feel sweet indeed, when our so-called
'sister country' had never missed out on a chance to remind us of its
superiority in all things football and spent most of the previous decade
poaching our best players by throwing liras at them like confetti at a
New York ticker-tape parade. But on penalties? We had won the lottery
all right.

At long last, the enthusiasm and belief which had been confined to
the die-hard supporters began to seep into the country at large, as erst-
while critics sucked pensively on their pens, wondering what was left
to be criticized. Jacquet, whose regular team-talks were a mixture of the
mundane, the garbled and the truly inspirational, used what venom was
left in the post-match notices to gee up his 'commando', claiming that
some of what was still said and written about his charges was true: they
created numerous chances but failed to capitalize on these openings.*
The forwards had often dithered when they could have taken a shot.
Next time, shoot, for fuck's sake. Pirès needed to 'muscle up' his game
. . . Even Blanc, who had been supreme so far, came in for some stick.
Deschamps alone walked between the raindrops, and with some justification. It's not just that, along with Lizarazu, whom I would gladly
select at left-back in my all-time eleven, he had been impeccable so far;
DD was to all intents and purposes an assistant coach to Jacquet and
far more precise in his instructions than his boss could be. Deschamps
it was who, before kick-off, would walk to a teammate and whisper
words of advice, as he did to Henry before every game. Switch flanks;
that guy is slow on the turn; press high; let him come at you; move
that way, drift wider. As Zidane, lying on the massage table, steadied
himself to enter the field again after scoring twice in the final's first half,
Deschamps went to him and, placing his right hand under Zizou's neck,
spoke to him as quietly as one would in a church. When greatness is

---

* France finished the tournament with the highest number of shots on target, and
by some distance: 41, against 33 for Argentina, 31 for the Netherlands and 29 for
Spain.

discussed, what is unseen (but known) is often discarded as irrelevant, and most of what Deschamps did was invisible. The web he spun on the pitch was so subtly woven that all you could notice, if anything could be noticed, was the size of the insects that ended up caught in it, flapping helplessly. Didier had been a manager-in-waiting throughout his whole footballing life. At Nantes, he would prop his elbows on his dormitory window, waiting for Jean-Claude Suaudeau to turn up on his customary walkabout around the training centre, and the two men, one of them a teenager, the other the most venerated French manager of his generation, would talk about football for up to an hour. It is no wonder that Deschamps became the closest equivalent to a cricket captain on a football pitch France had ever seen. Thierry, that most reflective of footballers, was very lucky to have such a master to learn from.

Two more games, two more victories, and France would be world champions. 'What we've done is good, very good,' Zidane said. 'But to go all the way would be . . . *grand.*' *Grand* means far more in French than 'great' in English: 'truly great' – 'almost unbelievable'; but belief was what this group of players possessed, or were possessed by. They hadn't yet blossomed as a football side: they lacked the panache and the silky interplay of Michel Platini's nonpareil 1984 Euro-winning team. In fact, this generation of Les Bleus would only reach its zenith at the 2000 European Championships, and, odd as it may sound, the victory of 1998 was in some ways a springboard, the foundation of a 'culture of winning' which sides that were just as talented as Deschamps' had failed to assimilate until then. Victories were obtained the hard way, by dipping the pail ever deeper in the well of fortitude, not by asserting technical or physical superiority, and none came harder than the 2-1 win over Croatia on 8 July.

That Croatian team had provided the biggest shock of the tournament so far by putting three goals past Andreas Koepke without reply in their quarter-final against Germany. As Jacquet reminded his players before their bus left Clairefontaine for the Stade de France, Miroslav Blažević's team had lost none of the creativity and skill that characterized Yugoslavian football before civil war led to the break-up of the country; but it now had another asset: a mental toughness that derived from fierce patriotic pride in a 'new', reborn nation. Jacquet's fears were well grounded. After an unbearably tense first half, in which Zidane had seen an astounding right-footed volley saved by Dražen Ladić, Croatia opened the scoring through, inevitably, Davor Šuker, whom Bizente Lizarazu wrongly assumed to have strayed offside. Then Thuram struck back almost as soon as the game had restarted, winning the ball off Zvonimir Boban in uncompromising fashion, then exchanging passes with Djorkaeff before curling a lovely left-footed shot in the bottom corner. Thuram, who scored one goal every fifty League games for his clubs over the course of his career, chose that afternoon in Saint-Denis to hit his only two for France – in 142 games, a record number of caps that will be very hard to beat. Thierry, who created only one real chance for himself in the hour he spent on the pitch after replacing an injured Christian Karembeu, was the first to congratulate his fellow West Indian. Less than a quarter of an hour later, in the seventieth minute, Thuram won a tussle with Robert Jarni and unleashed another powerful angled shot from just inside the area. France were – almost – through, thanks to the most improbable of goalscorers. It is often forgotten that the miracle of 12 July wouldn't have happened without the one that happened four days earlier at the Stade de France. 'Lilian saved us,' Deschamps said. But, with only seconds to go, Fabien Barthez still had to claw a deflected Croatian strike from underneath the bar. France, reduced to ten men after Blanc's harsh sending-off,* had trembled until the very end. Henry, who had supplied the ball that led to Thuram's second goal, was ninety minutes away from becoming a world champion, having scored three times in five attempts, easily the best ratio in the competition. Back in La Désirade, where she had gone on holidays, his mother

---

* Slaven Bilić was vilified – and not just in the French media – for clutching his face and falling to the ground rather theatrically after Blanc had brushed his face with his right hand. Getting the French defender dismissed was not uppermost in Bilić's mind, however: the future manager of the Croatian national team had been tugging at Blanc's shirt and feared receiving a booking that would have led to an automatic suspension. Instead of which it was the Frenchman who was punished by FIFA and missed the final as a result.

hadn't dared to watch the game, fearing her beloved Titi might get injured. Not so President Jacques Chirac, who walked down from his box to mingle with the players in the dressing-room. Clad in an oversize French jersey bearing the number 23, the head of the *République* planted a kiss on Fabien Barthez's bald head, just as Blanc did before every game. It was now only a case of beating reigning champions Brazil.

This book is not an account of French football's finest hour and a half, but of the life of one man who was ultimately deprived the chance to take part in it. As he had done when the opponent was Italy, Jacquet, fearful of the threat favourites Brazil posed on the flanks, deployed a conservative 4-3-2-1 in which Karembeu and Petit would help Lizarazu and Thuram to block the forward runs of full-backs Cafu and Roberto Carlos. There could be no place for Henry in such a set-up, something which the youngster accepted, hoping that he would come off the bench late in the game. Desailly's sending-off, two minutes after Dugarry had replaced the exhausted Guivarc'h, prevented that from happening, however. Thierry had been warming up, waiting for a call that never came. He was too caught up by the drama of the game to harbour any sense of resentment. France, exploiting the 'laziness' of the Brazilians on set-pieces (which Jacquet had drawn attention to in his last team talk), held an improbable 2-0 lead at half-time. It wasn't just the score-line that was improbable. The manner in which it had been achieved verged on the bizarre, as nobody could remember Zidane ever scoring from a header at a corner-kick. And he had done it twice. Corner-kick, Zidane, header, goal; and again – that was a winning combination nobody could have possibly dreamt of before kick-off. With Desailly gone and France reduced to ten men, the tension became so unbearable that Trezeguet burst into tears on the touchline, hugging Thierry with something like despair. 'When we were 2-0 up,' Henry recalled, 'I knew it was over, but I couldn't help thinking: "They're going to come back."' They didn't. The Arsenal duo of Patrick Vieira and Emmanuel Petit even combined gloriously to add a third goal in the third minute of added time. From then on, French players could wear a star above the cockerel on their blue jerseys.

So much, and probably too much, has been written about Ronaldo's mysterious 'epileptic' fit shortly before the game, and how it affected the mindset of the *seleçao* so catastrophically that France only defeated the ghost of Brazil. What the conspiracy theorists forgot is how, on one hand, the French had executed Jacquet's game plan to perfection and how, on the other, the Brazilians had had more than their share of luck against Denmark (whom the French reserves had beaten far more convincingly in the group phase) in the last eight, and could only win on penalties in their semi-final confrontation with the Netherlands. In truth, in the Stade de France nobody cared about Ronaldo. In the Stade de France – and everywhere else in the country, where Bastille Day was celebrated two days early, in an explosion of collective joy unparalleled since the end of the Second World War. I'll come back to these scenes later on, as they had to be seen from afar – from South Africa, after twelve years had passed – to be properly understood. There and then, the doubts one could have about a country united behind a so-called 'multicultural' team were blown away at the sight of white bourgeois mingling with black and Arab youths of the *banlieues* on the Champs-Élysées, dancing wildly in front of a huge portrait of Zidane beamed onto the Arc-de-Triomphe. Columnists, sociologists, philosophers and politicians dared to suggest that France, through sport, had become Jean-Marie Le Pen's worst nightmare: a rainbow nation that could embrace its sons and daughters of every race and every creed in the folds of the tricolour flag. A British paper printed a map which showed which parts of the world each of the twenty-two heroes of 12 July had come from. Wrong as it was – Zidane was born in Marseilles, not Algeria, and was of Kabyle, not Arab extraction; Djorkaeff, the 'Kalmyk/Polish/Armenian' whose father Jean had represented France at the 1966 World Cup, came from Lyons; etc., etc. – it nevertheless imbued the French 'new' identity with a sense of universality that chimed in with the most exalted ideals of the Republic's founding fathers. It was an intoxicating notion. It was magnificent, as magnificent as the picture of Deschamps' hands locked with Desailly's on the golden trophy. The euphoria wouldn't last; but it had a redeeming quality that outlived the onset of disillusionment: it showed what our true aspirations were, and these had a nobility and a grandeur that even the tragi-comedy of Knysna, years later, could not deface.

The players themselves never claimed to have been the torchbearers of a renewed sense of nationhood, which doesn't mean that they failed to realize the extraordinary impact of their victory. The bus trip back to Clairefontaine, with Zidane, Dugarry and Candela sitting at the back, traditionally the space reserved for the most popular players in the group, was a procession followed by tens of thousands of delirious supporters; it took the driver José Alegria almost half an hour to cover the last hundred yards before finally reaching the entrance of the team's headquarters. This is how Thierry recounted those glorious hours to Amy Lawrence in 2004.

A lot of amazing players never won the World Cup, so to do it at 20, and have that medal in your bag, is a difficult feeling to explain. I don't think I will ever realise what happened during that World Cup. The day after the final, I was watching TV and saw on the Champs-Élysées guys in suits getting out of their Mercedes to party with total strangers dressed in their underwear, and letting them dance on their car bonnets too. I said to myself, 'it's fabulous to see Paris and the whole of France come together'.

The decision to eschew the official party that had been organized for the winners and head back to the sanctuary of Clairefontaine was Aimé Jacquet's last as the manager of France. His departure had been planned long before the triumph of his 'commando'; he had become head of the *Direction technique nationale*, overseeing the development strategy of French elite football, to be replaced at the helm of the national team by his assistant Roger Lemerre. This harmonious transition was in keeping with the calmness that had been shown by the FFF ever since the project of hosting the 1998 World Cup had been launched by the far-sighted Fernand Sastre, a football administrator of exceptional integrity who had sadly passed away twenty-nine days before the coronation at the Stade de France. French football was on top of the world, then, and not just on the field. So were the players who had represented it magnificently over the last month.

The cameras stopped rolling, including that of Stéphane Meunier, the director of *Les Yeux dans les Bleus*, who had been a constant companion of the team from the first day of the competition. This was a moment players and staff wanted to savour together, with only their wives and girlfriends for company. As Youri Djorkaeff put it, 'The

relationships between us were magical,' and the strength of that collective bond was such that none of them experienced the emptiness which
often follows an achievement of such magnitude for sportsmen; one
thinks of an emotionally drained Bobby Charlton passing out in his
hotel room after Manchester United exorcized the demons of Munich
by beating Benfica on the Wembley pitch in 1968. Wine and champagne
were consumed in prodigious quantities; Jacquet danced a *paso doble*
with Zidane's wife Véronique among the empty bottles; everyone sang,
reprising a wordless version of Gloria Gaynor's 'I Will Survive', a song
(apparently championed by Vincent Candela) that had become the
team's unofficial anthem throughout the competition. 'All the players
ended bare-chested,' Djorkaeff recalled. 'The World Cup [trophy] was
in the middle of the makeshift dance-floor. We danced like crazy. I
improvised Russian dance steps.'

Nobody slept that night, not in Clairefontaine anyway, and in many
a French home, I guess.

6

What's his position?
What's the point?

A SEASON IN HELL

I have sought an English equivalent to the French expression *la traversée du désert*, literally 'the crossing of the desert', in vain; a pity, as it is how Thierry himself later described the strange year that followed the miracle of 12 July, a 'miracle' that had a personal as well as a collective dimension in his case. His inclusion in Jacquet's World Cup squad, coming off the back of a less-than-convincing season with Monaco, hadn't been expected by everyone, and the fact that he would end the tournament as the world champions' leading scorer had been predicted by none. These achievements would surely launch Thierry's career at ASM for good, wouldn't they? But they didn't. The player in whom Tigana believed as much as anyone else, but had been reluctant to make the lynchpin of his club's attack, for perfectly understandable reasons it must be said, actually regressed in the months that followed his greatest triumph at the Stade de France. This is the 'desert' Henry had to cross, with little sense of which direction to take, and which, for a man as proud as he had always been, must have resembled hell at times.

It is not unknown for footballers who have just come out of a successful international competition to find the readjustment to the routine of their domestic league a struggle. Some never properly recover from the demands made on them during the tournament proper, and even more fail to cope with the far greater attention they command in public opinion and media alike. This, however, might not be why Thierry's stock collapsed so dramatically after he was crowned champion, at which point great care must be exercised, as this fall from grace attracted at the time a number of comments whose motivation was often unclear and sometimes reprehensible.

Monaco was the only club, French or otherwise, to hold the registration of three World Cup winners, all of whom had played a prominent part in the conquest of the title: Fabien Barthez, David Trezeguet and Henry. ASM chairman Jean-Louis Campora convened an extraordinary meeting of his board on 15 July, making it clear that his priority was that none of these players should leave the Principality. Just as he had dug his heels in when Jean Tigana had requested permission to talk to the French federation after the departure of Aimé Jacquet, Campora resisted the temptation to find a buyer for footballers whose market value had rocketed over the last month. But it is precisely at this moment that Arsenal – through David Dein and Arsène Wenger – made their first approach for Thierry, which was met with a courteous but firm rebuttal. The player himself took the blow badly, as did his agents Marc Roger and Jean-François Larios, who stood to make a small fortune from the deal (a then colossal 120 million francs, the equivalent of £12 million, a figure later dismissed as 'fantasy' by Monaco). Henry's dearest wish was to join the growing French contingent at Highbury, whilst Wenger dreamt of associating him with his Clairefontaine schoolmate Nicolas Anelka at the point of the Arsenal attack. Failing to do so, Wenger later told me, remained one of the greatest regrets of his managerial career.

What could Henry do? Nothing. Which is precisely what some of his harshest critics alleged he did. According to them, the player started turning up late for training, dragged his boots whenever he was called to the first team, all the while conniving with his advisers to leak misleading stories to the media to force Monaco's hand, with the complicity of Arsenal FC. Campora assured friendly journalists that he had made an official complaint to FIFA on the matter; but the letter he claimed to have sent must have been lost on its way to Zurich, as no action of any kind was taken. Henry, it is said, requested a meeting with his chairman, purportedly to negotiate a salary, in fact to demand a transfer to the London club. Campora didn't yield, leaving Thierry with one way and one way only to find his way out of the club (or so his enemies contend). The press had reported that Henry's contract with Monaco contained a clause which triggered an automatic one-year extension should the player take part in a given number of matches. According to the conspiracy theorists, it is to prevent such a thing happening that Thierry wilfully 'destroyed' his own game, forcing Tigana to select Victor Ikpeba and David Trezeguet ahead of him.

I for one do not buy into this reading of Henry's spectacular drop in form in the first half of the 1998–9 season. He would sometimes coast through a match or two (as he did repeatedly in his last two seasons at Arsenal), either because the game was inconsequential in itself and he wished to conserve energy or, more often, because he could feel that putting his usual effort into those ninety minutes could precipitate an injury. Nearly all players do likewise, and it could be argued that only a fool would not realize that self-preservation goes hand in hand with the greater good of a team, when the player concerned happens to be one of its most valuable assets. Sabotage is a different matter altogether. That Henry's game was adversely affected by ASM's refusal to sanction his transfer to Arsenal cannot be doubted. A slight but lingering back injury might also have contributed to a decrease in efficiency. That he decided to play so badly he had to drop out of contention is a very serious accusation to direct at a professional footballer, for which there is no other objective grounding, if objective is the word, than the manner of his subsequent exit, and the spiteful reactions which followed. Thierry may have turned his back on people who deserved better on occasions; but he never betrayed football. He loved it far too much for that. Moreover, he paid a heavy price for his repeated failures in the first five months of the new season: within two months of dispatching a vital penalty kick in the World Cup quarter-final against Italy, he had lost his place in the French national team.

As expected, Roger Lemerre put Thierry in the starting line-up of the team that faced Austria on 19 August, in a friendly that was as much a celebratory occasion as a rehearsal for the forthcoming Euro 2000 qualifiers. These started a couple of weeks later with an inauspicious 1-1 draw in Rejkavik, where France failed to deal with an ultra-defensive Icelandic side despite fielding a team replete with attacking talent – but which Henry only joined for the last twenty-two minutes of the game, without adding significant threat up front. He would have to wait another eighteen months to collect his twelfth international cap.

It is not as if *Les Bleus* had suddenly hit upon another new winning formula, swept everything before them during that period, and an out-of-form Henry had become surplus to requirements.* On the contrary: it was clear that Lemerre wished his team to play a more enterprising game than had been the case under Jacquet's regime, in which aggression and caution made for an efficient but not always seductive blend. The new manager constantly chopped and changed his under-performing forward line, calling on Christophe Dugarry, David Trezeguet, Tony Vairelles, Sylvain Wiltord, Lilian Laslandes, Florian Maurice, Stéphane Guivarc'h and Nicolas Anelka in the year-and-a-half that elapsed before Thierry was called on again at last, in March 2000. None of the combinations and permutations Lemerre tried game after game proved particularly convincing; still, Henry remained on the sidelines for reasons that went beyond the poor quality of his performances with Monaco – and, soon, Juventus – as we'll see.

Henry would often mention this long exile when people later questioned his capacity to 'knuckle down' when times were challenging. He accepted his demotion to the French under-21 team with remarkable good grace, seeing it as the surest way to rejoin the senior squad, in which he wasn't entirely correct. Other interests were at stake, which delayed his return to the 'A' team. The greatest hope of French football

---

* France would do well at first in Thierry's absence, beating Russia in Moscow (3-2), then Andorra (2-0), after which Nicolas Anelka scored a memorable double in a friendly against England at Wembley in February 1999 (2-0). A scoreless draw in Ukraine followed in March, then a 2-0 win over Armenia in Saint-Denis later in the same month, and a 2-3 reverse at home on 5 June against Russia, the first defeat in twenty-seven competitive games for France, who hadn't lost since 17 November 1993 – the infamous loss against Bulgaria (1-2) which cost them a place at the 1994 World Cup. *Les Bleus* struggled badly afterwards, edging Andorra and Northern Ireland 1-0, scrapping a 0-0 draw against Ukraine on 4 September, playing with no less than three defensive midfielders. Difficult 3-2 victories in Armenia and against a a tenacious Iceland in Paris placed them back in contention for automatic qualification which was achieved when, fortunately for Lemerre, Russia fluffed their lines against Ukraine in Moscow, conceding a comical goal in the last minutes of their game. France finished top of Group 4, one point ahead of Russia, two of Ukraine, and would not have to endure the play-offs to take part in Euro 2000. France's progress had been as laboured as this paragraph.

had become an *Espoir* again, an irony that wasn't lost on everyone. Thierry drifted further and further away from public attention: a World Cup graduate who had been forced to go back to school and who was now playing with qualification for the 2000 Sydney Olympics in mind, not the senior European Championships, which would be held in Belgium and the Netherlands in the same year. The question was no longer: 'How far can he go?' but 'When will he come back? Will he come back at all?' Among the few who still watched him as closely as before was one Arsène Wenger, however, who, on one of his trips to follow *Les Bleuets*, told Henry that he was 'wasting [his] time on the wing and would have a different career as a centre-forward'. Thierry was nonplussed. 'I won the World Cup as a winger,' he later recalled. 'People all over the world recognized me as a winger. So for me it was kind of strange. I'd already been in the national team, and Arsène was telling me I could have another career as a centre-forward. It was difficult to understand.' It would take another eighteen months for Thierry to realize that Wenger had been right.

What was even more difficult to understand, or accept, was how quickly the chorus of 80,000 voices Henry had heard at the Stade de France had faded away. The young man who, shortly after the World Cup, had said that signing autographs was, 'somehow, a way to give something back to the fans who've supported you in times good and bad, as our duty is to make people dream, on the field and off it', found himself schlepping through Europe with the *Espoirs*, visiting Russia, Ukraine and Armenia in front of tiny crowds, scoring the odd goal, doing what had to be done to show Roger Lemerre that he warranted a return to the 'A' team. It is as if he had been a musician who, having enjoyed a couple of hits and seen the spotlight move to someone else, had buckled up and attempted to 'break' America in second-rate venues with a guitar and a clapped-out van. 'Have ball, will travel.' It wasn't quite thus, however. At the heart of Henry's sudden fall from favour was his complex relationship with Raymond Domenech, for whom success with the under-21s in Europe and at the Olympics represented the best chance to continue his climb within the French football nomenklatura.

As we've seen, Domenech had consistently argued Henry's case for inclusion in Aimé Jacquet's World Cup squad, which was far from the open-and-shut case that hindsight would have us believe. Thierry knew it and, then as now, had a long memory for genuine favours as well as for perceived slights. Domenech, his elder by a quarter of a century, had acted selflessly, or so it seemed: why recommend the 1996 'French Young Player of the Year' to Jacquet when he could have him bolster his own group of players? Even those who see in Domenech an imposter of the first order and an incompetent careerist do not deny that his love of football is genuine; the man they depict as a brazen manipulator, both shameless and machiavellian (a potent mix), is also an obsessive fan, who, just like Wenger and Tigana, had recognized an exceptional talent in Henry and wanted to help him blossom.

A change had occurred since then, however. If Henry needed Domenech's *Espoirs* to relaunch his international career, Domenech needed Henry just as badly. He had already been in charge of France's under-21s for over five years, a job he had inherited from the gentle Marc Bourrier in 1993, and had won nothing with them. The 1994 and 1996 European Championships had ended with France reaching the semi-finals, which could be seen as honourable failures; but they had been eliminated in the group phase in 1998, and their coach could sense that the Federation, much as its panjundrums enjoyed having a man they could control (or so they thought) in charge, might look elsewhere should they be disappointed again.

Was it a case of Lemerre dropping Henry, or of Domenech insisting on having him? Numerous sources within the French hierarchy – all of whom were already in place at the time – have told me that the manager of *Les Bleuets* did his utmost to have the striker rejoin the youth team, and that Lemerre wouldn't have waited so long to bring Henry back into the fold had it not been for Domenech's insistence on keeping him. This would explain why the player, who certainly hadn't committed any cardinal sin, had been left in purgatory when the world champions were searching for a solution up front and had trouble finding one. The call didn't come, even when the French only just beat Andorra 1-0 on 9 June 1999 – thanks to a far from clear-cut Frank Leboeuf penalty, scored in the eighty-sixth minute. Trezeguet and Anelka had got in front of Henry in the pecking order, which was understandable in view of

Thierry's patchy form with Monaco and his subsequent failure at Juventus, a move which a number of observers deemed ill-conceived from the outset. But could Tony Vairelles really be thought of as a superior alternative to Thierry? Or Lilian Laslandes? Or Florian Maurice? Or Stéphane Guivarc'h, again? None of these players, effective as they were at League level, could be thought of as strikers who commanded by right a berth in the best team in the world. They were at best experiments, and all of them failed.

That is not to say Henry was the dupe of Domenech's manoeuvring. A constant in the two men's relationship has been their awareness of how much they ultimately relied on each other. What little they appear to have in common in their upbringing (such as divorced parents, or a 'working-class' background, which , in France, is a foggy notion) pales in comparison with what distinguishes them, the list of which is inexhaustible. Ambition drives both, but the ambition of a supremely gifted athlete bears no relation to that of an aparatchik for whom 'playing the system' had become second nature. The former's selfishness will ultimately benefit those around him as he flourishes; the latter's will be destructive in that insidious, inexorable way in which mediocrity seeps in and corrupts what it comes in contact with. Domenech had some talent as a player. But even then, he cheated. He built a reputation on a lie; the so-called 'butcher' (a nickname which he derived great pride from) never broke the leg of an opponent as he was reputed to have done at the very beginning of his professional career. He was only eighteen at the time of the incident. On 12 August 1970, the Austrian playmaker of OGC Nice, Gabriel Metzner, suffered a double fracture of the leg on the first day of the season, the victim of an awful tackle by Domenech's teammate Jean Baeza, Lyon's answer to Chelsea's 'Chopper' Harris. Raymond took the flak, instantly seeing the benefits he could derive from someone else's 'hardness'. He would later claim: 'I love being called a murderer' and would reprise that awful chorus: 'Football is war.' He grew a handlebar moustache so that nobody would mistake him for one of the good guys and refined the old Italian trick of dissimulating safety pins in his shorts to prick his opponents with (a bit crude) by growing and sharpening his fingernails for the same purpose. In those days of pitches surrounded with metal fences, he would hit the ball as hard as he could against the wire mesh during the warm-up, to startle and antagonize rival fans, who never failed to raise to the bait. Domenech couldn't care less if existing in the eyes of others meant being almost universally despised; and what was true of the player remained true of the manager.

His gamble didn't pay off. On 17 November 1999, in Tarenta, Italy, inspired by a superb Andrea Pirlo, saw off France 2-1 after extra-time in the return leg of a winner-takes-all play-off which Domenech remained convinced was fixed by the Italians. According to him, they had bought that match's referee, one Lucilio Cardoso Cortez Batista, who had sent off French defensive midfielder Christian Bassila, later of Sunderland AFC, after only ten minutes had been played. Repeating this utterly unproven allegation would earn him a one-match ban and a 10,000 Swiss francs fine in 2007. Domenech had failed again, but survived, as he always did. Thierry, fortunately, had already turned the most important corner in his career; but he first had had to go through a period of his life which is hardly ever mentioned in accounts of his rise to the very top of the world game. I have to go back in time to tell that story, which starts at the beginning of 1999, when Henry, still marooned in Monaco, by now in open conflict with Jean Tigana and further away from the French 'A' team than at any other point over the two previous seasons, had to break free not to become another casualty of premature fame; this meant leaving France behind him, not for England – not yet – but for Italy's Serie A, as was announced on 18 January of that year – to almost unanimous disbelief. .

Remarkably, not even his agents had the faintest idea that their client was on his way to Juventus, with whom Henry agreed to sign a four-and-a-half-year deal; his agents – or, if you prefer, the two men who thought they were his agents, Marc Roger and the former French international midfielder Jean-François Larios – reacted furiously to the announcement of the transfer. Roger exploded: 'To think that, last Tuesday [12 January, six days before the move to Juve was publicly announced], I was in Monaco with Thierry to talk about his dad opening a restaurant in Guadeloupe!' The chairman of ASM, Jean-Louis Campora, and Juve's chief executive, Luciano Moggi, had short-circuited Henry's representatives, using the notorious Lucien D'Onofrio* as a go-between, to whom a gargantuan commission of £360,000 had been paid. Documents were leaked to the press, which appeared to show that Thierry, contrary to what he believed, was still under contract with Roger and Larios until 20 February. A fine mess, and a dangerous one too for the player, as less than two years had passed since he had been fined 400,000 francs by FIFA for signing an illegal pre-contract with Real Madrid. Larios made no accusations against Thierry, concentrating his fire on his former club instead. 'Monaco had it all sewn up,' he told *France Football*. 'This contract was not negotiated, but forced [upon Henry]! Campora had already used the same methods when he tried to sell Lilian Thuram and Emmanuel Petit to Inter. Unfortunately, Thierry hasn't quite got the strength of character of these players, and let himself be manipulated.' Seventeen years later, Gilles Grimandi, who had joined Arsenal a season

---

* To clarify the use of the adjective 'notorious': D'Onofrio is not nicknamed 'Lucky Luciano' for nothing. Born in Italy, he grew up in Belgium. When his footballing career failed to take off there, he played for a while in the USA, then in Portugal with First Division side Portimonense , where a double fracture of the leg forced him to retire at the age of twenty-eight. D'Onofrio, who had gone to Italy for treatment, somehow became a 'sports adviser' at Internazionale. He moved from Milan to Porto in 1985 and enjoyed a spectacular rise in that city's flagship club, right up to the position of general manager, which he left in 1991 to become one of the most powerful agents in European football. Players like Alen Bokšić, Victor Baía, André Cruz, Victor Ikpeba, Marcel Desailly, Didier Deschamps and Zinedine Zidane had used his services before he handled Thierry Henry's transfer. D'Onofrio was quite open about his methods, which he summarized thus in a 1997 interview with the Brussels daily *Le Soir*: 'the agent makes do as he wishes. FIFA has not defined a payment structure. There's no such thing as an official fee.' This relaxed attitude landed him before a French tribunal a number of years later, when investigators found proof of serious irregularities in the accounts of Olympique de Marseille. In October 2007, the Appeal Court of Aix-en-Provence sentenced D'Onofrio to two years' imprisonment (eighteen months suspended), a fine of 200,000, and a two-year ban from any activity in football. This didn't prevent him from retaining his position of vice-chairman at Belgian elite side Standard de Liège, of which his brother Dominique was head coach until 2011. 'Lucky Luciano' has now gone back to what he knows best: being an agent.

and a half before Henry's sudden departure, would concur with Larios. 'Campora had a relationship in place with Juve,' he told me, 'and Thierry did what he was asked to do. Campora and Monaco also decided to sell Thuram [to Juventus]. Lilian didn't want to go, and they made life impossible for him, and it took him incredible strength to resist and have things his own way. The players were going where Campora wanted them to go, where it was in his interest that it should happen.'

Henry himself was quite happy to present his move as a personal decision, or at least as a decision that hadn't been taken without his express consent (I can't help but think that he had his move to Juve in mind when he said, in 2008, 'Every decision I've made in my life, I've made on my own'). In the first interview he gave after signing for the *bianconeri*, this is what he said to *France Football*'s Jean-Michel Brochen, who asked him why the agents he had been advised by for two years had been left out of the move they had tried to engineer all along. Jean-Michel noted the 'sarcastic' tone of Henry's answer:

Yes, it's bizarre, eh? (pause) As if by chance. My transfer happened when nobody expected it. I was sometimes announced in a club because 'someone' knew another one was interested in me. So that I wouldn't go there. This time, I chose. It was my decision. It's a bit like . . . I cocked a snook (pied de nez*) and it might also serve as an example.*

    Believe me, I've learnt a lot recently.

Henry was not yet twenty-two years old when he made his first career choice as a grown man. He had come to it very quickly indeed – in a matter of hours, after a phone conversation with Campora. His immediate assent demonstrated a measure of courage, a great deal of self-confidence and a certain talent for dissimulation. It was also a final, decisive step away from his father Tony – who seems to have been kept in the dark until the very last moment – the moment when the string finally snapped in their tortuous relationship, which had grown even more volatile ever since Thierry's botched negotiations with Real Madrid. 'You have to be the man you carry inside,' Thierry told an English journalist in 2008. Going to Juventus might not have been the wisest of decisions, but it enabled that 'man' to step out in the open; no one else was going to carry him but himself, free, at long last.

What astounded Roger was that Henry appeared to forfeit a lot of money by operating on his own. 'At Monaco, Thierry earned 150,000 francs [£15,000] a month,' he said. 'Even if he's going to multiply his wages by five or six, we could've got more for him: they were offering 800,000 francs a month to [Christophe] Dugarry.' Both he and Larios stated their intention to pursue the matter with Juve. Had the agents not taken Thierry and his father Tony to Barcelona at their own expense? Hadn't they been told by Arsène Wenger that Arsenal were willing to put £12 million on the table for the player, £5 million more than Juventus were rumoured to have paid? What's more, as Grimandi recalls it: 'after I moved to Arsenal, he kept pestering me about it – because his dream was to play for them. I remember seeing him in the car park at the Monaco training ground in La Turbie. "Gilles, tell Wenger I want to play at Arsenal!"'

Larios also wondered how Henry could have signed a contract drafted in Italian, a language the player didn't speak at all. But he would learn to, and very quickly. Within a few weeks of his arrival, he was able to converse with his teammates and, towards the end of his stay at the Stadio delle Alpi, could conduct interviews with *Tuttosport* as well as most of the nineteen other Frenchmen – seven of them world champions – who had chosen to play in Serie A.

Henry never thought he would waltz in and instantly claim a spot in Juve's starting eleven. 'The first two months will be difficult,' he warned. Saying, as footballers do, that it was a 'dream' to wear the jersey two of his idols, Michel Platini and Zbignew Boniek, had made him long for when he was a child did not prevent him from confessing that Spain (Barcelona) and England (Arsenal, who, thinking Henry couldn't be brought to Highbury, chose the Nigerian Kanu instead) would have been his destinations of choice if Juve hadn't called. Half an hour before he signed his contract with Juve, Thierry called Wenger, but, 'by that time, he had no choice', his mentor recalled. 'I had to be patient . . . as I'd been with Kanu'. AC Milan and Internazionale had made enquiries too. But if it had to be Italy, why not opt for the club where he would find three other Frenchmen: Zidane, Deschamps and the former Metz midfielder Jocelyn Blanchard, who had been one of the revelations of the 1997–8 season in France?

Thierry wasn't under any illusions as to the magnitude of the challenge that was ahead of him. Juve were going through a turbulent period, both on and off the field. 1999 had started for them with three draws in the League and a humiliating 1-2 home defeat to Bologna in the Coppa Italia. The Serie A leaders, Fiorentina, were eleven points ahead in the championship table. Italy's best-supported club hadn't found itself in such a precarious position since Marcello Lippi's appointment in 1994. One objective remained, and one only: the Champions League, which Thierry couldn't take part in anyway, as he had already played in the UEFA Cup with Monaco. Fiorentina's best striker, the Argentinian Gabriel Batistuta, had only scored one goal less than all of the other Juventus players put together. One reason for this paucity of goals was Alessandro Del Piero's unavailability through a knee injury that would sideline him for most, if not all, of the season. Del Piero's reaction to Henry's arrival was, shall we say, not exactly ecstatic. 'I was surprised,' he said. 'I hadn't heard of it. The other day, someone on television called him a *bidone* ('fraud') . . . It made me cry with laughter – he's a very good player, who plays mostly on the wing. We could think of an attack with him, Inzaghi and myself, plus Zidane just behind. But Thierry Henry shouldn't take me out of the team!'

Del Piero's suggestion – joke, rather – made little sense in tactical terms, which was precisely the point the Italian player wanted to put across: Henry would have trouble fitting in, and he shouldn't count too much on others to help him do so. 'Football is an individual game,' as I once heard a French international quip to a nonplussed fan. At the age of twenty-four, on the back of what would remain the best campaign of his career at club level (thirty-two goals in forty-seven games), Del Piero had established himself as the finest *trequartista* of his generation in Italy, a supporting striker, a link between midfield and attack, certainly, but who would be wasted in the 4-2-1-3 formation he suggested, knowing perfectly well that it could never become Juve's default set-up. Prudent coaches like Lippi or his – already anointed – successor, Carlo Ancelotti, would not deploy such an adventurous formation, which ran against the grain of Juventus's tradition of 'realism' and contradicted their own convictions. Henry would also soon face competition from Gianluca Zambrotta, a wide midfielder with a more defensive outlook, whom Ancelotti, already pulling strings in the background, had asked Juve to purchase from Bari. The more one looked into it, the less one could see how and where the young Frenchman would slot in, and why Juve had spent more money to acquire him – the equivalent of £7.5 million – than any other Italian club had ever paid for any of his compatriots, Zidane included. Juve needed not just goals – like the one Thierry had scored against them in the previous season's semi-final of the Champions League – but, more pointedly, a goalscorer, which Henry wasn't yet and, in his opinion, would never be.

'I'll play as I did at Monaco, on the wing, either on the left or on the right,' he explained. 'I'm not like David Trezeguet. People shouldn't expect bagfuls of goals from me.' Later on, Henry's lack of headline-making success in Turin would be blamed on his 'repositioning' on the left flank, which blunted the sharpness of a natural finisher. In truth, only Wenger had thought of him as a centre-forward in waiting, so to speak. I remember a conversation I had with the Arsenal manager shortly after Samir Nasri had been brought from Marseille in the summer of 2008. 'It's sometimes a good idea,' he told me, 'to deploy a player who has a future in the middle of the park on the flank. He gets used to using the ball in a smaller space, as the touchline effectively divides the space that's available to him by two; when you move the same player to the middle, he breathes more easily and can exploit space better.' What Wenger said of Nasri could be applied to Henry, though I doubt it was uppermost in Lippi's mind when he advised his employers to make an approach to Monaco. The 'repositioning' of Henry was a red herring; at the root of his incapacity to settle in Turin were the demands that are made of a wide player in the safety-first environment of Serie A in the 1990s. As Blanchard told me, 'Juve was a team in which you were not necessarily asked to play in your natural position. You had to fit in a tactical system that might not suit your own qualities. Thierry was a forward – and Juve asked him to play in midfield, on the left – a position in which you need to have great stamina, in order to fulfil your defensive as well as your attacking duties,' a role for which his teammate felt Henry wasn't ready: he would have to learn to defend, something none of his previous managers had asked or taught him to do. Reflecting on those few months spent in Italy, Thierry himself said, in 2002:

A football player must be a good actor today. He must adapt to every kind of role. There [at Juve], it was a role that was too much against nature for me. We played 3-5-2, with all of the left side for me. When we were attacking, I was the second or third forward. When the ball was in the middle, I had to be the fifth midfielder. And when the ball was at the back, I was the fourth defender!

'Given his young age, even if you take what he'd done at Monaco into account,' Blanchard adds, 'he was still a newcomer in football terms. So it wasn't easy for him to integrate the demands that were made, or to accept them. When you're signed by as big a club as Juve, you feel proud, you want to shine, show your worth. And sometimes, when you don't find yourself in a situation where your qualities are not made the most of, things get difficult.' And they did get difficult, very quickly, despite Zidane's prediction that, being a 'smart, clever and quick player', Henry would be 'very comfortable at Juventus'. Not so: Thierry made his debut on 24 January 1999, playing the last twenty minutes of a 2-1 win over Perugia, started the next game, a less-than-crucial Coppa Italia tie against Bologna – and that's about as good as it got, with the exception of one truly superb performance at a rainswept Stadio Olimpico on 17 April, where Sven-Göran Eriksson's Lazio was utterly outclassed by Juve. Thierry contributed two goals (with the complicity of the Lazio 'keeper Luca Marchegiani, it must be said) to his team's 3-1 victory. But his total goal tally was a mere three in sixteen games, the majority of which he only played in part.

This doesn't necessarily mean that the time Henry spent at Juve was wasted, or can even be considered a 'failure'. It had been Thierry's first move as a professional. How many twenty-one-year-olds immediately impose themselves in a foreign culture, and a culture as conservatively minded as *calcio* then was, at that? The Italian nucleus of that Juve side had made no more effort to make the youngster feel at home than was their habit with foreign imports; in other words, they made none. Lippi's and Ancelotti's tactical set-ups negated Henry's qualities as a game-changer. With this context in mind, it is remarkable that Thierry didn't lose every ounce of confidence he had in his talent. Blanchard, who found the going even harder than his new teammate, insists on the fact that neither Henry nor he were 'unduly worried'. 'We hadn't been taken on by Juve by chance,' he says. 'If you were with them, it meant that you had qualities. Some things you have no control over – the decisions taken by your coaches or our board, the team's form, and so on; others you do – your level of individual performance, regardless of the context in which you have to deliver them, and which is not always favourable. Thierry and I didn't worry about that. What mattered was to try to play, and to take Juve as high as we could. In a club like Juve, failure is not an option.' And don't let us forget that, if Thierry 'failed', others did too that year in Turin. As he put it in 2004:

Zidane and lots of other players weren't playing well either. It was a test. Obviously, you're going to have some bad moments in your career and that was one of the bad moments, but it depends how much you want to use it to make great moments later. How much do you want to erase that from people's memories? I tried to make people forget about that time. Because of what I've done since it seems to some people as if I have only played for Arsenal. They maybe remember I played for Monaco when I was young, but sometimes they forget I even played for Juve.

'I remember his frustration,' Blanchard says, 'when he had to play in that position . . . He wouldn't produce as much effort as he could have at times. I talked to him about it. "Tell yourself how lucky you are to play," I said to him. "Give everything you've got. Whether you're satisfied or not . . . that's not the problem. You'll be able to go wherever you want to go whenever you want to go. But what you're living now is exceptional, as you'll realize later in life." That game against Lazio, when he scored two goals, that was his way of saying, "When I am fully integrated, and people trust me, I'll be able to do great things for this club." But he wasn't given the time to do so. I'll tell you: Juve rued letting Thierry go far more than Thierry rued leaving them.'

It is not as if Henry had suffered from 'collateral damage' after Lippi was replaced by Ancelotti in February 1999. If anything, this managerial change should have helped him to settle. What Florent Malouda later said of his Chelsea coach was already true at the time: 'Ancelotti has the character to be close to every player, the ones who play and the ones who don't. He knows the ones who don't play have different feelings and he tries to keep everyone together,' something with which Blanchard agrees. 'I'd say that Ancelotti was a little bit closer to the players than Lippi. But his methods and Lippi's were almost the same, their behaviour too. They'd known this squad for a long time and tended to trust what they knew rather than what they didn't know too well,' especially if these players they 'didn't know too well' showed as little natural inclination to defend as Henry did.

Years later, some of Highbury's loudest cheers would erupt when Thierry, having lost the ball, would harry defenders in their half of the pitch, chasing one, then the other, sprinting madly across the turf – to good effect, it must be said. It was a startling and oddly beautiful sight: the opposing centre-backs lost the script, paused for a moment in their confusion, wondering what to do with the ball, giving Henry time to close down on them. The ball would then travel to a full-back, who wasn't expecting that gift, panicked and hoofed it forward (sometimes straight into touch), where the patrolling Arsenal midfielders rarely failed to regain control of the play. Some of my best memories of Thierry Henry at Arsenal are these manic, anger-fuelled sprints which proclaimed his love of the club better than any speech might have done. But that was Arsenal, not Juve. Just as Thierry would complain of the extra defensive work he had to shoulder in his first season at Barcelona, he struggled to adapt to the demands made of him as a 'wide midfielder' in *calcio*.

When I got a chance to ask Carlo Ancelotti to explain why, in his opinion, Henry made so little impression in the six months he spent in Italy, I got this reply: 'He was very young, and lacked a bit of maturity. It isn't easy for a young player to come into as strong a team as Juventus and immediately show his qualities.' And to be fair to Thierry, opportunities to 'show his qualities' were scarce; the Monaco star was reduced to a series of cameos, in which he shone too intermittently to force his manager's hand. At no point did it cross Ancelotti's mind that the World Cup winner who had been signed at his predecessor's request would show rather more of his talent in a different position. 'I didn't think I could play him in the middle,' he chuckled, 'and he never told me he could. Yes, of course, when you see what he did at Arsenal, you have regrets – but he didn't leave Juve because he had a problem with me, or me with him. His problem was with the club.'

Thierry later referred to 'a lack of respect on the part of Luciano Moggi'. as his main reason for leaving Italy, not his lack of first-team football or his displeasure with Juve's prudent approach. Ancelotti was more precise when we talked about the circumstances of Henry's departure. The player had become a pawn in his chairman's game, which Moggi wanted to move across the board on loan to Udinese Calcio, so that Juve could acquire their Brazilian striker Márcio Amoroso, who had outscored everyone else in the 1998–9 Serie A season. But the Stadio Friuli held little attraction for Henry, who flatly refused to move to an unfashionable club whose list of honours was two lines long: the 1978 Anglo-Italian Cup and the 1980 Mitropa Cup. From then on, it was just a question of finding a buyer. Thierry was on his way home. To Arsenal.

7

Not just a new jersey; a new skin.

THE METAMORPHOSIS

It has often been said that Henry's first steps in England were tentative, in keeping with what had happened to most other imports before him. According to common wisdom, the 'hustle and bustle' of the Premier League was bound to be a disconcerting experience at first for any foreign player, regardless of what he had accomplished beforehand, and particularly so for a striker, as it was agreed that English defenders were somewhat more vigorous in the challenge, and referees more lenient in their judgement of what constituted a foul, than their continental counterparts. After all, hadn't Dennis Bergkamp himself, Arsenal's surprising capture in June 1995, struggled to adapt to life at Highbury? Well – perhaps not as much as was made out. The Dutchman broke his duck with a brace in his seventh Premiership match and ended his first season in England with a return of one goal in every third game, finishing with eleven in the League alone – as many as he had got in his previous two seasons with Inter put together. Adapting to Serie A had been more of a challenge to Bergkamp than getting accustomed to the 'rough and tumble' of English football, it seems. I make no apologies for borrowing these clichés, as they were used liberally in Henry's case as well; with hindsight, what they demonstrated was that the understanding of the nature of that game had evolved at a slower pace than the game itself. The dilution of the League's 'Englishness' was not a columnist's worry any more, but a fact. The erosion of cultural frontiers within English football had proceeded as spectacularly as that of the Suffolk coastline: when Thierry arrived from *calcio*, an elite English club without a foreigner in its ranks would have been as strange a sight as the sunken city of Dunwich rising again from the sea. But somehow, the mystique of a 'different' game or, more precisely, of a game that, by nature, was 'more alien' to footballers trained abroad than, say, Italian, Spanish or German football, endured well beyond the point when it had changed irrevocably. Thirty-eight French players had already appeared for Premier League clubs before the start of the 1999–2000 season, of whom five* had been brought in by Arsène Wenger, before it was announced on 4 August 1999 that Arsenal had paid a then club record £10 million plus to secure the Juve part-timer on a five-year contract.

The correct figure, £11.5 million, £4.5 million more than what Arsenal had paid Ajax for Marc Overmars in June 1997, might not appear to be that much money thirteen years on, 228 goals later. Sums far greater than this are routinely exchanged between leading clubs when trading players of an age and status comparable to those of Thierry in 1999, a world champion about to celebrate his twenty-second birthday. The picture changes somewhat when putting that transaction in context. According to Paul Tomkins's study *Pay As You Play*,† the average Premier League transfer fee increased by 234 per cent between 1999 and 2010, which makes Henry a £26.9 million player in current terms, that is to say a fortune, considering how his progress had been checked since he had ended the 1998 World Cup as France's most prolific goalscorer. Davor Šuker, who had finished that tournament with six goals for third-placed Croatia, earning the Golden Boot award in the process, had been brought from Real Madrid for £1 million the same summer, £2.3 million in adjusted terms, agreeing to a substantial pay-cut in order to join the London club. Wenger had huge resources at his disposal following Nicolas Anelka's protracted sale to the Spanish club, which raised £22.5 million, the equivalent of £54 million if Tomkins's Current Transfer Purchase Price index is used. To spend that much of these proceeds on a 'failing' forward like Henry represented a gamble nonetheless, not that dissimilar to the decision taken by Liverpool to spend 70 per cent of the £50 million made by selling Fernando Torres

---

*   Rémi Garde, Patrick Vieira, Gilles Grimandi, Emmanuel Petit and David Grondin. Garde and Grondin had left by the time Henry signed for Arsenal.
†   GPRF Publishing, 2010.

to Chelsea in January 2011 to secure Andy Carroll's move from New-castle. The 'Henry ready to reign at Highbury' headlines were misleading. He patently wasn't: Arsenal would have to be a springboard before it became his stage. And Arsenal had not one, but two, vacuums to fill.

Anelka had gone in acrimonious circumstances, when he seemed on the verge of establishing himself as one of the most potent strikers in world football. Dennis Bergkamp's aerophobia prevented him from taking part in almost any away Champions League fixture Arsenal would be involved in, much to the distress of the club's fans. One of them, a friend of mine, went as far as combing European train timetables to find out how it would be possible to get the Dutchman to Ukraine by land in record time, an option Wenger weighed for a while, apparently. Kanu could be added to the equation, as he would miss up to seven weeks of the coming season in January and February, when his home country, Nigeria, would host the 2000 African Cup of Nations. According to Wenger, his team's 2-1 victory over Manchester United in the FA Charity Shield on 1 August had shown that 'Arsenal didn't depend on one player', namely the Madrid-bound Anelka. Those who remembered how the young Parisian had tormented English defences with his athleticism, technique and composure in front of goal reserved their judgement. Thierry couldn't escape comparisons with his former under-20 teammate. Both were graduates of Clairefontaine, both were black of West Indian parentage, both came from the *banlieue* – and had two brothers, even though Claude and Didier Anelka had very little in common with Willy and Dimitry, then an infant. Henry brushed these similarities aside. 'Nicolas is his own man, I am mine,' he said on his arrival at Highbury; but the expectation wasn't dampened by what Wenger himself had to say about his acquisition. 'As well as having the qualities of youth, pace and power, I think he is a good finisher,' the manager stated. 'That is some-thing he hasn't worked on enough in the last two years, because he has played more wide, but I think he can become a central striker again. That is what we will try to develop together.'

Henry wasn't given much time to acclimatize to the English game before he was named in Arsenal's starting eleven. After replacing Freddie Ljungberg at the interval in his first match for the Gunners – a season-opener against Leicester which proved trickier than expected for the second-best team in the land – Arsenal prevailed 2-1 but narrowly escaped their first home defeat of the calendar year. Thierry was given eighty-five minutes in another 2-1 win, at Derby this time, in which he appeared short of fitness and struggled to keep up with the tempo of the game. One of his shots shaved Mart Poom's goal-frame, another brought a good save from the Estonian 'keeper. He also earned his first caution in English football, and that was that. After a forgettable 0-0 at Sunderland, Manchester United, who had only won one of their past nine games against Arsenal – a famous 2-1 victory in the semi-final of the 1999 FA Cup, admittedly – sent Wenger's team to their first defeat on their home ground since December 1997. Thierry was still feeling his way; not that he was alone in doing so. With Emmanuel Petit injured and Nicolas Anelka gone to Spain, Arsenal could be likened to 'a piece of film being developed', as the *Guardian*'s Kevin McCarra put it, whose 'true appearance may emerge only gradually'. Against Bradford, on 25 August, a match in which the visitors conceded twenty-nine attempts on goal, Henry wasted a host of chances when he should have earned the match ball by half-time: Marc Overmars replaced him just past the hour. It was even worse three days later, when Gérard Houllier's Liverpool, fresh from a superb win at Leeds, were well worth their 2-0 success. Robbie Fowler, who crashed a stupendous twenty-five-yard strike off the bar and into the net to open the scoring in the eighth minute, gave a lesson in leading the line and finishing that contrasted with Henry's gaucheness. The fact that Thierry had played three times in six days, and that four weeks had not yet elapsed since he had been presented to the British press, did not prevent criticism being voiced from some quarters, criticism which, Henry being Henry, did not go unnoticed by their target. 'Some people were a bit harsh,' he recalled in 2004. 'All that money [spent] for a guy who can't cross the ball, can't score, can't do anything.' But he also knew he had been 'awful' (his own choice of word) against Liverpool and could not help asking himself whether the critics had a point. Yes, 'it takes time to relearn how to move, to bend your run and find the right angle to score goals', but this was 'the moment when I doubted that I could impose myself as a centre-forward', he later confessed. Like a pianist who has been unable to practise because of a hand injury, Henry, the boyhood centre-forward, long exiled to the wing and beyond at Monaco and Juve, had to relearn his craft and assume a role for which he didn't necessarily think himself fit. There was nothing coquettish in his assertion that he 'wasn't a natural goalscorer', which he made time after time after his statistics had gone from the remarkable to the prodigious.

Even though Wenger kept on encouraging him, Henry's confidence can't have been helped when, following a short international break in which he played no part with France, it was another striker who ensured – and in brilliant fashion – that Arsenal, already defeated in August by two direct rivals for the title, beat Aston Villa 3-1 at Highbury. Davor Šuker scored twice, earning this comment from his manager: 'You feel that when he's inside the box, he'll find the target.' Not that many people would have said that of Henry at the time. He had only played seven minutes of that win. He only played nine of the following match, perhaps Arsenal's most important of the season so far – an away trip to Fiorentina, to which Bergkamp had been driven by his godfather. Could Thierry, the record signing, the world champion, really be ranked fourth in the hierarchy of his new club's forwards, behind the Dutchman, Šuker and Kanu? And why had Wenger put him on the right side of midfield when he finally chose to use him in Florence? The 0-0 in Italy had been his eighth game for the Gunners, by which time his statistics read: goals, 0; assists, 0; cautions, 2.

By his own admission, Henry had missed 'fourteen, fifteen chances' since Arsène Wenger had first sent him on the field on the opening day of the season. If he carried on in that vein, it wouldn't be long before some chanted 'What a waste of money' in the stands. Maybe he wasn't made to be a striker after all, despite what his manager told him day after day on the training ground, where a programme of specific exercises had been devised to sharpen his decision-making and his accuracy in front of goal. Wenger never doubted that the cause of Thierry's hesitant finishing was to be found in Turin, and nowhere else. 'They pushed him wide,' he reminisced in 2007, 'they kept him wide, they played him as a winger. He lost his appetite for scoring goals. He convinced himself that he couldn't score goals. That's what everybody reproached him with. I thought, "Let's have a go and start through the centre, like when you were a boy."' All Thierry needed was a stroke of luck, an opponent's mistake, a flash of genius. It was the latter. The trigger was not one of these chancy tap-ins which never seem to come to the rescue of under-performing centre-forwards, but a spectacular long-range effort which must rank among the finest he struck in his eight seasons with Arsenal. It didn't immediately transform Henry into a scoring machine; but it bought him valuable time.

18 September, 1999. With little more than a quarter of an hour to play, Henry's team was still locked in a 0-0 draw at Southampton when Kanu made way for the misfiring Frenchman. Eight minutes later, Thierry received the ball some forty yards away from Paul Jones's goal, evaded the Portuguese defender Marco Almeida and curled a twenty-five-yard shot in the top corner. A goal, at last, and a splendid one at that. But there was no explosion of joy, no expression of relief. Henry raced towards the right-hand corner flag, grabbed the post and made a mock military salute – then, and only then did he allow a smile to light up his expression. He was reprising a routine which had been familiar to Monaco fans, which he had borrowed from 'Batigol' – his nickname for David Trezeguet, in homage to Gabriel Batistuta. Watching footage of this celebration, I'm reminded, once again, of Jacques Crevoisier's irritation at the way Henry and Trezeguet rehearsed their double act with the French under-20s and under-21s. 'They were spending a lot of time thinking of what they'd do after they'd scored. So I said: "Do you know what would really be original, lads? Next time you score, drop your pants and piss on the corner flag. I'm sure it's never been done before."'

Jacques wouldn't be the only man to feel aggrieved by Henry's lack of spontaneity; in fact, Thierry confessed on a number of occasions that, watching himself on video, he too felt puzzled (and, at times, not a little embarrassed) by his behaviour, for which he couldn't find a ready explanation. 'I see myself,' he told me, 'and I think: "Can't you just relax, man?" But no, I can't, and I don't know why.' As has already been mentioned, he had been influenced by the theatricality of the American sportsmen he most admired – Michael Jordan, whom Henry idolized, being a case in point – which manifested itself either in the most exuberant of fashions or in a display of indifference

intended to 'get under the skin' of the opposition. The 'yes' sign celebration (V-shaped fingers, pointing at the heart), initiated by Nicolas
Anelka, adopted by Thierry Henry, also had an American origin: it
had been patented, so to speak, by the Chicago Cubs right-field base-
ball player Sammy Sosa. Such gestures grated with the management,
but were lapped up by the public at large. When, in July 2000, the
French players gathered on the balcony of the Hôtel Crillon to salute
the huge crowd who had come to celebrate victory at the European
Championships, a chant rose up from below. 'The sign! The sign!'
Henry and his teammates obliged, naturally.

If one thinks ahead to a stage in Thierry's career when he couldn't
be suspected of immaturity – the wonder goal that beat Real Madrid
at the Bernabéu, in 2006, for example – it is clear that this inability to
enjoy the ecstasy of scoring accompanied him to the last, with the
glorious exception of the goal he scored against Leeds United on his
brief return to Arsenal in 2012. As he put it in a *Sun* column, dictated
late in 2008, 'what happens is that I don't understand euphoria'. How
sad that sentence was, how revealing too; and, as ever, his father Tony's
shadow loomed large in the background. Thierry continued:

*I was ten years old. I finished a game in which I scored six goals. I got into
my father's car and I saw he was very serious. I asked him what had happened and he asked me if I was pleased. I answered yes but he started
counting out my mistakes, that I had missed a cross in the tenth minute, I
missed a chance in the 14th minute and another time I failed to control
the ball. Every game was like that. Ever since then when I scored a goal I
thought of what I had done wrongly previously in the game instead of
celebrating.*

There were occasions on which Henry, by his own admission, 'lost it'
(his pitch-long sprints after scoring against Liverpool and Tottenham
at Highbury are two instances that all Arsenal fans will be familiar
with), but these can be counted on the fingers of one hand. 'I'm driven
by anger,' he famously said towards the end of his English career. In
which he's not alone: so is Wayne Rooney, to an extent. But Henry's
anger could not be released in the kind of physical battle relished by

the Manchester United player; he sought to elude his markers, not confront them directly. Those who have accused him of 'lacking appetite for a fight' have missed the point. Yes, Thierry was blessed with an imposing physique; and, had his game been that of a traditional 'target man', which it never was and never could be, he might have used it more purposefully than he did. But this would have blunted, perhaps even negated, the qualities that made an exceptional footballer, first among them the speed of thought and limb that prevented defenders from getting close to him. This ability to distance himself from what was happening around him on the field was a tremendous asset; sometimes, watching him bear down on goal in one of those trademark left-sided runs, with one defender to beat and the opposite corner of the goal to aim at, you could picture Henry as one of these part-human, part-machine hitmen so loved of science-fiction film-makers, whose perception is transcribed visually in row after row of digits scrolling at blinding speed on the screen. A personal fancy? Not quite. Henry could analyse his own movement and deconstruct his thought process with a precision and a detachment no player I have come across has matched. But objectification of that kind also has an emotional component – and impact. The regal footballer of the mid-2000s had acquired the kind of self-assurance that would have passed for cockiness in his younger self; but the Henry of 1999 was already, strangely, *beside* himself when he played, or scored, not with joy – but literally, a spectator as well as an actor. 'When you're a striker,' he once said, 'your game is based on instinct, and I'd say 40 per cent of my game is. But I always know where my teammates are before I receive the ball. If you can win time on the pitch – have a look before you receive the ball, see things before everyone else – that's the difference between an average player and a player who illuminates the game.' It's easy to guess which category Henry has long felt he belonged to, and rightly so. Self-awareness is precious in more than one way, however: it pays off, but also comes at a cost.

Not much was made of Thierry's first goal on English soil at the time, as headline writers had bigger fish to fry that weekend: Bobby Robson had celebrated his take-over from Ruud Gullit at Newcastle with an 8-0 win over Sheffield Wednesday, with Alan Shearer scoring a quintuple. Far more notice was taken of Henry's contribution to Arsenal's 3-1 win over AIK Solna at Wembley four days later. Once again, Thierry had started on the bench, only leaving it with a little over twenty minutes to play, when the score was still tied at 1-1. Arsenal had garnered four points from a possible nine at the national stadium in their previous Champions League campaign, and it seemed as if they would be jinxed by the arena once more. Most of the players resented the financially motivated move to Wembley, none more so than Martin Keown, who, on that occasion, complained about the choice of pre-match music, the temperature in the dressing-room and the length of the grass before kick-off.* Wenger's argument that 'if we pass the ball well, the ground is the same everywhere' was one which even he, in private, recognized to be spurious. What's more, the Swedish champions had made Barcelona work very hard to earn a 2-1 victory in the previous round of matches.

Enter Thierry, in one of these unsubtle moves which will be familiar to all Wenger-watchers. We need a goal? Let's add a striker or two to the mix. Henry and Kanu joined Bergkamp and Šuker, and, in the ninetieth minute, the two subs combined to put the Gunners ahead, Thierry slotting a neat drive low into Mattias Asper's goal. Henry added an assist to his goal in the dying seconds, offering Šuker a chance he couldn't miss. 'I would have felt as if I'd let everyone down if we hadn't won the game,' Henry told reporters in his already excellent English after the game. Before you rush to the conclusion that the young man was getting ahead of himself when saying that, be aware of the fact that he had missed a golden opportunity to score in normal time ('I looked at the clock and knew I had nine minutes to put it right'), and that he felt genuinely indebted towards those who had welcomed him at Highbury. London wasn't yet the 'home' it would quickly become for Thierry, once he had left his digs at Sopwell House. But, coming after six difficult months in Turin, not one of Italy's most obviously charming or welcoming cities, and a rigorous, not to say rigid, football environment,

---

* Was it a coincidence that it was a poor clearance by the same Keown which gifted Solna their equalizer?

Henry could enjoy a far more relaxed attitude to his trade than had been the case in the past. Wenger's so-called 'scientific' approach concerned itself with diet, physical preparation, short but intense training routines and, especially, the creation of surroundings in which players could express themselves to the full extent of their natural ability. Very little time – if any, judging by what a number of his former players have told me – was devoted to the kind of tactical drills a Tigana, a Lippi or an Ancelotti would have put his charges through. Emmanuel Petit recalled his delight when his manager sometimes dispensed with the customary exercises and asked his whole staff to repair indoors in order to play half an hour of basketball. This was as good a way as any to sharpen the footballers' awareness of space, practise movement off the ball – and guarantee they would have fun.

Winning the Double in 1997–8 had united a squad that, despite its growing cosmopolitanism,* retained the English core inherited from the George Graham era. Later on in Thierry's career, when age had caught up with the famous old guard, that balance would be lost and, with it, some of the camaraderie of those first few years; on the field, some of the team's competitive edge was blunted as well. Wenger was conscious of this. I remember how he told me, at the very end of the 2000–2001 season, how he felt he now needed to 're-anglicize' his squad. Sol Campbell, Richard Wright and Francis Jeffers were soon brought in, but, with the exception of the former Tottenham defender, the experiment failed. I'm not sure that managers can exert a great deal of control over dressing-room politics, qualitatively that is. Clans will always be formed along national lines as much as in accordance with personal affinities, drawing invisible but sometimes impenetrable border lines within a club. This became the case at Arsenal, as it did elsewhere. Back in 1999, however, power had not yet shifted away from the English contingent, whose fierce loyalty to their club made a deep impression on Henry. To use an – alas – antiquated expression, Seaman, Adams, Keown, Winterburn, Dixon and Parlour were true 'Arsenal men', whose love for, and dedication to, their colours was not that markedly different

---

* Of the twenty-four players signed by Wenger before Henry arrived at Arsenal, only two were English: Matthew Upson and Jermaine Pennant.

to that of the Bastins, Hapgoods and Males of the Chapman era. Adams in particular felt it was his responsibility as club captain 'to tell everyone, including Thierry Henry, what were the requirements at this great football club'.

Walking into the training-ground canteen – a privilege long since revoked for all journalists – I could see how the English would congregate at one table, whilst the 'French guys' ate their steamed broccoli at another. They didn't look like boarders about to start a joyous bread fight; but neither did they seem to live in different worlds. There was a palpable sense of togetherness. The pivotal role that Patrick Vieira and Emmanuel Petit had played in securing the second Double in the club's history had convinced the English contingent that their manager knew a thing or two when it came to gauging the potential of a footballer, something Henry drew benefit from when he struggled in the first few months of his Arsenal career. As Martin Keown put it with telling simplicity: 'If Wenger was backing [Henry], we thought he must be a very good player.' Just as importantly, the open-mindedness of stalwarts like Keown drew the newcomers within the fold, provided they were willing to earn the respect of their elders. These newcomers could expect a robust reception, as Thierry later acknowledged. 'The guys were letting me know what [you] needed to do to play for Arsenal FC,' he said, remembering his days as a Highbury apprentice. 'You can imagine what it was like in training, sometimes, with the likes of Tony [Adams], Lee [Dixon], Nigel [Winterburn] and Martin [Keown].' These grown men were accustomed to give as much as they got; they were also willing to give as much as you deserved, and that included an initiation into what it really meant to wear the cannon-crested jersey. It cannot be a coincidence that, to this day, personalities as diverse as Petit, Vieira, Grimandi, Pirès and Henry himself have retained a sense of belonging to Arsenal that many of their successors would be unable to comprehend. A generational gap? Superficially so. Rather the consequence of a failure to bridge it.

Henry later claimed to have been an Arsenal 'fan' some time before he put on the red-and-white jersey, a claim that shouldn't be viewed with the scepticism with which we greet all such declarations of love today. It is part of Arsenal's folklore that, on the day Thierry signed for the club, David Dein, then vice-chairman and, then, still one of its main shareholders, presented him with a video retracing the career of Arsenal's record goalscorer, Ian Wright, adding: 'This is what you've got to do.' Henry's fascination for Wright and his club pre-dated that gift, however. It had to do with a much-fancied PSG, Henry's childhood team, being eliminated by the Gunners in the semi-finals of the 1993–4 European Cup Winners' Cup. It had to do with Wright's remarkable record of scoring in every round (bar the final) of the following edition of that tournament. It had to do with the iconic look of the Arsenal shirt itself. It had to do with a desire to be part of a history that was bigger than himself and rewrite it, as Wright had done. As Thierry later said:

I said to myself, 'he's no bigger than me, no faster, no more muscular, but he scores more goals'. I watched him closely. He put 100% into everything. When he called for a pass, he shouted at the top of his voice, and when he got it, he'd smack it into the back of the net. I just [kept] thinking: 'this is a goalscoring move'.

What Henry tried to learn from watching the exuberant Wright in action he still found hard to put into practice, however. Watford, 25 September: subbed after seventy-two minutes, missing several decent chances. Barcelona, 29 September: back on the bench, unable to make a difference in the twenty minutes he spent on the pitch. West Ham, 3 October, on the day Chelsea inflicted a famous 5-0 defeat on Manchester United: taken off after another unconvincing display, with eighteen minutes to go. Preston, 12 October: in the starting eleven, but guilty of a bad miss at the death, in a one-on-one with 'keeper Moilanen. Everton, 16 October: unused substitute (Šuker scoring a brace). Barcelona at Wembley, 19 October: on for Freddie Ljungberg, with whom reporters noted that he didn't seem to enjoy the warmest of relationships, too late to have an impact and prevent Guardiola's temmates from winning a fiery encounter 4-2. Chelsea, 23 October: Kanu's match, in which the Nigerian scored a remarkable hat-trick in the last quarter, earning a 3-2 victory at Stamford Bridge; Thierry was again a bit-part player, coming on for, again, Ljungberg. Fiorentina, 27 October: the game Arsenal had to win, but lost 0-1 to a brutally beautiful Batistuta finish which Thierry watched from the touchline. The Gunners couldn't progress past the Champions League group stage any more. 30 October, Newcastle: a starter, this time, but replaced by Bergkamp at half-time after suffering an injury that would keep him away for the best part of a month. Perhaps it was for the best. This period of forced inactivity allowed Henry to work on his fitness, which had been sorely tested by a far tougher schedule than he had been accustomed to in France and Italy, and when he came back in late November, goals started to flow, no fewer than thirteen (including three braces, against Derby, Sunderland and Deportivo La Coruña) in the space of three and a half months in which he proved Wenger's intuition to be correct and established himself as Arsenal's number one striker. By the time Arsenal had edged Spurs 2-1 in a typically tough derby, on 19 March 2000, Henry had scored sixteen goals in all competitions for his club, only one fewer than Nicolas Anelka in the whole of the previous campaign. What must have been especially gratifying for Wenger was that some of these goals owed more to a rediscovered instinct than to outstanding skill, such as the strikes against Wimbledon (December), Deportivo La Coruña (March) and Werder Bremen (March, again, a prolific month in which Thierry hit the target on six occasions). Each time, Henry had shown that he could lose defenders thanks to the smartness of his running rather than by sheer pace, finishing from close range with the coolness of a seasoned goal poacher. He also exploited his natural attributes with greater efficiency than before, positioning himself on the shoulder of the last defender with devastating effect. Ex-Gunner Steve Bould felt every one of his thirty-six years of age when, in January, his Sunderland visited Highbury; twice, Thierry surged past him to score with such grace and ease that the excited television commentator proclaimed Henry to be 'world-class', the first time this epithet had been used to describe him in England. He had grown stronger as well, as Chelsea's 'Rock', fellow World Cup winner Marcel Desailly, learnt to his expense when, at the beginning of May, Henry bundled him off the ball in the box to score a rare left-footed goal.* There were some stunning strikes as well – a twenty-five-yard volley against Bradford in February, and, perhaps the most aesthetically pleasing of them all, another long-distance shot, struck with hardly any back-lift from the corner of the box, to beat the Sheffield Wednesday 'keeper on 9 May, the last goal he scored in a season that had seen the Juve reject become one of the most feared centre-forwards in English football. 'Turnaround' would be too weak a word to sum up this transformation: Thierry, who had scored just the once in his first twelve League games, ended up sixth in the Premiership's 'hotshot' charts, with seventeen goals. The Nigerian Kanu was the only other Arsenal player to reach double figures, with twelve. It was not a rebirth, as Henry had never experienced sustained success of that kind before, and as no one – bar Wenger – believed he could do, not in that guise anyway. It was a revelation, an epiphany rather than a redemption.

Back in France, where many had considered Wenger's £11.5 million gamble something of a folly to start with, the media were now busy rewriting Henry's move as an inspired one. In no small part thanks to Manchester United's dramatic win over Bayern Munich in the 1999 Champions League final, the Premier League was well on the way to establishing itself as the foreign championship to follow, at least on a par with Serie A, whilst Germany remained a *terra incognita* and Spain the playground of a handful of clubs which garnered support from fanatical Real Madrid and Barcelona supporters, and few others besides. The Cantonas and Ginolas had paved the way on which the Vieiras, Petits and, now, Henrys could strut. English games had become part of the weekend menu for French sports broadcasters. A type of football that had seemed exotic, remote, even, ensconsed in values and traditions that contrasted so vividly (at least in terms of how the French public had long perceived them) with those of other European leagues was now considered *cool* by Canal+'s subscribers. Thierry's timing had been impeccable. He had shown the very best of his new self on the occasion

---

* Of the twenty-six goals Henry accumulated in his first English season, twenty-three were scored with his right foot, two with his left, his solitary header coming against Deportivo la Coruña on 9 March.

of Tottenham's visit to Highbury on 19 March, the first win in a series of eight on the trot for Arsenal in the League, which enabled them to climb from fifth to second, their final position. That game was televised live in France, where the debate as to whom should lead the attack of *Les Bleus* at the forthcoming European Championships was keeping columnists and supporters busy as never before. Could Henry, who hadn't been selected in the 'A' team for over a year and a half, still be ignored? Could Roger Lemerre carry on calling underperforming strikers when a world champion had indisputably been the star man in one of the biggest, most pressurized occasions in the English football calendar? Henry hadn't caught the eye by hitting a wonder goal (the one he scored came from the penalty spot, the first time he had taken that responsibility in England), but by his eagerness to ask for and fight for the ball, by his ability to keep hold of it under the pressure of Sol Campbell, as uncompromising a marker as the Premiership could provide. A French journalist spoke of the metamorphosis of a *picador* into a *torero*, for whom Highbury truly deserved the word 'arena'. To ignore him any longer would be an insult to common sense. As was widely expected, and hoped, Henry's name was included in Lemerre's squad for a friendly played against Scotland at Hampden Park, on 29 March. Thierry seamlessly transposed his superb form with Arsenal to the national team, playing the ninety minutes of a 2-0 victory, scoring a finely crafted goal from the edge of the area to cap a performance that ensured he would not be overlooked again; which he never was, unless he was unfit or suspended, until he retired from international football ten years later. A long, painful parenthesis had been closed at last.

Thierry's on-field persona had changed, too. He looked both more relaxed and more eager, filled with a *joie de jouer* that he demonstrated with – as yet – no hint of self-consciousness. If he played for an audience, to be sure, he didn't play *to* it, as he was accused of later on in his career. The entertainer yearned for praise, earned it but didn't milk the applause as a true showman would, a 'true' showman being the very opposite of true, of course. What I recall with most clarity from that game against Spurs is Henry's smile at the final whistle, as he drank in the applause raining from the stands. It was clear, even then, that a very special bond now linked the young Frenchman and the Highbury crowd. Later on, when we went down the players' tunnel to meet Henry, a unanimous choice for the Man of the Match award, he spoke in words we would hear a number of times over the next seven years – and beyond.

'To play here is an extraordinary privilege. Even when you miss something, when you lose the ball, people don't boo, people clap. This was my first derby, and it is something truly extraordinary. The fans were red-hot. And that's what I love: people are aware that you've given everything you had in your guts. That's why I do things I wouldn't have attempted back in France, because the fans push me, and make you feel that you want to give everything for them. There is at Arsenal – and undoubtedly everywhere else in England – a communion between player and public which doesn't exist anywhere else in the world.'

Like Vieira before him ('When I hear my name being sung in the stands, I get a hard-on,' is the way Patrick once put it to me), Thierry had discovered the type of passionate support that Monaco could not inspire, of a more visceral type than the devotion that Juve attracted in Italy, of which he had hardly partaken in any case. He could also see that many opposing fans quickly came to respect his impeccable sports-manship, his refusal to embrace the role of the diving, rolling, cheating pantomime foreigner. England as a whole loved an entertainer as much as any country, perhaps even more, as this species of performer was thought to be thinner on the ground there than elsewhere, perhaps unfairly. The Premier League had quite a few of those crowd-pleasers then – Matthew Le Tissier at Southampton, Gianfranco Zola at Chelsea, Paolo Di Canio at West Ham, David Ginola at Spurs, Ryan Giggs at Manchester United, to name but five – but Henry was alone in that he was now recognized as a genuine centre-forward, if of an unusual kind. 'Entertainers' had tended to be wingers in Britain. Why this is the case has been explained, quite convincingly in my opinion, by the poor state of English pitches during the winter months, back in the days before groundsmen adopted a more scientific approach to their trade. The fields on which a Best shone couldn't survive the constant pounding of studs in the middle, especially in the 'D' and close to the goalmouth. What little grass there was left in February grew on the flanks, where a ball could be teased this way and that by a skilful operator. Elsewhere? Better aim for the big man.

In 2000, the stereotypical British-style number nine was still sup-posed to be one these 'big men', adept in the air, capable of 'mixing it' with hard-tackling defenders, a fighter/finisher rather than a creator. This image is reductive, of course. The Premier League didn't want for genuine goalscorers whose skill extended far beyond their ability to shield the ball or outjump their marker, Dwight Yorke being a case in mind. But for one Yorke, there were also many Quinns, Heskeys, Dub-lins and Suttons. Henry offered a new template. He ran faster with the ball at his feet than most wingers do racing after a long-distance punt; he tried flicks, backheels, shots from outside the area, revelling in the freedom he had been granted by his manager and by a style of football that encouraged and rewarded those who dared to dare. So much of what Henry had been taught and told in France and Italy had to do with the fear of being beaten. The spring had been uncoiled and, having been uncoiled, initiated a subtle shift in the way the mechanism of Arsenal functioned as a whole.

One of the reasons why no one would argue against Wenger's claim to be called a 'great' manager has been his ability to mould a succession of superb sides during his fifteen-year tenure at Arsenal, shuffling hun-dreds of players, coping with departures and retirements, integrating a remarkably high number of untested talents within his first team without compromising his club's ability to compete, at least until very recently, even when hamstrung by the financial constraints of the move from Highbury to the Emirates Stadium. The second Double squad of 2001–2 bore little resemblance to the one which had achieved the same feat four seasons previously. The 'Invincibles' of 2003–4 were another avatar, by which time the connection to the Graham era had all but disap-peared, save for the last and increasingly rarer appearances of Martin Keown and Ray Parlour in an Arsenal shirt. The under-rated crop of 2007–8, which won nothing but produced, perhaps, the most delightful, at times ravishing, football of the Wenger era, had none of the genes of the 2004 monster. Nothing too surprising in that, you might say; all teams have to go through a process of renewal, forced or otherwise. What sets Arsenal apart, though, is that the changes affected the overall playing style of the team to a lesser degree than could have been expected, despite the relatively high turnover of players throughout this period.

Why that is, and why it matters when discussing the evolution of Thierry Henry during his Arsenal years, even at this very early stage of his career, has to do with the mindset of Wenger himself. Not all great managers are great tacticians, just as assistant coaches who possess great tactical minds can fail when they're called on to manage human beings rather than parameters in a complex collective equation. I wouldn't dare to call Wenger 'tactically inept' but must admit that there have been occasions on which this thought has crossed my mind. His substitutions can be baffling in their crudeness. His refusal to alter Arsenal's default game-plan when confronted with unexpected circumstances, often presented as an inability to conceive a plan 'B', when it is more likely to be sheer pig-headedness, can infuriate the most patient of his admirers. He will spend hours poring over statistical data – to give himself an objective corroboration of his intuition, rather than to alter his judgement – but will prefer graphs and figures which have to do with individual performance, such as the variation in high-intensity sprints of a given player over ninety minutes, for example. By contrast, he will devote surprisingly little time to the analysis of future opponents. I remember how, a couple of days before the 2006 Champions League final, Wenger casually let drop in conversation that he and his staff would have a good look at Barcelona's shape on the eve of the game. I was astonished. Hadn't they done that already? A Mourinho would have had his scouts filing report after report on his team's adversaries for weeks, if not months. Perceived weaknesses would have been identified, specific training drills would have been designed to exploit them. For Wenger, however, attention to such details would have been an admission of inferiority, a denial of his footballing credo. Only in one instance did he break that rule: when he realized his depleted team could not possibly prevail by playing its own game against a superior Manchester United in the 2005 FA Cup final. Arsenal won, but that victory tasted sour to their manager, who promised himself he would never compromise his principles again.

Why bring this up when dealing with Henry's very first season at Arsenal, then? Because the impact of a new arrival can go well beyond the goals he scores. As soon as Henry became his club's number one striker – which he did from late autumn onwards – Arsenal had to evolve, if subtly at first, to tune to a different 'A', as Thierry established himself as the focal point of the attack. This is a point we'll come to again and again: if Wenger did a great deal for Henry, Henry did a great deal for Wenger as well. Most people would characterize the French manager as a romantic, but this, if true, doesn't make him less of a pragmatist in the implementation of his principles. A dreamer who follows his dreams to their rational conclusion, guided by an unshake-able faith in their validity, can end up corseted in his set of beliefs. Should he fail, he'll appear too rigid by half in his approach. A coach whose priority is to maximize the talent he has at his disposal, rather than bend it to suit his own designs, will do the opposite and adjust his system to suit individuals. It's jazz. When it works, you get Duke Ellington. When it doesn't, you feel like you've gatecrashed an improv-isation workshop. Wenger's genius is that he ensured it worked almost all of the time.

Thierry didn't play Anelka solos, that much was clear from the beginning. The 1997–8 and 1998–9 Arsenal teams created danger pri-marily through their capacity to react at speed as soon as the ball had been won back. It was geared towards the kind of swift, lethal counter-attacking that would have won the blessing of Herbert Chapman. George Graham's defensive quintet played from memory, the duo of Vieira and Petit patrolled the midfield, clear of thought and precise in their distri-bution, a seamless combination of steel and imagination. Overmars scorched the left flank, Bergkamp found space wherever it could be invented *ex nihilo*, Parlour ran and ran and ran, Anelka surged to sign off with a flourish. The 1999–2000 incarnation of Arsenal, whilst retaining many of the virtues of its immediate predecessor, wasn't an extension of its previous self but, rather (as the 2000–2001 version would also be), a transitory ensemble, a bridge thrown from one period to the next. Wenger, though he hasn't admitted it publicly, let it be known to friends at the time that he felt in a sense held back by the impossibility of dispensing with what was left of the 'old' Arsenal, namely the strongest back-five in the country. These players, for whom their manager felt genuine admiration, were, paradoxically, too good to be kept out of the team; they had also shown their willingness to espouse the training methods of a Frenchman they hadn't heard of before David

Dein brought him from Japan to England. 'These guys don't know when they're beaten,' Wenger once told me in a tone that suggested that their hunger and self-belief reached depths with which he wasn't entirely familiar. Wenger, however, had visions of a team that was also able to build from the back, to use a rather simplistic formulation, in which the heart of the defence could beat to the same pulse as their supposedly more creative teammates. The Arsenal of 1999–2000 wasn't the possession machine it gradually became in the mid- and late 2000s in particular. Its full-backs were not averse to bypassing the midfield and directing long passes towards Henry and whoever was partnering him in attack that day. It's not that the players Wenger inherited from the Graham era were poor footballers; that they were able to enrich their game as they did, when all of them had long entered their fourth decade, brought conclusive proof of the opposite. It is more that they had been shaped by a type of football that bore little or no relation to the game Wenger aspired to, of which the 'Invincibles' would provide the best expression, with Henry the supreme example of what a complete player should be – intelligent, fast, strong and skilful. Wenger, the pragmatist dreamer, realized that the new Arsenal he wanted to build could take shape around the axis of the prodigious talent he had first seen at Monaco. If that meant breaking up the team that had achieved so much already, so be it. A common question around Arsenal FC at the time was: 'How long can they last?', they being Adams and Co., naturally; another: 'What will happen when they go?' But there was no catastrophe. The old guard made way gradually, as winter turns to spring. Henry himself was entering a magnificent summer.

8

It's all about balance:
Thierry's first hat-trick for Arsenal.

THE BLOSSOMING

Few modern footballers progress from miscast to top of the bill as swiftly as Henry. It took him less than a year. The highs and lows experienced by almost all elite sportsmen generally have an easily identifiable cause, which, more often than not, is injury, which Thierry had been spared. So what exactly happened? Had he even really 'improved' as much as his record for Arsenal suggested? Or was it not rather a simple case of a man having to physically up sticks and move away in order to find himself again? In that sense, Henry's lengthy absence from France's national team might have been an unexpected blessing. Much as he enjoyed the praise that journalists were not slow to give him, the scrutiny he had been under ever since his debut with Monaco had clearly had a detrimental impact on his career. Too many hangers-on had been allowed to gravitate around the new star. Too many rumours had circulated as to which big European club he would eventually join, leading to an unsavoury parting of the ways with Monaco and a rash move to Juventus in which each party ended up a loser. England now provided Thierry with fiercer day-to-day competition than he had ever experienced before, something he quickly came to relish, whilst granting him peace off the field. These were two subjects about which he never tired of speaking. 'In the beginning,' he said, six months after playing his first game for Arsenal, 'when I was hit [by a defender], I stopped playing, I was convinced that the referee would blow his whistle. No. Play carried on. Now, I too use my elbows, because, otherwise, I'm dead. It is an obligation to tune in to the English traditions. Six months ago, I'd have been horrified, now, I do what the others do.'

And there were the fans, those fans who 'when they ask for an autograph, always do it with a smile' and 'let me have a coffee with a friend, living their own life, and letting me live mine', fans who didn't wait for him to score his first goal before singing his name to the tune of 'Tom Hark', a minor hit in 1980 for the Brighton punk/ska band The Piranhas. One day, walking the streets of London, Henry came across a man wearing a suit and tie who, after staring at him for an unnerving length of time, undid the buttons of his shirt to reveal an Arsenal jersey underneath. The player never forgot that encounter. 'We feel loved,' Thierry said in January 2000. 'When the fans sing your name after you've messed up, you really want to bury the next chance, just for them, to give them pleasure. In England, if I make a technical mistake, I forget it more quickly, because of the public . . . We may be pros, but it does a lot of good to be pushed that way. Because of that, we surpass ourselves.' Talking about his memories of the Highbury crowd, Emmanuel Petit once put it this way to me: 'They make us discover more about ourselves,' he said, a phrase that could easily apply to the twenty-three-year-old Henry, for whom this discovery also meant that he had a clearer idea of who he could become. Once the early nerves had been conquered, there was barely a hiccup in his first season in London, which he finished with twenty-six goals for his club alone, when his best total thus far had been the fourteen he struck for ASM and France in 1997–8.

Despite what Arsenal supporters might have felt on the night of 17 May 2000 – especially those who were caught in some vicious fighting in downtown Copenhagen – even the dreadful 0-0 draw and subsequent loss on penalties in the UEFA Cup final, against outsiders Galatasaray, was little more than a disappointing footnote to what had otherwise been a satisfactory season for their evolving team and, for Henry, a remarkably successful introduction to the English game. In Denmark, Thierry hadn't been the worst player in an Arsenal side that, for once, found that the well from which they normally drew their desire had run dry. The Turks sat back, leaving Hakan Şükür on his own up front, their *fantasista* Gheorge Hagi content to thicken a mid-field bent on breaking up play and little else. Arsenal huffed and puffed, Martin Keown missing a good chance to decide the game as it neared its conclusion. Thierry it was who had supplied that ball, Thierry who soon had to leave the field after suffering a slight injury and could only watch his teammates fluff their lines in the shoot-out. 'Our heart wasn't in it,' Wenger told me, 'which is why it didn't hurt as much as it would have in other circumstances,' certainly not as much as elimination from the Champions League had done. Thierry had been full of fighting talk before the final; but I cannot recall him ever mentioning the Copenhagen game of his own accord afterwards, whereas he would, for example, often bemoan his own lack of sharpness in the 2006 Champions League final; for once, defeat didn't seem to sting as much, as the true loss had happened months before, when Batistuta's rocket had beaten Seaman at his near post at Wembley, and Fiorentina had put an end to Arsenal's progress in the competition. And what pain Henry might have felt didn't affect him in the least when he rejoined the French team and prepared for the European Championships, the stage on which he truly established himself as one of the continent's finest attacking players, cementing his place in Lemerre's starting eleven as he had done in Wenger's. 'He's got a turbo in his legs,' his Arsenal manager had said. That's probably what the Danish defenders thought when, in the competition's opening game, Henry, receiving an anodyne pass from Zinedine Zidane inside his own half, accelerated irresistibly towards Peter Schmeichel, leaving all his pursuers for dead, to score as prodigious a goal as any he would score in the rest of his footballing life. Five days after France's 3-0 victory, Thierry added another goal to his tally against a dangerous Czech team, not quite the show-stopper of the previous game, but of greater significance in the context of the tournament. The resulting 2-1 win guaranteed the passage of *Les Bleus* into the quarter-finals and enabled their manager to rotate almost his entire squad in their last group encounter. Henry was among those rested for a meaningless 2-3 loss to the Netherlands, a sure indication that he was no longer the 'joker' of 1998, but an essential cog in the seductive machine that had been put together by Roger Lemerre. France, who had marched towards the 1998 final under the guidance of a tightly organized defence, protected by no fewer than three defensively minded midfielders, and which had had to rely on goalscorers as unlikely as Laurent Blanc and Lilian Thuram to make progress, was now as potent going forward as it was difficult to upset at the back. The threat of Sylvain Wiltord, who had been in splendid form with Bordeaux, had been added to the goalscoring instinct of David Trezeguet, while the combination of Henry and Anelka as the two spearheads of *Les Bleus*, of which France would unfortunately see so little in the years to follow, worked as well as Arsène Wenger was convinced it could. 'Nico' was nominally the centre-forward, Titi being told to play on the left wing, as he did against Denmark, or on the right, as he did against the Czech Republic – with equal success.

Some journalists were exercised by Henry's 'wrong' positioning, so much so that Thierry, who had been France's brightest player so far, fed up with being asked the same questions over and over again ('Wouldn't you prefer to play in the middle?' and variations on that theme), decided to give a wide berth to anyone carrying a press card. His teammates and most of the French team's technical staff took his cue and became near-invisible in their luxurious headquarters of Le Château du lac, near Brussels, sprinting through mixed zones and skiving media engagements, leading to a farcical stand-off which was the only sour note in an otherwise near-perfect tournament. Incidentally, it was when Henry was restored to his 'natural' centre-forward position – in a 2-1 win over Spain in the quarter-finals – that he had his least convincing game of the competition. Thankfully for Lemerre's team, Zidane chose that afternoon in Bruges to give one of the greatest recitals of his whole career, and France found themselves two wins away from becoming only the third team in history to hold a continental and world title simultaneously, as West Germany and Brazil had done after respectively winning the 1972 European Championships and the 1997 Copa America.

Lemerre restored the Anelka–Henry tandem for the semi-final against Portugal, but this time in a classic 4-3-1-2 – and it was the understanding between the two Clairefontaine scholars that allowed France to cancel Nuno Gomes's early opener – the Real Madrid player sending a low, accurate cross from the right to the Arsenal striker, who swivelled and shot from twelve yards through Fernando Couto's legs to beat Vitor Baía. A Zidane penalty scored deep into extra-time gave the French another victory. Just as in 1998, when Paraguay were the victims, *Les Bleus* had taken maximum advantage of Fifa's short-lived 'golden goal' rule, as they would in the final against Italy. Just as in 1998, Thierry would end up as France's top goalscorer in the tournament, with three successful strikes, which he would dedicate to the memory of his grand-father Teka, who had died earlier in the year; but it was a different Henry whose achievements made the headlines in his home country. His status had changed irrevocably, both within the team and without, all the more so given that he had spent so long away from the national squad. As Vieira later said, 'Thierry gained a lot of confidence during the tournament. He attempted a lot of new things. When he played for France, I could sense, because I know him so well, that he held himself [back?] a little bit. With Arsenal, he was capable of taking the ball, beating two or three players, crossing it or scoring. For France, he didn't feel free enough mentally to do that. But at Euro 2000, he did.' I would add: more than he had done before, but also more than he would do afterwards, too.

As a number of players from the old guard were about to step out of *Les Bleus* (such as Laurent Blanc, who had entered his thirty-fifth year, and skipper Didier Deschamps, now thirty-one, whom many argued was holding back the more dynamic Patrick Vieira), Thierry fed the hope that France's supremacy could be sustained in the near future and beyond; that there would no hiatus comparable with the decline that followed the retirement of a Raymond Kopa or of a Michel Platini. Henry himself downplayed the expectations of the public, saying that he was 'satisfied to see that the way [his] teammates looked at him had changed' and that it was 'enough for his own enjoyment' – even if he must have been aware that others had far loftier ambitions for him, such as Platini himself, who singled him out as 'the most skilful' of all the French players, blessed with 'the pace of an Anelka and the sense [of goal] of a Trezeguet', who could 'do everything' and possessed a certain 'something that no French footballer has ever had'. With Zidane at his peak, Vieira the clear leader-to-be of a reshaped, more dynamic midfield and a surfeit of talent in the forward line, France could look forward to dominating for years to come. How the team eventually failed to do so is a story we'll soon come to, as Thierry's complex relationship with a number of senior players, Zidane in particular, undoubtedly had a bearing on the squad that imploded in humiliating fashion at the 2002 World Cup. We haven't come to that yet, however. France had retained the togetherness of the Jacquet 'commando', whilst opening its ranks to younger elements, some of whom – Anelka in particular – had disproved the notion that they held football to be an individual sport, and played the expansive game which the 1998 side had only shown in fits and starts before the final against Brazil.

Of the five wins Lemerre's team registered in Belgium and the Netherlands, four had finished with a 2-1 scoreline, the last two, against Portugal and Italy, after having conceded the game's first goal. The fortitude the French had shown, especially against *la nazionale*, when substitute Sylvain Wiltord equalized only in the fourth minute of added time, and Pirès combined with Trezeguet to shatter Italian hearts in the 103rd. It was a credit to the players themselves, but also to their manager, whose dour public demeanour and aversion to small talk concealed a man of great charm and humanity, as well as a coach with a fine grasp of tactics; Lemerre could certainly think on his feet from the dugout, as his match-changing substitutions had proved in the final. It is not to the French media's credit that his contribution was systematically belittled then and later. In private, some senior journalists poked fun at the near-sexagenerian falling in love with a young Dutch woman, Jeanette, whom he had met at the time of the 2000 Euro semi-final and married three years later. They mocked his accent, his odd turns of phrase (when the supposed malapropisms were more akin to flicking two fingers at his questioners), his background as a manager of the French military team (which he had led to a world title). And on, and on. One French reporter went as far as to suggest that Lemerre's sole modus operandi was to ask himself 'What would Jacquet have done?' and replicating his former boss's formula as closely as he could. Nonsense. But then, so much of what surrounded that team was nonsense.

'The Blossoming' would be a misleading heading for this chapter if the player's performances in his second Arsenal season were its main topic. In fact, it could be argued that the 2000–2001 campaign was one of – relative – stagnation for Henry, compared with what he had shown in the last two-thirds of the previous one. The numbers bear this out, showing his second year with the Gunners to have been his least prolific in London until 2006–7, when injuries restricted him to twenty-seven appearances in all competitions. He was now an automatic starter in Wenger's evolving eleven, which hadn't been the case for the first few months of his career at Highbury; but despite this, and taking part in six more games than in 1999–2000, he ended the 2000–2001 campaign with twenty-two goals, compared with twenty-six, and exactly the same return in the Premier League: seventeen. These were still the statistics of a top striker but did not constitute a 'blossoming' as such: it is the man who blossomed, rather than the footballer, and the footballer only showed the full benefit of this when the team he was part of found a new, stable identity. The Wenger reinvention of Arsenal had entered its second phase but hadn't yet progressed past the experimental stage.

The team that opened the season with a 1-0 defeat at Sunderland featured a back-line composed of David Seaman (a month away from his thirty-seventh birthday), Lee Dixon (thirty-six), Martin Keown (thirty-four) and Tony Adams (thirty-three), with only the Brazilian Sylvinho on the right side of thirty, in lieu of Nigel Winterburn (thirty-six), who had been sold to West Ham in the summer. George Graham's defensive unit couldn't be expected to carry on indefinitely – in fact, couldn't be expected to perform at the highest level past that season, which would already test what was left of its physical resources. Wenger's dilemma was that he couldn't do away with the ageing core of the side without endangering the foundations on which the achievements of the past four years had been built, whilst being aware he had no choice but to do exactly that. The manager wisely opted for evolution rather than revolution, but at a price: 2000–2001 would be a season of transition, all the more so as its make-up had been shaken rather more than expected – and certainly not in the way that was expected – after the European Championships.

In the end, the defence remained much the same as it had for over a decade. The arrival of Mallorca's Cameroonian Lauren signalled increased competition for Lee Dixon at right-back, but not a complete upheaval of the old order, as the second defensive recruit, Skonto Riga's Igor Stepanovs, could only be thought of as cover for Keown and Adams. Arsenal's midfield was a different case altogether, however, with both

Emmanuel Petit and Marc Overmars being sold for a combined fee of £30 million to Barcelona, enabling Wenger to purchase two of the newly crowned European champions: Robert Pirès, who had never settled in Marseille, and Sylvain Wiltord, France's leading goalscorer with the Girondins de Bordeaux, who could play on the right flank as well as at the apex of the attack. Back in France, some had started to refer to Arsenal as *le championnat*'s twenty-first team, not always kindly it must be said, as columnists deplored the 'pillage' of their league by the Premier League in general (Fabien Barthez had joined Manchester United, Franck Leboeuf was on his way to Chelsea) and the Alsatian manager in particular, a criticism that would only intensify as time went by.

In England, however, the impact of Wenger's summer deals in the transfer market provided a more pressing topic of discussion than the cultural shift to come within the Arsenal dressing-room. The partnership of Petit and Vieira in what the French refer to as a *double pivot* had been one of the manager's most inspired moves: it joined fire with fire in the zone where the game burns most intensely. That duo could out-fight, out-think and out-play any other in the Premier League. Why break it now? Then there was the twenty-seven-year-old Marc Overmars, one of Arsenal's finest performers in the 1997–8 Double season. He had not been quite as trenchant in the two campaigns that followed but had still taken part in forty-seven games in 1999–2000, contributing thirteen goals and as many assists – two more than Thierry – along the way. The Dutchman had a well-known history of injuries but would still play forty-five games for Barcelona in his first season there, exactly as many as he had done for the Gunners in 1997–8. Wenger didn't get rid of a 'crocked' footballer: he weighed his options carefully and saw that Barcelona's remarkably generous offer would enable him to carry on rebuilding his squad without putting the club's finances under undue strain. Both transfers were concluded without any of the fuss that had accompanied Nicolas Anelka's move to Real Madrid – or, indeed, Wiltord's acquisition from Bordeaux, where the player staged a comical strike of sorts before his club agreed to the deal. Once it had been concluded, none of the players who had beaten Italy in the Euro 2000 final were playing football in their native country. A reminder of what would be missed was given when Petit and Overmars lined up for Barça against their former club in a pre-season friendly played at the Amsterdam Arena, which the Catalans won 2-1. No one gave the Gunners a realistic chance of challenging Manchester United for the title, with Chelsea, who had just spent £15 million on Jimmy Floyd Hasselbaink, thought much more likely contenders after their 2-0 victory over the champions in the Charity Shield.

Henry had to do the same as everyone else: adapt, as his side struggled to assume a more clearly defined shape. Arsenal's early results bore witness to this, as did Thierry's own contributions. The defeat at Sunderland, in which Ray Parlour had twice missed a gaping net, was followed by a rare victory over Liverpool, in which Graham Poll distributed eight yellow cards and three reds – Patrick Vieira, already sent off against Sunderland, collecting his second within three days. Henry, who had earlier forced Sander Westerveld into a difficult save when his shot seemed bound for the top corner, wrapped up Arsenal's victory a minute from time. Twisting in the area, he managed to create just enough space to hit a stinging left-footed shot that Westerveld parried back to him; Thierry, reacting so quickly that the cameras failed to keep pace with him, wrapped a gorgeous shot in the opposite corner of the goal – with his right foot, this time. 'Bang goes the 0-0 draw,' said the message on the T-shirt when he lifted his jersey in celebration. It's only fair to say that that scoreline looked very unlikely throughout the season. Arsenal could seem irresistible one minute, vulnerable the next, as they did in a harum-scarum 5-3 win over Charlton in their next League game, in which Vieira, about to start a five-game suspension, produced a display that still sends shivers down the spine of all who witnessed it. By the end of a match in which both teams had seemingly lost all tactical sense, Thierry was leading the country's 'hotshots' list, with thirteen efforts on goal, eight of them on target, and two more – splendid – goals to his credit. First, a minute into the second half, receiving a Tony Adams pass outside the area, Henry flicked it with his left boot, then bounced the ball on his right thigh to tee it for a spectacular dipping strike on the volley. He then concluded a beautiful counter-attack initiated by Kanu and Pirès by placing a fierce strike past Kiely from a tight angle to give Arsenal a 4-3 lead. Next game? A 2-2 draw at Chelsea, after being 2-0 down, only secured through a late Sylvinho thunderbolt once Henry had put Arsenal back in contention,* denying the hosts what would have been their first win in the last ten derbies between the two London teams. Wenger's team clumsily sought for a yet-to-be-defined equilibrium in unpredictable fashion. Bradford, thrashed 6-0 by Manchester United a week previously, threatened to take all three points at Highbury before Ashley Cole salvaged a 1-1 draw. The net result of this chaotic start to the season was that Arsenal found themselves below United, Leicester, Newcastle, Liverpool and Spurs in the League table by 11 September.

The whole of Arsenal's year followed a similar pattern, and so did Thierry's – the electrocardiogram of a healthy patient peaking when placed under too much stress. Let's take Manchester United's visit to Highbury on 1 October 2000, when Thierry hadn't scored for seven games in all competitions, one of the longest barren runs of his Arsenal career. Alex Ferguson had tinkered with his side for a midweek encounter with PSV Eindhoven in the Champions League, changing no fewer than six players from his previous eleven, a gamble that failed to reap dividends: the Dutch champions won 3-1. Ferguson's decision to rest key players was understandable, however: a victory in London would have seen United open a six-point gap over Arsenal in the title race after eight games, which Wenger himself thought would prove too big a handicap to overcome. In truth, the 'top-of-the-table clash' was a dull affair redeemed by an unforgettable moment, the prodigious goal that

---

* I should add a word about Thierry's goal at Stamford Bridge, the thirtieth of his Arsenal career: it was also the first example of a trademark move, already familiar to the coaches of his previous teams, from Palaiseau to Monaco, which he would repeat time and again for the Gunners from that day on. This time, receiving a delightful pass from Sylvinho, he set off on an angled run on the left side of the box, forcing the 'keeper to leave his line before passing the ball with deadly precision into the opposite corner of the net. As we've seen, he had practised that run and that shot for hours on end with Claude Puel at Monaco, achieving such a degree of mastery in its execution that, to the observer, it seemed inconceivable that the target could be missed. 'If it looks easy, it's because I worked very hard at it,' he once told a reporter who perhaps hadn't fully understood the coolness, balance and technical excellence the player had to display to replicate that strike on so many occasions, with the same deadly result.

Henry scored in the thirtieth minute, a finish that was 'so spectacular that it took the breath away', as Alex Ferguson put it.

Nothing seemed to be on when Gilles Grimandi gathered the ball from Sylvinho on the left flank and sent it towards Thierry on a wing and a prayer. His back to goal, with Dennis Irwin clutching his shirt, Henry flicked the ball with his right foot, pivoted 180 degrees and produced the volley of a lifetime, which, for a fraction of a second, the striker thought 'would be too high'; but the ball dipped just enough to fly beyond Fabien Barthez, who might have advanced ever so slightly too far off from his line. 'It was one of the best goals I have ever scored, not only because of the way it went in, but also because it was against Manchester United and my international team goalkeeper,' Henry said. 'Whenever I see that goal, I'm always like: "Did I do that?" I'm all about instinct . . . I felt like doing this . . . and it went in.' Wenger commented: 'It was beginning to play on [Thierry's] mind that he did not get the goals he wanted to score. Maybe if he had been in a one on one with [Fabien] Barthez he would not have scored. Sometimes you just need to do something completely crazy without thinking about it. You just do it.' A remarkable goal it was, no doubt about that. But another statistic: of the eighteen outfielders chosen by Wenger in that season so far, Henry had been the least precise in his passing: 33 per cent of the balls he had attempted to give to teammates had ended up at the feet of an opponent, something that gave substance to the opinion that he was not and could never be an authentic target man. If there were a template for Thierry, it had yet to be defined, and would only be by himself, in moments such as his near-miraculous strike against the champions.

If Arsenal was a patient, that's not to say that 2000–2001 was a season entirely spent in the waiting-room. Signs of improvement could be detected along the way, especially in Europe, now that the exile in Wembley was mercifully over. Arsenal, who had been drawn with Sparta Prague, Shakhtar Donetsk and Lazio, moved past the Champions League first group stage at the third attempt – in more laboured fashion that their first place in that group might suggest, if convincingly enough in the end. Pushed by a raucous Highbury crowd, Wenger's team, who had enjoyed a comfortable 1-0 win in their first match against Sparta in the Czech Republic, could thank Martin Keown for an improbable double against the Ukrainian side, which put the Gunners on top of their group (with the same number of points as Lazio at this stage) from the second round of games onwards. Keown, who had scored a mere six goals in his 333 appearances for the Gunners up to that point, planted his imposing body in Shakhtar's box for the closing ten minutes of the tie, when it looked as if Arsenal, bereft of ideas, would be unable to overcome the two-goal deficit they had conceded in the first half. This one-man rebellion, which proved successful when the central defender bundled the ball over the line for a 3-2 victory in the closing seconds of the game, showed how much Arsenal still owed to the blood-and-guts approach inherited from George Graham – the one reason why I have singled out that game out of the twelve Wenger's team had to play before, at long last, it reached the quarter-finals of the Champions League. That night, similarly, Sylvain Wiltord's rather crude hustling and bustling and Henry's own anonymity had exemplified the transitory nature of this Arsenal side. For one thing, Wenger seemed unsure of who should partner Thierry upfront. Should it be Kanu, Wiltord or Bergkamp? Was the manager's rotation policy the best possible use of the options at his disposal or a manifestation of indecisiveness?

Take Bergkamp, for instance. The Dutchman hadn't scored for five months when he beat 'keeper Richard Wright – soon to become an Arsenal player, at least as far as his registration was concerned – to salvage a 1-1 draw at Ipswich on 23 September.* Six days later, the thirty-one-year-old gave a magnificent demonstration in the art of link-up play off the main striker, offering two goals on a golden plate to Freddie Ljungberg in a 2-0 defeat of Sven-Göran Eriksson's Lazio at Highbury, which all but assured Arsenal's progress in the Champions League. The first goal was a thing of beauty, a flowing movement that linked Henry to Kanu, then Kanu to Bergkamp, finally Bergkamp to

---

* This is the game after which Henry publicly voiced the wish to see Man of the Match (for the fourth time running) Titus Bramble, who hadn't given him an inch of space to move in or a second to react, play for Arsenal one day. If it was generous praise towards the player to whom he gave his shirt after the game, it was also indicative of another trait in Thierry's personality: when you're under par, offer compliments to your opponent. It won't make you look worse, for one thing.

Ljungberg, Bergkamp who found the Swede with a perfectly weighted, perfectly placed cushioned header, the ball landing precisely where its intended target could meet it on the half-volley with the most effect. Still, Wenger couldn't quite make his mind up as to who would provide the most efficient foil for Thierry. That season, Bergkamp made twenty-five appearance in the League, Wiltord twenty-seven, the same number of matches as Kanu, and I would argue that it was no coincidence that the 2001–2 Double was achieved when Arsenal's number ten resumed his precedence in the forward line ahead of his competitors.

In the meantime, the Arsenal team gave accounts of itself that ranked from the mediocre (by the standards they had set since Wenger's arrival) to the inspiring (on a fairly regular basis), followed no other logic than that of a living organism still searching for a settled modus vivendi. Which direction it would eventually set its compass on could be guessed, but not the interferences that would lead it astray at times. Having hauled themselves back in contention with a series of fifteen undefeated games in all competitions from August to early November, Arsenal then stumbled badly, drawing one and losing four of their next five, by which point Manchester United were eight points clear at the top of the League; hic-cuped past the new year with four victories in eleven (the gap with the title-holders had now widened to fifteen, with Sunderland briefly snatching second place from the Gunners); and relaunched their campaign with a perfect six out of six from 27 January to 18 February. It was a contrasted but by no means disastrous record, with enough signs of encouragement along the way to speak of growing pains rather than of failure; the same could be said of Henry's own contributions to his mutating team; unex-ceptional at times, breathtaking at others, he remained a variable in his manager's equation, and it would take another year for that variable to become a near-constant on the field as it already was on the team-sheet. I should add that I use those scientific words, 'variable', 'constant' and 'equation' loosely, as Wenger, so often described as a 'professor' obsessed with data, GPS and the like, is anything but a cold, detached logician. 'I'm an educator, first and foremost,' he once told a group of *France Football* readers (almost all of whom were coaches themselves) I had taken to London Colney; an educator, not a lecturer: a distinction which is too often lost in these days of over-analysis.

This is not a digression: logic is often picked out of thin air where there is none to be found. I am increasingly worried by the contemporary trend (which is in danger of becoming a default setting among sports writers) of denying that football is inherently chaotic. We are told that we must 'read' football as much as watch it, or that we can only watch it – and speak about it with any kind of authority, as if authority was the only thing that mattered! – if we've learnt our *ABC* to start with. Pre-determined grids, be they tactical, statistical or otherwise, are nailed onto the undulating surface of the game. Unwanted asperities, one of which is enough to prove the absurdity of the whole system, are erased for no other reason than convenience. What's it got to do with Thierry Henry? Rather a lot, I believe, certainly in the context of a book like this one, which I have always thought of as a biographical essay rather than a biography.

A game-per-game account of Thierry's career would weigh down (not just lengthen) this narrative to such a degree that the detail, instead of providing the necessary devil, would more often than not obscure its purpose, which is to try to understand how and why such a magnificent footballer, whose achievements should be beyond criticism, has inspired such extremes of feeling; not just an admiring ambivalence – which would be my own stance – but, as we've already seen, mistrust, detestation as well as unconditional love. Almost all accounts of a man's life understandably assume a linear form, as adherence to chronology provides a clear and, in most cases, the clearest thread. A date is a date is a date, as a goal is a goal is a goal, burdens of proof as incontrovertible as the stone Dr Johnson kicked away to disprove Berkeley's negation of the existence of matter. But add date to date to date and goal to goal to goal in Henry's case, and you would end up – I believe – with a series of 0s and 1s instead of the music these 0s and 1s somehow conjure into being in the digital world. That's not to say it isn't the way he, the seeker of records, would choose to present his achievements himself. Quantification has a semblance of neutrality; but we should be wary of the kind of unanimity it gives superficial justification to. Football's relationship to numbers, in any case, is far more confused than we have grown to accept, when our reliance on them often only demonstrates a reluctance to proffer an opinion and risk being exposed as incompetent when we are only being true to our own perception.

There came a point at which I realized that, should I use all the material I had assembled over two years of research, this book could well be 250,000 words long, if not more, as Henry's professional career, which spanned three decades and seven major international tournaments, was so rich that it wouldd soon make me lose myself (and, just as importantly, the reader) in an inextricable wilderness of facts, rows upon rows of 0s and 1s. An English-speaking reader's awareness of Henry's progress at Monaco, Juventus and with the French national team will, quite naturally, be less sharp than what he will know and remember of Thierry's years in the red-and-white of the London club. Every goal is there to be watched and watched again on the internet; every match report is one online search away. What matters more? That Thierry played a goalless friendly with France in South Africa in October 2000 or that, on that occasion, he joined the beeline of celebrities who shook Nelson Mandela's hand? That, the same month, Henry couldn't shake off the attentions of Lazio's Alessandro Nesta and Siniša Mihajlović at the Stadio Olimpico, and Arsenal had to rely on Robert Pirès's first goal for his new club to secure the 1-1 draw that confirmed Arsenal's qualification for the Champions League second group stage? Or the brace he scored against Manchester City at Highbury on 28 October? Scoring his first that day, an improbable half-volley flying off his right boot after using the same foot as a tee, Henry unveiled another of his celebratory T-shirts, inscribed with the word 'Babe', a coded message to his future wife, model Claire Merry. He could be irresistible, as Leicester City found out on 26 December 2000 at Highbury, the day of the first of his nine hat-tricks for Arsenal:* a quite ridiculous volley from outside

---

* Eight of these were scored in the Premier League, which places Henry, as of end of the 2011–12 season, equal third (with Michael Owen) in the list of hat-trick-scorers in the history of the competition, behind Alan Shearer (eleven) and Robbie Fowler (nine). Thierry's other treble came in the Champions League, in a 3-1 victory over Roma at the Stadio Olimpico, on 27 November 2002. He's been often credited with another hat-trick in Arsenal's spectacular 5-1 win against Internazionale at San Siro, but only scored a brace on that occasion.

the box, directly from a Robert Pirès corner-kick, was followed by a less spectacular left-footed effort from inside the area, which nevertheless showed how he could use his physique to outmuscle a defender, Matt Eliott on this occasion. Henry's treble was completed when Nelson Vivas sent him through on goal, past defenders who were so demoralized by that stage (it was the fifth of the six goals City conceded in that match) that the striker had the time to tease, and tease, and tease again Tim Flowers until the 'keeper had to commit himself to some kind of save, ending on his backside as a result, Henry skipping away to roll the ball in the empty net with his left foot. By then, Thierry was well on his way to fulfilling one of the prerequisites of greatness in a footballer: to make the exceptional look ordinary. Do watch if you can a film of the goal which gave Arsenal a 1-0 win over Ipswich in the League on 10 February 2001. I can't decide what is most admirable in that understated masterpiece: Bergkamp's eye-of-the-needle pass to bisect the Ipswich back-line or Henry's two touches, the first with his left foot, the second with his right, to secure the winner. Writing this, all I can feel is gratitude towards the authors of this gem. Bergkamp and Henry as Rodgers and Hart, Avenell Road our own, precious Broadway – what beautiful music these two made together, and we, adoring fools, felt it would last for ever.

There were discords and bum notes too, none as resounding as the utter destruction of Wenger's elegant team at Old Trafford on 25 February, which was all the more unexpected in that it followed well-crafted wins over Lyon in the Champions League* and Chelsea in the FA Cup, Thierry hitting the target on both occasions, including a rare header against the French champions. As Gilles Grimandi and Patrick Vieira told me, this was one of a handful of occasions when the odd teacup felt Wenger's wrath at half-time. A back-four composed of Luzhny, Stepanovs, Grimandi and Cole was perhaps a tad frail to face a full-strength United attack, for whom Dwight Yorke scored a

---

* Arsenal had been drawn with the French champions, Spartak Moscow and eventual winners Bayern Munich in the second group phase, which saw the two best-placed teams of each of the four groups qualify for the quarter-finals of the competition.

nineteen-minute hat-trick, but to concede five before half-time smacked of something more severe than unfamiliarity between part-time defenders. Oddly, the one goal the Gunners conjured in this 1-6 annihilation was perhaps their finest of the campaign in terms of its build-up, as eye-catching and efficient an illustration of Wenger's principle of 'collective improvisation' (an expression Cesc Fàbregas used when I asked him to provide a succinct definition of 'wengerball', many years later) as Arsenal had given since he took over in November 1996. Who remembers it? I didn't, until watching the video of that match again. The one-touch move, started by Vieira in his own half, involved Pirès, Luzhny, Pirès again, who exchanged passes with Wiltord on the right flank before squaring the ball to Henry, who struck it first time with the outside of his left boot. A gorgeous goal, but of no consequence: Arsenal, now sixteen points behind the leaders with ten games to go, clung on to their second spot in the League table only because of the tameness of their rivals' challenge. There was brittleness as well as brio in that team, both of which were in evidence until the conclusion of the season. A farcical 0-3 home defeat to Middlesbrough on 14 April – in which two of the visitors' goals were scored by Arsenal players, namely the Brazilians Edu and Sylvinho – extinguished any hope Arsène Wenger might still have had of catching up with the leaders; in fact, he had forsaken any such aspiration a while ago already. To say Thierry and his teammates freewheeled until the end of the season would be an exaggeration, but they were obviously more con-cerned with their FA Cup run, which saw them overcome Blackburn and Tottenham in the spring to set up the first of three consecutive finals at Cardiff's Millennium Stadium, and, especially, with their tie against Valencia in the last eight of the Champions League, a stage Arsenal hadn't reached since Frank McLintock's side went out to Ajax in 1971–2, when the competition was called the European Champion Clubs' Cup.

The double-header was a tight affair, in which the Gunners, who had scraped through the second phase only by virtue of having a better head-to-head record than Lyon, held the advantage until the seventy-sixth minute of the return leg, when John Carew placed a header past

David Seaman to send his side into the semi-finals.* The away goal scored by Roberto Ayala in Valencia's 1-2 defeat at Highbury two weeks beforehand had proved as costly as Wenger had feared. I remember seeing Vieira and Henry shortly afterwards at the London Colney training ground, both looking sombre and, in Patrick's case, still seething with anger. 'We got done like kids,' he told me. 'We only started playing like we can when we were one-nil down.' Wenger himself put it down to the fact that Arsenal were still pursuing their apprenticeship in Europe. Thierry had more personal reasons to feel bitter at this narrow loss: yes, he had scored the equalizing goal in the first fixture, thanks to a glorious piece of improvisation by Robert Pirès, who backheeled the ball from the edge of the box to find the striker. Standing on the shoulder of the last defender, Henry concluded with a flourish. But he had also missed a golden chance to make it 3-1 when clean through on goal towards the end of the game, only to lose his composure at the very last moment. A week later, placed in a similar situation in a 4-1 win over Everton, he made no such mistake, scoring what would be his last goal of the 2000–2001 campaign with another five games to go. Not much was made of rare lapses like his miss against Valencia at the time, but it wouldn't be long until they were highlighted as evidence that Thierry was not quite the 'big game player' he aspired to be. Liverpool's 2-1 victory in the FA Cup final, which took place on 12 May, was added to the body of evidence compiled by those detractors who claimed, and still do, that, cometh the hour, the man tended to be late – the man who famously didn't score in any of the nine major senior finals he played in† – with the exception of the 2003 Confederations Cup trophy match, the least notable of all these occasions. It is too early to discuss

---

*   It was Thierry's second visit to the Mestalla Stadium in less than a month. On 28 March, the French national team (for whom Henry played the full ninety minutes) had lost 1-2 in a rematch of their Euro 2000 quarter-final against Spain, the first defeat of *Les Bleus* since they'd won that tournament.

†   With France: Euro 2000, 2003 Confederations Cup and 2006 World Cup; with Arsenal: the 2000 UEFA Cup, the 2001, 2002 and 2003 FA Cups, and the 2006 UEFA Champions League; with Barcelona, the 2009 UEFA Champions League. The 2009 Copa del Rey is among Thierry's list of trophies, but he wasn't in Pep Guardiola's squad for the final against Athletic Bilbao (4-1).

what is almost an accusation; but it might be useful to remind these critics that, had Stéphane Henchoz not stopped a goal-bound Henry shot on the line with his arm in the sixteenth minute of Liverpool's victory (an offence which was overlooked by referee Steve Dunn), it is a statistic they wouldn't have come up with in the first place. It had been a disheartening experience for Thierry, which I have mentioned before at some length – you may remember the 'fox in the box' episode – but it provided a fitting full stop to the narrative of this transitional season, in a number of ways. Arsenal had been fitful, taking three steps forward, one step back, which indicated progress, but also imperfection. Old Trafford, Valencia, Cardiff were harsh reminders of that.

I won't withdraw my statement that that year was one of personal blossoming for Henry, however; certainly not as far as his adoption of and by London is concerned. By the spring of 2001, he had bought himself a £5.95 million home – completed just two years previously – in Hampstead, a 7,000 sq ft creation of former RIBA president Richard McCormac, located on leafy Templewood Green, a few paces away from the heath.* It featured an internal swimming-pool, a 'partially subterranean glazed hall' (to quote from the architect's blurb), three garages, a 'suspended staircase, designed to be reminiscent of Frank Lloyd Wright's Fallingwater', six bedrooms and, naturally, an array of giant TV screens which invariably showed football games. Thierry enjoyed his gadgets. When the first MP3 players appeared on the market, an astonished French colleague told me that Henry's own could store ten times as many tunes

---

* Henry, who retained the ownership of Templewood Avenue after his 2007 divorce from Claire Merry, requested permission from the local council to demolish this home in early 2012, in order to build a larger, taller structure, much to the displeasure of McCormac and neighbouring Hampsteadites. One detail of the new plans provided tabloids with splendid copy: Thierry intended to install a giant vertical aquarium which would bissect all four floors of the house. The structure was said to cost £250,000 to build and £12,000 a year to maintain. Fish-keeping seems to have become quite a popular hobby (or status symbol) with modern footballers: David Beckham, Joe Hart, Micah Richards and Steven Ireland have all fitted huge tanks in their homes, Ireland being rumoured to have considered digging a shark tank under his kitchen.

as what manufacturers claimed for their top-of-the-range products. Oh well.

Hampstead's faux-bohemian appeal seemed to exert an irresistible pull on Arsenal players at the time. Patrick Vieira had already settled in Branch Hill, a few hundred yards away from Thierry's spectacular mansion. Freddie Ljungberg was another neighbour, Robert Pirès would soon follow suit. Emmanuel Adebayor too chose to live in NW3 when he joined the club. George Graham had been a resident for nearly a decade when Thierry settled in the area, which the relative proximity to Arsenal's training base at London Colney made even more attractive to its players. It was also London without the hassle of London, teeming with wealthy expatriates, coming with a sheen of safe cosmopolitanism and 'class' that seduced the young millionaires of Highbury. The son of Arsenal's vice-chairman David Dein, Darren, who had quickly become a central figure in the lives of many of them, also ran his business from Beaumont Gardens (exit Thierry's house, walk down to West Heath, third street on the left, you're there), and – so Robert Pirès told me – provided advice on real estate deals to his footballer friends and clients on several occasions.

Henry soon found his marks. He could sometimes be spotted enjoying lunch at Base, an unpretentious bistro which had long been a favourite of exiled French sportsmen. Rugbymen Thomas Castagnède and Rafael Ibanez would sometimes join the likes of Vieira and Pirès for a drink on its terrace. Journalists too – French ones, that is – were welcome to join their company for a cup of coffee and an informal chat. In the mid-2000s, on one of these beautiful spring afternoons which turn Hampstead High Street into a village fantasy (more akin to Marie Antoinette's Petit Trianon than Wodehouse's Market Blandings), I remember all of the above joining Pirès and me, one by one, and Vieira waving at . . . could it be Ashley Cole carrying shopping bags on the other side of the street? Yes. Minutes later, another wave – it was directed at Jens Lehmann, pushing a pram. No wonder footballers love London so much. Passers-by recognized them, nodded, sometimes – rarely – summoned the courage to ask for a quick autograph, then scurried away like church mice spotting the beadle sneaking out of the sacristy. Such scenes would have been unthinkable in Milan or Madrid.

It was a peaceful, unremarkable existence which, in Henry's case, was only disturbed once, but in dramatic fashion. On 5 December 2001, burglars took advantage of his playing in a 3-1 victory over his former club Juventus to break into his home, tied up his terrified housekeeper, 'ransacked the property and left with a quantity of property', to quote a Camden police spokesman. This incident, fortunately, was the only cloud that darkened the Hampstead horizon throughout Thierry's stay.

If he enjoyed the respectful distance fans, Tottenham fans included,* kept from their idols as much as anyone, Henry was not quite as gregarious as his teammates. He spent much of his time at home nearby, or patronized more exclusive establishments, of which his favourite was The House on Rosslyn Hill. There were few professional footballers in his 'crowd', what Gilles Grimandi calls his 'bubble'. Within the 'bubble' were some old friends, many of whom he had met through his half-brother Willy, such as Franck Nema, a family acquaintance (but not his cousin, as has been written elsewhere), who was also a decent footballer himself and played a few games for Levallois. He would encourage former teammates from Clairefontaine and Monaco to visit him in London, like Robert Camara and the magnificently named Haitian international Ernst Atis-Clotaire, now retired from football and eking a living as an electrician in a northern Paris suburb. At one point, Atis-Clotaire was thought of as a 'great of the future', after collecting numerous caps for France's under-18s and winning the 1996 under-19 European Championships alongside David Trezeguet and Henry himself. But he only ever played one game in the *championnat* with Monaco and quickly disappeared from view – but not from Thierry's world.

A few celebrities would join in, like the Cameroon-born rapper Pit Baccardi, or singer Sharleen Spiteri, as we have seen. Within a little over

---

* Thierry described one of his many encounters with Spurs supporters in those terms: 'One day, I am at the airport and I see a couple of Tottenham fans running at me. The lift is going to close, so I put my hand, to prevent the door from shutting on them. They are in a hurry, the husband is running, he puts his hand out as well, but without looking inside the lift, and his wife makes a little sign to him, raising her eyebrows. He turns back, looks at me . . . and they go to the stairs.'

a year of arriving in a city he didn't know before, Henry had found a balance that was previously lacking in his life, and it showed: to us journalists who tracked him from game to game with Arsenal, he appeared more mature, more relaxed, chattier than what we had been told by those who knew him through following Monaco and, especially, the French national team. Whether he could shake off his essential remoteness was a different matter, however. 'I agree with him that, had we been from the same generation, we would have been friends' – but Arsène Wenger wasn't talking of Henry. Emmanuel Petit was the player with whom the Arsenal manager had 'exchanged secrets', 'who has an extreme side in his character which I understand and value, because, in this respect, we're the same'. Wenger's relationship with Thierry was of an altogether different nature, despite the obvious parallel between the career paths of both footballers. Wenger had given them their first chance to play at the highest level, Titi when he was seventeen, in 1994, Manu at the age of eighteen, in 1989. My own guess would be that Petit's character, which can't be understood without reference to the tragic death of his brother Olivier, who collapsed from an aneurism suffered in a football game when Manu was a teenager, chimed in with an often-overlooked trait of Wenger's personality: a passionate desire to live life to the full, bordering on recklessness. This is not to say that no fire burns in Henry's soul; but it is not the uncontrollable blaze that can consume Petit, and which Wenger, by his own admission, only learnt to channel after he spent two seasons in Japan, in many ways the formative experience of the cerebral 'professor' of his Arsenal years.

Wenger and Henry grew closer over time, acknowledging a debt they shared, united in their desire to fight for the club they loved, assured of each other's trust. The older man valued one of his junior's qualities above all others: 'his generosity, on the field and in life'. 'Thierry is a sensitive guy,' he said, shortly after the final of Euro 2000, 'and I like that; but sensitivity cuts both ways. In this milieu, people make you pay a heavy price for your vulnerability.' Henry would have concurred, he who confided to a French journalist a year later: 'I don't like to talk about my life, even if you sometimes have to open up to other people. But you have to keep certain things to yourself.' In that, in the way Thierry 'opened up' to Wenger at one of the most difficult moments in his young life – the breakdown of his marriage, which was one of the reasons why he finally yielded to the temptation of Barcelona – you could say that what had been a harmonious working relationship, though by no means devoid of tiffs and quarrels along the way, had evolved into a genuine complicity over the years. One of the things that struck me the most when Henry's statue was unveiled at the Emirates Stadium in December 2011 was the body language of the supposed mentor and pupil. Deep in conversation, they seemed to inhabit a space within which both were completely at ease, oblivious of the crowd around them. These were two equals talking to each other. But two friends? Not quite. Another recent memory of Thierry comes to mind. The Football Writers Association honoured him at its annual gala dinner in January 2011. Walking to the rostrum to acknowledge the black-tied audience, Henry, never the most fluent of speakers in occasions such as these, spoke awkwardly for a few minutes, which, to those who know him, only meant that he was tangled up in his own emotions and struggling to convey them, alone in front of several hundred people who hung on to his every word. An uneasy feeling rippled through the room when Thierry thought it necessary to make a rather cutting remark – in terms of tone if not of vocabulary – about Arsène Wenger's absence. 'I don't know why he isn't there,' he said, and not in jest. My neighbours and I exchanged an embarrassed glance.

Player and manager gave no indication whatsoever of the difference in their respective statuses. But a genuine friendship? As the song goes, it's lonely at the top. And this is where Thierry was now.

9

His ball, his team, his garden.

THE HENRY PARADOX I

The numbers are prodigious. Between 15 August 2001 and 25 June 2004, Thierry Henry took part in 189 games for club and country, that is sixty-three per season, scoring 120 goals along the way, giving him a strike rate of 0.63 per match over that three-year period. The records started tumbling, beginning with Ian Wright's total of thirteen goals in European competitions for Arsenal, beaten when Thierry scored a brace against Schalke 04 at Highbury on 19 September 2001. Milestones were passed at an accelerating rate, making it obvious that it was a question of when, not if – barring injury, and provided that another club didn't lure Henry out of Highbury – the most prolific European goalscorer of that period would, at least in terms of raw statistics, set standards that no Arsenal player of the future could improve upon. His hundredth League goal for the Gunners was scored on 10 February 2004, in a 2-0 defeat of Southampton. A little over two months later, the first and only quadruple of his career, against Leeds United, enabled him to reach the 150 mark in all competitions. Personal honours and distinctions followed with an air of inevitability: the Premier League Golden Boot, twice, in 2002 and 2004; the PFA and FWA Player of the Year and Footballer of the Year awards in 2003 and 2004, which made him the first-ever player to be distinguished twice in succession by the Football Writers Association; the consolation of being named French Footballer of the Year in 2003, having narrowly missed on being voted that year's *Ballon d'Or*. Innumerable Man of the Match awards, including that given in the 2003 FA Cup final, which Arsenal won at the expense of Southampton. Genuine trophies, too – the 2001–2 League/FA Cup Double, the 2003 Confederations Cup, of which he was both Golden Shoe and Golden Ball winner, and, to cap an astonishingly consistent three seasons of prowess, the 2004 Premier League as part of one of English football's greatest-ever teams, Arsène Wenger's 'Invincibles'. Henry had not just laid an unquestionable claim to being considered a giant in Arsenal's history, he could now be counted among those exceedingly rare players who come to embody an era of English football as a whole, as George Best or Éric Cantona had done before him.

Talent, consistency of performance and goalscoring exploits are not enough to achieve this status; we will take artistry as a prerequisite, and charisma as a given; yet even all those attributes taken together do not necessarily suffice to produce that peculiar aura which, in Thierry's case, also had to do with the easy grace he showed on and off the field. I was not particularly taken with the 'va-va-voom' catchphrase which advertisers had picked for the Renault Clio campaign that Henry fronted from 2002 onwards,* but I must concede that it certainly caught a mood and offered a new template for 'Frenchness' which was quite distinct from those provided by, say, Éric Cantona or David Ginola. The footballer-poet and the suave charmer fitted traditional stereotypes which, when you think of it, were not that much subtler than the image of the chap in a Breton shirt, cycling with a string of onions around his neck. Thierry was something else altogether: a young West Indian man who had grown up in the *banlieue*, whose 'Frenchness' I recognized as self-evident, but who made me ask myself: 'What is it to be French? What do Thierry Henry and I have in common that make people recognize us as French?' This was a kind of triumph for the post-1998 ethos of *black-blanc-beur* – to the British at least, Thierry cut across distinctions of class and ethnic origin whilst remaining essentially French. How do you reconcile the slightly awkward black teenager who was photographed in Monaco, carrying a huge ghetto-blaster and sporting would-be dreadlocks, with the suave, über-cool metrosexual who later modelled his

---

* The expression did not enter the OED because of Henry, as is commonly believed. It had been included as early as 1989 in the dictionary, and was also the title of a Gil Evans composition featured in the film *Absolute Beginners* (1985).

own line of clothes for the American designer Tommy Hilfiger* and
seemed born to glide from one VIP lounge to the next? He had an air
of unstudied sophistication about him, which the advertisers seized upon
with relish. Like many top athletes, he also moved unhurriedly, almost
lazily, when he was away from the football field. He had the ideal physique, both lithe and powerful, to make casual wear look sharp and
elegant. He was just perfect, in that, for what would be a very short
time for other mortals, he lived on an enchanted plane where it all
seemed as natural as sunshine: the goals, the glory, the celebrity friends,
the adoring fans and all the paraphernalia of success. The joy he took
in giving joy to others was obvious. He spoke about his own achievements with engaging humility, putting them down to the faith everyone
at his club had in him, feeling as proud in his ability to make others
shine – twenty-three assists in the 2002–3 League season alone – as in
his own accuracy in front of goal. He had genuine greats alongside him
– Patrick Vieira, Dennis Bergkamp – whose presence protected him
from conceit; and he had other teammates who, for a while, flirted with
greatness themselves, none more so than Robert Pirès, who, if only for
a season, in 2001–2, before he sustained a serious knee injury, was in
Arsène Wenger's opinion the best attacking midfielder in the world.
Those were heady days, which we probably didn't appreciate as much
as we should have.

This was especially true of the way France now looked at Henry,
which grew more and more ambiguous as time went by, and this,
cruelly, when Thierry had become an almost unanimously respected
ambassador of his native country in England. There was obviously
pride at seeing one of our own succeed with such brio, as part of the
Musketeers (Titi, Pat, Bobby and Nino, Nino being Sylvain Wiltord)
who, with the gradual retirement of Graham's old guard, assumed an

---

* The collection was unveiled in October 2007 in the designer's Regent Street
shop, Thierry modelling some of the clothes in the shop window, to the great
surprise of passers-by. All profits from the sales were to be channelled towards
Henry's One 4 All foundation, which aimed 'to help underprivileged kids in
underprivileged areas', in the footballer's words. I have failed to find any trace of
that charity's activity since then.

ever-more important role in defining the club's identity. There was also frustration. Henry's willingness to talk to visiting journalists was taken as a proof of his self-regard and his appetite for – positive – publicity, which must have been voracious, as the clippings I have collected for these few years could provide enough material for a substantial book on their own.* It was also felt – how many times did I hear this debated! – that Henry didn't really 'try' when he was on national duty, that he expected to be the main man wherever he went, and that he couldn't stomach Zinedine Zidane's pre-eminence within *Les Bleus*, a subject I'll devote more space to later on. That Henry's efficiency suffered when he turned up for Roger Lemerre's and, from July 2002, Jacques Santini's team is beyond doubt; but to hold the footballer solely responsible for this is unreasonable, whatever some carefully selected figures may suggest.

From the summer of 2001 to that of 2004, Thierry scored exactly a goal every two games for France – seventeen in thirty-four, to be precise – and of these seventeen goals twelve were scored in UEFA or FIFA competitions, which constitutes a handsome return for a supposedly struggling centre-forward. It is true that Henry often filled his boots against opponents that were easy fodder for the World and European champions of 1998 and 2000, scoring four in a 10-0 aggregate demolition of Malta home and away in the 2004 Euro qualifiers, for example. Israel, Cyprus, New Zealand were some other victims of his marksmanship. Whether it is fair to pick and choose which games were 'significant' and which ones were not is a different matter, and how could scoring a goal, any goal, be used as evidence of the scorer's ineptitude? I can't remember people making acidic comments about Zidane putting two past Maltese 'keeper Mario Muscat in March 2003, or subtracting them

---

*   A book which, I should add, would be monotonous, as all questions Thierry was asked invariably led to the same three themes: his love of Arsenal, his love of life in London, and his role in the French national team. Henry, probably through boredom, developed stock answers to all three, with the result that the wonderful interviewee of his first Arsenal years gradually turned into a bit of a bore himself – unless it was the game itself that was talked about, in which case a lovely light was immediately switched on.

from the French captain's total in their otiose calculations. Something must have happened; if I had to single out a turning point in France's uneasy relationship with one of its best-ever footballers, I would choose the masquerade of the 2002 World Cup. So let's leave England's green fields for a while and head for South-east Asia, where the golden legend of *Les Bleus* was turned into a soap opera of the cheapest kind.

France approached the tournament as favourites, which seemed logical enough. They held the two most prestigious titles in world football. Their strike force looked frightening, with the Golden Boots of Serie A (Trezeguet), the Premier League (Henry) and *le championnat* (Djibril Cissé) to call upon. Their unimpressive performances throughout the first five months of 2002, with three wins to show in five games, two of them laborious, were largely ignored in the previews of the competition. It was only when Zinedine Zidane suffered a muscular injury five days before France's opening game that the first alarm signals started to flash. The French management had agreed to play a meaningless friendly against South Korea at this extraordinary late stage in the team's preparations to please their main Korean sponsor, who had insisted that France should select as many of its stars as possible. The French federation obliged. Zidane himself was in no fit state to play any part in that match but did, lasting thirty-eight minutes before his exhausted body gave up the ghost. He had had no time whatsoever to rest: his season with Real Madrid had ended only eleven days previously, when he had scored a glorious left-footed volley to give his club a 2-1 win over Bayer Leverkusen in the Champions League final; after which he had rejoined his wife, Véronique, who was about to give birth to their third son, Theo; Theo being born, on 18 May, the sleep-deprived Zidane then boarded the plane which delivered him safely in Japan nineteen hours later; only to take another plane to go to Suwon, in Korea, where France's scrappy 3-2 victory over the Asian 'red devils' was overshadowed by their playmaker's early exit. Still, with Senegal, Uruguay and Denmark in their group, it shouldn't be beyond the world champions to finish in the top two and progress to the round of sixteen, should it? Zizou's minor thigh tear would soon heal, and all would be well.

What followed was an unmitigated disaster. First-time qualifiers

Senegal rode their luck to earn a 1-0 victory. Thierry was sent off for a reckless tackle on Marcelo Romero in the twenty-sixth minute of their next match, against Uruguay, and ten-men France conceded a 0-0 draw. Even the return of Zidane, at least as a name in the starting line-up, failed to inspire *Les Bleus* in their win-or-die encounter with Denmark. Tomasson and Rommedahl scored, France couldn't reply, and the holders had relinquished their title in the most abject of fashions, goalless, clueless, leaderless, pointless, finishing bottom of Group A. The post-mortem was even uglier than the death itself.

The French journalists who had travelled en masse to Japan and South Korea, tagging along with the bloated caravan of the French delegation, felt they were no longer duty-bound to keep what they had witnessed at first hand to themselves. The *omertà* rule which had always been de rigueur as far as the national team was concerned was lifted. Revelling in the freedom they were now granted by the abysmal quality of the team's performances on the field, the chroniclers of France's humiliation turned their pens to descriptions of such luridness that, libel laws being what they are in the United Kingdom, I can only scratch at the surface of what was printed in my home country at the time. The most stinging criticisms were directed at those amongst the fifty-odd FFF officials for whom this World Cup was said to represent an all-expenses-paid vacation, judging by the bills they ran up in the swankiest bars and restaurants they could find. Claude Simonet, the chief panjandrum of that delegation, thought nothing of ordering a £4,000 bottle of Romanée-Conti to wash down one of his dinners in Korea and ran a personal £50,000 expense bill for a tournament that was over in less than two weeks as far as France was concerned. Later convicted of fraud – he had massaged the FFF's 2003 accounts to show a €63,000 loss when it actually amounted to over €14m – Simonet was sentenced on 24 April 2007 to a six-month suspended jail term and fined €10,000. But to single out Simonet, whilst not unfair, would be hiding the extent to which the national team's administration had become corrupted. The triumphs of 1998 and 2000 had fed a sense of hubris which could no longer be kept in check. Sponsors were falling over themselves to court players and administrators, not many of whom seemed to show too much resistance to endorsing the most disparate range of products or services you could think of. Franck Leboeuf was paid to promote French beef, Marcel Desailly and Bixente Lizarazu mobile telephone operators, Zidane a brand of spring mineral water. In total, no fewer than forty businesses struck up individual deals with Lemerre's players, who would also each receive a very generous bonus (rumoured to be the equivalent of £400,000 per player), whatever the final result may be, to which should be added the fifty-four 'official part-ners' of the national team, who contributed €38 million to the FFF's coffers – more than double the amount earned by the 1998 world-title-winning side. These paying friends of *Les Bleus* naturally demanded their pound of flesh, and not just in the form of tickets to the team's games. Their representatives enjoyed access-all-areas status in the French bases, both at Ibisuki in Japan and Seoul in Korea. Agents infested the place as well. Looking back at what happened then, Emmanuel Petit has said how he felt shame at having become drunk on his own fame and having – almost – forgotten what had made him such a valuable commodity to start with. Many shared his feelings, but the collective ethos fostered by leaders such as Didier Deschamps and Laurent Blanc, both of whom had retired from national service, had disintegrated completely by that stage, to be replaced by self-absorption and its natural companion, paranoia.

Nothing was too good for the future world champions, as they were bound to become according to the FFF's accountants, who had tailored their budget accordingly, making no provisions for other scenarios. Six tons of equipment were shipped to the Far East, plus food and drinks, which included twenty cases of Domaine La Lignane 1998 and Domaine de l'Echevain 2000 to be served at the team meals. The head chef of Juventus had been recruited to prepare pasta to Zidane's and Trezeguet's specifications. The FFF considered installing a temporary satellite link which would enable players and staff to watch French television before deciding that an outlay of €400,000 might be a tad excessive – one of the few sensible decisions taken on this trip taken on the road to nowhere. The hotels they stayed in were the most luxurious available, which might explain why the daily food and accommodation cost for each member of the delegation amounted to €534 in Korea – and why the total budget went over the €15 million mark.

Then there were the late, late nights at the Sheraton Grande Hill

Walker Hotel and Towers, to give this five-star residence its full name, where a separate building, the Douglas Executive Club, had been put at the disposal of the team. The manager of Italy, Giovanni Trapattoni, had initially considered making this hotel the headquarters of *la nazionale*, before noticing that it boasted of harbouring Seoul's only casino and a 'fun-bar', the Sirocco, where last orders were taken at 2 a.m. This is where, according to what the bar's resident band-leader, a Bulgarian named George, told a correspondent of *Le Parisien*, Roger Lemerre and his assistants had dinner on the eve of France's last game in the competition. There was nothing wrong in that *per se*, but not everyone visited the Sirocco for the sole purpose of a quiet, in-depth football discussion. It soon filtered out that several players had been regular late-night visitors and fought off boredom by making friends with some of the girl dancers employed by the hotel. A private lift enabled guests to access bedrooms straight from a karaoke booth without having to go though the main hall. I should add that none of the players concerned were regular starters in Lemerre's eleven. This should, however, give a measure of the laissez-faire which now characterized the atmosphere within the team and their support staff, a number of whom were regularly seen the worse for wear in the small hours of the morning.

Some players tried to react. Marcel Desailly and Patrick Vieira both attempted to convince their manager that the 4-2-3-1 he had decided upon wasn't best suited to the personnel available, with Robert Pirès absent through injury and Zidane unavailable for two games at least. They could see how Lemerre was visibly losing his grip in this environment. He had always been suspicious of outsiders, of journalists in particular; and he couldn't countenance the presence of so many hangers-on in the French camp, not that he could do anything about it. His response was to withdraw further into himself to the point that he lost communication with his own players, with disastrous effect. His decision-making betrayed a man lost in the lurid circus which had surrounded the national team even before it had flown out to the Far East. Experienced footballers looked on, aghast, losing confidence in the coach whose clear-thinking and decisiveness had had such a clear impact throughout Euro 2000. 'We were knackered (*claqués*) before the tournament,' Youri Djorkaeff recalled. 'Zizou got injured, unsurprisingly:

Lemerre had insisted on putting him through laps and laps of the training ground when he should have tried to get over jet-lag.' Petit, who is fond of his former manager, speaks of his 'stubbornness', taking Thierry as a prime example of what Lemerre did wrong in 2002.

Ah, Thierry. If I've barely mentioned him in the last few pages, it is because he had become near-invisible. On 23 May, three days before France's match with Senegal, Henry had played no part in a warm-up game won 5-1 against J-League club Urawa Reds. He had suffered a minor knee injury in the friendly played in South Korea a week before-hand, which hadn't healed in time and which Lemerre made more of than he should have, implying that his medical staff were fretting about the striker's fitness for the World Cup itself. His words ('It'd be very worrying if we weren't completely reassured by Sunday') made the next day's headlines, quite legitimately. Thierry, infuriated, decided to boycott the media, a choice he would have reason to regret later on: journalists would not be so keen to find mitigating circumstances for the footballer who had scorned them. The knee injury was no less real for that and had clearly impaired him in the Senegal match, even if he had struck one of Tony Sylva's posts in the sixty-sixth minute. Then, in the match against Uruguay, Henry was asked by Lemerre to play on the left wing, when he had expected to be deployed upfront with David Trezeguet. 'That,' Emmanuel Petit says, 'is what "killed" him.' With less than a third of the game gone, losing all sense of discipline, Thierry took out his anger and his frustration on Marcelo Romero, ramming through the Uruguayan defender, studs showing, in an act of violence of which no other example can be found in the rest of his career. From then on, Henry could only be a guilty party, not just as the author of a reckless tackle, but as a symbol of all that was wrong with that team of prima donnas – all of them tarred with the same brush, whether they deserved it or not – for whom the French jersey could as well have been a patchwork of sponsors' logos. Zidane, exhausted, injured, helpless, escaped the ensuing storm. Henry had no such luck. From then on, it seemed as if one would always be judged in comparison with the other; but in the odd couple they formed together one half always held the upper hand, whatever the merits of the other might be. The winner could only be Zizou.

*

In the history of football, only a very small number of countries have been blessed with the near-simultaneous emergence of two outstanding footballers such as Zinedine Zidane and Thierry Henry, and those lucky few have almost always enjoyed a period of pre-eminence on the world stage as a result. It would be tempting to say that this was true of France as well, as a World Cup and a European Championship were won when both players were at their peak or approaching it with *Les Bleus*. This couldn't be a mere coincidence, could it? But it isn't a gratuitous taste for paradox that makes me wonder whether this unprecedented success was achieved despite, rather than because of, the presence of these two exceptional talents in the same team.

In France's case, the privilege to be able to call on both of them was nothing short of a miracle. It had been a long-lamented characteristic of our game that it produced so-called 'world-class' players in fits and starts only, and just one at a time at that. As a consequence, the decline of that player unavoidably led to a decline of the team as a whole, and to years, sometimes decades, of underachievement, until a new sun appeared on the horizon. The late 1950s and early 1960s had been the age of Raymond Kopa, who had superbly gifted teammates – Roger Piantoni was probably the best of them, Just Fontaine the deadliest – to play with, but none whose ability to shape a game could be compared to that of the 'wizard' of Reims and Real Madrid. The 1980s belonged to Michel Platini, who could also count on first-rate support from the likes of Alain Giresse or Jean Tigana. But both Kopa and Platini inhabited a higher world, to which their contemporaries could only aspire from afar; they were the stars around which orbited lesser lights, as well as the focus of their countrymen's fantasies. With Zizou and Titi, despite the age difference – the Marseillais was five years older than the Parisian *banlieusard* – we had at last a measure of synchronicity. What's more, whereas Zidane only truly established himself as a footballer of the first rank after his move to Juventus in 1996, when he was twenty-one years old, Henry had already shown enough of his potential at a very young age for Real Madrid to instigate their botched transfer from Monaco before his nineteenth birthday. Neither should it be forgotten that Thierry scored his first goal in the final phase of a major tournament before Zinedine did and that, in all, even allowing for the elder's temporary retirement after Euro 2004 and his heir apparent's fall from grace shortly after the 1998 World Cup, the two greatest icons of France's golden era spent no fewer than six full seasons together in the national team, during which both reached the apex of their careers. But put them on a pitch together and you couldn't help but share the opinion expressed by French journalist Vincent Duluc a few weeks before the last tournament they played together, the 2006 World Cup: 'they look like two magnets which are repelling each other, because they share the same polarity, the same talent, the same ego.'

When one of them shone, the other seemed to recede into the shadows. Zidane would ultimately emerge as the hero of France's World Cup campaign in 1998, by dint of two headed goals in that competition's final; but he had been below his best until then, getting himself sent off – and suspended – for that cowardly stamp on a South African player in France's opening match of the tournament. Henry, by contrast, had revelled in the occasion, scoring three crucial goals and showing commendable composure in a penalty shoot-out against Italy in the quarter-finals. Two years later, at the European Championships, Zidane had been close to his best form, but intermittently, whereas Henry could claim to have been the competition's most consistently effective player, until the strain he had put on his body on the back of an exhausting campaign with Arsenal deprived him of much of his powers in the decisive encounter against Italy. And so it went on. Those fires couldn't be kindled at the same time, it seemed. As time went by, and what had been merely odd became a matter for speculation and, indeed, suspicion, much was made of that astonishing fact: Zinedine Zidane had never provided an assist for Thierry Henry, unless you took into account the almost inconsequential pass that the striker received from the playmaker sixty yards from goal in a 3-0 win over Denmark at the 2000 European Championships. Thierry had embarked on one of his exhilarating raids, leaving every defender in a heap before slotting the ball past the Danish 'keeper: a prodigious solo, an extemporization executed without the guidance of a conductor. Later still, at Euro 2004, it was Zidane who made the headlines by pinching victory from under the noses of the English in their opening group game, scoring from a free-kick and the penalty spot in the last minutes of a match that meant the world to

Thierry. But Thierry it was who had drawn the crucial foul in the box, after exploiting a stray back-pass from Steven Gerrard; yet hardly anyone bothered to stress his contribution in France, where people were too busy lauding ZZ for yet another decisive intervention in the face of certain defeat. The bare fact remained: in the fifty-one games Zidane and Henry played together with France before the 2006 World Cup, not once had the Arsenal striker scored a goal set up by the *galáctico*, despite finding the net on thirty-two occasions; in the meantime, Zidane had helped twelve teammates to get on the scoresheet – including Jean-Alain Boumsong and Mickaël Silvestre. Thierry must have been maddened by the constant sniping he was the target of from those journalists who pointed at the discrepancy between his efficiency in the Premier League and his supposed lack of success with the French team.

Statistically speaking, this was utter nonsense: prior to the 2006 World Cup, Thierry had an overall strike ratio of 0.41 goal per game with the French national team; but, remarkably enough, this ratio rocketed to 0.63 when only the fifty-one games he played alongside Zidane were taken into account.* None of his countrymen came close to it, but nobody seemed to pay attention to that fact, blinded as they were by Henry's exceptional form with the Gunners in the same period. It wasn't goals that were missing; it was the fluency and authority that the Arsenal player exuded week in, week out with the club he loved and which eluded him too often when he was playing for his country. The question had to be asked: how could it be that the most gifted creator in world football could fail to work in harmony with one of its greatest finishers, to the extent that he had never been the last link in the movement leading to one of his numerous goals?

Regardless of the rumours that deduced enmity from perceived differences between their characters, Zidane and Henry held each other in respect, if not affection, at least at the outset of a relationship that was strictly limited to the exercise of their profession. Just as he had done when a teenager at Monaco, where he had tried to ingratiate

---

* This average was even superior to the 0.61 goal per game (in all competitions) which Thierry scored in his Arsenal career, and this when the task of taking penalties – his prerogative with the Gunners – was given to Zidane in the French team.

himself to Sonny Anderson, the younger of the two frequently sought the company and the advice of his elder at the regular get-togethers of the France squad at Clairefontaine, sipping coffee by Zidane's side at the end of the communal supper, listening, asking questions when he summoned up the courage to do so, eager to hear what the reserved, secretive even, undisputed leader of *Les Bleus* had to say. The opposite wasn't necessarily true – but then, Zidane always preferred his own company to that of others, whoever they may be, a facet of his character with which Henry, the self-confessed 'loner', could empathize readily. 'He is such a great player,' Thierry said in 2005. 'His aura is so immense that I've never succeeded in talking to him. He makes too strong an impression on me, and he's not that expansive either.'

How much their lack of natural sympathy for each other led to conflict is a matter of conjecture or, worse, gossip, of which there was plenty. They couldn't deny a certain coolness in their relationship but always spoke of each other in a conciliatory tone, with Thierry accepting that he hadn't earned the right to be mentioned in the same breath as the player he called 'God' in at least one interview. The rift between the *Zidaniens* and Thierry's supporters was much more pronounced outside the French camp than inside and was drip-fed by constant innuendo in the media. Zizou had been remarkably successful at crafting the image of a humble, painfully shy family man with the public at large, helped in no small degree by an impressive retinue of behind-the-scenes advisers. 1998 had made him a secular saint in the newly built cathedral of French football, stood on a pedestal chiselled by his many sponsors, a monument which always looked to me more like William Beckford's Fonthill Abbey than Canterbury. In contrast, Henry could appear brash, aloof, too clever by half. And what couldn't be denied was that Zidane never illuminated a football field more than when he put on a blue jersey. The star sewn over the cockerel in 1998 was his dominion. When he wore the same shirt, Thierry, albeit scoring freely, struggled to show the brilliance familiar to all followers of the Arsenal.

By 2002, some journalists were alluding to a '*Clan des Gunners*' within *Les Bleus*, whose objective was to make Henry the pivotal player within the national team – at the expense of Zidane, naturally. One journalist, Bruno Godard, devoted the equivalent of a substantial chapter to those behind-the-scenes parleys in a book that sold quite well in France prior to the 2006 World Cup, as vicious an attack on Thierry's character as I have ever read, in which the paucity of evidence was used as a proof in itself – of Henry's consummate talent at covering his tracks. There were rumours of secret dinners held by Vieira, Pirès, Petit and Henry in their Hampstead haunts, at which these modern-day Catilinas would devise the best strategy to undermine Zizou's privileged situation. When I mentioned this to Pirès, all he could do was shrug his shoulders and go '*pff*. . .' The Arsenal players had sat down at the same table, that's true, just like Manchester United and Liverpool players used to keep themselves to themselves at England get-togethers. As in every national team in the world, clubmates associated with those they knew best. And Patrick Vieira, one of the suspected plotters, actually played a key role in persuading Zidane to put an end to his international retirement in 2005, without wrecking his relationship with Henry in the process. As for Bobby, anyone who has ever been lucky enough to be in his company for any length of time will know that he was just as incapable of fostering treason as an apple tree is of bearing a peach, or a wolf of giving birth to a baa-lamb.

Thierry probably felt more frustrated by his – imagined – lack of efficiency with France than anyone else and searched for an explanation, sometimes publicly, giving his critics ambiguous quotes to feed on. 'The sooner I get the ball, like at Arsenal, where we play without a playmaker, the better it is,' he said in 2004. 'I'm not aiming this at anyone in particular, but sometimes it would be better if the strikers got the ball before the two banks of four opposing defenders had closed us down. We do not play wide enough to create breaches. We should move the ball more quickly.' As ever with Henry when he talks about football, what he said made perfect sense. The barb, if barb it was, was aimed at his then manager – Jacques Santini, a strict devotee of the 4-4-2 'wingless' formation – rather than at any of the footballers who carried out his instructions on the pitch. But people had learnt to listen to Thierry differently by then, as if the language he spoke required the addition of subtitles to be understood. There was an unmistakable tone of frustration in his words, a subtext that couldn't be ignored, a suggestion that the unimpeachable status of Zidane grated with him (as, I should add, it grated with many, myself included). Was Henry pointing at a genuine weakness in France's game or was he simply jealous?

By the time the French players had rejoined their clubs after a disappointing, but arguably not catastrophic, Euro 2004, where 'that wily old fox' Otto Rehagel (Arsène Wenger's expression) turned Greece into an unbreakable wall against which the French, and others, broke their teeth, the 'conflict' between the two stars had been blown by the media to such a ridiculous extent that Thierry felt compelled to call Zidane on his Spanish mobile phone (something he had never done before) to assure the Real Madrid maestro that he wasn't the instigator of a plot to usurp him. 'We understood each other well,' he said, showing that this 'private' conversation was ultimately meant to be a very public gesture, in typical Henry fashion. 'It's a good thing that I don't have any problem with Zizou and that we know each other well.' But there *was* a problem with Zizou, at least on the field, where their games seemed so ill suited to each other that it wouldn't have been an exaggeration to label their rapport as dysfunctional. And know each other well they didn't, even if they may have been similar in many respects, such as their conviction that each of them could be the main instrument of France's resurgence after the humiliation of the 2002 World Cup. How much space should be left to the other in that mission was a grey area, which anyone could fill in with the colours they desired, or which served their interests best.

Matters came to a head in 2006, once Zidane had been reinstated as captain of *Les Bleus*, after a brief hiatus during which the team, now managed by Raymond Domemech, had found it impossible to fill the vacuum left by the departure of its most iconic figure, but also stalwarts like Claude Makelele and, more pointedly, the revered Lilian Thuram, who commanded unquestioning respect among his peers and had so often played the role of peacemaker in a dressing-room where tension could be transmuted into communal aspiration once he had put factions back in their place. The World Cup in Germany would be the last chance for Zidane and Henry to prove whether their inability to dovetail on a football field was nothing but a statistical freak or, as I believe is the case, a genuinely unsolvable tactical equation, far more than the consequence of personal dislike or machinations. Thierry had welcomed his skipper's return to the French squad the previous year so fulsomely that he had achieved the very opposite of what he had intended; he had given more ammunition to those who portrayed him as a hypocrite, a Machiavelli in shorts and long cotton socks. It is only natural to infer that, if praise is applied so copiously, it is because too much needs to be covered to start with. Whatever there is of sincerity in the eulogy is thinned to the extent that the canvas shows through. Zidane, for whom silence had long been a weapon, had no need for manoeuvring of that kind. Suspect as Henry's panegyric was, it also betrayed some naivety on his part. Had he been a subtler operator, the 'Machiavelli' his enemies liked to describe, he wouldn't have laid it on so thick, so to speak, as the hyperbole betrayed puzzlement as least as much as bruised vanity.

It can't be denied that Zidane's first exit from *Les Bleus* had given Henry a chance to occupy centre stage alone, probably earlier than he had expected, and that he hadn't seized it. Many of the 1998 world champions were now reaching the end of their careers, and it was expected of Thierry, the youngest of them all, that, at the age of twenty-eight, he would establish himself as the mentor of a new generation of French players. It was also plain to see that this prospect thrilled him. It was a natural step in his extraordinarily smooth ascent to the very top of the game: hadn't he been the captain of every national youth team he had been part of before? But France had appeared rudderless after their defeat to Greece at the 2004 European Championships, and it would have taken a remarkably prescient mind to guess that it was also due to the fact that the French federation had chosen a manager – Raymond Domenech – who would explore previously unknown depths of crassness and incompetence in the six years to come. Henry presented a much more visible and much easier target to the worried masses. As so often, he tried too hard, with predictable results.

Zidane's return shook him, shocked him, even. The *Clan des Gunners*, whatever it really was, or more probably wasn't, hadn't kept him au fait with the efforts made by Vieira – who had left Arsenal for Juve at the end of the 2004–5 season – to bring the *galáctico* back into the fold. A story circulated at the time that Henry had only found out about this by accident, so to speak. One of the rapidly diminishing group of journalists he trusted had naively asked him how it felt to welcome back the hero of the Stade de France. According to that journalist, Thierry uttered an expletive then said: 'Are you sure? Are you sure?'

What I didn't know then, of course, was that some of Henry's confidants, whilst being careful to flatter him in their articles, could also put the boot in and viewed him with a cynicism that I'm tempted to think was their own to start with. Thierry's legendary distrust of outsiders, which he often confessed to and was the first to regret, should have extended to those who had made a pact with him out of interest and disguised it as admiration. They did Henry a great disservice, of which their 'friend' was, and perhaps will always remain, unaware.

What's more, whoever scratched the sacred image of Zizou, the living symbol of a 'rainbow nation' that conquered the world, was bound to be found guilty of blasphemy before anyone had heard what he or she had to say. It was a photograph of Zidane's face that had been projected on the Arc de Triomphe on the glorious evening of 12 July 1998, not Lilian Thuram's. Not Thierry Henry's. As one who has harboured doubts about 'God's' persona for a long time (maybe as a result of a sometimes irrational distrust of unanimity), I can testify to the extremely tetchy character of his proselytes. Let's agree – for argument's sake – that Henry had plotted to take on the role of the providential man, and that Zidane (and those who profited from his elevation) felt that he represented a threat. When it was obvious that France could do with one such 'providential man', what on earth could be wrong with that? Thierry was careful, too careful maybe, to exculpate Zidane from any dark intent, when quite a few of the less blinkered observers of France's team thought that the playmaker could and should have done more, perhaps, to make one of the most feared strikers in Europe shine more brightly on the field. It certainly didn't seem to bother Zidane that much when the subject was broached in interviews and press conferences. His answers would be vague, or casual, or both. Most put this down to Zidane's well-known diffidence, his uneasiness of speech and manner when confronted with people he didn't know intimately (but which didn't prevent him from becoming a board member of the multinational Danone and an ambassador for Florentino Pérez's Real Madrid after his retirement). Coming from another man, the throwaway nature of his remarks, some examples of which are given below, would have been interpreted as indifference bordering on silent hostility. But Zizou's smiling inscrutability, be it studied or not, protected him from accusations of that kind. Rather than prejudge intent on one side or the other, it was simpler and far more fruitful to – simply – watch and try to comprehend what happened on the field, the one place where it is impossible to hide; for whoever tries to do so is instantly, mercilessly found out.

Spain had changed Zidane, for one thing. Prior to his transfer to Real Madrid from Juve for a record €77 million in July 2001, he used his prodigious skills to accelerate the game in the opposition's half, often opting for first-touch passes, striving for simplicity and efficiency in the transmission of the ball through compact and generally well-drilled defensive blocks. La Liga, with its more languid tempo and its emphasis on possession, coupled with the reluctance of lesser teams, of which there were not a few, to press high up the pitch, encouraged the virtuoso to retain the ball for seconds at a time (an eternity in football) and to work narrow spaces in such a way that he could exploit the full range of his individual technique to the benefit of his team. This he could do – and to great effect – better, and more ravishingly, than any of his contemporaries. The 'artist' Zidane was truly born at the Bernabéu, not at the Stadio delle Alpi; there, in Madrid, surrounded by the likes of Ronaldo, Roberto Carlos and Luís Figo, he could give free rein to his gorgeous mastery of the ball without diminishing his impact on the game itself.

But Real Madrid was not France, and neither was Arsenal; but whilst Henry was repeatedly asked to cut his cloth to the fashion of *Les Bleus*, no one dared suggest that Zidane should meet him half-way in that respect – unless they were part of Thierry's entourage, in which case their opinion was, of course, tainted by their favourite's supposed desire to become the fulcrum of the national side. Arsène Wenger told me on several occasions how frustrated he was that France – which he cares passionately about, more than he ever cared for any player – was missing a trick when it failed to recognize that the Thierry of the 'Invincibles' could become the focus of its tactical set-up. This was the view of an exceptional reader of the game; it was taken to be lip-service paid by a clever manager to a moody player who craved attention and praise. Henry couldn't win. 'I can make 35,000 runs, [but] if I don't get the ball, nothing happens,' he said. 'Compare the number of goals scored by Andrei Shevchenko with AC Milan and Ukraine, there's no relation between the two.'* Interestingly, even Thierry, who has got a better head for numbers than any footballer I've ever encountered, didn't realize that his proficiency in front of goal had not been affected by Zidane's increased deliberation – if that's the word – when nursing the precious ball. What he remembered were the countless occasions on which, having won it back in their own half, his French teammates had opted for a patient build-up, ignoring the calls of their striker who had been screaming down the touchline, anticipating a longer pass that almost never came. What made it all the more galling was that Sylvain Wiltord and Robert Pirès, who found him with such ease at Highbury, managed to do the same with France – but not Zidane, despite his protestation that 'it wasn't difficult to find Titi', a quote that had to be taken with a large pinch of salt, when the same man could also say, in June 2004: 'maybe Titi simply doesn't need me? . . . He brings the ball up from very far back, and he manages to do extraordinary things afterwards. In fact, he starts from so far back that it's easier to work in one-twos with him than to provide him with an assist.' *Maybe Titi simply doesn't need me?* Could I be the only one to detect a cruel put-down in these words? Ironically, in a friendly against Ukraine which took place a few days later in Saint-Denis, it was Henry who nodded the ball back for Zidane to score France's late winning goal. Titi could provide for Zizou, even if the opposite wasn't true. 'Titi and Zizou' would never be a double act like Lock and Laker, Bebeto and Romario, and, well, Bergkamp and Henry. Germany 2006, would be the last opportunity both of them had to prove the world it was wrong; and, against Brazil, Zizou, at long last, delivered the ball that Titi had been waiting for for so long. It was too late, however, to alter the Henry paradox.

---

* Henry was wrong. Whilst at Milan, 'Sheva' scored 173 goals in 296 games (strike ratio: 0.58); during the same period (1999–2006), his goalscoring record for Ukraine was 27 in 46 (strike ratio: 0.59).

10

It can't get any worse, can it? Oh yes it can.
(France–Senegal, 0-1, 2002 World Cup.)

THE HENRY PARADOX II

I was tempted to choose 'The Road to Perfection' as the title to this overview of Thierry's most successful years at Arsenal, which also marked the high-water mark of Wenger's tenure at the club. But 'perfection' would have been misleading, as what I had in mind was not so much the football on display at Highbury and the trophies it brought to the club as the bond that was created between a team whose heartbeat was in sync with Henry's and fans who embraced it with a sense of hope and a joy of which I have not witnessed an equivalent in the quarter of a century I have spent in England. This is not to say that other English sides didn't reach similar heights in that time – in terms of plain achievement, Manchester United and Chelsea did better, whilst Liverpool added to their myth at Istanbul as only Liverpool could – or that the faith Arsenal supporters had in their club was, somehow, stronger or 'better' than that of others – that would be insulting as well as incorrect. But those were truly special years, three seasons in which a team that had, perhaps, overachieved in 2001–2 in adding a third Double to those of 1970–1 and 1997–8, evolved into the majestic title-winning side of 2003–4, the only side to complete a thirty-eight-game League campaign unbeaten in the history of Europe's major championships until Antonio Conte's Juventus emulated that feat in 2011–12.*

---

* Of the other 'Invincible' sides, Milan only played thirty-four games in their 1991–2 unbeaten season, as did Ajax in 1994–5; Perugia, who finished second in Serie A in 1978–9, thirty; Benfica (in 1972–3 and 1977–8), Porto (2010–11) and Besiktas (1991–2), thirty as well. Galatasaray, runners-up in the 1985–6, clocked up twenty wins and sixteen draws in the 1985–6 Turkish championship, but failed to win the title.

Three years is often given as the maximum lifespan of a great team, the third of these years having even been deemed 'fatal' by the Hungarian manager Bela Guttman, for whom the word 'peripatetic' could have been invented. Some would undoubtedly question whether the Arsenal of 2001–4 would warrant the epithet 'great', when it surrendered an eight-point lead over Manchester United in the 2002–3 season and failed to transfer its imperious domestic form into Europe when a first Champions League title was well within its reach a year later. But I defend the right to use 'great' nevertheless. If evidence can't be brought out on which to rest such an imponderable qualification, examples can be given to add substance to what is essentially an emotional judgement, informed by moral and aesthetic considerations as much as by figures and statistics. I'll give such an example later, which, though a defeat, was also a manner of apotheosis, the memory of which is preternaturally clear in my mind: the 2-1 reverse against Chelsea in the return leg of the quarter-finals of the 2003–4 Champions League. It may seem an odd choice; but I can't think of a better illustration of how Arsenal, masterful at times, delighted in delighting their audience to such a degree that failure was always a risk they thought was worth taking.

Those three years were a build-up to nights such as these, in which flesh was added to Wenger's ideal of an Arsenal built not as a 'dream team', a collection of stars, but as a dream of a team, playing what could be rightly called 'fantasy football'. The squad that started the 2001–2 season was not markedly different from that which beat Leicester City 2-1 on 15 May 2004 – Henry scoring the equalizing goal, Vieira adding a victorious full stop to the story of the 'Invincibles'. The most telling addition to the playing staff had been made in the summer of 2001, when David Dein and Arsène Wenger had convinced free agent Sol Campbell to cross the line which divides North London football. Kolo Touré, who soon became a regular starter, joined in February 2002; Gilberto Silva, who had just had a superb tournament with World Cup winners Brazil, followed suit in August of the same year. Finally, Jens Lehmann came in to replace David Seaman in July 2003. Four major signings (not that Touré's arrival from the Ivory Coast was considered as such at the time) in the space of three seasons can hardly be described as an upheaval. Compare this turnover with that of Manchester United in the same period, when Ruud van Nistelrooy, Juan Sebastián Verón, Laurent Blanc, Diego Forlan, Rio Ferdinand, Tim Howard, Louis Saha and Cristiano Ronaldo were recruited by Alex Ferguson. Arsenal's re-invention was the fruit of an evolutionary process – not far from a managerial masterpiece. Its gradual nature can be highlighted by the individual cases of four English players who, while still playing a sig-nificant role in the successes of these three seasons, each of which brought at least one trophy, found themselves gently pushed towards the sidelines without creating the dressing-room unrest that might have been feared. David Seaman was first put in direct competition with newcomer Richard Wright and understudy Stuart Taylor, starting a mere seventeen League games in 2001–2, taking advantage of Wright's failure to impose him-self to enjoy a comeback of sorts the season after that, only to make way for Jens Lehmann in the summer of 2003. Tony Adams, hampered by back problems, only made ten appearances – just enough to obtain his champion's medal – in 2001–2 before retiring and passing on the captaincy to Patrick Vieira. Martin Keown, still the fourth-most-used defender in Wenger's second Double team, saw fringe players Pascal Cygan and Gaël Clichy feature in a greater number of League games in the 2003–4 unbeaten side. Lastly, Ray Parlour, at thirty-one in March 2004 the youngest of this quartet, was a starter in fewer than half the Premiership games of that team.

The smoothness of this transition owed a great deal to the tact and the clear-mindedness of its main strategist; but Wenger couldn't have implemented his three-year-plan without the consistent excellence of a handful of key players, with Sol Campbell – whose contribution I don't think has been recognized as it should have been – Patrick Vieira and Henry maintaining a level of performance throughout that was utterly admirable. Others shone, but more intermittently. Robert Pirès, fighting back from a cruciate ligament injury suffered in March 2002, had a splendid 2003–4 season, providing fourteen goals and ten assists in the League alone, but never quite recaptured the form that saw him voted Footballer of the Year in 2002. Freddie Ljungberg, whilst still effective, faded somewhat after crowning a terrific 2001–2 campaign by scoring Arsenal's first goal in their 2-0 victory over Chelsea in that year's FA

Cup final. Dennis Bergkamp, to whom genius was a regular visitor,* partnered Henry up front less often than the willing, more direct, occasionally decisive but one-dimensional Sylvain Wiltord, who accrued seventy-three League starts to the Dutchman's sixty-six in those three seasons. The main thread remained Thierry's continued presence and threat at the forefront of Arsenal's attack, which, in the modern game, can only be compared to the freakish success enjoyed by Cristiano Ronaldo at Real Madrid and Lionel Messi at Barcelona; and this in an Arsenal side that could not call on resources, financial or otherwise, on a par with the two Spanish clubs.

The numbers are scarcely believable. Between August 2001 and May 2004, Henry, who had also taken part in a World Cup and a Confederations Cup, only missed seven out of 114 League games for his club, clocking up more appearances than any other of Wenger's players, goalkeepers included. In Europe, where Arsenal, despite a puzzling inability to fulfil their potential away from Highbury early on, still went past the first group stage of the tournament three times out of three, Thierry failed to feature in only one of the thirty-four matches in which his team was involved.[†] The goals flowed – seventy-eight in 107 Premier League encounters, nineteen in thirty-three in the Champions League – most of them spectacular, such as his solo effort against Spurs on 16 November 2002 (which BBC viewers made

---

* 'The' goal scored against Newcastle on 3 March 2002 immediately springs to mind. But a better reminder of what the Dutchman – and no one else – could do on a football pitch would be the 'blind' pass he gave Henry with the outside of his right boot to open the scoring in their 2-0 victory over Celta Vigo on 10 March 2004. Seemingly closed down by two Galician defenders, Bergkamp stopped time until the perfect moment came to roll the ball in the Frenchman's path. No wonder Thierry could say: 'I've never seen a player like Dennis Bergkamp. I moved right, a caviar, I moved left, a caviar. I was squeezed by two defenders, another caviar. Moving deep – another one.' Caviar, in French footballese, is used to describe a pass from which missing the target would be unforgivable. Henry didn't waste many of these.

† A 1-3 defeat at Schalke on 30 October 2001, in which Wenger used a shadow side, Arsenal having already secured qualification to the second group phase of the competition.

their Goal of the Season, the only time Thierry won that award), which he celebrated by sliding on his knees in front of the travelling supporters and striking the pose which sculptors Margot Roulleau-Gallais and Ian Lander cast in bronze for the statue that was unveiled at the Emirates in front of a tearful Henry on 9 December 2011. It was yet another of these bursts of speed, punctuated by ten touches of the ball, the eleventh, with his left foot, sending it past Casey Keller's reach. This goal, and not a few others, have led some to misuse the word 'effortless' when describing Henry's unique gift – the dream of every schoolyard footballer – to beat *everyone* and score. As he has said himself, 'Everything that looks instinctive in a player's game has been worked upon. If, beyond the gift, I were stripped of all I've worked upon in my career, I'd be the little boy from Les Ulis again.' That little boy had grown up in many different ways. Surrounded by teammates he recognized as his equals and, in the case of Dennis Bergkamp, his superior in terms of football intellect, he flourished as a creator of chances as well as the man most likely to transform them into goals. In 2002–3 alone, a season at the end of which, in the eyes of many, he deserved the *Ballon d'Or* he craved and never got,* he provided twenty-three assists in the League, a feat that he told me on several occasions had given him as much pride and pleasure, if not more, than a number of his individual efforts. 'Without the *vista* of the last passer of the ball, the goalscorer is nothing,' he said, 'and I am not one of those players who suffer when they haven't scored in a game.'† More posing from the humble-arrogant Henry? Patrick Vieira

---

*   He finished second, sixty-two points behind winner Pavel Nedvěd, the highest position he attained in the classification of the *France Football* award in his career. In other years, he finished third once (2006), fourth twice (2000, 2004), fifth in 2005, sixth in 2002 and ninth in 2001. No other player has featured as regularly or accrued as many votes as Henry did in the first decade of the twenty-first century.

†   This is one of the reasons why Thierry often celebrated an assist with greater effusion than a goal. An example of this would be his complete absence of reaction when he headed home a pinpoint cross from Bixente Lizarazu in a 3-0 defeat of Germany on 15 November 2003, whereas he celebrated with abandon David Trezeguet's goal in the same game, of which he had been the main creator.

didn't think so: he characterized him as 'a very unselfish player, a reserved guy who can be charming and engaging nonetheless'.

As I've said before, going through every season of Henry's with Arsenal with a fine-tooth comb was an easy temptation to resist: a litany of goals doesn't make for pleasant reading (or writing, for that matter). Henry's oeuvre is, in any case, only a click away for everyone, and it makes more sense, once salient facts had been given their due place in this narrative, to concentrate on those events that reveal enough of the man and the player to avoid the pitfalls of mere enumeration. I have made an exception in the case of the 2002–3 season, however, precisely because it demonstrated better than any previous or subsequent campaign how Thierry had now reached a level of consistency and excellence which he could maintain regardless of the dips in form that affected his team as a whole. It was perhaps the year in which he reached his absolute peak as an individual player, whereas, for the Gunners, it represented something of a stutter, bookended as it was by the Double of 2002 and the remarkable run of forty-nine League games without defeat that was ended in contentious circumstances by Manchester United on 24 October 2004.

The notion of a 'power shift' from Manchester to London had gained credence throughout the summer and the early autumn of 2002, until Everton's Wayne Rooney scored a wondergoal at Goodison Park in mid-October, provoking a mini-collapse during which Arsenal lost four consecutive games by an identical scoreline (1-2). As Manchester United built up a head of steam, picking up thirty-six points out of forty-two between 28 December 2002 and April 2003, the prospect of the Gunners winning back-to-back League titles for the first time since 1934–5 dimmed, to dissipate for good late in the spring. If it was a genuine disappointment, and another indication of the fact that Arsenal's most significant weakness was not an in-built frailty, but a temptation to yield to complacency, there were also many moments of brilliance to celebrate – including in Europe, where Thierry, having already hit a brace in a 4-0 win at PSV Eindhoven in late September 2002, launched his team's second group phase with a fine hat-trick at the Stadio Olimpico two months later. Arsenal's 3-1 win over AS Roma was the English club's first victory on Italian soil for twenty-two years, Henry's treble his first in the Champions League. This unexpected success should have provided the momentum for a push towards the quarter-finals, but two dull draws against Ajax proved costly, and, as in 2001, Valencia's Norwegian striker John Carew provided the fatal blow, beating Stuart Taylor twice at La Mestalla, where Henry's equalizer only sharpened the sense of frustration of players, fans and manager alike. Yet, again, there was much to celebrate, starting with both Dennis Bergkamp and Thierry passing an increasingly rare landmark in modern football, that of a century of goals for a single club.

Henry, who had felt a twinge in a hamstring during a 3-2 win over Chelsea on New Year's Day, 2003, was rested for Arsenal's next outing, a routine 2-0 victory over Oxford United in the third round of the FA Cup. Thierry, enjoying a rare five-day break in the Alps, was filling his lungs with the mountain air when Bergkamp scored his hundredth goal in all competitions for the Gunners, a figure the Frenchman reached a few days later, on 12 January, when it was the turn of Christophe Dugarry's Birmingham City to face an Arsenal team in full cry. The Blues took a pounding: 0-4 at home, with Henry's name appearing twice on the scoresheet. Only one French player had scored a century of goals in a foreign league before, and Thierry now found himself within four units of Michel Platini's record 104 at Juventus. He knew this – of course he did – but barely celebrated this new milestone. 'The nature of the goal explains why,' he told *L'Équipe*. 'Robert [Pirès] did something extraordinary on the left wing, Sylvain [Wiltord] had the presence of mind to pass the ball to me. It was another team goal – the symbol of Arsenal. That's something I never forget. I'm surrounded by players who are there to make me shine. So, if I shine, it's thanks to them. It sums up Arsenal.'

An aside: it was hard not to see in the praise he gave to his teammates a barb directed at the management of the national team, and at what was a not necessarily innocent reluctance to exploit his qualities as they ought to be: Zidane was France's playmaker in more than one sense. I've already spoken at length about the peculiar dynamics of the relationship between the two players, and the two men. I'll just add at this point that it couldn't be a mere coincidence that the one international tournament in which Henry was at his most effective with the national team, scoring four goals in five games, winning both the Golden Boot and the Golden Ball awards, was the FIFA Confederations Cup held in France between 18 and 29 June 2003. Jacques Santini, who had taken over from Roger Lemerre after the disaster of the 2002 World Cup, had chosen to rest Zidane for this tournament and selected a young squad of which Henry was the de facto leader, even if someone else – Marcel Desailly – wore the armband. In a tournament overshadowed by the death of Marc-Vivien Foé, the Cameroon midfielder, who suffered a fatal cardiac arrest at the seventy-second minute of the Indomitable Lions's semi-final against Colombia, Thierry showed all of the qualities that made him such an exceptional performer with Arsenal and, sup- posedly, a lesser avatar of himself with France. Well, not on that occasion. With two other Gunners, Sylvain Wiltord and Robert Pirès, enjoying fine tournaments as well and supplying him with the first-class service he fed on at Highbury, Thierry blossomed in the blue jersey and was fully embraced by the French public, if only for two weeks, if only in the least prestigious of all official international competitions. As he told a journalist from *L'Humanité* shortly after scoring the winning 'golden goal' in a final that neither France nor Cameroon believed should have taken place after Marc-Vivien Foé's tragic death, 'who hasn't fan- tasized, playing in his parents' garden, of being acclaimed by a crowd?' At Saint-Étienne, as he warmed up before a group game against Japan (which France won 2-1), that crowd sang his name; a crowd that, in Lens, five years earlier, had booed him – and asked for local boy Tony Vairelles to take his place on the field – when he had headed the ball against a post in France's round-of-sixteen game versus Paraguay. But that honeymoon was brief and only lasted as long as the absence of the true king, Zinedine Zidane, had enabled Henry to become the undis- puted focal *patron* of *Les Bleus*. ZZ not only conducted the flow of play on the field, he also dictated its shape, its mood, its organization. With Zidane back in the conductor's chair, Henry resumed a role that he was convinced did not suit his qualities: that of an all-out striker. 'I am not a goalscorer, as I have always said. Goalscorers are guys like [Jean-Pierre] Papin and [Bernard] Lacombe yesterday, and David [Trezeguet] today. I don't think only about scoring. I think about scoring – that's the difference. A true goalscorer only thinks about it, even when his team is losing.' But let's go back to Arsenal and their new centurion.

The 'deep [personal] satisfaction' he had felt at hitting the hundred-goal mark couldn't match the joy of simply being there – an Arsenal player, an Arsenal man.

'Everyone knows it: I cannot forget that, when I left Juve, a number of people were asking themselves questions about me – rightly, by the way. That's why I will never be able to forget what's happened with Arsenal and Arsène. He had no guarantee that his gamble [on me] would pay off. I worked without saying a thing, I went back to play with the [French] under-21s for a year and a half after our World Cup title. When you remain humble, work, and can look at yourself in the mirror every morning, it has to pay off. There are people here who offered their hand and trusted me. The least I can do is score goals and be of use to them. Here – I have a contract with my own heart.'

And this heart had changed. Then, in early 2003, all the players I had a chance to chat with at the London Colney training centre would comment on Henry's growing maturity, which could sometimes translate into a certain hardness towards outsiders, even if courtesy never deserted him. 'Now, when somebody bores me, I tell him,' he said. Vieira, who used to 'room' with Thierry at Arsenal, concurred: 'Like Manu [Petit], when he likes you, he [Henry] really likes you – for him, it's all or nothing when it comes to relationships with people.' At the age of twenty-five, Thierry had found stability in his private life – Claire Merry had moved into his Hampstead house* – kicked into a different orbit many of the human satellites who had been gravitating around him since his move to Monaco, for their benefit rather than his, dis-

---

* The couple were married on 5 July 2003 at Highclere Castle, Berkshire. Darren Dein served as Henry's best man at a private ceremony in which the football world was represented by Arsène Wenger, Emmanuel Petit, Ashley Cole and Patrick Vieira. 'I didn't want photographs in the press, nothing to do with the [celebrity] magazines,' Thierry explained. 'I don't know who could be interested by that. The only thing I want people to remember of me is what I show on the pitch, not my haircut or my dress style.'

tanced himself from his father and gained a confidence in his own powers which could, at times, be confused with arrogance if you were minded to perceive it that way. It could sound as if Thierry Henry owned Arsenal as much as Arsenal owned Thierry Henry. When he said: 'When I came here, what I wanted more than anything else was not to disappoint Arsène – his credibility was at stake,' wasn't he belittling the achievements of a manager who had won the Double in his first full season in England, and without Henry's help?

That would be far too harsh a judgement. The extent to which the Highbury crowd had embraced Thierry moved him to a degree that made him, or so we're told, a rarity among contemporary footballers: a genuine supporter of the institution which, week after week, swelled his bank account with tens of thousands of pounds, as sincere and as committed as the North Bank season-ticket holders who wouldn't have dreamt of earning that much in a year. The way he expressed his attachment to 'his' fans and 'his' club, awkward, jarring as it was (and would always remain), *trying too hard*, in other words, was not indicative of duplicity in his character, or a cynical means to court popularity. We all love being loved. The truth is that Henry (who, in February 2001, could still say: 'I'm not English. I'm here for my job, not for fun') had fallen in love with Arsenal by then – and what he could express best by scoring goals, or chasing defenders when he had lost the ball, he was unable to verbalize as well as he, or rather we, might have hoped. The words we confide to the person we love lose their ring when someone else overhears them, unless we're blessed with a gift for poetry or music. Thierry was blessed with a gift for football, and made it sing. What else should matter?

That sharp, tender shock was as unexpected to him as it was welcome. Professional footballers are expected to 'kiss the badge' not just when they score, but when they speak, too. It is asked of them precisely because the surrender to a sentimentalized tradition of 'belonging' has become an irrelevance to most of them. Why should they be blamed for that? Hypocrisy is bred by those who hanker for a golden neverland of proletarian heroes making a beeline from t'pit to t'pitch. In truth, now as ever, the furthering of a footballer's career depends on severing ties as much as forging them. A 'modern' phenomenon? I'm not so sure.

One-club men were often denied the chance of being anything else by their chairmen. For every Tom Finney, there are a dozen Billy Merediths. And the 'Preston Plumber' would have moved to Palermo in 1952 if it hadn't been for his masters demanding a ludicrously inflated fee from the Sicilian club. Thierry is not alone among those foreigners who came to England and found their true home there. Éric Cantona did at Manchester United, and so did Patrice Évra, another child of Les Ulis, who once told me how he had 'learnt' about his club, and had grown to see himself as part of a story that was bigger than he could ever be. Gianfranco Zola did likewise at Chelsea. Patrick Vieira, Robert Pirès and Dennis Bergkamp all fell under the spell of Highbury. In truth, a remarkable number of so-called 'imports' found themselves swept away by the fervour emanating from the stands. Thierry was, perhaps more than anyone else, to an extent that thrilled him and should thrill us too.

Around that time, in the winter of 2002–3, I had a chance to talk to Wenger about the criticisms that were now levelled at his recruitment policy – how he was stifling English talent, how, in the name of sound management, he was sacrificing the 'spirit of the game' by shopping for cut-price talents abroad. The emergence of Ashley Cole, thanks to an injury to the Brazilian left-back Sylvinho, of which the young Englishman took full advantage, was a one-off, a happy accident, not a harbinger of things to come. Wenger was acutely aware of this and, for a while, as we have seen, attempted to 're-anglicize' the club: Sol Campbell, Richard Wright and Francis Jeffers were all bought in the summer of 2001, 'so that English would remain the first – and only – language spoken in the dressing-room' (his very words to me). With the glowing exception of Campbell, these transfers had proved failures, and Wenger was no longer willing to pay inflated transfer fees for English players. He had also become convinced, passionately so, that Arsenal was, in its own patrician, archaist-modernist way (this oxymoron had defined Arsenal ever since Herbert Chapman was called in by Sir Henry Norris in 1925), an entity that transcended nationalities. 'Is Patrick Vieira English?' Wenger told me, in that rhetorical fashion he's fond of. 'Of course not. Is he Arsenal? Of course, yes.' The fans, 'the most implacable of judges', knew best: they cared as little for passports as their manager did. No Englishman could love Arsenal as much as Thierry did, or so Thierry had come to believe.

On 8 March 2003, with nine games to go in the League, Arsenal looked well set to hold on to their title. Manchester United remained five points adrift, Chelsea and Newcastle were struggling to remain in their slipstream, whereas Liverpool had all but imploded during the winter and the early spring. But, as Thierry then remarked with his customary precision, 'on 2 November Liverpool were seven points ahead of us; today, they're fourteen points behind. This can happen to anyone. Nothing should ever be taken for granted in the championship of England. Ever.' He had remained in majestic form throughout, scoring a so-called 'royal hat-trick' against West Ham in Arsenal's 3-1 win in January: left foot, right foot and – that rarity in his repertoire – a header, the first of his career on the Highbury pitch. Had it not been for a fine display by opposing 'keeper David James, Thierry could well have challenged Ted Drake's English record of seven goals in a single top-flight match, scored for the Arsenal at Villa Park on 14 December 1935. It was to be a constant in Arsenal's oddly frustrating campaign; time and again, they created chances, were offered opportunities to annihilate whichever challenge was thrown at them, only to spurn them, inexplicably. The storyline didn't change much until the end of the season. Arsène Wenger had plenty to ponder: it seemed that his team sometimes took the first line of Freddie Ljungberg's song ('You're just too good to be true') too literally for their own sake. An unprecedented 'double Double'* had been in sight until the thirty-first game of the campaign, when Villa held Arsenal to a 1-1 draw on 7 April, which enabled a revved-up Manchester United to join them at the top of the table. Two other draws within the following three weeks altered the dynamics for good. In each case, the Gunners had held the advantage before throwing it away. First, United took a point from the Gunners at Highbury after Thierry had beaten Fabien Barthez twice to give them a 2-1 lead which

---

* I.e. two consecutive League/FA Cup Doubles. Liverpool had been one win away from achieving it before Wimbledon beat them 1-0 in the 1988 FA Cup final.

lasted but a single minute. Ten days later, an identical 2-2 scoreline at Bolton, when the Gunners had been two goals to the good until the last quarter of an hour of the match, gave Ferguson's team a lead they did not relinquish. The pendulum had swung. The fatigue, mental as well as physical, of Wenger's players, who had been chasing three trophies for the greater part of the season, had played its part, as had the strength of their main rivals' resolve. But Thierry was perhaps closer to the truth when he said that the Double of 2001–2 couldn't be taken as 'a point of reference' and that the consistency they had achieved then, scoring in every single game, going a whole season unbeaten away from High-bury in the League, winning at St James' Park, Anfield and Old Trafford – where Sylvain Wiltord memorably secured the title – without conceding a goal, was 'something that could [only] happen exceedingly rarely'. He couldn't have guessed that what followed, the year in which he became one of the 'Invincibles', was even more remarkable.

It must seem odd to choose a defeat as the game that perhaps showed best why that 'Invincible' Arsenal deserved to be called 'great' in its time and beyond, and not just just because of the magnitude of the feat it achieved; but that is precisely what the return leg of their UEFA Cham-pions League quarter-final against Chelsea was to the 35,846 spectators who were at Highbury on the evening of Tuesday, 6 April 2004, if only for forty-five minutes; or rather forty-six, as José-Antonio Reyes scored as the first half was entering its first and only minute of added time, slotting the ball between Marco Ambrosio's legs after a Thierry Henry shot had been blocked close to the goal-line. But what forty-six minutes they were: breathless, furious, intoxicating. As referee Markus Merk hit the 'pause' button, the correspondent of an Italian newspaper was heard to say something on the lines of 'This is not football,' shaking his head at the outrage he had witnessed; but his smile gave him away. He had loved it, just like everybody else. What we had seen was the glorious proof that it was possible to combine the frenzied rhythms of English football with sweeter continental harmonies (there were only seven British players among the twenty-two starters) and produce a spectacle as thrilling as anything the game could offer. Chelsea, missing its 'rock', the suspended Marcel Desailly, had offered stubborn resistance and threatened on a couple of occasions; but it had been Arsenal's show, Arsenal who, for one half, had looked destined to sweep everything placed in front of them and a good bet to be crowned European champions at last, more than seventy years after Herbert Chapman had first dreamt about a competition that would pit him against the likes of his friend Hugo Meisl.

Over 120 European Cup and UEFA Champions League games have been played in London to this day – discounting the qualifying rounds – but only one tie has pitched one representative of the British capital against another, despite the regular presence of Arsenal and Chelsea in the latter stages of the competition in recent years; that was the one. Arsène Wenger later confessed he had dreaded being drawn against Claudio Ranieri's team and still feared the worst after Robert Pirès had given Arsenal a deserved 1-1 draw in the first leg. Superstitious, Wenger? Maybe. The London rivals had already met each other four times that season, Arsenal winning both League matches and an FA Cup quarter-final by two goals to one. What's more, Chelsea had failed to beat Arsenal in any of the seventeen games they had played against each other since November 1998, and every series must come to an end, of course; but the Gunners were flying high in the Premiership, leading Chelsea by four points at the top of the table, only eight matches away from achieving a feat that no one had thought could be achieved in the 'modern' English game: to emulate the Invincibles of Double-winning Preston North End and finish a League season unbeaten, but in a championship that comprised twenty clubs, not the twelve of 1888–9.

It is of course possible to play too fast. But is it possible to play too well? To be so good that, like a musician who is flying on a guitar neck, you get caught up in your own virtuosity and end up playing far too many notes, forgetting to strike the right chord? Watching Arsenal that evening, the answer to that question had to be a puzzled 'yes'. To start with, the constant pressure exerted by Chelsea's midfielders on whoever carried the ball for the Gunners seemed to disrupt the rhythm of their hosts. Arsenal's response was to increase the tempo when it seemed barely possible to do so. Passes whizzed across the turf, most of them hit first time by players caught in a *perpetuum mobile* of their own invention. As might be expected, some of their attempts went astray.

Shots missed Ambrosio's goal by yards, with Henry the worst of the culprits. What was remarkable, however, is that, shortly after the quarter-hour mark, Wenger's men found a way to breathe in this asphyxiating atmosphere. It was as if they had managed to slow down whilst maintaining the same blinding speed, a phenomenon which is not as paradoxical as it would seem: a batsman who has reached the 'zone' can sometimes treat a 90 mph delivery as if it were a gentle off-spinner and miraculously take the watching audience to that most precious of places with himself. In an astonishing passage of play, in the thirty-seventh minute, Arsenal created no fewer than three excellent chances. First, Henry had a shot blocked in the penalty area following terrific play by Robert Pirès on the left flank. A few seconds later, another of the French forward's strikes skidded inches from the post. Marco Ambrosio's goal-kick having gone straight to Arsenal, it was Reyes's turn to find Pirès in the box, no more than six yards away from the goal-line – but the Frenchman headed the ball into the side-netting. This is not to say that Chelsea had no opportunities of their own: in fact, immediately after these sixty seconds of beautiful madness, an unmarked Eiður Guðjohnsen should have scored. But his header from a pinpoint cross by Wayne Bridge, who didn't look a lesser left-back than Ashley Cole that night, was misdirected.

In a game as frantic and as open as this one, chances were bound to be thirteen to the dozen. Frank Lampard took pot-shots from outside the area, most of them close to or on target, and the audacious Damian Duff scorned perhaps the best opening of the half, missing Lehmann's right post by no more than a foot. But did Arsenal ever play a better forty-five – forty-six – minutes than on that night, in the greatest season in their history? It is doubtful. Vieira, ably supported by Edu, was at his most dominant in midfield. Reyes, who had scored a brace against the Blues in the FA Cup two months previously, fizzed on the left flank. Henry, suffering from back spasms and replaced by Dennis Bergkamp late in the game, and who was so harshly judged in the following morning's reports, was a constant danger in front of Ambrosio's goal, spreading the play quite gorgeously at times, until tiredness caught up with him and the rest of his teammates. It is true that the two legs of this quarter-final bookended a double-header against Manchester United which had sapped the resources of Wenger's team: a 1-1 draw in the League and a 0-1 defeat in the semi-finals of the FA Cup for which Henry – who had featured for France in a 0-0 against the Netherlands in between – and Reyes had been rested by their manager.

The criticism that was levelled at Henry, and the way in which this game was seen as a warning to Wenger's men, a reminder of their mortality, tell us more about the way football history is written in the twenty-first century than they do about what happened that night. The demands of modern communication, the first of which is to make sense of chaos as it happens, as if its witnesses were merely transcribing a truth that had already been written, are such that journalists can sometimes lose sight – literally – of what is happening before their own eyes, when these eyes are not riveted on a computer screen, a TV monitor or a barely discernible keyboard. Most of the copy that was sent at half-time from the exiguous Highbury press box was ripped and binned an hour later, once Wayne Bridge had secured Chelsea's passage to the semi-finals with a wonderfully constructed goal as the game seemed destined for extra-time. Roy Hodgson has said that football matches are not decided over ninety minutes, but in a handful of incidents which barely last more than a matter of seconds, when something akin to logic, or fate, can be superimposed on a mass of conflicting events. How to make sense of this whirlwind of a game presented a challenge that could not be properly addressed once Chelsea had survived Arsenal's waves of attacks, unless what had unfolded in the first half was considered inconsequential. In the end, it was all but forgotten. As Claudio Ranieri's side had won, displaying admirable courage and steadfastness throughout, reasons had to be found why that particular verdict had been reached. What was forgotten was the football that had been played at Highbury when that verdict still hung in the balance, and, indeed, the jury appeared to favour the Gunners, as if football didn't matter, and only the result did. It is not necessarily a romantic notion to hold the opinion that this view is essentially flawed.

It is possible that Arsenal overreached, stung by their poor recent results against Manchester United in domestic competitions, too eager to reach the semi-finals of the European Cup for the first time in the club's history. Their unusual status of favourites, not just for this tie, but for the competition as a whole (alongside Real Madrid and Milan, who also exited the tournament at the quarter-final stage), didn't sit too comfortably on their shoulders; for three-quarters of an hour, however, their sense of daring and the sharpness of their focus were such that the apprehension shared by many fans before kick-off disappeared. The Gunners were a blur of red and white, passes arrowing at blinding speed on a perfect surface, all of them aimed at a runner, punctuated by the ferocious tackling of the Chelsea midfield and defence. It was as if the magnificent machine created by Wenger was trying to find an extra gear that perhaps wasn't needed, if winning was the sole objective. The tempo was so high, in fact, that this half could be seen as an aberration. Following Arsenal's and Manchester United's repeated failures in Europe (barring the miracle of Barcelona 1999), the consensus was that, to succeed in the UEFA Champions League, English sides had to alter their DNA and adopt a more deliberate style. Not that evening. And in that regard, if the first half was indeed a magnificent aberration, the second could be seen as the vindication of a more purposeful, more 'continental' approach to the European game. Claudio Ranieri replaced Scott Parker with the much quicker Jesper Gronkjaer at half-time, a purely tactical substitution which proved decisive. The shrewdness of the Italian manager had altered the physiognomy of the game as a whole. With one change, and the subtle reorganization of his team that followed from it, he had reclaimed a kind of authorship on events, whereas Wenger, despite or more properly because of his side's brilliance, couldn't do so any more. His players had gone further than he had hoped or feared, so far that they couldn't turn back. Their manager had become a spectator. He had seen a supreme example of the type of football he wished to create, which could be described as simultaneous improvisation. Once fatigue had set in, Chelsea's resilience turned into domination. Ranieri had sought to restore some logic in the proceedings, and succeeded; Wenger could only watch, and feel powerless. Of the three substitutions he was allowed, he made only one – Bergkamp on for Henry, in the eighty-first minute – when it was clear that his team badly needed freshening with new legs. Lampard equalized when Lehmann could only parry a very rare strike from distance from Claude Makelele into the path of the Englishman; Bridge scored the goal that forced

Arsenal to reply twice in less than five minutes to avoid elimination – when for a while even one goal had looked unlikely. Perhaps our Italian journalist was ultimately right when he said 'That's not football.' He had been wrong for only forty-five minutes. Leaving Highbury, I knew I had been in the presence of greatness and felt cheated, much as Dutch fans must have after their blessed team lost the World Cup finals of 1974 and 1978.

Thierry never spoke of 2003–4 – the season in which he was voted Player of the Year by the PFA and Footballer of the Year by the FWA for the second time running and received another Premier League Golden Boot award* – as his best-ever year, despite scoring thirty-nine goals in fifty-one games for his club, compared with thirty-two in fifty-five in the previous season. Perhaps it had to do with his slightly lesser efficiency with France (which coincided with Zidane's return to the side) since a superb Confederations Cup, with a run of three goals in eight matches in the run-up to the 2004 European Championships. There was also the manner of Arsenal's exit of the Champions League, of which I've spoken at length, all the more bitter since Didier Deschamps' Monaco and José Mourinho's FC Porto would not have presented insurmountable obstacles for that Arsenal side. Manchester United had put paid to Wenger's hope of sending his team to a fourth consecutive FA Cup final at Cardiff's Millennium Stadium by winning 1-0 in the semi, a game in which Henry, coming off the bench in the fifty-seventh minute, had no discernible impact. Nevertheless – it was that year that Thierry produced two of his greatest performances for club or country, the first of which earned him an almost unheard-of ten out of ten from the *Gazzetta dello Sport.*

No one gave much of a chance to the Gunners when they came onto the San Siro pitch on 25 November 2003. Their record so far in the Champions League read: played four, won one (and that, a 1-0 victory against Dynamo Kyiv, thanks to a rare Ashley Cole goal scored two minutes from time), drawn one, lost two. Elimination wasn't a likely prospect, but a near-certainty. The first of these defeats, in

---

* This constituted a unique 'double double'.

Arsenal's opening game of the tournament, had been a 3-0 spanking by Inter at Highbury, that same Inter who could ensure qualification for the round of sixteen if they achieved a positive result in their own stadium. Instead of which Henry engineered the evisceration of the Italian side. He scored the visitors' first goal in the twenty-fifth minute, a composed side-footer from the edge of the box to conclude a harmonious one-touch build-up by Ashley Cole and Robert Pirès. Christian Vieri responded quickly, thanks to a deflected shot that looped over Lehmann's head. Thierry then turned provider, twisting and turning on the left flank, to send a cross towards Freddie Ljungberg, who, taking one touch to tee himself up, restored Arsenal's advantage – the Swede's third goal in a row for his club. But what everyone remembers, naturally, is Henry's second strike, straight from an Inter corner kick that Sol Campbell had hoofed in the general direction of – wherever. Thierry, still ten yards within his own half, let the clearance bounce, then drove the ball forward with exquisite timing, taking seven touches in nine seconds to bring the ball into Inter's box, slowing down for the briefest of moments (long enough for Arsenal supporters to risk apoplexy), then switching from right foot to left to slide his shot into Francesco Toldo's net, opening a narrow angle into a much wider space that only he could see. Javier Zanetti, a master of his craft, had shadowed him all the way, but had been utterly powerless to stop the Frenchman who, that night, truly played like the best footballer in the world. Arsenal added two late goals through Edu – another assist from Henry, from the right flank, this time – and Pirès to complete the rout.

Then there was that afternoon at Highbury, on 9 April 2004 – Good Friday – when Liverpool, lagging twenty-five points behind Premier League leaders Arsenal, threatened to transform what is remembered as one of the greatest seasons in Gunners history – one which saw them chosen as 'the team of the first twenty years of the Premier League' in 2012 – into one of chokers, eye candy that dissolved as soon as it was dipped into something stronger than lukewarm water. If Arsenal survived that acid test, it was entirely due to Thierry, who, incidentally, had not quite got over the back problem that had led to his substitution a few days earlier against Chelsea. Pushed out of the FA Cup and out of the Champions League within a single week, the Gunners – should they not take all three points – risked opening a door through which Chelsea or even Manchester United could sneak with seven games to play. In the fifth minute, Steven Gerrard headed a Harry Kewell corner across the goal for Sami Hyypia to hurl himself at the ball and put Gérard Houllier's team ahead. Pirès and Henry (who had already had a 'goal' ruled out for offside) combined for Arsenal's equalizer, which happened to be Thierry's 105th in the Premiership, a new record for his club. But when Owen, sent through on goal by Gerrard five minutes before the break, made it 2-1 from six yards for the visitors, a brief hush descended on Highbury. I remember it so clearly; as I remember the wave of noise that started rippling in the Clock End almost instantaneously and coursed through the rest of the stadium like a river breaking its banks. Players sometimes say that, through habit or strength of concentration, they develop an ability to cancel out the barrage of sound that descends from the stands. Thierry, as befits a showman, rarely sought to isolate the stage he performed on from the stalls – or the gods. 'I've never *felt* Highbury like this, before or since,' he told me six and a half years later, my italics but a crude approximation of the stress he put on that word. The Gunners drew level soon after the second half was under way: Henry found Ljungberg, who, first time, found Pirès, who, first time, found the net. Then, one minute later, came the goal that, more than any other of Thierry's, more than the volley against Manchester United in 2000, the scorching run against Spurs in 2003, the slalom at the Bernabéu in 2006, Real Madrid defenders falling to ground like so many skittles, or the backheel against Charlton in February 2004 (which Thierry once called 'the most elegant of my goals'), must lead all cynics, critics and doubters towards the nearest exit. Henry scored goals that, in terms of technique, were better examples of his mastery of the game; in terms of speed of thought and feet, demonstrated his alertness and explosiveness in more obvious fashion; in terms of sweetness of strike and perfection of timing, spoke more highly of the familiarity that, through natural gift and ceaseless work, he had developed with the ball. That goal had all of these hallmarks, it's true, but it was first and foremost an act of willpower, anger fuelling every twitch of the footballer's muscles. Hamann and Carragher ending up on their backsides as Thierry's run evaded them could have given that goal an almost comical quality, but it had none. I want to score, therefore I will score: the *cogito, ergo sum* of a supreme striker. When Tom Watt, speaking at the gala dinner which the FWA organized in Henry's honour in January 2011, mentioned that goal, which effectively gave Arsenal the title by rekindling a faith that had been shaken by previous results, Thierry's face showed barely any emotion. I may have mentioned this before, but make no apologies for mentioning it again: an hour or so later, when I met Henry by chance at the taxi rank by the back exit of the Savoy, we spoke about that goal. Thierry's face lit up. He knew, I knew, as all Arsenal fans who were there that afternoon knew: in the year of the 'Invincibles', he had showed us that invincibility was not just a matter of numbers and statistics, but something that could be conquered, and which he had.

11

The sound of silence.

FROM TEAM-MAN
TO ONE-MAN TEAM

Great things were expected of Arsenal in the 2004–5 season, and with good reason: the spine of the 'Invincibles' had been left untouched, despite a flood of departures from Highbury during the summer: twenty-two in total, a staggering number, even if most of those who left were youth and fringe players who had barely played any role in the previous campaign's triumph. The additions to the squad were modest; taken together, Manuel Almunia, Mathieu Flamini and Emmanuel Eboué (who joined in January) cost little over £1 million and seemed a long way away from challenging for a place in the first team. Not everyone was convinced that twenty-year-old Robin van Persie, then as well known for his rebellious character as he was for his undoubted talent, would 'cut it' in England – which might explain why Feyenoord agreed to let him go for a cut-price £2.75 million. What no one fully realized then was that, if Wenger's strongest eleven could still compete with any side in England, injuries and suspensions would have a far greater effect on its ability to do so than previously. The loss of Martin Keown (who had retired at the grand old age of thirty-eight), Kanu, Sylvain Wiltord, Ray Parlour and Giovanni van Bronckhorst, all of them players of great experience and, in the case of the two Englishmen, wardens of the most uncompromising traditions of the club, was bound to be felt at some stage in the season. But it could have been much worse – Patrick Vieira could have become a Real Madrid player; and such was the relief felt by Arsenal fans when this cloud vanished for good that the awkward questions raised by some about Wenger's unwillingness or incapacity to strengthen his squad were airbrushed out of public debate in no time.

On 10 August – two days after a young Arsenal team, bereft of their injured captain, had beaten Manchester United 3-1 in the Community Shield – David Dein had told Vieira that an agreement had been reached between both clubs, but that there was still time for him to change his mind. Torn between the prospect of playing alongside Luis Figo and Zinedine Zidane (who had encouraged him to come to Spain) and the desire to remain in a club and a city he loved, Vieira sought the advice of the two players he trusted the most: Dennis Bergkamp to start with, then, hours before he had to make his final decision, Thierry, who he knew would 'tell [him] what he really thought'. Henry knew nothing of Vieira's intentions, but, like everyone else, had seen the headlines and the back pages in the British press over the last month. The newly re-elected chairman of Real, Florentino Pérez, had used his tried and tested strategy of baiting his prospective catch with a public announcement, after which Arsenal's vehement denials that anything was afoot carried negligible weight. Vieira's self-imposed silence – with the media as well as with his own teammates – made for an uneasy atmosphere during the club's truncated pre-season training camp. Until then, not once had the Arsenal skipper opened up to Thierry; and when he did, a troubled night before he finally made his mind up, Henry showed great intelligence and tact in his response. Of course he wanted Patrick to stay: their club was on the way up, he felt, and would be diminished by the loss of their captain; but he wouldn't advise his friend one way or the other. Vieira had to look within himself to find the right answer.

Inter-season turmoil was nothing new to Arsenal fans or board members: the memory of Nicolas Anelka's departure to Real Madrid in the summer of 1999 was still fresh in everyone's mind. But the indecision around their captain's future, and even the manner in which a resolution was reached, pointed to a deeper malaise within the club, who had long sought a way out of its financial uncertainties – some of which derived from the success Arsène Wenger's stewardship had brought to an institution renowned for its cautiousness. The rewards brought by three Premier League titles, three FA Cups and year-after-year qualification for the Champions League were cancelled out by the inflation-busting rise of players' wages, which affected English football as a whole. Some leading clubs – Leeds being the most infamous example – borrowed recklessly, mortgaging future revenues to keep afloat; then sank. Chelsea had Roman Abramovitch. Others sought to increase revenue by developing their stadiums, as Manchester United did, by carrying out work on the North, East and West Stands of Old Trafford from June 1995 to January 2000, bringing the arena's capacity from an all-time low of 44,000 to over 68,000 in that space of time. Arsenal, shackled by the regulations that protected its listed Art Deco stands, at odds with neighbouring residents, local councillors and planning officers over what could and could not be done with the dear old stadium, faced the stark choice of either moving to Wembley – where they had regularly attracted over 70,000 spectators in the two seasons when they played their Champions League games there – or building a new stadium from scratch.

This is not the place to delve too deeply into the politicking that went on within the Arsenal board, and which ultimately resulted in David Dein being ousted in April 2007,* which doesn't mean it should be ignored, as those convulsions were bound to have an impact (and did) on the one player who linked, if imperfectly, two epochs in the club's history. To sum it up in – very – broad terms, once it had become clear that the redevelopment of Highbury was not a viable option, Dein championed the Wembley option, whereas shareholders such as Danny Fiszman (who had bought a significant portion of Dein's original stake) were in favour of moving the club to Ashburton Grove, a brownfield site located less than half a mile away from the club's historic home.

---

* Henry's decision to join Barcelona one month later must also be seen in the context of that departure. Dein Sr, an 'Arsenal man whose blood runs red and white', to quote Arsène Wenger, had always had a weak spot for 'flair', flamboyant players (Tony Woodcock, Anders Limpar, Ian Wright, to name three), leading him at times, in the words of a long-time friend, to 'turn a blind eye' to some of their less-admirable behaviour. He had taken Thierry under his wing as soon as he had arrived at Arsenal, doing his utmost to make the young Frenchman feel welcome at Highbury. That relationship was strengthened by Henry striking a close friendship with Dein's eldest son Darren (Thierry's best man at his wedding with Claire Merry), whose role went far beyond the remit of a legal adviser within Jerome Anderson's SEM agency, which represented the player. Darren Dein, assisted by Henry's solicitor Stuart Peters, took sole charge of Henry's affairs after the transfer to Barcelona was concluded on 22 June 2007.

Despite his very close personal relationship with Dein, whose Totteridge home was only a short walk away from his own residence at the time, Arsène Wenger supported that choice. One problem remained unsolved, however: Arsenal, who lagged well behind neighbours Tottenham when it came to exploiting the club's commercial potential, had nowhere near the funds required to embark on the move to what would become the Emirates Stadium. Back then – the planning permission to build the new ground got its final approval in December 2001, four years after the project had first been sanctioned by the board – Arsenal FC was not yet the model of self-sustainability which is now justly praised throughout the football world. The demise of ITV Digital in April 2002 (a company whose part-owner Granada had acquired a 5 per cent stake in the club in September 2000) highlighted the fragility of Arsenal's funding: they had committed £30 million to the project, which had to be found elsewhere.* The fact that, between 1996 and 2002, AFC's net spend on new players (£24 million) was less than half of what Spurs committed to transfers (£53 million), and a quarter of Manchester United's 'investment' (£99 million), could not be solely attributed to the well-known prudence of its directors. In 2001–2, the season of Wenger's second Double, the club had filed a pre-tax loss of £22.3 million at Companies House. By committing to building the new 60,000-seat arena, Arsenal and their manager knew full well that they were entering a period of increased austerity that would adversely affect their ability to recruit established players and, conversely, make it far more difficult to hold on to their best elements. It would be foolish to believe that Henry could be impervious to the convulsions that were shaking his club to the core. The shift in the club's recruitment policy meant a shift in his own position as well, figuratively but literally too, as we would see in Arsenal's 2005–6 Champions League campaign.

A few days away from his twenty-seventh birthday by the time he walked on the pitch of the Millennium Stadium in Cardiff on 8 August

---

* Construction work had to be delayed or interrupted on several occasions before it started for good in February 2004, pushing back the inauguration by one year, when it had been hoped that Arsenal would move into their new home before the start of the 2005–6 season.

2004, where a young, Vieira-less Arsenal side beat Manchester United 3-1 in the Community Shield, Thierry was entering what are supposed to be the peak years of a striker, with this proviso: many coaches prefer to have a look at the number of competitive games played than at the birth certificate when assessing a player's career parabola. He had already accrued 478 games for club and country – over 500 if his appearances for France's under-19s, under-20s and under-21s were taken into account. Many forwards do not reach such figures in a whole career. Regardless of his natural fitness and exemplary lifestyle, Thierry was bound to start feeling the strain of having played non-stop football for the best part of ten seasons, punctuated by all-too-rare holidays. In fact, France's exit at the quarter-finals stage of the 2004 European Championships had allowed him to enjoy some downtime at last.* Still, it was a tired Henry who started that season, still impaired by an injury suffered towards the end of the previous one, a Henry who considered himself 'at 70 per cent of his capacities'. 'I have the feeling I've only been playing one uninterrupted season since I turned pro,' he confided a few months later, still complaining about the nagging pain that prevented him from expressing himself fully. He had trained for a couple of days, not more, before playing the first forty-five minutes of the win over United in Cardiff, and only resumed what can hardly be called his 'preparations' after Arsenal's first League game of that campaign, a 4-1 win at Everton that seemed to indicate that the champions of England had lost none of the swagger of the twelve previous months; and, up until 24 October 2004, the date of their trip to Old Trafford, it looked as if they could even better the record of that golden period. With eight wins and a solitary draw in their first nine League matches, in which they had scored twenty-nine goals – most of them of the dazzling kind, such as Thierry's famous back-to-the goal backheel in a 4-0 demolition of

---

* He had answered NBA star Tony Parker's invitation to visit him in the USA, spending two weeks in the home of the San Antonio Spurs player, a stay during which the bond between two Frenchmen strengthened into an intimate friendship. The son of an expatriate American basketball player, Tony Parker Snr, and a Dutch mother, Tony Parker (Jnr) was born in Bruges, Belgium, but moved to the north of France when he was only a few weeks old.

Charlton on 2 October – Wenger's team found themselves at the top of the table again, with only Chelsea in close attendance, two points adrift (having played one game more), and Manchester United a further nine lengths away. Invincible they had been, invincible they looked – until Alex Ferguson's team put a brutal stop to their progress, the word 'brutal' not being chosen at random, as José Antonio Reyes, singled out for 'special treatment' from the outset, could certainly testify.

It is not necessary to spend too much time on the details of that infamous game in the context of this book. Whether it was Cesc Fàbregas or another player who hurled the slice of pizza that 'hit Fergie straight in the mush'* in the aftermath of Arsenal's 2-0 defeat, only those present in that dressing-room know for sure. What matters is that more than a game of football was lost – the impetus that had driven Arsenal forward for over a calendar year dissipated like mist rising from a battlefield. A series of three draws, one defeat (at Liverpool) and a single win (a crazy 5-4 victory at White Hart Lane) followed in the League. By 28 November, José Mourinho's Chelsea had launched a breakaway run that would lead to the Blues's first League title in a half-century. Wenger's men were five points adrift of the new leaders then, looking more likely to fall further behind than to close the gap. Thierry himself, still struggling to regain full fitness, performed as well as could be hoped for in testing circumstances, still scoring with his customary regularity until Boxing Day, 2004 – eight goals in nine League games, including a precious brace in a 2-2 draw with Chelsea, plus three in three Champions League matches – but the spring had gone from Arsenal's increasingly hesitant step. In the past three seasons, Henry had been the spearhead of a team gathering collective speed; he now looked too often like the last resort of a group of players that had become over-aware of its own limitations. More ground was lost in January and February, with Thierry suffering from a rare dip in form, going six games without scoring, the last of these being a sobering 2-4 defeat to Manchester United at Highbury which briefly pushed Arsenal down to third place, thirteen points behind Chelsea. As if to stress the growing dependency of the no-longer-invincibles on their most valuable player, no sooner had he found a

---

* To quote from Ashley Cole's autobiography.

second breath* than his team followed suit, enjoying a fine spring – at least in the League – which enabled them to secure second spot behind Chelsea, with a points total (eighty-three) that would have been enough to tie with champions United in 2002–3 and win the title outright in 1999–2000 and 2000–2001. Thierry himself, with twenty-five goals in the Premier League, despite missing six games through injury, had done enough to earn the English and European Golden Boot award for the second consecutive year.† A disaster it wasn't, far from it, not for a club that its board and manager knew was entering a phase of transition, both to a new economic reality and a new stadium, and even less for their star striker who, despite having signed a four-year contract extension with the Gunners in May 2003, was more coveted than ever by every leading European club, it seemed.

Seen from further away in time, however, that season had been less of another movement in Wenger's third Arsenal symphony than an unsatisfactory coda; or, if we're to draw another musical parallel, the last and least convincing recapitulation of a theme first exposed four years previously. Just as was the case with 2003–4, the memory that sticks most vividly in my mind of 2004–5 is that of a defeat, and in Europe as well; but whereas Chelsea's win at Highbury had highlighted the intrinsic beauty of Wenger's creation, the 1-3 reverse Arsenal suffered in Munich on 22 February 2005 showed we were not witnessing a short-term reverse, but a decline. The scoreline itself gave but a faint idea of Bayern's superiority on the night. In Sol Campbell's absence, and with Ashley Cole restricted to a place on the bench after he had failed to recover fully from a viral illness, the deficiencies in the visitors' defence, which had already been exposed in domestic competitions,‡ would have been exploited by lesser

---

* Henry, despite being sidelined with injury on two occasions, scored nine goals in the five games he played in the Premier League from 5 February to 2 April, including hat-tricks against Portsmouth (3-0, 5 March) and Norwich (4-1, 2 April).

† Thierry shared the second of these distinctions with Villareal's Diego Forlan. It was the first time in the history of this award that a player had been its recipient two years running.

‡ Arsenal conceded thirty-six goals in the 2004–5 Premier League season, ten more than in the previous season.

opponents than the German vice-champions, of which, by the by, there had been more powerful incarnations.

Outplayed in every department, bereft of imagination on the rare occasions they managed to venture out of their own half, Arsenal were lucky to have been offered a lifeline by a Kolo Touré goal scored with two minutes left on the clock of the Olympiastadion. There had been instances in the past when Arsenal had lost their footing on foreign soil, certainly; but those disappointments could be interpreted as irritating but necessary steps in their apprenticeship of an unfamiliar competition. This was different. There was nothing to learn from that occasion, unless it was that, judging from that night's experience, this group of players looked unable to compete at the requisite level. It is true that Arsenal's reaction in the return leg of the tie showed pride and bravery; Henry's sixty-sixth-minute goal, greeted by one of the most deafening roars I've ever heard at Highbury, even restored hope for a moment; one more goal without reply, and the Gunners would advance to the quarter-finals. It is also true that this unlikely qualification would have been achieved against the run of play, as well as against a patently superior opponent who had shown that the glorious team of 2001–4 had reached the end of its three-year cycle. Henry's continuing excellence couldn't hide that the process of renewal Wenger had to embark upon, for economic as well as for sporting reasons, must begin in the guise of a decline, and not just in terms of plain, measurable achievement. It is inconceivable that any Arsenal side of the previous nine years would have adopted the negative tactics which earned them – just – a 'victory' of sorts over Manchester United in the 2005 FA Cup final, and which Wenger promised himself never to adopt again. Patrick Vieira's successful strike in the penalty shoot-out, his last-ever touch for the club he had served for close to nine years, added a trophy to Arsenal's honours list but gave little joy to his manager. It had been a confession of weakness: the team that had become renowned for its flamboyant football throughout Europe could not or would not attempt to play it in the absence of its main striker. The age of 'Henry dependence' had started for good.

'I'm nothing without the team,' Thierry was fond of saying. But was his team anything without him? Little changed if statistics alone are taken into consideration. From August 2001 to May 2005, Henry had had a hand, so to speak, be it as a finisher or a provider, in 155 of the 324 goals scored by Arsenal in the Premier League, that is in 47 per cent of them. In the 2005–6 season, this proportion rose slightly, to reach 50 per cent (thirty-four goals out of sixty-eight), a ratio you wouldn't find anywhere else in English football during that period – not even Cristiano Ronaldo reached that mark in 2007–8, the year in which he was awarded the *Ballon d'Or*. But Thierry had done even better in 2003–4: 53 per cent of the goals scored by Arsenal in their unbeaten League campaign bore his imprint. Yes, 2005-6 saw a crucial shift in Henry's status and influence at Highbury, but it is a story that cannot be recounted in numbers, not those anyway. Other figures are more telling, which speak of an unsettled team, struggling to cope with the departure of not just their 'gladiator' Patrick Vieira, but also the elegant (and universally popular) Brazilian playmaker Edu, and the dimming of that glorious light called Dennis Bergkamp, who was deemed worthy of a mere eight League starts that year. Age was also catching up with Robert Pirès and the injury-prone Freddie Ljungberg, who scored a total of thirteen goals between them in all competitions in 2005–6 when they had added thirty-one to Arsenal's total in the previous season.

Only four outfield players made twenty-five starts or more in the Premier League: Sol Campbell, Gilberto Silva, teenager Cesc Fàbregas and Henry himself. In 2004–5, there had been seven; in 2003–4, no fewer than nine, including four defenders. Uncharacteristically for Wenger, who has always expressed doubts about altering his squad mid-season, January 2006 saw the arrival of four recruits: Carlos Vela, Abou Diaby, Theo Walcott and Emmanuel Adebayor,* following the acquisitions of Nicklas Bendtner, Vito Mannone, Armand Traore and Aleksandr Hleb in the previous summer. The dressing-room of which Thierry was now the undisputed leader was filled with newcomers, not all of whom – we'll make an exception for Bendtner – had the force of character to claim a space of their own. They were too young, too raw, too fragile for that. Several spoke only rudimentary English – or French. I remember a former Arsenal player telling me then about his fears about a 'personality vacuum' taking hold

---

* Estonian 'keeper Mart Poom would be added to that list if it hadn't been clear then that he was purely taken on as cover, on a temporary basis.

of that team; I didn't contradict him then and wouldn't now. Thierry's elevation to the captaincy seemed logical enough. Now Vieira had gone, and with Bergkamp likely to watch most of the football from the bench, Henry was the longest-serving player at the club, its unchallenged figurehead, the living embodiment of Wenger's ambition, the link that would keep the chain unbroken. But a leader of men – or of boys – he wasn't and didn't claim to be, preferring to be a 'captain by example', a 'technical leader', as Gérard Houllier called him when presenting him with the keys to the French under-20s. Not for him the rousing speeches at half-time, the dressing-downs, the 'arms round the shoulders' which, supposedly, are the hallmarks of the ideal captain, alongside excellence on the field and impeccable conduct off it. Two of this squad's younger players – who didn't wish to be identified – told me that the only times Thierry spoke to them either as individuals or as a group was on the pitch, in full view of spectators, as if captaincy was first and foremost something to enact in public. Neither dared to go to their elder and seek advice. 'Speaking to Thierry . . .' one of them said, 'no, no. He lived in his own world, and us in ours.'

The harsher critics of Henry would see in this another illustration of his self-serving duplicity: it was his image he was taking care of, not the youngsters he had been asked to guide.* I would argue that it said as much about the timorousness of these youngsters as it did the aloofness, *hauteur*, egotism, call it what you want, of the French, English, European and world champion who kept on banging in the goals that kept a dying/nascent Arsenal competing at home – with some difficulty – and abroad – beyond all expectations. And while every care was taken

---

* To counterbalance this view, I should stress that Henry could also show genuine interest in others, including scholars from the academy, such as Fabrice Muamba, who signed his first professional contract with Arsenal in 2005. Another case of 'damned if you do, damned if you don't': shortly after Muamba, who had become a Bolton player by then, suffered cardiac arrest at White Hart Lane on 17 March 2012, Thierry flew from New York to visit his convalescing former teammate at the London Chest Clinic. This was widely reported in the British press, Henry earning praise for his gesture – but also stinging criticism for having made sure everyone was aware he had done the 'right thing'. The facts? Thierry entered the hospital through a back door and left as discreetly as he could: it was Bolton Wanderers FC who alerted the media to his presence in London, not Henry's PR consultants.

by Wenger to provide his charges with a near-perfect environment in which to learn their craft, his finishing school could look like a crèche to outsiders, a far cry from the 'jungle' Thierry had grown up in. It is true that Henry's last two seasons in London looked at times as if they were a procession of personal milestones, and not much else. Highbury provided the backdrop, Wenger the extras. Who should be blamed for that? Was there indeed reason to blame anyone? The manager-crusader, hamstrung by financial constraints, but spurred on by a passionate faith in youth and what could be built on its virtues – hunger, eagerness to learn, lack of fear, even lack of respect – had to balance two needs that appeared contradictory: the radical transformation of Arsenal as a team and as a club and its upkeep as a competitive force in England and Europe. He had no alternative – yet it was his choice.

As the contrast between the individual achievements of the club's only global superstar and the travails of his team quickly grew, so did, inevitably, the perception that Henry was retiring ever higher to the peak of his own Mount Olympus, godlike and unapproachable. Chelsea beat Arsenal twice in the space of two weeks in August, first in the Community Shield, then in the League, in which the Gunners suffered a second defeat at Middlesbrough in early September – which Thierry had to sit out though injury. By 15 October, when West Brom beat the still Henry-less Gunners 2-1, Wenger's team now lay eighth in the table, fourteen points behind an all-conquering Chelsea team whose record read: played nine, won nine. The 'Invincibles' had moved from north to west London, it seemed, so swiftly, so inexorably. As if it were necessary to remind us of what had been lost in little over a calendar year, it is then, when all hope of challenging for the title had vanished, that Thierry broke the record he craved most. I have heard it said that he craved it so much, in fact, obsessed as he was by his desire to write himself into history, that it explained why he had refused to listen to offers coming from other clubs, as if this somehow devalued his decision to remain at Arsenal, and showed his loyalty in an unflattering light. Turning this argument over and over, I fail to understand how it stands to reason, unless pride in one's achievement is a capital sin, in which case I defy you to name me one player of Henry's magnitude who hasn't been guilty of it.

He wished it had happened at his own fiefdom, Highbury, not in a near-empty Letná Stadium, but it was in Prague, on 18 October 2005, that Henry finally went past Ian Wright's 185 goals in all competitions for Arsenal. 'He didn't even expect to be on the pitch,' beamed Wenger afterwards. Still troubled by the ankle problem that had kept him idle for thirty-eight days, Thierry had been forced onto the field by an injury sustained by José-Antonio Reyes as early as the fifteenth minute. Whatever discomfort he might have felt was undiscernable to the untrained eye. As Wenger had told me on a number of occasions, no other footballer was as aware of his own body as Henry, and none was as adept as he to know how far he could push it without risking further damage. As ever with Thierry, instinct and intelligence both informed the myriad decisions a footballer must take within ninety minutes; what made him stand out was that, as Wenger told me, 'faced with a multitude of choices, a truly great athlete like Thierry takes the correct decision almost every single time, within a timespan that is so brief that "thinking", as we understand it, cannot come into it'. 'He's thinking like a chess player,' Sol Campbell once said of his teammate, 'four, five, six moves ahead.' That night, Henry played 'with the handbrake on', as he owed it to his team and to himself; Arsenal, who had battled through two 2-1 victories over FC Thun and Ajax in Henry's absence, had a 100 per cent record to protect in the Champions League, and no one could step up from the bench, should their striker suffer a recurrence of his injury. He knew when to release the spring, however, and did so on two occasions; firstly, when, sprinting forward, he channelled a long Kolo Touré clearance into the stream of his run with an exquisite backheel, and, hitting the ball with the outside of his foot, imparted so such side-spin on it that the Sparta 'keeper must have thought that the shot would sail wide of his far post – instead of which the ball jagged like a Shane Warne leg-break to nestle in the corner of the net. His second goal of the night, if not as spectacular as the first, was as good a demonstration of the striker's art as any he had scored. Robert Pirès – fittingly – had spotted him racing into a huge gap left open by a distended Czech back-line, and fed him a sumptuous ball, which, running at full pelt, Henry controlled with his right boot, teed up in two quick shuffles of both feet, and hit past Jaromír Blažek, with the help of a deflection off Adam Petrouš. He instantly turned towards his teammates, calling them to join him by the right-hand corner flag to celebrate his 186th goal for the Arsenal. The new record-holder smiled like a child. 'I'm over the moon,' he said afterwards, and, for once, the cliché rang true. It had taken him 303 matches in little over six seasons to reach that mark, which gave him a ratio of 0.61 goals per game in all club competitions in that period. That would have been a remarkable ratio for any top centre-forward over the course of a single campaign; over such a long timespan, it was truly phenomenal. Which other striker had shown comparable consistency in the modern game until then? The three-time *Ballon d'Or* winner Marco van Basten, widely recognized as the supreme finisher of his age, ended his six years at Milan with 125 goals in 198 games – a ratio of 0.63, virtually identical to Henry's, if admittedly in a league boasting more accomplished defences. But, if numbers mean anything, and they do in sport, this is the kind of company Henry could claim to keep, he who so many are reluctant to count among the greats of the game. They will use statistics to give substance to their appraisal – Thierry's failure to score in cup finals, for example – but will choose to ignore others, which are far more numerous and certainly no less significant. Who is right and who is wrong I'm quite happy to let others decide, as my own views fluctuate, according to whether my judgement is about the player or about the man, towards whom my ambivalence should be clear by now to readers. And judgement means two very different things: evaluation and verdict. The former can be fair, the latter cannot be appealed against in the context of a book.

So? So let's go back to the pitch, a place where liars never fail to be instantly exposed. Arsenal were sparked back into life for a while by that victorious night in Prague, with a series of eight wins and one draw* which enabled them to ensure qualification for the last sixteen of the Champions League and, taking advantage of their rivals' inconsistency, climb back into the Premiership's top three by the end of November. But the revival was brief. A pitiful run of three defeats, to Bolton, Newcastle and Chelsea, saw them drop back to eighth, twenty points behind

---

* That solitary draw was a 1-1 at Tottenham, the only League or Champions League match Henry missed in that period, in which, still short of match fitness, he still scored six goals in six games, including a famous free-kick in the 3-2 victory at Wigan (Arsenal's first away win of that season): this was the occasion on which, having been asked by the referee to retake his shot, he sent his second attempt into John Filan's top corner. Cameras then caught him turning to the official to ask: 'Good enough?'

their latest victors. The rest of the domestic season would follow a similar pattern: brief moments of success, in which it was difficult to discern whether they were a memory of a recent past or the promise of things to come, alternating with increasingly predictable disappointments. Eleven defeats by the time fourth place was guaranteed, on the very last day of the League season, tell their own tale: you had to go back to the 1994–5 campaign to find an Arsenal side that conceded more. Thierry, meanwhile, kept claiming more club records: when Blackburn Rovers were beaten 3-0 on 26 November 2005, he became the first player in Arsenal's history to score 100 goals at Highbury; in fact, the first player in the Premier League's history to score a century of goals on his home ground. Having equalled Cliff Bastin's tally of 150 League goals by scoring a hat-trick in a 7-0 annihilation of Middlesbrough on 14 January 2006, he passed that mark on 1 February, deflecting a Robert Pirès shot into the net in a 2-3 loss at home to West Ham. Three days later, Henry, making the most of a luminous pass by Cesc Fàbregas, attained his double-century of Arsenal goals in all competitions at Birmingham, where the Gunners won 2-0. No matter how others performed around him, and how his body language betrayed increased exasperation with lesser mortals – the looks to the heavens, the 'teapot' posture, the chin bent downwards, a catalogue of attitudes that will be familiar to all Henry-watchers – Thierry carried on, the embodiment of success within a club that wasn't quite sure of what success really meant any more.*

---

* Thierry's equalizing goal six minutes from time at White Hart Lane on 22 April is another example of this. Cesc Fàbregas was lost for words. 'I don't know how he did it. He just fought for the ball . . . and scored.' Adebayor had won a fifty-fifty ball with Spurs' Canadian right-back Paul Stalteri, and nothing much seemed 'on' when the Togolese rolled the ball in the box. Henry, steaming in from the right, sent the ball ninety degrees away from his angle of running without breaking stride, an astonishing feat of skill which – of course – he made look ridiculously easy. This particular goal is seldom singled out when Henry's contribution to Arsenal's cause is discussed by their fans. The only reason for this must be that it didn't bring victory to the Gunners. But it not only preserved a proud record against Spurs in the League, it also prevented Arsenal's bitterest rival from snatching fourth place in the Premiership and, with two homes games to follow, from denying Arsène Wenger's men their now customary spot in the next Champions League draw.

Yes, it was an odd year, one that didn't quite make sense, whichever way you looked at it. Arsenal fans were already in mourning for Highbury: allow me to speak for all for a moment. It was as if, every time we walked to the ground, we had to read another chapter in the chronicle of a death foretold. It couldn't be, could it, that, in a matter of months this would be rubble? Never did those stands look more beautiful. So we suspended disbelief for another ninety minutes. Only the present matters, we told ourselves; but no, it doesn't; or, rather, what lies ahead is part of the present, which can be a bitter truth when you know that what lies ahead is oblivion, not amnesia. We took the same steps down Avenell Road, up the stairs, up to the seat we had believed was ours and ours alone – yes, including me, a journalist who always made his way to D42, East Stand. We visited the same pubs, ate pizza at the same Italian, met our friends by the clock on Highbury Hill, in the knowledge that, soon, all this would be gone for ever. *'Encore un moment, monsieur le bourreau.'* But the blade would fall, and we knew exactly when: on 7 May 2006, when Wigan were to be the last-ever guests in our home. The world, well, some of it, remembers that Thierry Henry, signing off the script with a flourish, scored a hat-trick that afternoon, kissing the turf when he buried – ha! – the third of his goals, a penalty, which seemed just perfection added on top of perfection: not only had Tottenham, half of its squad incapacitated by food poisoning, succumbed 1-2 at West Ham to grant Arsenal passage to another year in the Champions League; but Thierry had been given a spot to put his lips to to bid farewell, and what a sweet spot it was.

Henry stayed long after the final whistle, chatting with Ashley Cole on the stand that had been erected in the centre circle, enjoying what he called his 'garden' for the last time. We stayed much longer. My memories of that evening – that night – are a bit confused. Crates of beer had been brought in by the club. All doors had been left unlocked. Accompanied by three friends, I set out to explore the stadium, sat in Peter Hill-Wood's chair in the boardroom, stepped into the bathing pool in the home dressing room, joined an impromptu kickabout on the pitch, lost my mobile phone, lost it, in short. The lights were still on, just. We could hear shouts, laughs, unseen people cracking up, just as at a wake, which it was. I must have cut a bizarre figure when I finally took the bus back home, truly tired and emotional. Beneath my jacket, I had concealed a red coat-hanger, the hook of which protruded from my shirt-collar. It was Thierry's, the red plastic triangle on which he had hung the cherry jersey for the last time. I'll not give it back anytime soon.

It wasn't over yet, however. In ten days' time, we would be off to Paris. Against all odds, in what seemed like what science-fiction would call an 'alternate universe', Arsenal had qualified for the Champions League final – the club's, and Thierry's, first.

12

Love hurts. Champions League final, Paris, 2006.

THE DIMMING OF THE LIGHT

You'll never win anything with kids. Well, Arsenal nearly did, and perhaps should have, on 17 May 2006, the day they became the first London club to play a European Cup or Champions League final. The giant screens of the Stade de France still showed Barcelona 0, Arsenal 1 with less than a sixth of the game to go. Reduced to ten men since Jens Lehmann's sending-off in the eighteenth minute, clinging on to the one-goal advantage which Sol Campbell's header from a corner-kick had given them eight minutes before the pause, Arsenal were on the verge of achieving something of a miracle; it's true that it was a miracle of sorts had taken them that far.

Four months earlier, back in February, in the earlier rounds of the competition, the very idea that a side depleted by injuries, dismissed as no-hopers in the Premier League, which had just conceded a draw at home to Bolton and a defeat at Liverpool, could come back from the Santiago Bernabéu with anything but a season-ending thumping at the hands of Real Madrid was not just fanciful, but an insult to reason. In one half of the pitch, an assemblage of *galácticos* named Roberto Carlos, Robinho, Beckham, Zidane, Raúl and Ronaldo. Facing them, Wenger's youth project, whose back-four was composed of an Ivorian right-back with a reputation for extravagance, Emmanuel Eboué, a twenty-one-year-old Swiss, Philippe Senderos, not the nimblest of centre-backs, partnered by good old Kolo Touré, a gentle soul who could, it is true, turn into a ferocious competitor, but struggled to pass the ball out of defence, and a largely unproven defensive midfielder, Mathieu Flamini, who had been converted into a left-back following a serious injury sustained by Ashley Cole four months previously. They didn't stand a chance, did they?

Wenger, fully aware that such an inexperienced back-line demanded maximum protection from its midfield, took a decision that, when considered in the light of the credo he had adhered to ever since he had become a manager, and came back to afterwards, amounted to more than a leap of faith, as it was based on a purely tactical appraisal of his team's capabilities, not on an ideal (or idealized) vision of the type of game it should play. Nothing changed in the Premier League, where Arsenal stuck to its traditional 4-4-1-1/4-4-2 with varying results; in Europe, however, using a dead rubber against Ajax* as a test run for his experiment, Wenger adopted a 4-5-1 formation which proved surprisingly effective throughout the rest of the tournament, never more spectacularly so than in that first leg of Arsenal's last-sixteen tie with Real. Why such a dichotomy, then? Henry explained it thus: 'In the Champions League, we played against teams – Juventus being the exception, perhaps – which came out of their half and wanted to assert their own game. When two teams are trying to impose themselves, it's always a different kind of game.' So Arsenal turned into a reactive team; which is not to say that they squandered their creative potential. In fact, they often played with a wonderful fluidity which could have justified using this set-up as a template for the team's organization in the future, including in England, a temptation that Wenger resisted. Of the five players who screened their back-four, only one could be described as an out-and-out defensive midfielder, even if the superb Gilberto Silva ('The Invisible Wall') was much, much more than a so-called 'destroyer'. The other four were chosen from a quintet composed of José-Antonio Reyes, Freddie Ljungberg, Cesc Fàbregas, Aleksandr Hleb and – the least-used in that European campaign – Robert Pirès, all of them footballers for whom the ball was a friend, not something to kick at in anger.

On no player did this system put more demands than Thierry himself, however. 'I had to learn how to play with my back to goal,' he

---

* On 7 December 2005: a 0-0 draw at home in the last game of the Champions League group phase, when Arsenal, having won five games out of five, were already assured of first spot in their group. 'A rather dull game,' was Thierry's verdict on that game, in which he had missed a penalty.

told *France Football* in December. 'I had to adapt to a way of playing which wasn't naturally mine. To play up front in a 4-5-1 implies a huge amount of mental work: you tell yourself that you might only get one ball, and that you must make something out of it. [This was especially difficult] for someone like me who needs to touch the ball to feel all right. I am not a John Carew, a Luca Toni. It's not what I like the most.' But it is something at which Henry proved most adept. More than ever, he was lonely at the top. His isolated role up front echoed his increased distance from those around him at the club, maybe, but also served to show how 'making a sacrifice for the team' wasn't a hollow pronounce-ment in his mouth. That 'sacrifice' added to his personal aura, to the mystique surrounding Arsenal's tutelary god, certainly; but I would call this a virtuous loop rather than a vicious circle. The more Arsenal relied on him, the more he gave – and got – back. If you wish to call this a trade-off, be ready to accept that it benefited both parties handsomely.

In two instances only have I lost all sense of press-box etiquette, and the first of these was on the night of 21 February 2006 in Madrid.* All of my English colleagues present at the Bernabéu did as well, I should add, including a number who were not known for their devotion to Arsenal. The insufferable arrogance of our *Madridista* counterparts before kick-off and throughout the first half, when they cheered every half-opening created by their team, had something to do with that, but so had the manner in which Henry, collecting a ball which Fàbregas had picked from Ronaldo's pocket, blasted through in the forty-seventh minute, swatting away defender after defender as if they had been flecks of white dust, and planted a firm angled shot past Casillas to give his club a 1-0 lead they didn't look like losing afterwards. Speaking about this goal nine months later, Thierry told me: 'I didn't score it on my own. In the first forty-five minutes, the team had put me in a mental state where I could attempt it. If we'd suffered, I'd have thought, "Thierry, keep the ball, don't lose it." But I felt we were solid. When your team sends you the right signals, you try more than when the guys at the back don't take the ball cleanly out of defence. If you look closely, I

---

* The second was when Clint Dempsey scored the goal that gave Fulham a 4-1 victory over Juventus in the 2009–10 Europa League, if you wish to know.

don't do anything extraordinary on that goal – each time, I go where there is space, and that's all.' That's one way of describing it.

I had the chance to speak to Wenger about that particular game on a few occasions. Each time, he used the same expression: '*le match de la prise de conscience*'– the exact moment when a group of youngsters united behind Henry and became aware of its outstanding potential. Their captain agreed: 'That result was crucial for us. Things clicked afterwards. The fact that we beat Real, with all that that club represents in world football, helped a lot of people to understand certain things. We discovered ourselves.' When pressed to explain what these 'certain things' might be, Thierry continued: 'Sometimes, what makes the difference is so minute . . . There is a very fine line between knowing what you can do and achieving it. Sometimes, you can have a big potential and finish your career without having fulfilled it. And the strength of a player is to know how to exploit his potential. At the time [i.e. before beating Real Madrid 1-0], I was far from thinking we'd play the Champions League final. Of course, when you're a fighter, you never think about laying down arms, but you also try to be realistic. Then – suddenly – you beat Real – and you feel invincible.'

This is indeed the feeling Arsenal, having held Real to a 0-0 draw at Highbury in the return leg, gave when facing Juventus in the quarter-finals, when their supremacy was exemplified by Robert Pirès producing a textbook tackle ('the first in my thirteen-year career', he said afterwards) to dispossess Patrick Vieira – now in Juve colours – an unlikely intervention that led to Cesc Fàbregas's opening goal in the Gunners' 2-0 victory. The 0-0 in Stadio Delle Alpi on 5 April was perhaps even more impressive. Perched high in that ugly stadium, at no point did I – or any of my neighbouring spectators – sense that the visitors were in any danger of yielding to whatever pressure David Trezeguet, *Ballon d'Or* winner Pavel Nedvěd (who got sent off) or Zlatan Ibrahimović tried to apply. The semi-final against Villareal, another unexpected guest at the Champions League high table, was not achieved with anything like the same comfort, as it took a save from Jens Lehmann – in tremendous form throughout the tournament – to deny Juan Riquelme from scoring an equalizer from the penalty spot that would have thrown the tie wide open. But, remarkably, Arsenal's makeshift defence had not conceded a single goal in 919 minutes of play since Markus Rosenberg had brought Ajax back to 1-2 on 27 September 2005: a new Champions League record, which still stands. Thierry himself had scored five of his club's ten goals, bringing his tally for Arsenal in European competitions to forty-one. It was a simple but unexpected recipe for success: to beat Ronaldinho's and Samuel Eto'o's Barça in Saint-Denis would require the same plain ingredients: doggedness and discipline at the back (where Sol Campbell and Ashley Cole were now available again), accuracy up front (which clearly put the onus on Thierry to perform as majestically as he had done in Madrid). The defenders stuck to their task admirably despite losing Lehmann so early in the game and held on until the seventy-sixth minute, when substitute Henrik Larsson, playing his last-ever game for the Catalan team, set up Eto'o for the goal that levelled the scoreline. As for Henry – better to let him speak about was probably the biggest personal disappointment of his career.

'I didn't make the difference. I'll be the first to say that. I've got two big chances. On the second one – not that I'm looking for excuses – we'd been playing with ten men for fifty minutes, and I had nothing left in my socks. But the first one . . . I have to put in the net. And I think about it often. It annoys me, because of what the consequences were. We'd made a super start, the game would have followed a different course, even if I'm the first to know that a striker cannot be judged just by goals and assists alone. I always have the feeling I've let my team down if I haven't made a difference. And that's what I felt then.'

Reading this again, I'm reminded of a conversation I had had with Thierry six months earlier, when he had collected his customary French Player of the Year award from a small delegation of *France Football* journalists. He had told us how he was driven on by his desire to win the Champions League, the only major trophy that had escaped him until then. 'What if you were to win with Arsenal, Thierry?' I asked him. 'Oh, that . . .' (the pause, in itself, told more than the words themselves) 'that would be . . . that would be extraordinary.' The tone of his voice, the way he looked down to the floor then, have stayed with me, and I remind myself of that scene whenever I hear it said that the one reason why he had chosen to stay at Arsenal when it seemed his club wouldn't be able to compete at the very top of English, let alone European, football again for a long time was that no one could challenge his regal status there. He had had the chance to fill in that missing line in the list of his honours, and he had fluffed it. He knew it, as he knew that it would take another, even more improbable miracle to be presented with it again. Yet, a few minutes after receiving his loser's medal in the Stade de France, he went up to Wenger and told him, 'I'm staying,' soon signing what he called 'my last contract', which made him – at least on paper – an Arsenal player until June 2010, when he would be two months away from his thirty-third birthday.

I'll be frank: I don't know quite what to make of the other final Thierry played that year, on 9 July 2006, in Berlin's Olympiastadion, fifty-two days after the heartbreak of Saint-Denis. It is not the Frenchman speaking here, still unable to digest that the combination of Zinedine Zidane's headbutt on Marco Materazzi and David Trezeguet hitting the crossbar in the penalty shoot-out prevented *Les Bleus* from sewing a second star on their jersey. It is more that that World Cup as a whole, and its last game in particular, seemed to pass Henry by, somehow. Expectations were not that high at home before the competition and dropped even further when France only qualified for the round of sixteen by finishing second behind Switzerland in Group G, huffing and puffing all the way. Henry, whom Raymond Domenech had chosen to deploy at the apex of a new-fangled 4-5-1,* had done what was required of him, scoring two of his team's three goals in performances that ranked from the uninspiring (a workmanlike 2-0 win over Togo in the game that ensured they would trundle on) to the frankly mediocre (0-0 and 1-1 draws against the Swiss and the South Koreans). Still: 'As game followed game,'

---

* Some of Thierry's teammates were of the opinion that this system significantly diminished his capacity to make an impact on the game. One of them, Louis Saha, who was part of the 2006 French World Cup squad, put it thus: 'When you play next to him in a 4-4-2 formation, it's a bit like following the yellow jersey in the Tour de France.' To further this parallel, in a 4-5-1, Henry, already exhausted by forty-five games played for Arsenal in the season leading to the tournament, could sometimes look more like a *domestique* than the *maillot jaune*.

he said in December, 'it became more and more difficult [for me]. But, at a given time, what's important for the team? What you prefer? No. If the eleven guys in the team do what they feel like doing, where do you go? Nowhere. In that World Cup, I gritted my teeth, and that's what I had to do. D'you think it was fun to be 75,000 times offside against Spain?* But in that competition, I knew that it was the way I'd be efficient for the team – since it was what the manager demanded.'

What the manager demanded? Yes and no. Domenech had come into the 2006 World Cup with a masterplan that quickly looked more like a botched strategy devised by someone who didn't master much, least of all his own players. Frustrated by their incapacity to overcome modest opponents in the group phase, senior members of Domenech's squad, a number of which feared an ingnominous repeat of the 2002 World Cup, decided to take the matter into their own hands and impose self-governance within the French camp. That, at least, is the way in which France's resurgence from the round of sixteen onwards is almost universally explained in my home country. That, and the last flowering of Zidane's genius, whose performances against Spain (3-1), Brazil in the quarter-finals (1-0) and Portugal in the semis (1-0 again) ranked among his finest in a blue shirt, despite having turned thirty-four shortly before the tournament. Henry, whose three goals equalled Zidane's return for the competition, couldn't be called a 'passenger', yet he was, inasmuch as the spotlight had moved to another when he must have hoped he had finally taken on the mantle of a leader. He had good reasons for that. If he hadn't been France's most prolific goalscorer during a fraught qualification phase[†] – Djibril Cissé was, with four goals to Thierry's two – he had provided his national team with a decisive contribution when it mattered most.

Let's go back nine months, to Dublin's Aviva Stadium, on 7 Sep-

---

*   In the quarter-final against Brazil, in which, airborne, he volleyed France's only goal in the fifty-seventh minute – the only instance of his scoring thanks to a Zidane assist – Henry registered more offisdes than attempts at goal.

†   France, with five wins and five draws in ten games, came top of Group 4 with twenty points out of a possible thirty, but both Switzerland and Israel finished a mere two points behind them, Ireland a further length behind.

tember 2005, where Henry scored the kind of goal that commentators call 'magical', an adjective that infuriates the man whose artistry inspired its use on that night. Thierry's graceful athleticism, his unnerving bursts of speed and the fluidity of his movements could make him appear nonchalant to the casual observer when his body-machine was locked in first gear through tiredness, injury and, let's be frank, lack of interest. We have been through this before: Henry has no time for 'effortlessness'. Domenech had picked him for that crucial game even though Thierry was carrying the groin injury that would make him miss over a month of the 2005–6 season for Arsenal. Henry knew he would be substituted, and soon. But the idea of not shooting at goal, just once, angered him as only he could be angered. Sylvain Wiltord cushioned a long pass from Claude Makelele on his chest, and screened the ball from the Irish defenders. In a flash, Henry noticed that Shay Given had marginally erred from his line, and curved the ball into the net with his right foot. Magic? Most definitely not. 'A goal like this comes from a long way away,' he explained, 'from upstream.' In this case, from the Monaco training ground, where, when he was not travelling with the first team, one of Wenger's coaches, Claude Puel, made a teenage Henry rehearse the same sequence until he was sick to the stomach. Run at full speed. Receive the ball. Cut inside, past a line of cones. Shoot from distance, ripping the outside of the big toe against the leather. Then do it again, and again, until that piece of skill had become as instinctive as walking. Henry dedicated the Dublin goal to Puel. Forgetfulness is not one of his faults.

This was a magnificent strike. More importantly, it was decisive, as six of the twenty-eight goals he had scored for *Les Bleus* had been until then. Every single one of these 'deciders' – i.e. goals that turned a draw into a win, or a defeat into a draw – had been scored in UEFA and FIFA competitions,* a remarkable feat in itself, but none had had a comparable impact, as this one more or less safeguarded France's passage to the 2006 World Cup, at a time when the talk was not of what Henry

---

* Those decisive goals had been scored against the Czech Republic and Portugal at Euro 2000; Colombia, Turkey and Cameroon at the 2003 FIFA Confederations Cup; and Switzerland at Euro 2004.

could bring, but of the contribution that could be made by the elders who had just come out of international retirement – Claude Makelele, Lilian Thuram and, of course, Zidane. 'A beautiful goal,' Henry would say after scoring – against the Faeroe Islands, on 13 October 2007 – the goal that took him level with Michel Platini's record mark of forty-one for France, 'is a goal which has a purpose.' From that night in Dublin on, his goalscoring record for France improved markedly, in terms of influence on a game's result if not of raw statistics. If only numbers are taken into account, Henry had never been more successful, somewhat bizarrely, than under the aegis of Jacques Santini, with fifteen goals in twenty-five games (0.6 per match), compared with a ratio of 0.33 with Jacquet (three in nine), 0.31 with Lemerre (nine in twenty-nine) and 0.45 with Domenech (twenty-four in fifty-two, just before France's infamous return leg of their play-off with Ireland, in 2010). But after the curling shot that gave France a precious 1-0 win in Ireland, eleven of those he scored from 2005 to 2009 changed the course of a game for good, or rather for the better, a fact that highlights the inanity of the notion that Thierry 'failed' when more than his own desire to shine was at stake. But when France lined up against Italy in Berlin, how many remembered that it owed its presence there to Henry? Barely anyone.

One of Henry's teammates at this 2006 World Cup, Vikash Dhorasoo, had kept a video diary during the competition, which was later edited into an arthouse documentary.* Vikash, who had been a regular starter for Domenech throughout the qualification phase, found himself pushed towards the bench for motives that were never clearly explained to him. More at ease in the company of books than of that of most of his fellow footballers, he had never tried to dispel his reputation as an outsider; he now found himself pushed further towards the periphery of the squad, whose everyday life he observed from afar with an affectionate, yet detached, eye. He wasn't particularly close to Thierry; neither was he to anyone else in football, it must be said. But I was struck by a comment he made when we met much later on: it looked to him as if Henry wasn't that close to anyone else either

---

* *Substitute*, co-directed by Fred Poulet, which was released in February 2007.

then. It was as if he had taken a step back, fulfilling his role without fuss, going about his business, far from the supposedly power-hungry and divisive figure that had been written about at length following Euro 2004; so much so that Didier Deschamps, now employed as a pundit by a French radio station, encouraged him publicly to 'invest more of himself [in the life of the group], have a laugh, take this team in hand'. 'He was right,' Thierry admitted. 'But I am who I am, I sometimes spend too much time in my own corner.' It's not that Thierry didn't get on well with other players. There was a natural complicity with Patrick Vieira; Louis Saha, one of football's angels, sought his company; David Trezeguet was there too. It's more that, with Zidane's light rekindled, a light that could blind those who followed it, Thierry had to accept living in its shadow. To his credit, he did so, with grace, selflessly, despite his conviction that he could have offered more in a system that didn't place physical demands as exacting as Domenech's did. Some read his visible displeasure at the end of France's 3-1 win over Spain as yet another demonstration of his inability to take pleasure in the achievements of others – when all he had done was to relive his own game and find fault with it, as Tony would have done in a fast-receding past. Tony gone – at least as his mentor – Thierry had taken on his father's role. 'I gave everything,' he said, recalling the final against Italy, in which, his legs gone, he was replaced by Sylvain Wiltord in the seventeenth minute of extra-time. 'Maybe it wasn't enough on the day, but I gave everything. I've played games in which I hadn't given anything, when I hadn't moved an inch, and I'd scored a hat-trick.' So? 'So – yes, there is a regret of not having won the final. But there is no regret of having not done something more.' And again: 'because I gave everything'. He had; but what should have been a source of pride was ultimately a frustration. Thierry had featured in that season's two grandstand finals, the only player to do so, but had scored no goals in those games, won no title and gained no recognition. The *Ballon d'Or* – which he would have given to Andrea Pirlo – escaped him again when it went to Italy's tattooed captain, Fabio Cannavaro, whose Juventus side had been stripped of its 2005–6 *scudetto* in July of that year, following the *calciopoli* match-fixing and referee-bribing scandal. Cannavaro wasn't guilty of any wrongdoing himself, but the jury might have made a more judicious choice nonetheless.

Once again, Henry had little time to draw breath before he was thrown into another domestic season with Arsenal. Once again, the team he had had so little time to prepare with had parted with players who had been central figures in its years of success: three more of the 'Invincibles', Ashley Cole, Sol Campbell and Robert Pirès, had gone, three players who, between them, had won a total of fifteen trophies while at High-bury, Campbell and Pirès joining their new clubs – Portsmouth and Villareal – without commanding a fee. The homesick José-Antonio Reyes, whom Henry was rumoured to show little respect for, but had delivered a number of match-winning performances for the Gunners, was sent out on loan to Real Madrid, his place in the squad being taken by *la Bestia*, the Brazilian man-mountain Júlio Baptista, who, on the rare occasions when he was part of Arsenal's starting eleven, looked hopelessly out of synch with his slighter, quicker-thinking teammates. In the case of Cole, then at his peak and considered the country's best left-back, Wenger engineered a last-minute cash plus swap deal with Chelsea, the experienced William Gallas switching from Stamford Bridge to the Emirates Stadium in the process. As we know, Gallas had been Thierry's fellow scholar at Clairefontaine and his teammate with *Les Bleus* and shared a date of birth and Guadeloupean roots with his new captain; but the many memories they had of their time together had not blossomed into the kind of easy-going intimacy Thierry had enjoyed with Vieira and, especially, Pirès.* Looking around him in the dressing-room or on the field of play, the twenty-nine-year-old Henry could see precious little experience and far too many untried youngsters to be

---

* The best example of their common sense of mischief must be the famous missed penalty incident in a 1-0 victory over Manchester City on 22 October 2005, when the two friends tried to re-create a one-two combination Johan Cruyff and Jesper Olsen had first used for Ajax in 1982. We all know what happened: Pirès fluffed his attempted pass from the spot to Henry (whose idea it had been), and the day's referee, Mike Riley (wrongly) waved play on. 'Maybe we shouldn't have done it,' Thierry said, 'but football is a game and it is entertainment.' Pirès was not amused.

confident of what lay ahead for his club. Alex Song, Fran Merida and Brazil's under-19 skipper Denilson were enrolled in Wenger's finishing school; of the recruits, leaving Gallas aside, only one, the Czech creative midfielder Tomas Rosicky, who had made a sparkling impression at the World Cup in Germany, could be counted as a genuine reinforcement for the team that had struggled to qualify for the Champions League in the previous season. Thierry had said that he had wished 'to lead Arsenal into their new stadium', but to do what? And when? 'In a way,' he told *France Football* when the new campaign was only a few months old, 'you never have the time to wait'. He went on:

I was already telling myself that when I was seventeen, eighteen, nineteen years old. There's an awful lot of quality in [this] group [of players], but it is not well exploited yet. It'll take a while – but I've always had this mindset, 'You should never wait.' I acknowledge that it's been like that [for me] since the start, I hope these youngsters can mature as quickly as possible.

Hearing which, the question had to be: why on earth, then, had he decided to extend his contract immediately after the defeat against Barcelona, when it should have been obvious to him, as it was to everyone else, that Arsenal had mapped their future by choosing to follow an uncharted path and would – precisely – need to show patience as much as resolve to succeed?

The offers had been there for him and for the club to take. David Dein confirmed that £50 million bids (which would have constituted a new world transfer record in absolute terms, Zinedine Zidane having cost £47 million when he moved from Juventus to Real Madrid in 2001) had been tabled by two Spanish clubs before the Champions League final, 'and you don't have to be a rocket scientist to work out who they were'. A Madrid-based friend who had the ear of Real chairman Florentino Pérez had told me in February that his club was 'willing to do everything it takes' to bring Thierry to the Bernabéu. Barcelona, coached by one of these Dutchmen whom Henry revered – Frank Rijkaard – might have been a graveyard for some French players Thierry knew well – Laurent Blanc, Philippe Christanval, Emmanuel Petit – but wearing the *blaugrana* jersey remained one of his avowed ambitions. 'It is the best team in the world . . . There are extraordinary players there, at the Camp Nou . . . It's true that when you hear sirens like these, it's hard to turn a deaf ear to their song.' A word would have been enough to make it happen, but that word, 'yes', Thierry kept for Arsenal.

Arsenal hadn't changed anything in the offer they had first made him in January 2006: a four-year-deal worth a rumoured £6 million a year, plus bonuses – and a signing-on fee (said to amount to £5 million) which both club and player were very discreet about. At the time, only Chelsea's Michael Ballack, who had been taken on as a free agent, earned more money in the whole of the Premier League.

'People [a word he was using more and more often to categorize those who were speaking from outside his inner circle] want to stick a label on your back when you're a footballer,' he said. 'Money, money, money. Of course, money allows you to have a certain lifestyle, which will end one day, but there's also love, emotion, a true love, a genuine emotion. Sometimes, you'd like to leave because you'd like to live elsewhere. It's not always money which decides whether you stay or not. I am a "man of heart", it is the heart that counts for me.'

It could have been the desire not to uproot his young family, and his fondness for the city he called 'home'; his appreciation of the fact that his club was intent to hold on to him when it had to make a huge financial sacrifice to do so; the 'extraordinary relationship' he had with fans 'who'd never put on the least pressure for me to stay'; it could be that David Dein's remark that 'I believe he also knew that if he went to a club like Barcelona or Real Madrid, he would just be a prince. Here he knows he is a king' struck just the right chord with him; it could be that the wish to be remembered as the man who linked two eras in the history of Arsenal FC proved more powerful than his *wanderlust* – and, conversely, that he feared being seen as a deserter in an hour of need. The likeliest explanation is that all of these arguments played their part; which proved decisive, only Thierry knows.

So it is that on 19 May a delighted Wenger could say that he 'had two aims at the start of the week: to win the European Cup and then to make Thierry stay. I only managed one of those but, for the future of the club, that's certainly the best one.' Most Arsenal supporters, who had sung 'Four more years! Four more years!' on the day Henry scored

Highbury's last-ever goal, felt the same. Even José Mourinho added his voice to the intoxicated chorus: 'Fantastic! Arsenal will be stronger with him, but we want the Premier League to be the best league in the world.'

But Arsenal were not the stronger for Henry's presence – principally because this presence was at best intermittent. He started the season decently enough, scoring six goals in his first ten games in all competitions. Then injury struck – not the kind of impact injury that would've sidelined him for a few weeks, after which normal service would have been resumed, but a succession of strains and pains that prevented him from regaining full fitness and eventually cut his season short in March 2007, consequences, it seems, of a chronic back condition that soon had tongues wagging on football's equivalent of the bush telegraph. One game stands out in my memory, the 2-1 defeat at Fulham on 29 November 2006, at the end of which Arsenal lagged in sixth place in the League, trailing leaders Manchester United by sixteen points.

Was it Thierry's worst game in an Arsenal shirt? Possibly – and certainly the poorest performance of his that I have ever witnessed. His control had deserted him completely. Balls he would normally have cushioned with ease rebounded off his feet, shins and thighs as if in an old video-game, when the screen turns into a blur of black-and-white pixels. He was patently unfit and made sure that all around him were aware of the fact; eyes raised to the heavens, hands on hips, Thierry became a question mark: 'What am I doing here?' If I could sense it from the wooden seats of the press box when the game was only a few minutes old, how must his young teammates have felt on the pitch? Some of them went to pieces, none more so than Alex Song, who would become one of Arsenal's most consistent performers within two years. Fulham too sensed Henry's disarray and seized their chance to inflict a merited defeat on the Champions League finalists. It wasn't yet widely known that Thierry was suffering from a debilitating inflammation of the sciatic nerve that did far more than hamper his movement on the field. As every sports doctor will tell you, the constant pain that sufferers of this condition (often described as 'back trouble' or 'back spasms' in journalistic shorthand) experience leads them to 'over-compensate'. To

withstand the efforts required of every elite sportsman, extra demand
is put on muscles that are already tuned to react to the slightest discord.
Repeated tears, pulls and strains invariably follow, especially when the
sportsman in question has passed his physical peak, which was becoming
clear in Thierry's case.

'I hate being injured,' he told *France Football* a couple of weeks later.
'But there comes a time when you've got to accept that your body is
telling you to stop.' It had done so before the game at Craven Cottage,
but Henry hadn't listened. His sincere desire to help his team was, as
ever, combined with an extraordinarily acute sense of how his own
contribution would be perceived. Thierry, I felt then, was playing to
prove he couldn't and shouldn't play, yet did all he could, hurting in
more ways than one when the Fulham fans jeered at another fluff in
the maestro's performance. He sought excuses. 'All the guys who've had
a big season, in their League, in the European Cup, in the World Cup
. . . I can't see many of them who're in top form [at the moment],' he
said, not entirely without justification. 'A good year, that's a year when
you win [something]. On the other hand, should you forget everything
when you haven't won [anything]? Put aside all you've done with Arsenal
and the French team? I don't think so. So, yes, even without a title, it's
been a good year.'

Until 9 July, it had been. But not since then. Thierry was fooling
no one, least of all the 60,000 spectators who filled their seats in the
vast oval of the Emirates Stadium, a huge expanse of air too rarely filled
with the noise that often rocked the so-called 'library' of Highbury.
Henry started only thirteen of the twenty-seven games Arsenal played
in its new arena and played no part whatsoever in the one competition
where they thrived – the League Cup, in which they were defeated 2-1
by Chelsea in the final.* There were some moments to cherish, like the
header that gave the Gunners a last-gasp 2-1 victory over Manchester
United on 21 January 2007 – oddly, Thierry, never renowned for his
aerial prowess, scored three headed goals that season, all of them from

---

* Arsenal exited the Champions League in the round of sixteen, PSV prevailing
2-1 over the two legs, and the FA Cup in the fifth round, beaten 1-0 by Blackburn
after a replay. Henry played in all three games without scoring.

crosses swung in by Emmanuel Eboué.* We had even seen the 'old' Henry tormenting one of his favourite victims, Liverpool's Jamie Carragher, slotting in Arsenal's third in their 3-1 win at Anfield on 6 January 2007, in the third round of the FA Cup: 'Henry . . . passes to Henry . . . who passes to Henry . . . who scores!', was how a friend of mine described the exhilarating run. He hadn't lost that rare quality of imparting tremendous speed and 'weight' to the ball, as cricketers would say, whilst using minimal backlift – a free-kick against Newcastle on 18 November and a stupendous first-time shot in the top corner at Blackburn on 13 January the two most spectacular examples of this. Each time this happened, a curtain was drawn back, revealing a scenery which had been Henry's kingdom in the past; each time, it was pulled shut again. Did he really wish to be there at all?

Then, on Wednesday 17 April, Arsenal FC published the following statement: 'Irreconcilable differences between Mr Dein and the rest of the board have necessitated a parting of the ways.'

Wenger, whom I spoke to in the training ground's car park two days after the announcement, was shattered by the news but determined to see it through and stay. Henry saw it differently. 'People join the club, others leave,' he said. 'But whatever is in store, what happened will always remain which could've been avoided. His [David Dein's] departure is a mistake. I'm saying it now, and I'll say it again in twenty years' time. If there was one person who ought not to have gone, it was him.' It didn't take a genius to guess that another person would head for the exit, where Barcelona was still waiting.

---

* The other two were scored against Sheffield United in the Premier League (3-0, 23 September 2006) and FC Porto in the Champions League (2-0, three days later, Henry's fiftieth goal in European competitions).

13

Exile, triumphs, heartache.

BARCELONA:
THE PARENTHESIS

France Football is still waiting for the summons that Henry's SEM agency had promised would come its way after the magazine had revealed on 12 June 2007 that an agreement had been struck between his player and Barcelona, following a meeting between Darren Dein* and the Catalan club's sports director, Trixi Beguiristain. 'Absolute rubbish,' fumed SEM's Jeff Weston. 'There has never been any question of him not being at Arsenal FC next season.' Thierry himself entered the fray a week later, speaking to *L'Équipe*'s Bernard Lions after taking part in his idol Sonny Anderson's jubilee celebrations at the Stade de Gerland. 'Everybody's talking about me? That's great,' he said, in the increasingly flippant tone he adopted when talking to the media. 'This palaver doesn't affect me in the least. I'll be thirty in August. It's not the first, and it won't be the last time that someone speaks in my place. In the meantime, I'm still an Arsenal player.'

He wasn't for long. By Friday 22 June, Barça was briefing reporters that an agreement had been reached and would be finalized within a matter of days.† On Saturday, confirmation came via journalist Pierre Menès, a long-time confidant of the player, who said that David Dein's ousting from the Arsenal board had been the deciding factor in

---

* As stated previously, Darren Dein became Thierry's sole representative after his transfer to Barça.
† The contract was signed on 25 June. Henry had committed himself for four years, and would earn an estimated £4.6 million per season (other sources stated £5.5 milllion, a discrepancy which might have been caused by the inclusion of bonuses in the second figure).

Henry's decision ('Had Dein stayed, so would have Thierry'). According to Menès, 'Arsenal no longer had any kind of sporting visibility.' Moving to Barcelona was 'his last chance to go to a big club', which, obviously, Arsenal wasn't or couldn't aspire to be any more, at least not in the course of the few years Thierry could still hope to play at the top level.

A surprise it was not, even if the news still came as a shock for Arsenal supporters who had had to live with constant rumours of their striker's departure for at least three years, and whose hopes of holding on to their beloved captain had been strengthened when all of these rumours had – thus far – proved to be unfounded. More puzzling, perhaps, was the modesty of the transfer fee – €24 million, equivalent to £16 million – for a striker who, even if his sell-on value was negligible, given his age, brought with him the guarantee of at least twenty goals a season (should he stay fit) and whose off-field worth hadn't yet been exploited to the full. *Time* magazine had named him among the 100 'most influential people' on the planet in May. His very last assignment as an Arsenal player had been a photo-shoot with Brazilian supermodel Gisele Bündchen. He now moved in a world populated with A-listers, an advertiser's dream, his now-former club's most bankable commodity; but that club had let him go for roughly the same amount of money they had parted with to buy Sylvain Wiltord from the Girondins de Bordeaux.

Doubts about his long-term fitness undoubtedly entered into the equation, and rightly so, as the events of the next few months would show, but were not the sole reason why Arsenal, or more properly Arsène Wenger, having fought tooth and nail to keep Thierry at the club beforehand, seemed quite relaxed at the idea of letting him go now. A sense of loyalty played its part, loyalty towards the player who had given so much to the cause over the eight previous seasons. You couldn't begrudge respect to a man and a footballer who had earned it so magnificently over what, in modern football, amounted to a lifetime; this also meant respecting a decision he wasn't prepared to reconsider. Wenger also knew of Thierry's marital problems and of his imminent separation and divorce. London was no longer Henry's 'home' as it had been before. We shouldn't be fooled, however. In situations such as these, 'your intelligence has to rule over your heart', Wenger said in late 2011, referring to the choice he made in Patrick Vieira's and Thierry Henry's cases.

'We sold them around the age of twenty-nine or thirty,' he told a gathering of Arsenal supporters and small shareholders. 'Why? Because we needed the money and [couldn't let them] go for free. What happens in football is that a player goes over his peak and you still have to pay him the maximum money. There is always a difference between the moment when a player is well paid and his performance [*sic*] – there is a delay. When you get to a player who is twenty-nine, thirty years old and you want to renew his contract, you pay mega money knowing that he will [only] give you two years at his best when he is a striker.'

As Elvis Costello sang, 'money talks / and it's persuasive'.

Twenty thousand *socios* attended Henry's official presentation at the Camp Nou on 26 June, a stage-managed occasion in which one cringe-making moment stood out. Having exited the players' tunnel, clad in the number fouteen shirt that belonged by right to Johan Cruyff, Thierry paused as he was about to come on the pitch to tie the laces of his Reebok Sprintfits boots in full view of the cameras. This didn't appear to be the Thierry we had known at Arsenal. His first public gesture in Catalunya could easily be interpreted as a nod towards one of his main sponsors, an exercise in product placement, a signal sent to consumers, rather than to his new fans. Still, for him, he told the club's website, this had been a day he would 'remember for the rest of [his] life'. He hadn't experienced anything like that before in football. It had been 'a huge shock'. The welcome had been 'crazy'. He would 'always be thankful'. This was another Henry, of which there might have been glimpses before, but not quite like this: he had slipped into his new jersey as if it were a corporate suit, spouting hyperbole like a Californian life coach. On the one hand, there was nothing feigned about his pride in being part of 'the only team in the world that had not varied their style of play over time', the team he had watched with awe when he grew up, 'the one that you always remember more vividly than any other'. On the other, there was something unconvincing about the tone of this gushing endorsement of all things Barça. Thierry said what was expected of him, to be sure, but tried too hard, succumbing to an all-too-human desire to please,* which seemed to become more pervasive in his character as he got older. It seemed obvious that Barcelona couldn't possibly play a front-four composed of Messi, Ronaldinho, Eto'o and Henry; one or two of these players would have to accept being deployed in an unfamiliar position, or even being left on the substitutes bench. For Thierry? No problem. 'I will play where the coach puts me because he will always do what is best for the team,' he said. 'When you play for a club like Barcelona, nobody can specify whether they want to play here or there,' etc., etc. We hadn't been used to Henry resorting to such platitudes in London. There was another slightly disturbing thing. He, the man who had said 'Football is not the Thierry Henry show' (and meant it then), now appeared to have fewer qualms joining in the celebrity circus he had been so careful to avoid in London. In July 2007, he appeared on stage at Le Bataclan, a Parisian club, to be serenaded, if that's the word, by rapper Snoop Dogg (wearing a Barcelona shirt emblazoned with Henry's name and number fourteen). One month later, still in Paris, it was the turn of another platinum-selling rapper – 50 Cent – to be presented with that jersey, which was also seen on the back of his 'friend' Spike Lee. A pity that, on the field, it wasn't all bear-hugs and high-fives for Thierry, whose first season in Spain was, by the standards he set at Arsenal, more than a disappointment.

I've come to see the three years Henry spent in exile (for an exile it was) at Barcelona as a parenthesis in his career, despite the incontrovertible fact that he won as many major trophies – seven – in this short space of time as he had done in eight years spent at Highbury and the

---

* This could lead to misunderstandings: a number of people were convinced that Thierry had converted to Islam after watching a – poorly translated, it should be said – interview he gave to the Al Jazeera network in December 2008, when all he had said was that he was 'interested' in that religion, and had talked about it with a number of teammates who had embraced it, such as Nicolas Anelka, Éric Abidal and Franck Ribéry, and should he be tempted to turn towards God, well . . . He hadn't converted; but he had given in to his penchant for offering the answer he thought his audience would like to hear.

Emirates.* The word 'parenthesis' might be considered inappropriate, but I shall stick to it nonetheless: it's as if he never quite belonged there, even though he recaptured his form in 2008–9. Perhaps it couldn't be otherwise, as very, very few players experience the communion Thierry had enjoyed while at Arsenal. In statistical terms, his first year at the Camp Nou was not an unmitigated disaster: with nineteen goals in all competitions,† he topped the club's 'hotshot' charts, recording his first hat-trick for Barça in a 4-1 victory at Levante on 29 September 2008, ten days after opening his account in the Champions League, when Lyon were on the receiving end of a 3-0 thrashing in Barcelona. He had expected far, far more, however. Frank Rijkaard had quickly made his mind up that Henry's best place was on the left wing, a position in which he had to assume defensive duties that did not come naturally to him and which he believed sapped his energy to such a degree that he couldn't contribute as much as he should have when Barça were on the attack – which, of course, was most of the time. But who could displace the prodigious Samuel Eto'o from the main striker's spot? Henry recognized that his friend 'Sam', whose advice he had sought before he completed his move to Barça, was 'a better centre-forward than I am'. Numbers bore this out: though sidelined by a meniscus injury until mid-December, the Cameroonian struck eighteen times in nineteen La Liga games on his return. As David Dein had predicted, Thierry couldn't be a king in Barcelona, at best a prince. Perhaps not even that, not then.

Meanwhile, tantalizingly, Arsenal seemed to flourish, which raised awkward questions about Thierry's contribution to 'his' team as a footballer and a captain in the previous season. By mid-October, with seven wins and a single draw in the League, the so-called 'baby Gunners' led Manchester United by two points – with a game in hand – prompting a number of observers to reflect that, once again, Wenger had 'got rid' of a star player at exactly the right moment when he had become a hindrance.

---

* Two Ligas (2008–9, 2009–10), one Copa del Rey (2008–9), one Spanish Supercup (2009), one UEFA Champions League (2008–9), one UEFA Super Cup (2009) and one FIFA Club World Cup (2009).
† Henry also recorded ten assists in the League alone, second only to Lionel Messi in that department.

Others even ventured that it would have been better for Arsenal to cut short their association with the most prolific goalscorer in their history twelve months beforehand, rather than agree a ruinous contract extension. Had Henry held Arsenal back? It is a paradox that, as many coaches less ruthless than Wenger have found to their cost, inhibits teams at every level of the game: a player's aura can grow as his powers decline. The impact that this fading of the light, almost imperceptible at first, has on the team's performance heightens that player's contribution in the recent past, and feeds uncertainties such as: are we doing all we can to make him shine? The longer that player has been in the limelight, the deeper the effect it has on the scene as a whole; and the sun had shone more brightly on Henry than on anyone else at Arsenal.

Marc Overmars, Emmanuel Petit and Patrick Vieira had been disposed of as soon as Wenger had felt that their level of performance was no longer on a par with their status – and salary. Each time, the manager, armed with statistics that supported his intuitive judgement, had come to the conclusion that the organic development of his young team risked being stifled by the decline of key elements whose physical capacities were on the wane. He did so with elegance, cunning and a measure of cynicism. I remember Patrick Vieira confiding that he hadn't quite understood how exactly he had gone to Juve. Had it been his decision? Had it been his manager's? Had a trick been played on him? I could see that he bore no grudge towards Wenger, but that these questions wouldn't find a ready answer. Thierry's case was different. The relationship between the two men was as strong as any Wenger had enjoyed with his previous players, including George Weah and Dragan Stojković, whose name I remember Arsène quoting with unfeigned emotion when we once talked about his personality-defining stay with Grampus Eight in Japan. Emmanuel Petit, too, had been one of these men whom, had it not been for the age difference (almost twenty-one years), Wenger would have been proud to claim as a friend. But Arsène had let 'Manu' go, whereas he had held on to Thierry. Maybe it had to do with the sense that he had a debt towards the striker-turned-midfielder he had rescued from Juventus. 'Everybody speaks about how much Henry owes to Wenger,' Christian Damiano told me. 'Nobody seems to realize how much Wenger owes to Henry.'

It is around that time that I had a chance to sit down with Cesc Fàbregas and ask him how it was that his team had been able to fill the void left by their captain's exit. 'You've got to do something when the best player in the world leaves you,' he told me. 'You cannot expect him to score a fantastic goal when things don't go too well any more. You must find different options. Thierry won everything here, and we do not have the right to say: it is because he's gone that we're better. This would be a total lack of respect towards someone who's won everything . . . when we . . . we haven't won anything. How could you say we're better? People forget things far too easily. If we win something – then we might be able to say something. Maybe. But we haven't done it so far.

'But what is true is that all of us – all of us – have improved.'

'I agree with him completely,' Thierry commented. 'Because of my seniority, the fact that I was captain and my habit of screaming for the ball, they would sometimes give it to me even when I was not in the best position. So in that sense it was good for the team that I moved on.' But was it good for him? When winter turned to spring, Catalan fans and media, who are not renowned for their patience, started questioning openly their chairman Joan Laporta's decision to 'spend a fortune' on a player who had clearly not recovered from the previous season's injuries. In March 2008, following a 1-2 defeat to Robert Pirès's Villareal in the Camp Nou, the Catalan daily *Sport* dissected Henry's contribution in that game, in which he had been replaced by youngster Bojan in the sixty-sixth minute. 'Dissected' is wrong; 'slaughtered' would be more apt. According to a poll published in the same paper, Henry was now Barcelona's third-choice attacking player in the minds of Barça's *socios*. There was also talk of the pernicious influence of 'cliques' within Rijkaard's team, one of them being the 'French', led by Eto'o and Henry, Ronaldinho and Messi being the top dogs in another. When interviewed by the BBC's *Football Focus* programme that spring, Thierry had clearly had enough.

'They signed the guy from Arsenal, so they want to see the guy from Arsenal. I'm only trying to explain to some people sometimes, "Don't expect the Henry from Arsenal" – it's not the same . . . thing! If you ask any kind of forward to play on the wing, he will do his best. But will he be as efficient as he

can be as a centre-forward? I don't think so . . . I'm happy here [in Barcelona] . . . but . . . how can I explain this to you? I'm happy here . . . I'm the same in training, I'm the same in life. I cannot act. That's sometimes something good about me, and it can also be something very bad. I cannot act. If I'm not happy, I'm not happy . . . After six months not training, not doing anything, I went straight into the group, without being good. My groin was still hurting, my back, my thigh, I was really like . . . out of form . . . It's not what I was doing at Arsenal, thirty goals and twenty-plus assists per season, but it's still fourteen goals and ten assists . . . that is not a bad ratio . . . There has been a lot of speculation from day one. There's only one team for me [Arsenal]. It took me a while to understand what that club meant. That's why I was so mad at times, because I was so into it. I became a fan. I don't regret leaving, I don't regret stuff in my life, stuff happens for whatever reason in my life, in my personal life also. I don't regret stuff . . . Highbury was my garden.'

But Highbury was now a pile of rubble. And regrets there were, aplenty. In another interview, with *The Times*'s Allyson Rudd, Henry confided that he missed 'everything' about England – the songs in the stands, the Saturday routine, the fans – even, God forbid, the press. His daughter Téa was far away. He had seen her only five times in the first eight months of his stay in Spain. 'If you know what it is to have a daughter then you can imagine what it is like,' he said.

When things had been tough in the past, there had always been a place where he could be confident to find a refuge: the French team. This was no longer the case. He still had Domenech's trust and had rewarded it by finishing top goalscorer – with six goals – in what had been a tight qualification phase* for the 2008 European Championships; but the French public had now turned against him, the same public that, not so long ago, had named him the 'nation's favourite sportsman'. On 3 June 2008, the day France beat Colombia 1-0 at the Stade de France in front of 80,000 spectators, Thierry became the sixth French

---

* France took second spot in Group B, behind world champions Italy, whom they had beaten 3-1 at home in the opening game of the qualifying phase, Thierry scoring his team's second goal.

player in history to reach the hundred-cap mark. All of them, Henry, Deschamps, Zidane, Vieira, Desailly and Thuram, the skipper on that night, belonged to the golden generation of 1998. But when Domenech signalled to the new centurion that the time had come to make way for Nicolas Anelka, with a quarter of an hour to go, the vast arena resounded with boos and whistling. In any other country, I thought, a presentation would have been made before the game – anything: a bunch of flowers, a commemorative football shirt, a memento of some kind would have been given to the man of the hour. Not here, not in Paris. The crowd barracked him. It was a shocking sound, even for habitués of the Stade de France, who might have become used to the fickleness of the supporters there. A striking feature of this crowd is its homogeneity: white bourgeois Parisians for the most part, more or less the same people you would expect to come across at a Six Nations rugby match, less the southern contingent. On the pitch, lined up to sing (or not, as it happens) 'La Marseillaise', eleven men in blue, most of whom happened to be black in that game; in the stands, well-dressed men and women, mostly white, looking forward to be entertained by the ex-world champions, their cheeks daubed ever so prettily in the colours of the tricolour flag. What have they got in common? Nothing. The *banlieues* from where most of these footballers come will never be visited by the thousands who only know one chant: 'Allez Les Bleus!' The way they booed Henry was a disgrace, even if, beyond Thierry, Domenech too was targeted. But disgraceful as it was, it was in tune with the shambles that followed.

France made their debut in the tournament ten days after the win over Colombia. With Zidane retired, for good this time, and his successor Patrick Vieira present but injured – and pushed to the sidelines of a team everyone knew he wouldn't be able to play for – thirty-six-year-old Lilian Thuram and Thierry Henry, the two elders of Domenech's dysfunctional family, inherited responsibilities that the former had never craved and the latter wasn't ready for. Of France's performances in that tournament, the less said, the better. *Les Bleus* plumbed unknown depths of ineptitude. In defence, they were awful. In attack, worse. At Zurich's Letzigrund, Romania were supposed to provide easy pickings for the World Cup finalists in their opening game on 9 June, even without

Thierry, who hadn't recovered from a small knock. But France could only rescue a 0-0 draw against a well-organized Romanian team that seemed to revel in their own negativity – or so Domenech said, failing to see, or, rather, refusing to acknowledge, that the French had shown no adventurousness themselves either. This left his team with the obligation to get maximum points in at least one of their two remaining group matches, in which their opponents would be perennial favourites the Netherlands and Italy.

There was no 'miracle of Bern' against the Dutch, who inflicted one of the most humiliating defeats France had suffered in living memory. The final scoreline – 4-1 to Holland – was, if anything, slightly flattering for the French. Still some way from full fitness, but back on the pitch, Henry watched the massacre from the apex of Domenech's 4-4-1-1, doing what he could to provide some focus to a performance so disjointed that it verged on the brainless. A fine brace of goals, by Kuyt and van Persie, gave the Netherlands the lead they deserved before one hour had been played. Hope, if that's the word, flickered briefly when Thierry brought *Les Bleus* back to 2-1, showing great composure in beating van der Sar from a tight angle. But within one minute of the restart, Sneijder and Robben had combined to restore the *Oranje's* advantage. Sneijder, provider turned finisher, stylishly completed the rout in added time.

Back to Zurich, backs to the wall. Remarkably, France still had a chance to qualify for the second round, as Italy, the world champions – whom they had beaten so convincingly in the Stade de France less than a year previously – also risked exiting the Championships in shame after taking a solitary point from their first two matches. Domenech juggled the pack one more time; out went Thuram, in came François Clerc, with Éric Abidal sliding from left-back to the middle of the defence, and Thierry being promoted captain in Thuram's absence. The ploy failed miserably. Luck certainly deserted the French when Ribéry, who had looked their most potent threat up front, was forced to leave the field with ten minutes on the clock; but luck had nothing to do with Abidal's desperate attempt to stop Luca Toni going one-on-one with Grégory Coupet. The Barcelona player was shown the red card, and Andrea Pirlo despatched the ensuing penalty kick. Ten against eleven, a goal behind, France were as good as out of the tournament. Sixty-six minutes later, it was confirmed.

France's ignominious early exit from the Euros left Thierry with plenty of time to spare in the early summer, a luxury he had rarely enjoyed throughout his professional career, when international tournaments nearly always came on the heels of a long domestic season. As often in the past, he chose to visit the USA, where paparazzi spotted him strolling in New York City's Greenwich Village, 'sporting a white T-shirt with a red tie silkscreened on it, along with a pair of distressed jeans and some retro-red high tops', as a British tabloid put it. The 'striker stud' was then followed to SoHo, where he lunched in a fashionable Italian restaurant, and . . . and so on, and so on. But Thierry's visit was not just an opportunity for celebrity trackers to feed their readership with titbits like these; disillusioned, it seems, with Barcelona, and mourning – very publicly – his departure from Arsenal,* Henry was already sizing up another future. America tempted him. Major League Soccer, where his former French teammate Youri Djorkaeff was adding a unexpected, but distinguished, last chapter to his long career, tempted him too, as he had confessed to journalists in June of that year. 'I so love America,' he had said. 'I love it here. And whenever I come here, I feel free. Hopefully, one day. You never know what's going to happen the next day.' Thierry eventually decided to stay, convinced, it seems, by what Barcelona's newly appointed coach Pep Guardiola had told him. It was the start of a parenthesis within a parenthesis, which was closed when Henry reached the end of a rainbow he had been chasing for over a decade and could call himself a European champion.

What had changed? Frank Rijkaard had gone, to start with, whom Henry might have admired as a Milan player and a member of Holland's

---

* It is at that time, in mid-July 2008, that Henry was given first place in the 'Gunners' Greatest 50' chosen by the visitors to the club's website. Six months later, he was also voted the Premier League's 'favourite player of all time' – ahead of Steven Gerrard – in a poll of 32,000 people conducted for the Barclays 2008 Global Fan Report.

1988 European Championship-winning side, but whose managerial approach was in marked contrast with the non-confrontational style of Arsène Wenger and who was certainly less tolerant of the mood swings of his star players than the Arsenal coach. Thierry had also found a new balance in his private life, having met Bosnian-born Andrea Rajacic* in the summer of 2008, his companion to this day. Guardiola, whilst a hard taskmaster on the training pitch, also wished his players to give free rein to their instinct and gift for improvisation in match situations: if for one season only, Henry recaptured the sense of fun that was so precious to him. The dazzling Barcelona team that is now routinely named among the greatest sides in football history didn't immediately settle into its distinctive shape, but was born that season nonetheless, and it shouldn't be forgotten that Henry was part of it, just as much as Xavi, Iniesta and Messi. The Argentinian, the Frenchman and Samuel Eto'o contributed seventy-two of the 105 goals Barça scored in the course of their conquest of La Liga, finishing nine points clear of Real Madrid. Seventy-two goals – six more that the all-time Spanish record for a trio of forwards, which had been set by Alfredo Di Stefano, Ferenc Puskás and Luis Del Sol in the 1960–1 season with the *merengue*. Thierry's own return bore comparison with some of his best with Arsenal: nineteen goals in twenty-nine appearances in the League, six in twelve in the Champions League, twenty-six in forty-two in all competitions. What's more, a number of these goals – and assists, of which he totalled twelve that season – had had a crucial bearing on Barça's march towards a Liga–Copa del Rey–Champions League treble that was unprecedented in Spanish football history. There was his headed equalizer in Lyon on 24 February 2009, which he followed with a brace in the return leg, opening a regal way towards the quarter-finals of the Champions League;

---

* The couple took advantage of the traditional Christmas break to celebrate the coming of the New Year in some style. Henry chartered a private plane to take him from Barcelona to Malé, the capital city of the Maldives, and to fly him back to Catalunya just in time to take part in Barça's first training session of 2010. Rumours that his divorce settlement had had a huge impact on his personal wealth must have been exaggerated: the French daily *Le Parisien* estimated the cost of his escapade at over £160,000.

there was a gorgeous pass to set up Messi for Barcelona's third goal in the 4-0 demolition of Bayern Munich, a match in which Henry concluded the scoring, making qualification for the semis a formality.

In La Liga, too, Thierry recaptured the brilliance of his Arsenal years, and when it mattered most. On 12 April, surrounded by teammates who looked blunted by the energy spent against Bayern, he set up Andres Iniesta for the first goal of a hard-fought 2-0 over Recreativo Huelva. On the 26th of the same month, it was he who denied Valencia a sixth consecutive victory in the League, stepping from the bench to equalize four minutes from time, when a defeat, which would have been Barça's fourth in that competition, would have enabled Real Madrid to move ahead of them in the League table. But he kept the best for the title-deciding *clasico* of 3 May, a clash which took place between the two legs of Barcelona's contentious Champions League semi-final tie against Chelsea.

Barça humiliated Real on that occasion, putting six goals past Iker Casillas, a feat that the Catalan club had never achieved in its rival's stadium. First, Thierry cancelled Gonzalo Higuain's opener; then, after Puyol and Messi had brought the score to 3-1 in favour of the visitors, Sergio Ramos gave fresh hope to Real. Within two minutes, Henry pounced again, taking advantage of their high defensive back-line to re-establish a two-goal advantage. He unfortunately took a knock to the knee in that game that prevented him from taking part in Barcelona's sulphurous 1-1 draw at Stamford Bridge a few days later; and I've often wondered if it is not his absence from that match, without a doubt the most dramatic of that whole European campaign, which has led many to undervalue what he had brought to Guardiola's side that year, as if he hadn't really been more than a fleeting presence, as if he hadn't really been there. And perhaps that is fitting, if unfair.*

*

---

* Henry, injured, played no part in Barcelona's 4-1 victory over Athletic Bilbao in the final of the Copa del Rey, which was held two weeks before their meeting with Manchester United (the 25th time the Catalan club had won this trophy). He had had a significant impact on Barça's progress, however, scoring their first goal in the home leg against Mallorca in the semi-final.

Thierry was back for the final played on 27 May 2009 in Rome's Stadio Olimpico, albeit without having been able to resume full training with Guardiola's squad prior to the game, of which he played the first seventy-one minutes. Barcelona weathered an early United onslaught to end up comfortable winners, Eto'o and Messi the goalscorers in a 2-0 victory in which Henry exerted as much influence as his fitness allowed him to.* At the final whistle, in a hoarse voice, still struggling to breathe, he said: 'It's unbelievable. I have no words to describe what we have done, what we have achieved this year. No team has ever achieved the treble, and we'll always remain the first one to do it, so . . . it's something amazing. Apart from the way we played all season is the way we fought all season. I went through pain to come and play . . . Iniesta came through pain to come and play. [The defeat in 2006] will always remain the disappointment in my career, but tonight, I'm happy, for my family, for all the stuff I've suffered since I've been playing football . . . and you know? That season, a lot of people were talking a lot – and I'm still alive. It's a double satisfaction for me, because . . . what time is it ? [He checked his watch with a smile] . . . it's still the birthday of my daughter, so . . . I'll always remember the 27th of May. I dedicate this to my daughter. It was a great, great, great night.'

How could he guess there would be no other night like this one at

---

* An aside: Henry had filmed an advertisement for Reebok prior to the Champions League final, in which he was shown exchanging 'funny' emails and presents with the bootmaker's 'brand ambassador' at Manchester United, Ryan Giggs. Thierry was shown relaxing alone in a slick, bland, impossibly 'cool' interior, all off-whites and tasteful beiges, grinning and shaking his head in mock disbelief as he unwrapped Giggs's latest 'cheeky' presents. It wasn't awful. And yet it was. I couldn't help but think of a legion of assistants (all of them equipped with radio and telephone headsets) scuttering around like worker bees, patting sofa cushions, checking how blue the pool looked on screen. Plastic, silicone, pixels: the materials that make a very modern icon. Thierry had done worse. There is an excruciating video of him, shot in 2007, again for Reebok, fooling around with the very photogenic Spanish actress Paz Vega on the pitch of the Camp Nou, pretending to take penalties against each other. No prizes for guessing that the star of *Sex with Lucia* ends up scoring, whilst Thierry goes through his whole repertoire of 'cool' (again) facial expressions that could be expected from him. How is it possible to look so laid-back and so awkward at the same time?

the club where he, at last, had become a European champion? Samuel
Eto'o left for Inter, Zlatan Ibrahimović crossing his path on his way to
the Camp Nou, and Thierry found himself frozen out. Why that happened, and so suddenly, I'll come to in more detail in a moment.
Faultlines and dynamics shifted within the team, dressing-room politics
played their part, the emergence of Pedro, injuries too, which ruined
the beginning of the new season – by which time Barcelona were moto-
ring along, Thierry forgotten in the last petrol station. The parenthesis
within the parenthesis was shut. What followed was months of frustration. When he returned to Arsenal as a guest, to watch his former
teammates annihilate Blackburn 6-2 on 4 October, Darren Dein in tow,
his daughter Téa on his knees, a half-empty stadium gave him the kind
of ovation that he couldn't experience in Barcelona any more, if he had
ever experienced it, that is. 'I was a bit embarrassed, to be honest,' he
said, after being presented to his crowd, 'I didn't know what to do, I
just felt like clapping.' He would have to wait more than a month to
score his first goal of the new campaign for Barcelona, in a 4-2 win over
Mallorca. Guardiola could say: 'I'm very happy with Titi – he brings
us so much.' Henry added his habitual 'What matters is Barça and not
Henry or Pedro or Messi,' but everyone could see through the posturing.
Infuriated by the constant sniping of the Spanish media, he had punctuated that goal with a ferocious kick at the post of 'keeper Doudou
Aouate's goal. He had had enough.

Five days after this rare appearance in a Barcelona shirt, Thierry was
in Dublin, where France, having failed to qualify directly for the 2010
World Cup,* was facing Ireland in the first of the two legs of a play-off
whose winner would progress to the final phase of the tournament. This
is what I wrote immediately after hearing him address the journalists
on the eve of the game:

*His pre-match conference gives a good idea of the tone he now employs with
the media . . . His facial expression is one of bored hostility. Or hostile*

---

* Serbia finished a point ahead of the French in Group 7. Thierry was, again,
the most prolific goalscorer of *Les Bleus* in the qualifying phase, finishing it with
four goals, though this total was matched by André-Pierre Gignac.

boredom, maybe. 'Why are you wasting my time?' he seems to say, slightly slouched forward, elbows on the table, eyebrows raised just a bit, like one of these civil servants whose job it is to provide you with a new passport. Whoever has travelled in Eastern Europe in the not-too-distant past (or queued in a French préfecture*) will be familiar with this peculiar kind of grumbling aggression. Until the last second, you wonder whether they're going to tell you that you've forgotten a trivial (but indispensable) piece of documentation. And you find yourself thinking, 'Couldn't he try a little harder?' Henry won't. The reporters sit uneasily on their chairs. The watching public feels their toes twitching with an indistinct feeling of discomfort. 'As I've said so* often *before' . . . 'as I* keep *being asked' . . . and it goes on, and on, cameras rolling, pressmen scribbling and typing away, transcripts already floating in cyberspace, while the French FA's publicists are choosing the shot that will accompany their publication on the federation's website. Nothing's asked, nothing's said. It's another tedious fifteen minutes in the life of one of the world's most famous and best-paid sportsmen. And the question you put to yourself is, 'Is this the real Thierry Henry?'*

Or was it the Henry we saw in the Stade de France, four days later?

14

'Say it ain't so, Thierry.'

THE HAND OF GAUL

'Le Cheat' (*Daily Express*). 'Le Hand of God' (*Sun*). 'Ireland robbed by cruel hand of Henry' (*Guardian*). 'French Nickers' (*Daily Mirror*). 'Hand of Henry shatters Ireland' (*Times*). 'Hand of God II' (*Daily Mail*). 'Hand Gaul!' (*Independent*). 'Hand of Henry cheats Irish' (*Telegraph*).

18 November 2009, the day before the headlines. We've reached the 103rd minute of France's World Cup qualifier against the Republic of Ireland, played in front of 79,145 anguished spectators in the Stade de France. Four days earlier, a Nicolas Anelka goal had earned the French a 1-0 victory at Croke Park, giving them the upper hand in this play-off for a spot in the final phase of the 2010 tournament. But the team Henry is captaining for the eighteenth time looks disjointed and fearful, incapable of shaking off the blow of Robbie Keane's thirty-third-minute goal. The tie is now all square at 1-1, and the Irish, a motley crew of English Premier League and Championship players, are giving an admirable performance, full of disciplined fire, with flashes of excellence, qualities which are both conspicuously absent from the display of their hosts. Then—

Then Swedish referee Martin Hansson doesn't see Henry handle the ball twice to bring a long free-kick by Florent Malouda under control, Henry whose cross is met by William Gallas at the far post. France have equalized, France are as good as through. The Irish protest in vain, then collapse on the turf. Hansson will soon receive the visit of FIFA refereeing controller Hugh Dallas, the man who officiated at the France–Italy quarter-final of the 1998 World Cup, when Henry scored one of the penalties in the shoot-out that took the French to the last four of the competition. A few words are enough to make Hansson understand the magnitude of his – all-too-human – mistake; and this, when his performance had been beyond reproach until then, worthy of a World Cup referee. But Hansson won't go to the World Cup now and he knows it. Neither will the Irish.

What followed can best be told in the present tense, I believe, if only to give an idea of the whirlwind in which Henry was caught, and of which he will never completely escape. The French broadcaster TF1, like its British and Irish counterparts, shows Henry's sleight of hand on a loop, at real speed, in slow-motion, super-slow-motion, from every camera angle at their disposal. 11.5 million French viewers watch this 'crime against football' with a mixture of disbelief, anger and nausea. As Gallas is engulfed by ecstatic teammates, Henry among them, a voice is heard in the box that has been reserved for former French internationals – 'Quelle indécence!' That word is not part of Raymond Domenech's vocabulary. The French manager soon appears in front of the television cameras: 'my prediction before the game was 1-1,' he says, without the least trace of irony. 'I was convinced we would qualify. Some things are written . . .'

The French players trickle into the mixed zone, ignoring the microphones thrust in their direction. The captain himself – who has briefly seen Arsène Wenger just after the final whistle – confesses: 'Yes, there was handball, but the referee didn't see it and I'm not the referee.' He also adds that he has said the same thing to Mr Hansson. But when? 'I'm sorry if I've hurt someone' – the very words that will appear on his Twitter timeline later on. Some well-known pundits find it difficult to control their indignation. My RMC colleague Jean-Michel Larqué, a former international who skippered a glorious Saint-Étienne team in the 1970s and now manages several football academies in his native south-west, can hardly speak, fighting for breath between each of his words. 'Shame . . . cheating . . . disgrace . . .' Twenty-four hours later, his anger will have turned into something else: helplessness. 'What am I going to tell the kids who come to my clinics? That you can qualify by cheating?'

The French politicians who have surfed on the wave created by *Les Bleus* since 1998 express rather less delicate feelings. The photogenic

Sports Minister Rama Yade tells reporters that she is 'proud, very proud'. Nicolas Sarkozy talks about his 'fear' that the national heroes wouldn't go through; the President of the Republic, however, will soon fall strangely silent, once it has become clear that the mood of his electorate is not one of relief and jubilation. A celebratory party has been organized. Henry shuns it. He is seen driving away in his brother Willy's 4x4. He has switched off his mobile. His father Tony – who has stayed in Guadeloupe – can't reach him.

Some rumours filter from the French camp. Watching his teammate Loic Rémy warm up on the touchline, Karim Benzéma, the Real Madrid striker shunned by Domenech in favour of Toulouse's André-Pierre Gignac, has said: 'At least, I can still hold my head high.' A good night to be – and remain – a substitute, it seems. On the FFF's website, as on UEFA's, and FIFA's, no mention of what the Argentinian daily *Olé* will tastelessly dub 'la mano negra'.

On Thursday morning, more politicians take their place in the pulpit. One of them, the Finance Minister and future IMF President Christine Lagarde, one of Sarkozy's most powerful Cabinet members, is the first to ask for the game to be replayed. Everyone has an opinion, including the former chairman of Marseille Bernard Tapie, a convicted fraudster who is no less influential in presidential circles for that. Henry has left Paris. Late in the morning of 19 November, he's boarded a flight for Barcelona to join his clubmates, but doesn't take part in the afternoon training session: he still feels pain in one of his knees after a clash with Shay Given in the first half of the game. As he leaves Barça's training ground, a female journalist dispatched by the Irish tabloid the *Sunday World* unfurls a banner on which can be read: 'I'M SORRY – I, Thierry Henry, apologise to the Irish people for using my hand to knock them out of the World Cup finals.' Henry drives by, stony-faced.

Éric Cantona is in Marseilles with his brother Joël, to promote a beach-soccer tournament. 'What shocked me the most,' he says, 'is not the handball, but that he [Henry] sat down next to an Irishman [Richard Dunne] at the end of the game and that he talked to him when he'd just tricked him a few minutes beforehand. If it had been me, that guy [Henry] would have lasted three seconds,' a point of view echoed by the former Irish manager Mick McCarthy. Cantona also has a few words for Raymond Domenech: 'the worst coach since Louis XVI'. With this caveat: Domenech's head, muddled as it is, would remain on his shoulders. No matter how numerous your enemies may be, you'll be all right as long as your allies are in the right places, which, in the case of *Raymond-la-science*, means: high up in the hierarchy of the FFF, starting with the organization's chief mandarin Jean-Pierre Escalettes, who defends – on Friday – his beleaguered coach in front of an assembly of Ligue 1 chairmen, most of whom feel French football has been sullied by Wednesday's events. Frédéric Thiriez, the League's CEO, asks whether maintaining Domenech in his current position is such a good idea. Escalettes is scandalized: 'He fulfilled his mission! The question shouldn't even be asked! In a week's time, anyway, everybody will have forgotten about it, you'll see.'

Not quite. Within twelve hours of the final whistle, the Facebook page 'We Irish hate Thierry Henry (the cheat)' has 34,000 followers. A day later, there are 80,000. The Irish retailer Currys offers a €50 rebate to any customer who will trade in a Thierry Henry T-shirt or jersey. The betting firm Paddy Power plasters the arrivals lounge at Dublin airport with posters on which can be read: 'Welcome to Ireland . . . unless you're called Thierry.' One of Henry's main sponsors, Gillette, alters the photograph that greets visitors on their website. Tiger Woods is still holding a golf club (not for long, however), Roger Federer his tennis racket, but Thierry's hand is no longer holding a football; it is slipped into his pocket. More seriously, an investigative piece is published on the following Friday by *France Football*, which reveals how much money the manager that eight out of ten French football supporters want to see sacked will make thanks to his team's qualification for the World Cup: nearly £800,000 (four times what the 1998 World Cup winners had banked) on top of his £45,000 monthly salary, an absolute fortune given the state of the FFF's finances and the track record of a coach who has never won anything in two and a half decades of management, bar a Second Division title with Lyon. And this, without taking into account the bonuses he can expect from the team's sponsors, in total a treasure chest of £9 million to be shared with his technical staff and all the players who have taken part in the qualification campaign. Henry himself will receive in excess of £200,000.

As in the aftermath of the 2002 World Cup disaster, journalists are fed with information coming from disgruntled (or plainly disgusted) members of the FFF's structure. They're told that Domenech has – twice – led a delegation of fourteen on a 'fact-seeking' mission to South Africa before qualification was ensured. The cost to the federation was over £100,000. Domenech, ever the political animal, could counteract the criticism he was receiving from alumni of the 1998 squad by asking some of them to join his staff. The former manager of Bordeaux Élie Baup was asked to approach the world champions' 'keeper Fabien Barthez and offer him the position of 'third goalkeeping coach'. This turned out to be a nebulous role that involved, apparently, the supervision of a morning training session, lunch, a quick chat with the players and little else – work billed at £6,300 a go. 'Fabulous Fab' unsuprisingly accepted the offer, and, on one occasion, had a taxi take him to the Clairefontaine complex, wait there and take him back to Paris. He had run up quite a tab: £620, for which he made an expenses claim (which was not paid).

I could carry on in this vein for a while. But let's go back to Thierry, who had finally found defenders, some of them unsurprising, others less so. A number of players, Gary Neville among them, came out in support of a colleague, who – at least in their eyes – had only done what most professional footballers would have. The Manchester United captain, who couldn't be suspected of having a soft spot for the opponent he had roughed up on so many occasions, said: 'To label Henry a cheat is wrong. Everyone who has played football will know that, when the ball comes up at your side, your arm can come out instinctively. We have all done things in football matches in the heat of the moment that we have regretted later. The referee has to spot these things.' A dissenting Irish voice could be heard in Ipswich, that of Roy Keane, who, prior to his team's game against Sheffield Wednesday, entertained (that's the word) a posse of reporters with a remarkable diatribe directed at his own country in general, and the FAI in particular, concluding with these words: 'Did [Henry] bend the rule a little? Maybe. You see cheating going on all the time. Nobody wants a cheat. I wouldn't agree that Henry is a cheat. He is a top, top player who took advantage of the situation.' Zinedine Zidane shared that view: 'he's only done a handball, that's all. It is a *fait de jeu* which doesn't deserve this madness.' I use the French expression on purpose, as it was used by a number of others, André-Pierre Gignac amongst them. Literally, 'a fact of the game', which could be translated as an accommodation with the laws of football, which the British would call 'clever' or 'cute' were it one of their own who had committed a similar offence against the 'spirit' of sport. Examples of that kind wouldn't be hard to find, as Gary Neville and Roy Keane knew; as everyone knew – bar, maybe, Henry himself.

For it is worth remembering that when British papers tried to find 'previous' in Thierry's career, and tried they did, they failed to do so. Henry's increasingly aloof demeanour may have grated with some, indeed with many, but he had never been labelled a 'cheat' before. He didn't dive. He never waved imaginary yellow cards when he had been fouled, and heaven knows he was fouled more than most, when defenders could get to him that is. I witnessed one of the rare occasions on which he remonstrated with a referee, at the conclusion of a 3-1 victory over Newcastle at Highbury, on 18 December 2001. Thierry was beside himself with anger that night, and with some justification: Sol Campbell's impeccably timed tackle on Laurent Robert was adjudged to be a foul by referee Graham Poll, who pointed to the spot. It was the turning point of a crucial game. It was also a poor call by the official. Henry's vituperations then – later referred to by a few columnists as an example of his volatile temperament – were not that of a 'cheat', but of a football player, and football lover, who couldn't be reconciled with the idea that unfair play could be rewarded. Had Robert protested (as Robbie Fowler once did, against Arsenal) that Campbell's challenge had taken the ball cleanly from him? Of course not. It had been a strange evening. Alan Shearer had tried to prevent Graham Poll from sending off Ray Parlour for a second yellow card offence – when Shearer himself, certainly no Mary Poppins on the field, despite what his Newcastle chairman Freddie Shepherd said, had been the target of the Arsenal midfielder's lunge. All that Henry was saying was: 'Ref, it's *unfair*,' with the passion of a child who has been wronged. A 'cheat'? Never. But that evening in Saint-Denis, Henry cheated, perhaps for the first time in his professional career.

It boils down to context. It is one thing to exaggerate a tumble when there has been what is euphemistically called 'minimal contact' in an ordinary League game, and another to – wilfully, unapologetically – handle the ball – twice – in a match that is worth £1 billion to your own country, a figure bandied by a British economist, which most French analysts deemed to be an under-valuation of the windfall qualification would bring to their country. Context must also refer to the player's own record in such matters; in Henry's case, it was unblemished. Henry Winter of the *Daily Telegraph* sensed it when he opened his column with this far from rhetorical interrogation: 'Thierry, why did it have to be you?'

Why indeed? The affable Christian Damiano, Claudio Ranieri's right-hand man at AS Roma at the time, and one of Thierry's first coaches at Clairefontaine, said: 'This is not the Henry I know, a respectful and loyal boy. What I fear is that he's been bewitched (*marabouté*) by Raymond Domenech. My own feeling then was that under a Hidalgo, a Jacquet, a Lemerre, Thierry wouldn't have done the same thing: he would have owned up if his 'instinct' had got the better, or the worse of him. Domenech, 'a man who doesn't understand anything about sport' (Bixente Lizarazu *dixit*), had built a team in his image: dysfunctional, ugly, unlovable, the very antithesis of what French football had stood for for decades: daring, imagination, fairness. Saint-Denis 2009 could not erase the memory of Saint-Denis 1998, Seville 1982, Guadalajara 1986. Or could it? With Domenech at the helm, anything was possible.

We had been the victims for so long. In a way, Harald Schumacher's act of GBH on Patrick Battiston at the 1982 World Cup (and France's admirable reaction to that act of thuggery) had contributed to create a purist's dream, a team that understood, viscerally, the meaning of the word 'play'. Thierry Henry grew up in a France where this perception of our national squad was unchallenged, and rightly so: there were no cheats in there. Like our rugby players, our cyclists, our fencers and sailors, our footballers embodied a vision of sport in which success – titles – was a reward, not an objective which belonged to the realm of the absolute. It is (I'm tempted to think) a very Catholic view of salvation. No idea of predestination taints it; it leaves space for imperfection, a fumbling progress towards truth and beauty. To British ears, this might sound pretentious, or worse. But, believe me, peel back our skin, and that's the flesh you'll find; that alone explains how a country which had just seen its football team qualify for a World Cup could be so riddled with guilt, which it was. Nowhere else could you find a mainstream TV station set up a debate around this question: 'Should we forfeit the World Cup?'

What's more, not a few answered: 'Yes.'

The night France and Ireland drew 1-1, thousands of people descended on the Champs-Élysées to celebrate their country's passage to the greatest football show on earth. They were French, but the team they fêted was not France: it was Algeria, who'd made certain of their qualification for the 2010 World Cup a couple of hours beforehand. They came from the suburbs in cars, trams and trains. The most famous avenue in the world was awash with green and white flags emblazoned with the red star and crescent. Their fathers might have been there on 12 July 1998, when a photograph of Zidane was beamed onto the Arc de Triomphe. That was then; this was – different. Around 11 p.m., when the Paris underground was still disgorging baffled France and Ireland supporters on their way back from the Stade de France, a friend of mine, reporting for RMC radio station, found himself in the midst of a near-riot. Exuberant Algerian fans, very few of whom had ever set foot on their family's ancestral soil, started to set fire to cars and ransack luxury shops. Police were called in. They were pelted with a variety of missiles. There were a number of casualties, some of them serious. The trouble lasted late into the night, largely unreported by the French media.

What could you say? It hadn't been a celebration, but a demonstration. A demonstration of the fracture within French society, in which millions are ignored because they live outside the walls of the city, the Barbarians at the gates of the Empire, the sculptors living in squalor by the walls of Gormenghast, skilful, ignored and presumed dangerous. Thierry Henry was born in that world, but had escaped it through football. In a painful synchronicity, he was shamed on the very night that part of the *banlieues* exulted because of the victory of a team that represented anything but France. You could draw parallels with Irish,

Scottish or Welsh supporters siding with whoever happens to play against the English, save that the 'Algerians' who rampaged in *les beaux quartiers* that night did not act as they did solely because of the weight of colonial history, but also because of a very tangible present, made of mutual incomprehension as much as of exclusion. The French national team balanced itself unsteadily on top of this pyramid of non-communication, when 'national' had palpably turned from an adjective synonymous with unity into an interrogation. Henry's double handball didn't simply cause a polemic whose subtext was incomprehensible outside of France. It was also a first step towards the unravelling of a fictitious equilibrium, a precursor to Knysna's 'bus of shame', a tremor before an almighty crash.

Henry himself felt worse than lonely: abandoned. Abandoned by the very people who, thanks to him, would be travelling to South Africa the following summer. Had it not been for the support of his family, he said, he might well have retired there and then. It is not his teammates or his manager that Thierry had in mind: the former had sympathized with his plight, the latter had told reporters that he was so upset at the vilification of his skipper that he 'hadn't slept for two days'. Henry was thinking of the men who ruled the FFF, such as its vice-chairman Noël Le Graet, with whom Thierry had spoken for half an hour on the phone the day after the game. Le Graet denied that the captain of France had been fed to the wolves, a point of view that might have carried more weight had the administrator not expressed it from the French West Indies, where he had repaired for a holiday almost immediately after the match. Torn between self-justification ('the ball hit my hand . . . the referee doesn't whistle') and guilt ('I shouldn't have done that [celebrate Gallas's goal]. But, frankly, it was uncontrollable . . . after all we'd been through . . . that, yes, I regret it'), Henry released the following statement on 20 November through his solicitor Stuart Peters, a former SEM employee who had been his legal adviser for over ten years:

I have said at the time and I will say again that, yes, I handled the ball. I am not a cheat and never have been. As a footballer you do not have the luxury of the television to slow the pace of the ball down 100 times to be able to make a conscious decision.

People are viewing a slow-motion version of what happened and not what I or any other footballer faces in the game. If people look at it in full speed you will see that it was an instinctive reaction. It is impossible to be anything other than that. I have never denied that the ball was controlled with my hand. I told the Irish players, the referee and the media this after the game.

Naturally I feel embarrassed at the way that we won and feel extremely sorry for the Irish, who definitely deserve to be in South Africa. Of course the fairest solution would be to replay the game, but it is not in my control.

There is little more I can do apart from admit that the ball had contact with my hand leading up to our equalizing goal and I feel very sorry for the Irish.

The Irish seized on these words to request a rematch, their captain Robbie Keane praising Thierry for having the 'courage' to confess. Arsène Wenger supported that idea as well. 'French football and France as a country have a duty not to leave Thierry out there alone against the whole world,' he said. 'France has to say: "Yes, it was a handball and we offer a replay."' But nothing came of it, if anyone seriously thought it could. And, more quickly than might have been expected, a strange kind of normality returned. Henry came back to Barcelona, where Andres Iniesta said that his teammate was 'all right' and 'focused on doing things well' for his club. 'I'll fight to the end,' Thierry told *L'Équipe.* 'Even if what's just happened will always stay in my memory. You can always forgive, but you cannot always forget.'

The crowd he faced when he played his next match did neither. On 21 November, coming on late for Xavi in Barcelona's visit to Athletic Bilbao, he was booed relentlessly by the 40,000 supporters of the Basque team. Three days later, injuries to Lionel Messi and Zlatan Ibrahimović meant that Henry was given the responsibility of leading Barcelona's attack in a crucial Champions League group game against Inter Milan. Rubin Kazan and Dynamo Kyiv having drawn 0-0 earlier on that day, the European champions were in less perilous a position than might have been feared, but the outcome of Group F remained uncertain, and, had José Mourinho's team prevailed, the Catalans wouldn't have looked forward to a trip to Ukraine at the beginning of December. In the end, weakened or not, Barcelona easily outplayed a timid Internazionale, for whom Henry's friend Samuel Eto'o was making an emotionally charged return to the Camp Nou. The British media were more generous in their appraisal of Henry's performance than the French, who seemed to have reached a consensus as far as the captain of the national side was concerned. On one hand, the idea that the culprit was also a victim had made some headway, mostly within the game's establishment, but also most of the national papers and television networks, who knew how much income they would derive from France's qualification for the World Cup; on the other, the opinion – voiced by one of my RMC radio colleagues – that there was 'nothing to say about Henry's game' and that he had become a peripheral figure at Barça was now shared by the vast majority of observers, professional and otherwise. Henry had done the dirty work and been reviled for it. What to do? To rush to his defence would be to condone an act that eight out of ten French people judged 'shameful', according to a poll published at the time. But to condemn him would run against the vested interests of his accusers. Take my own paper, *France Football* (which creditably stayed true to its principle that it should defend what is good for football, not just for *Les Bleus*): The difference between France being in South Africa or not was €5 million added or subtracted from our turnover at the very least. An uneasy balance was found, by necessity. Empty-hearted, sickened and angry as we might have felt, we also had to live with the fact that Henry's handball had contributed to keeping us in a job. Thierry was right when he said that he had been treated unfairly; but what was perhaps the most unfair was the affected indifference with which he was now judged as a footballer, more than the attacks he had been subjected to. It is as if his decline was now accepted as fact, and the double handball as proof of it, even when what was happening on the field could contradict what was primarily a perception in which moral judgement played no small part.

That game against Inter, for example. In truth, Henry had performed well in a Barça victory that had given substance to the belief that the European champions remained favourites to win the trophy for the second time running. It was his flick from a Xavi corner-kick that had enabled Gerard Piqué to score the opening goal as early as the tenth minute, and Henry it was again who tested Julio Cesar with a decent shot a quarter of an hour later. He faded somewhat after that, and I couldn't help but notice his reaction to the Pedro volley which all but ensured that Barcelona would beat Inter and, at last, take command of their group. Standing near the penalty spot, Henry had seen Xavi dissect the Italian defence with an angled pass towards the advancing Dani Alves. He was already calling for the ball to be crossed to him – instead of which the Brazilian chose to loop the ball towards the further-positioned Pedro, well above the head of a clearly frustrated Henry. When the young Catalan's volley beat Inter's 'keeper, Henry remained rooted to the spot, his face still expressing a mixture of surprise and disappointment at Alves's instant decision. No smile, no arms raised in the air, the barest of acknowledgements. And whilst Pedro, joined by the other Barça players, rushed towards Alves to thank him, it took Henry a very long time to amble towards his celebrating teammates. He had never been the most demonstrative of footballers. But it was hard to resist the temptation of seeing in his coolness another illustra-tion of his growing isolation within Guardiola's squad – which coincided, a slightly misleading word, with Lionel Messi's elevation to godlike status at the Camp Nou, and with Barcelona inventing what I would call a type of 'meta-football' of which there was no precursor, fully justifying its claim to be 'more than a club'.

The Barça Henry had joined was well into transforming itself into an entity that, despite obvious connections with its past – its debt to Dutch football, for example – bore little resemblance with the team, or club, that a much younger Thierry had dreamt of playing for. It was an environment in which individualities could be glorified, but not in the fashion a Cruyff or a Ronaldinho had been. Their superstars were of a more unassuming type, modest, humble, to the point of dullness in some cases. It had to be thus for Guardiola's training methods to succeed, depending as they did on the daily repetition of drills designed to turn his team into an eleven-cell organism. His players had to strain their minds as much as their bodies in order for their on-field thought process to be akin to instinct. No player could expect preferential treatment, which led the unsettled Zlatan Ibrahimović to tell Guardiola: 'I'm a Ferrari, but you drive me as if I were a Fiat!' No player – bar Lionel Messi, according to numerous sources within the Catalan club. It's not that the Argentinian was allowed to turn up late for rehearsal; it's more that his truly unique talent, unique being taken here in all meanings of that word, demanded a unique kind of accommodation which his manager, a pragmatist as much as a poet, was happy to grant him. Messi's positioning or, to be more precise, repositioning from the right wing to a free, mainly axial role in the front-line became one of the keys of Guardiola's tactical thinking, ultimately leading to a system in which there was no longer a recognizable number nine. The consequence of that shift was that Henry, Zlatan and, later, David Villa, all of them centre-forwards of a more traditional mould, found themselves pushed towards the sidelines, literally as well as figuratively. Ibrahimović has told how, in 2009, Thierry once turned to him and said, 'Ciao, Zlatan, has he [Guardiola] looked at you today?' 'No, but I saw him from the back,' was the answer.

'Good luck,' retorted Henry. 'Things are getting better.'

15

'The bus of shame'. Driver: R Domenech.

THE SHATTERED MIRROR
OF KNYSNA

Things didn't get any better when France lined up against Spain at the Stade de France on 3 March 2010, in what could be Henry's very last game for his country in front of what could no longer be called 'his' public. 'A good Spanish lesson' was one of the more generous comments that could be read in the following day's papers. Barely five minutes had passed when the home crowd started to greet every pass from the visitors with cruel *olés*. It hurt, as the boos and catcalls must have done when Domenech called off his captain after sixty-five minutes of mediocrity. 'We had the feeling that they [the Spaniards] were untouchable at times, from another planet,' Thierry said afterwards, adding, perhaps too generously, that he could 'understand' why his so-called supporters had given him the bird in such a shocking fashion. True, he had been at fault for Spain's first goal, giving the ball away in a dangerous position; true, he had never tested 'keeper Iker Casillas; but neither had any of his teammates, most of whom had entered this game with a far sharper level of fitness. 'I had no rhythm,' he confessed, 'I was short in terms of physical condition, and, when you've got to chase the ball against a big team, that's tough.' There was resignation in his voice, as if he had come to accept that he was no longer judged as a mere footballer, but also as a symbol, maybe *the* symbol of that wretched business called the Domenech era.

Domenech himself attempted to draw the sting out of this clearest of defeats in that unflappable, disdainful way of his. He had seen 'interesting things', he said, quite breathtakingly, but didn't specify what they were. This is not a wreck, gentlemen, he assured his disbelieving audience, this is a fine ship, and you'll realize I was right in a couple of months' time. But I was not the only person to notice that his comments on Thierry's performance contained a veiled threat to one of the few allies he still counted (on the fingers of one hand) in the dressing-room, one of the very few men who had genuinely tried to give him some kind of vicarious legitimacy, through self-interest and fidelity to a shared past. 'Everybody's seen a better Titi on the field,' the manager said. 'But the fact that he's played [fewer games] is a problem for him when he has to come into a high-level match like this one . . . It raises a few questions. But I don't have any concerns for the time being.' But wasn't time running out? And what were those 'questions'? As usual, Domenech didn't elaborate. The art of non-elaboration was one of the few things he had learnt to master in his six years at the helm of the 1998 World Cup winners.

The final score, 2-0, could only be explained by the reluctance of the European champions to expend unnecessary energy as most of their players approached season-defining ties in the Champions League and in their domestic championships. Regardless of the injuries that had prevented a number of regular first-teamers – such as William Gallas and Éric Abidal – from playing on that chilly night in Saint-Denis, France had shown, yet again, a pitiful image of itself, devoid of poise, imagination and desire. It had all been said before: Domenech's rigid 4-2-3-1 didn't allow Yoann Gourcuff the space to impose himself as the genuine number ten most observers – not just journalists – thought he could become. As Henry insisted he must play on the left (that was part of his Faustian deal with Raymond-Mephistopheles, after all), Franck Ribéry found himself isolated on the opposing flank, in a position that not one of his club managers had ever thought was suited to him. It was a shambles. Domenech was hammering square pegs into round holes like a manic child whom no one dared to chide any more. As the now-jettisoned Patrick Vieira said, 'The problem with Domenech is that he thinks he's the centre of the world.' It'll go in, because I want it to. I'll break the whole damned thing if I must, but it'll go in, because, for me, there is no other way than my way. And there wasn't, as Domenech was all of these: the pupil, the teacher, the headmaster. If he had been able to, he would have set the papers and marked the exam himself. Unfortunately, on that depressing evening, Spain had, and had awarded him a perfect nil.

Back in Spain, where Lionel Messi rescued Barça from defeat at lowly Almeria on the following weekend, Guardiola carried on praising Thierry (and vice-versa) whenever a microphone was thrust under his nose, which, given the access that the media are granted to footballers and managers in La Liga, was almost every day. As Henry – taking advantage of Zlatan's suspension – showed with fine personal individual performances against Valencia on 14 January, then Stuttgart four days later, he hadn't become an embarrassment for Barça. His movement off the ball was good, his attitude impeccable, and some of his touches as subtle and imaginative as ever. It's just that the pace had gone – his capacity to 'explode' over the first few yards, and, crucially, to sustain a burst of speed like a one-lap sprinter, something that Dani Alves, Pedro and the unstoppable Lionel Messi did with astonishing consistency over ninety minutes, game after game. Henry inhabited a different space on the pitch. The former king looked benignly on the new rulers, offering encouragement, applauding the rare passes that were meant to reach him and went astray, dutifully moved to the position on the field that his undiminished power to read the game told him he should occupy. But he no longer made the difference as he had done a year previously.

There were signs, however, that Guardiola was reshaping his team in a way that could benefit the declining striker, even though Henry's well-being wasn't his manager's prime objective. The 4-3-3 system that had brought Barcelona an unprecedented six titles in a single season was evolving into an ever more fluid and dynamic formation which, seen from the top of the stands in the Camp Nou, players no bigger than dots on a green canvas looked at times like an updated version of Brazil's 1958 4-2-4 – then changed, with bewildering speed, to a 4-2-3-1 or, even, a 4-5-1 when their opponent had the rare luxury of having the ball in their feet; but not for long. Once Barça had regained possession, the full-backs would rush forward, leaving Valdes with just two defenders to protect him.

The main aim of Guardiola's reinvention of one of the game's basic set-ups was to maximize the contribution of a player who was now routinely compared to Johan Cruyff and Diego Maradona by *socios*, journalists and opponents alike: Lionel Messi, of course, who, by 21 March, had scored twenty-five goals in twenty-four Liga games (plus another twelve in the Copa del Rey and the Champions League), including a phenomenal eleven in his club's previous five outings. The *Purga*'s latest hat-trick – at Zaragoza – featured a solo goal of which the *Pibe de Oro* himself would have been proud. Barça's chairman Joan Laporta, talking in exclamation marks as he had been doing since he had launched his quixotic political career, told the world that Messi was now football's 'greatest-ever player' (meaning: it's also thanks to me that he became supreme). The diminutive 'Leo' was undoubtedly the most effective of the Barça forwards at this point in time: Guardiola had released him from his accustomed position on the right flank, whence he would dart inside, creating space for the overlapping Dani Alves. The twenty-two-year-old Argentinian now had the freedom to run wherever his instinct told him to go. This meant that, suddenly, there was space for four genuine attacking players in Guardiola's starting eleven, not three. Pedro could be stationed on the right, the more static and, in some ways, more old-fashioned target man Zlatan in the middle, Henry or Iniesta on the left; alternatively, Thierry could occupy the central position that most people – at least in France – felt was the most suitable to his qualities and to his physical condition. Messi himself would drift in from the right wing, popping up wherever he could hurt the most – that is: everywhere. Guardiola's evolutive conception was not exclusively his: Louis van Gaal was doing much the same (with Arjen Robben in the role of Messi) at Bayern Munich, and José Mourinho had experimented with a similar system at Inter, at least on the all-important occasion of the return leg of their Champions League tie with Chelsea, when Wesley Sneijder was deployed with tremendous success in a 'free role' behind a trident composed of Pandev, Milito and Eto'o. It could be argued that Andrei Arshavin, nominally a left-winger at Arsenal, fulfilled a similar role for Arsène Wenger – when Cesc Fàbregas didn't position himself so far up the field that he became a virtual second centre-forward. And what was Cristiano Ronaldo for Real Madrid, if not the most devastating of *faux-ailiers* ('false wingers')? I use the French expression here as this 'position', so hard to pinpoint that it isn't a position as such, had been a vital weapon in the armoury of coaches such as Michel Hidalgo when France finally established itself as a major force in international football. 'There is nothing new that is but forgotten,' goes the French proverb; nothing triggers invention like memory.

Late on the morning of Friday 18 March, Thierry heard the news he had dreaded: Arsenal and Barcelona were drawn together in the quarter-finals of the Champions League. Within minutes, every agency wire, Twitter feed and internet blog was announcing the 'return of the king', who, judging by what the 'king' himself had told journalists a few days earlier, must have felt that the cruellest of tricks had been played on him. 'I'll be an Arsenal fan until I die,' he had said. 'And if you ask me how that makes me feel about the possibility that Barcelona might meet Arsenal in the next round of the Champions League should we both qualify, I have to say I find the idea unthinkable. It's always the same on the day of a Champions League draw. Until I see that Arsenal have been paired with another team, I can't breathe. Proud though I am to be a Barcelona player, I dread the thought of having to oppose Arsenal. I would hate it. I pray for it not to happen.' But happen it did.

His old club decided to locate the nearest mound of sand and bury every head that could talk in it. A stern press officer reminded journalists who had been granted a quick chat with Cesc Fábregas after a 2-1 win over West Ham that all questions related to Thierry or Barcelona were off-limits, and would signal an immediate end to the interview. Wenger himself, whom I finally reached on the phone after numerous attempts, chose to downplay the importance of the occasion. He had had enough of the British media's obsession with 'personality stories', when Arsenal were fighting for their first Premiership title in six years, and a second successive spot in the semi-finals of the Champions League. There was no place for memories, however sweet they might be, no room for emotions other than the excitement at the prospect of the two most eye-catching sides in Europe battling against each other. It was a sign of how much Arsenal had matured on the pitch and in the dressing-room. Though no one dared say it, playing – and hopefully beating – Barcelona would be an act of almost Oedipal catharsis, a full stop rather than a caesura.

I attended Pep Guardiola's press conference at the Emirates on the eve of the game; as usual, when not answering in his excellent English, the manager of Barcelona (who, with every day, looked more and more like a Capuchin monk who had stepped out of a painting by Zurbarán) expressed himself in Catalan, baffling the Castillian speaker who had been hired to provide simultaneous translation. Like many others, I put the headphones down, and my mind wandered elsewhere – some fifty yards away, to the visitors' dressing-room. There, Henry was readying himself for a short 'training session' on the pitch where he had last played precisely three years and twenty-seven days earlier, when a late goal by the PSV defender Alex had knocked Arsenal out of the Champions League. What must he have felt in the strange surroundings of the 'wrong' dressing-room? There were no memories for him there. But there were many attached to the lush field outside, where he finally stepped out in the lashing rain, followed by the lenses of dozens of photographers. I had sneaked out pitchside in the company of a TV crew and, at first, could barely make out Thierry's silhouette in the downpour. He had also chosen to roll up a snood, which covered most of his face, as if to make himself as inconspicuous as possible.

Barcelona's coaches had separated the squad into two groups, who soon engaged in what the continentals call *toros* and British schoolchildren 'piggy in the middle' – quite an extraordinary sight, when you can watch Lionel Messi, Zlatan Ibrahimović and Dani Alves fooling around at close quarters. As all around him called out to each other, joking, laughing and attempting every trick and flick they could think of, Henry, hands in pockets, barely made any effort to keep possession of the ball. Maybe it was the artifical character of this photo opportunity that bored him so; this exercise had no purpose other than provide a backdrop for television previews and a few shots for photo agencies. Or maybe he shared the confusion of so many of the Arsenal supporters I spoke to during the build-up to the game. One of them, the novelist Nick Hornby, had said: 'I'd still love to see him warm up for us in an Arsenal shirt, with our team losing 1-0 fifteen minutes before the final whistle. This is all so bizarre.' Who could have imagined then that this would indeed happen in January 2012?

But I am getting ahead of myself. On that day, there was no chance of a quick word by the touchline. When our eyes met for a few seconds,

Henry's expression remained inscrutable. He didn't want to play, he had said. But he also wanted to play, especially as an injury suffered by Andres Iniesta had increased his chances of reclaiming a spot in Guardiola's starting eleven. And in the end, when he did play, he didn't really play at all. Bizarre was the right word. Thierry's state of mind could be guessed at during the warm-up, when he trotted towards the centre circle, acknowledging the loving reception of the crowd. He had a long look at his former teammates assembled on the other side of the halfway line, and noticed Sol Campbell doing stretching exercises some thirty yards away. The nutmeg he attempted rebounded off the left leg of the huge defender, and Thierry smiled like he must have done in the days when he had played the same kind of trick on Arsenal's training-ground.

With thirteen minutes left of one the most thrilling games ever seen at the Emirates (the incandescent Theo Walcott had reduced the scoreline to 2-1 in Barça's favour eight minutes previously), Zlatan Ibrahimović made way for the returning 'king', who heard his Arsenal song sung for what he thought would be the last time as he took position on Barcelona's left flank. As welcomes go, this was all he could have hoped for: as fervent, possibly even more so, as David Beckham's when he had produced a fine cameo for Milan at Old Trafford a few weeks beforehand. But whereas Beckham had immediately stamped his mark on a game that was lost, Henry disappeared in a game that appeared to be won. In sixteen minutes and fifty-six seconds of presence on the field, Thierry attempted a mere four passes, one of which went astray. Every single of his touches was greeted by pantomime boos. Bizarre, again. Two shows were played on the same stage. Whilst a tiring Barça and an Arsenal reinvigorated by sheer anger were offering a stirring spectacle to the world, Henry was engaging in a private dialogue with the fans, which ended in a long ovation when the final whistle blew. Thierry was – of course – last to leave the pitch, reminding me of Dionne Warwick taking bow after bow in one of her comeback tours, when she had long lost her ability to hit the impossible intervals devised by her songsmith Burt Bacharach but could still, somehow, suggest them through subtle inflections of her declining voice. It was a touching moment, but it had little to do with the splendour of what had been seen beforehand.

Walking back to Holloway Road tube station, a fellow journalist expressed his unease at what he called 'a stage-managed farewell'. 'What must have Guardiola felt when he saw that?' he asked. I didn't answer, but thought, 'Guardiola won't play him next Tuesday.' And he didn't. Henry all but vanished from the team that captured its second consecutive League title a few weeks later, signing off with a twelve-minute cameo on the very last day of the season, when Barça already led Valladolid by four goals to nil.

It's not just that Thierry, when he had been called upon, had been unable to contribute as much as Pedro or even the inconsistent Bojan, although his statistics for the 2009–10 season made for grim reading. In La Liga, he had scored a mere four goals, two of them headers, from a pitiful total of thirty-five attempts in twenty hours spent on the field. By comparison, Messi had registered 158 shots – and thirty-four goals – in just over twice as much time. Is it unfair to compare Henry's performance to that of a reigning *Ballon d'Or*? Perhaps – but only if one forgets that the Henry who was taken to the Camp Nou was not supposed to play second fiddle to anyone and that, in the end, he could not even command a spot in the third chair.

Catalonia – Spain – hadn't liked what it had seen at the Emirates. A *Madridista* friend called me to say that even supporters of Real had been shocked by Henry's very public love-in with the north London crowd, when no one could guess that Lionel Messi's genius would turn the second leg of this quarter-final into a mere exhibition. I thought of David Beckham earning another cheap cap as a substitute at Wembley a few months previously, and how uneasy I had felt at his soaking in the fans' adulation after the final whistle, clapping in that desultory fashion footballers have made their own. 'I love you,' he meant to say to these tens of thousands of people who, had they turned up at Milan's training ground, would have been turned away by security guards. Liberace at Las Vegas. What kind of love is that?

There is no reason to disbelieve the sincerity of a Beckham or an Henry. Their remoteness, their egotism, their pursuit of wealth and power, fanned by hangers-on and starfuckers, would be as devoid of sense and purpose as the screams of a madman in an empty room were it not for that essential truth: they never stopped caring – they just lost all sense of proportion. Imagine an airbrushed picture of yourself blown up to cover the whole side of a skyscraper on Madison Avenue. Imagine coming home to find one of your gophers sifting through a six-foot-high pile of fan mail (as I saw Cristiano Ronaldo's brother-in-law do at the Manchester United striker's home in Alderley Edge). Imagine how tall you would feel then (as tall as a tower block in New York must be the answer). And imagine what it must be like when, knowing the end credits are about to roll, you step on stage for the last time, as Thierry did at the Emirates. 'Henry is an entertainer,' George Best had told me. Like all true entertainers, he milked it for what it was worth, and more.

We – that is, my *France Football* colleagues and myself – had been convinced for some time that Henry, whose contract had another year to run, would not remain at Barcelona beyond the end of the 2009–10 season. As early as December 2009, persistent rumours had reached us that a gentleman's agreement had been found between the player and the New York Red Bulls, one of the more glamorous sides in American Major League Soccer, for which Thierry's former France teammate Youri Djorkaeff had played with great distinction in 2005 and 2006. The captain of the 1990 German world champions, Lothar Matthäus, had also worn that jersey but left few lasting memories when his cameo came to an end. In fact, Djorkaeff himself told *L'Équipe Magazine* in May 2010 that he had been coopted by the ambitious New York club to establish contact with Henry's adviser (in all likelihood Darren Dein) in the early autumn of the previous year. It had since become one of the worst-kept secrets in world football. As long as Barcelona agreed to cut their losses and waive a transfer fee, Henry would become MLS's second truly global star, in rank as well as in order of appearance – second to David Beckham, of course. The financial situation of the Catalan club was not as healthy as might have been assumed from its recent results on the field; laden with structural debts which, shortly before the June election, presidential candidate Sandro Rosell said amounted to €489 million, Barcelona had spent lavishly nonetheless, and were intent on continuing to do so. One year after Zlatan Ibrahimović had been purchased for €49 million (plus Samuel Eto'o, an outstanding candidate for the title of 'worst transfer operation in the history of football'), David Villa was prised from Valencia for €40 million, with Cesc Fábregas said to follow shortly for an even greater sum. According to the Catalan magazine *Sport*, Henry commanded a £6.8 million annual salary – plus bonuses – which was inferior only to that of Messi and Ibrahimović's; to let him go for nothing made sense in economical terms as well.

American media (at least those who could be bothered with soccer) assumed that the deal was all but done, as they showed when they asked Sir Alex Ferguson about the Frenchman whilst the Manchester United manager was promoting a forthcoming pre-season tour in May. Ferguson's answer was polite – up to a point. 'He may not have the blistering speed of five years ago,' he said, 'but he would be a success here,' meaning 'in the USA', of course. But if not America? A return to England, still an alternative not that long ago, could be dismissed out of hand – or so we thought. West Ham's co-owner David Sullivan invited ridicule, not for the first time it must be said, when he announced that he had made a bid for Henry towards the end of the 2009–10 season. This 'bid' amounted to nothing more than an embar-rassing attempt at regaining the favour of fans who had been shocked by the dismissal of Gianfranco Zola from his managerial post a few weeks previously and was greeted with the derision it deserved. Thierry's answer to Sullivan's proposal was never made public, not that it needed to be.

The Bulls – well, that was a different story altogether. Austrian billionaire Dietrich Mateschitz hadn't made his fortune by flogging smut and pornography to the British working class as Sullivan had done via publications such as the *Daily Sport* and VHS cassettes of his wife-to-be Eve Vorley. Together with his Thai business partner Chaleo Yoovidhya, Mateschitz had built one of the biggest soft-drink companies in the world, and invested over £200 million in a new stadium for the New York club. He was understandably keen to fill it, not that easy a task when your star player, Colombian striker Juan Pablo Angel, late of Aston Villa, was fast approaching his thirty-fifth birthday. And as we have seen already, Thierry loved New York. He had loved New York for a long time. This is what he had said in June 2000: 'I love concrete. I love the idea of a city that never sleeps. I love being there, in the heart of the city, even if I have nothing to do. Because something always happens in the big cities . . . I enjoy simple pleasures: sit in a café, watch people go by . . . I went to New York last summer. There is no night, no day-time, everybody lives all of the time.'

He even had friends there, as we have seen. On his return from the trip to visit NBA star Tony Parker, back in 2003, Henry had told *GQ* magazine: 'Everything is attracting me to America . . . I know I'll end up there.' Director Spike Lee and rapper Jay-Z, whom he had met in February 2004 at the Madison Square Garden, were also 'friends' of his. New York was covered in snow then, but Thierry 'felt fine in [his] forest of skyscrapers'.

The Barcelona reject had more pressing matters to attend to before he could lose himself in his New York dreamscape, starting with his uneasy position within the French national team. How uneasy it was was demonstrated in the lead-up to the South African World Cup, when Raymond Domenech chose to play Henry from the bench in France's warm-up games against Costa Rica and Tunisia, in which the hitherto 'captain for life' was a mere passenger. In the first of these two encounters, in which *Les Bleus* actually showed a surprising degree of enterprise and imagination, the armband had been given to Patrice Évra – who had kept it on when Thierry entered the fray in the second half. Domenech poo-poohed the idea that this was proof of Henry's declining status within the squad. But more people would have been inclined to take the manager at his word if a French TV network hadn't found out that he had visited Thierry in Barcelona shortly before this game, in order to strike a deal that would preserve both men's self-regard and ambitions. True to his obsession with secrecy, Domenech denied it had been the case, only for Henry to confirm, a week before the start of the tournament, that, 'Yes, the coach has come to see me, and told me I wouldn't be in the starting eleven at the World Cup.'

The agreement gave Thierry a chance to exit the international stage in as dignified a manner as possible. Domenech had decided to redeploy his team in a 4-3-3 formation* that he had hardly ever put to the test before. In theory, this bold system would have suited Henry perfectly, so much so that it was widely believed that the striker had lobbied the French management to implement this tactical change. Standing at the tip of an attacking trident, Thierry would have been able to exploit his undiminished technical abilities with greater effect than on the left side of a 4-2-3-1 set-up, in which he expended too much of his declining energy covering one of the game's more enterprising full-backs, Patrice Évra. But when France finally adopted their new formation, in that 2-1 win over Costa Rica, it was Nicolas Anelka, not Thierry Henry, who found himself in the position of a number nine. Some were surprised and interpreted this as a snub; but not Thierry, who had been forewarned by Domenech. He had been told that his role would be that of what the French call *un joker*, a luxury substitute, and that, should he refuse to play that role, he wouldn't be part of France's final squad. Domenech held the stronger hand by far, as he could play the card that would earn Henry another line in football's history, one that the player was desperate to add to his own, as no French player had ever featured in four World Cups. In fact, only one outfield player had taken part in five: the German Lothar Matthäus, who finished his career as a *libero*, of course. Only four footballers who could be categorized as strikers had achieved this remarkable quadruple of appearances: Pelé, Uwe Seeler, Diego Maradona and (one for the quizmasters) Saudi centre-forward Sami Al-Jaber.[†] I'm sure that Thierry would have been able to reel off the names on that list, just as I'm sure he couldn't possibly wave away the chance to add his own to it.

---

* Domenech, who favoured a 3-5-2 formation when he was in charge of the under-21s, had used the following set-ups in the seventy-six games he had taken care of before the 2010 World Cup (by order of frequency): 4-2-3-1 (31 matches): 17 wins (55%) / 10 draws (32%) / 4 defeats (13%): 1.97 pts/match; 4-4-2 (28 matches): 14 wins (50%) / 8 draws (29%) / 6 defeats (21%): 1.79 pts/match; 4-3-1-2 (9 matches): 7 wins (78%) / 1 draw (11%) / 1 defeat (11%): 2.45 pts/match; 4-3-3 (6 matches): 3 wins (50%) / 2 draws (33%) / 1 defeat (17%) : 1.83 pts/match; 3-5-2 (2 matches): 0 win (0%) / 2 draws (100%) / 0 defeat (0%): 1 pt/match.
† The Brazilian Ronaldo would have been on that list had he left the bench in the 1994 tournament.

Domenech's decision was prompted, as ever, by expediency, political nous and a measure of sporting logic; to which I'm tempted to add: as was Henry's. The destiny of both men had been closely entwined since 1998, when the up-and-coming coach had defended the player's cause within the French camp as forcefully – and skilfully – as he could, something Thierry never forgot. It was fitting that the last act in Domenech's chaotic reign should coincide with Henry's swansong. It should also be said that the agreement made sense in pure footballing terms. Short of match fitness as Henry undoubtedly was (through no fault of his own), he remained a potent presence in front of goal, a vastly experienced international whose knowledge of France's future opponents was unequalled in the French camp. That quality alone made dispensing with his services a risk that Domenech was not willing to take, notwithstanding the controversy that would have certainly erupted if Henry had been left behind. Thierry accepted his de facto demotion with good grace, at least in public. 'Je me mets minable pour l'équipe,' he said, which can roughly be translated as: 'I sacrifice myself for the team,' or even 'I'm willing to grind myself into the dust for the team.' Long-time observers of Henry had their doubts about the sincerity of that statement; the two-faced 'manipulator' wished to show his best profile in the most flattering of lights, once again. This seemed harsh to me. Of course, there was an element of calculation in Thierry's stance; but, as Jacques Crevoisier and Gilles Grimandi reminded me at the time, he was also a very rare beast: a footballer who could evaluate his own performances – and physical condition – with as much objectivity (and in deeper detail) than any of his coaches. He'd lost speed? He knew it. He couldn't launch his runs with the same frequency as before? He knew it. Anelka could – just possibly – offer more playing with his back to goal? He knew that too, as he knew that a successful team is more often than not a blend of the older and the new. By his own admission, back in 1998, he and David Trezeguet hadn't felt 'pressure' when their turn had come to take centre stage during the penalty shoot-out against Italy. Twelve years later, *Les Bleus* needed fresher blood, players who ignored fear – but who would benefit from the guidance of those who had been the young, three World Cups earlier. Thierry could be that guide and accepted the role.

True, a part-time role in France's campaign might benefit him in more ways than one. It would distance him from the reviled Domenech. His humility would wrong-foot a number of critics. In the stands of the Felix Bollaert Stadium, where France had taken on Costa Rica, he had heard his name sung in the stands with genuine affection. The sight of Henry warming up on the touchline whilst his younger teammates were playing against Mexico and Uruguay in South Africa would lead many to wonder whether they had misjudged him after all. And, regardless of the furore that had followed the 'Hand of Gaul' incident, Thierry's popularity remained high within that part of the French population (the overwhelming majority) for which football was something that only mattered when young men in blue battled in an international tournament and barely registered otherwise. In January of that year, pollsters from the KantarSport institute had found that Henry scored a remarkably high 47.3 per cent on their popularity index, ahead of Franck Ribéry and, surprisingly, David Trezeguet. Bruno Lalande, the head of that institute, argued that his findings could be explained by Henry's 'media ubiquity', which had turned him into a 'true celebrity icon'. It would be easier to protect this 'ubiquity' by being present at the World Cup, even with a walk-on role, wouldn't it? However, when RTL, one of France's most popular radio stations, asked its listeners what would be their French 'Fantasy eleven' in the World Cup, they ignored Henry altogether and placed Karim Benzema at the apex of France's attack. Benzema had been left out of Domenech's longlist of thirty players, of course. Make of that what you will.

The French team had retired to a five-star fortress on the shores of the Indian Ocean, the Peluza Hotel in Knysna, which was only accessible if you could get hold of a boat or show the proper identification documents to the policemen manning a roadblock on the one road leading to the luxurious compound. Henry kept as low a profile as possible, which, given the scant access the media were granted, meant he was invisible. Unverifiable – but persistent – rumours soon circulated of a 'breakdown' between France's new playmaker, the introverted Yoann Gourcuff, and disgruntled old hands, of which Thierry was said to be one, and Franck Ribéry another. Not that it mattered much: when

Patrice Évra had been given the armband against Costa Rica, *France Football* ran the headline: 'A true captain, at last' on its front page. Henry, the most successful French player in history (a tag that only seems to acquire value when you repeat it time and time again), had mutated from cosmopolitan record-breaker to some sort of pipe-and-slippers grandad within the course of a single year. This is not to say that he was resigned to his fate.

Despite Domenech's best efforts to keep the media at bay (some of which verged on the ridiculous),* every day *L'Équipe* and other publications painted a disquieting picture of what was happening behind the ramparts of France's fortress. Henry could no longer consider himself the leader of *Les Bleus* but could place himself in the slipstream of those who had taken on that role, namely Ribéry, Évra, Abidal, Gallas and, up to a point, Anelka. So he did. As in 2002 and 2006, small self-appointed committees met in private to discuss the team's performance and the options at their disposal. Domenech was lobbied to replace Gourcuff with the more defensive-minded Diaby on the right side of midfield. That proposal could be defended in tactical terms, but also hinted at racial faultlines within a squad in which players of West Indian and African origin outnumbered Caucasians by two to one. The 'sacred union' of *blacks, bleus et beurs* that had so captured France's imagination in 1998 belonged, alas, to history – or, for the more cynically minded, was shown *a posteriori* to have been a fantasy. Other players favoured reinstating Thierry in the starting eleven and deploying Anelka on the right, in a position similar to that which he occupied at Chelsea. In truth, the subject of these conversations mattered less than what they revealed of the deleterious atmosphere within the camp, and of the dire consequences any slip-up in France's opening game – against Uruguay

---

* Batches of journalists were shuttled to and from the hotel in blacked-out vans, accompanied by armed guards, and photographers were prevented from placing themselves less than a full fifty yards from the training pitch on the rare occasions when they could enter the compound. The local population was denied any access to the players, which contrasted with the relaxed attitude of the Danish team, also based in Knysna, and whose training sessions were sometimes attended by over 8,000 people.

– would have on the team's chances. A number of people might press the self-destruct button. In the end, despite a desperately disappointing draw in which Thierry featured for less than twenty minutes (when the *Celeste* had been reduced to ten men), and could – maybe – have earned a throroughly undeserved penalty when his volley crashed against a Uruguayan arm in the box (the source of much merriment in Ireland), the 0-0 scoreline – a repeat of the encounter between these two teams in the 2002 World Cup – came as something of a relief. At least we hadn't lost.

Back home, the mood was sombre; defeatist, even. Sixty per cent of *L'Équipe* readers believed that Uruguay, Mexico and South Africa stood a better chance of qualifying than France. It hadn't helped that the pre-tournament preparation in Tignes (a ski resort in the Alps), Tunisia and the island of the Réunion had been marked by a series of bizarre incidents: Lassana Diarra's unexpected withdrawal from the squad, due to an obscure medical condition that got tongues wagging in the game; William Gallas's comical crash in a dune-buggy race; Nicolas Anelka falling from his mountain bike in another of Domenech's stranger attempts at team-bonding. It didn't get much better once the team reached its base in Knysna. Sports Minister Rama Yade castigated the FFF for housing squad and delegation in one of South Africa's most palatial (and most expensive) hotels; on the eve of the opening match against Uruguay, the news filtered out that the same FFF had chartered a private plane for the players' wives and girlfriends so that they could be in the Green Point Stadium on 11 June, at a cost of £220,000; and so on. The numerous sponsors of *Les Bleus* did all they could to drum up support in the French public, but in vain. As Arsène Wenger remarked, whilst it seemed that every other white van and black cab was adorned with the flag of St George in London, the tricolour was noticeable by its complete absence from Paris streets. It was yet another sign that France had fallen out of love with its team on that shameful night in Saint-Denis; every setback was and would be perceived as deserved retribution for cheating Ireland out of a place in the World Cup. And to many, including myself, it was fitting that the team that would avenge the Irish also wore green jerseys: Mexico, who, on a chilly night in Polokwane, beat France for the first time in their history and all but guaranteed that *Les Bleus* would leave the World Cup in humiliating fashion, as in 2002, and as they had exited the European Championships of 2008, having shown nothing that resembled courage, skill or organization.

There is no need to give you a translation of *L'Équipe*'s headline of 18 June: *LES IMPOSTEURS*. A photograph of Franck Ribéry tangling with Mexican striker Guillermo Franco was accompanied by a scathing editorial, in which Fabrice Jouhaud exhorted his readers to laugh at Domenech's pitiful crew. No sadness should be felt, he said, no tears should be shed. The 'imposters' didn't deserve them. They didn't care – why should we care about them? In England, a reporter from the *Times* found a new way to cook an old chestnut when he remarked that if there was no 'I' in 'team', there was certainly one in *équipe*. In France, it was thought there were eleven, or even thirteen, as Gignac and Valbuena were introduced to replace the hapless Anelka and Govou in the second half. With the honourable exception of Florent Malouda, goalkeeper Hugo Lloris and possibly Patrice Évra, so overwhelmed by being given the captain's armband that he could not hold back the tears when 'La Marseillaise' soared above the vuvuzelas in the stadium, it was a case of every man for himself, with Ribéry – the man many had speculated was involved in plotting Yoann Gourcutt's removal from the starting eleven – multiplying brainless dribbles and impaling himself on Mexico's lightweight but well-organized defence, as if deliverance could only come from him alone. Anelka's shocking performance should have warranted a 123rd cap for Thierry as a substitute, but the call never came. France's record goalscorer hardly bothered to warm up on the touchline and watched impassively as André-Pierre Gignac (four goals in seventeen matches for France, eight in thirty-one for Toulouse in the 2009–10 Ligue 1 season) was brought on at half-time to replace the Chelsea striker, who, we would soon learn, had spoken to his manager in the crudest terms imaginable in the interval. From time to time, the cameras would cut to Henry, arms folded on his knees under a chequed blanket, his face almost invisible under a wooly hat; the bench might as well have been a bath chair wheeled to a deserted beach. The look on his face was not one of bewilderment, but of barely disguised boredom.

He had seen it all before, and so had we. Or so we thought, until 19 June, when *L'Équipe*, again, broke with over a century of tradition to print in huge block letters the following words on its front page: 'GO GET FUCKED UP THE ARSE, YOU DIRTY SON OF A WHORE'.*

The players were already caught in a bubble created as much by themselves as by the FFF aparatchiks who looked after their every need. Their paranoia was increased by the knowledge that a 'mole' had betrayed Anelka to *L'Équipe*. At the breakfast table on the morning of 19 June the main topic of conversation had been the identity of the 'submarine' who had infiltrated their ranks. A member of staff? An agent? A team-mate? Instructions were passed on by the team's big swinging dicks not to phone or send text messages to friends, family members and personal advisers. As was obvious from what Patrice Évra said later that same day, in an unedifying press conference staged by the panic-stricken management of *Les Bleus*, the incident itself came a distant second in the players' preoccupations, a long way behind this unanswered question: who had broken the *omertà*? Who could you trust? No one.

French radio station RTL had already broken the news that Anelka – who had refused to apologize to his manager – would be sent back as soon as he could be given a business-class ticket to his favoured destination. The Chelsea striker finally landed at Heathrow in the early hours of Monday morning, sunglasses and hoodie on, smiling like a naughty schoolboy at the paparazzi. He had spent an inordinately long time (over one hour) bidding farewell to his teammates, which told the most alert of the FFF staff that something was afoot. But what? Unbeknown to them, and despite a number of conversations that took place between management and players on the Saturday afternoon, senior members of the squad consulted their lawyers to compose a long-winded statement in which they sided unequivocally and 'unanimously' with the disgraced striker. Hubert Monteil, an FFF official who saw the text, commented: 'I don't think the players wrote it themselves. It was

---

* *L'Équipe* had got carried away – but only just. Anelka's words had been: 'Go and get yourself fucked up the arse, you and your "tactics",' which I must say pretty much summed up what most French people felt about the manager of their national football team at the time.

printed from a computer, and there wasn't a single spelling mistake.' Monteil, in case you were wondering, didn't intend to be humorous: in Knysna, there was much to laugh 'at', not 'about'. The decision not to attend the next day's training was taken there and then. A genuinely contrite Florent Malouda later told me that, 'We wanted to express that we'd had enough . . . we didn't inform the staff of our decision, because we wanted to make something surprising and spectacular of our strike.' They certainly didn't fail in that respect.

The 'strike' – which, in truth, amounted to nothing more than a symbolic downing of tools in a Sunday-morning training session – was played out in full sight of the cameras, on one of the few occasions when they had been allowed on the 'Field of Dreams', around which a few hundred children from the area were also gathered. Ribéry and Évra signed a few autographs for them before getting on with the serious business of not playing. Yes, the 'Field of Dreams': such was the name of the pitch on which Évra and fitness coach Robert Duverne were close to coming to blows after the team's intentions had been made clear to the management. The new captain strongly denied that their altercation was caused by the conviction that Duverne, who later rejoined his former Lyon manager Gérard Houllier at Aston Villa, had been the 'traitor' he and his teammates were obsessed with. This 'traitor' was never properly identified, in fact, and people were left with their suspicions, which pointed in more directions than one. It is far likelier that Duverne, who was seen hurling his accreditation badge (some say his stopwatch, others his whistle) to the ground in disgust, had been so appalled by the players' refusal to train that he had made his feelings clear to Évra. He and goalkeeping coach Bruno Martini were later seen in tears, hidden behind a lorry, a few paces away from the bus where the mutineers had barricaded themselves (and on whose sides this slogan could be read: '*all together towards a new blue dream*').

The scene veered towards the surreal. The FFF chairman, seventy-five-year-old Jean-Pierre Escalettes, sporting a ridiculous-looking coaching tracksuit, boarded the bus – to be confronted with stony-faced players who withstood his gaze and didn't utter a single word. Domenech too – who had been heard shouting 'Wait! Wait!' to what weren't 'his' players any more, and hadn't been for some considerable time – failed to engage them in anything resembling a conversation. Soon afterwards, shouts and screams could be heard from outside the vehicle. Some players banged their fists on the smoked windows, ordering their driver to pull away immediately. The farce lasted for half an hour, after which the 'bus of shame', escorted by four police cars, finally left the Field of Dreams for the Peluza Resort Hotel. It was left to an ashen-faced Domenech (who later explained that he had agreed to act as the spokesman of the rebels 'out of a sense of duty', believe it or not, when the French press officer François Manardo had refused to do so) to confront the media and read what follows from a crumpled sheet of A4 paper:

All the players of the équipe de France, *without exception, state their opposition to the decision taken by the FFF to exclude Anelka solely on the basis of facts reported by the press. Consequently, and to mark their opposition to the attitude of the highest authorities, [they have decided] not to take part in the session programmed for today.*

'Without exception' – very few observers of *Les Bleus* heard those two words without raising an eyebrow. Within hours of Domenech's humiliating performance as a loudspeaker for players who despised him, in which it was France itself that was humiliated in the eyes of the outside world, the football equivalent of the bush telegraph was alive with rumours that were founded on what had been known for a while as much as on what had just been revealed. That very same morning, a tearful Ribéry had invited himself 'spontaneously' on *Telefoot*, France's most popular, and populist, football programme, broadcasting live and exclusive from South Africa, to deny that he had schemed against Yoann Gourcuff, almost breaking down completely when he voiced his admiration of, and affection for, a player that everyone within the game knew he saw as his most dangerous rival and who had been the butt of his practical jokes ever since the two men had been part of the national team. In a World Cup campaign scarred by internecine conflicts, smears and politicking of the most squalid kind, the timing of Ribéry's *cri du cœur* had an unsurpassed nauseating quality. Gourcuff, whom Henry had spoken of before the tournament as '*la nouvelle star*' as if it were a derogatory phrase, was as introverted as he was handsome, a dangerous combination in the macho world of football.

'Without exception' – really? A number of the younger players had been pressured into putting their names down on the riot act, the consequences of which they couldn't fathom, all the more so since nothing in what they had experienced in their careers so far could have prepared them for such an event. You went along with your elders, you knew your place, you manoeuvred to find a cosier one – fine. But what to do when you, a mere mortal, have to stand up for yourself, and demigods are going mad? Djibril Cissé, in so many ways an archetypal 'bling' footballer, was seen drifting round the lounges of the Peluza, beside himself with – genuine – grief, apologizing to distraught FFF officials. Others – Hugo Lloris, Gaël Clichy, why not name them? – were soon identified as rebels *malgré moi*, who had stayed on the train hurtling to its destruction because they had been too scared to jump off it.

The 'clowns, cowards, hypocrites, bullshitters' of the French team (four epithets chosen at random in the list of *seventy-eight* featured in my editor Denis Chaumier's column on 22 June, the day South Africa put an end to the nightmare by kicking France out of the World Cup for good) hadn't got a clue of the impact that their behaviour was having on the French public. They had carried out their threat of a strike on television as much as on the Knysna training ground, unaware that, by doing so, they had hardened the conviction of many that what was unravelling before our disbelieving eyes was not just a once-great footballing side, but a whole age, in which reality was defined by representation, and human beings were reduced to mere ciphers, all substance drained from them, puppets dangling on a broken string.

This very public meltdown of the national team became an affair of state in France, which should have alerted commentators that this was not only about football; in fact, it had little to do with football, or even Anelka's appalling language, Domenech's laughable self-regard and incompetence and some of the so-called 'senior players' using *Les Bleus* as a means to their personal ends, scheming, plotting, disgracing themselves whilst pretending they were rebelling against the 'system'. It had to do with a fractured society, ridden with post-colonial guilt and neuroses, which had desperately wanted to believe in the 1998 *black-blanc-beur* utopia and was now forced to smell its own shit. This is what was said then, everywhere. This is what is still said now: we, the French, had been cheated by a crew of young men from the *banlieue* who constantly spoke about 'respect' and gave it to no one but themselves. Who valued nothing but diamond earrings, big wheels, easy girls, or girls who were easy enough once they had been paid; who didn't sing the 'Marseillaise' and could only think with two parts of their body: their feet and their prick. A friend called me after South Africa's victory in Bloemfontein, whom I told that – maybe – it would be for the best. Laurent Blanc would step in. He would find a team in ruins, yes. But he would be given the time to build something new, to identify the right players, the next leaders, and . . .

He interrupted me. 'Don't fool yourself,' he said, 'the next generation is even worse: *la racaille.*' *Racaille* – the awful word that Nicolas Sarkozy had used to describe the feral youths of *la banlieue*, a hyperbolic version of 'riff-raff', the dregs of society that should be 'washed away with a Kärcher', as the then Home Affairs Secretary had said. And, to my disgust, I found a part of myself agreeing with him.

Disgust. With the overpaid starlets, with the clown Raymond, with the fat panjandrums of the FFF. Disgust with ourselves for having let the whole lot get away with it for so long, supporting them, even, when it was plain to see that they were not *us*. What this 'us' means was hard to articulate. Our recent history is such a mess. Why did Zidane, the son of Kabyle immigrants, become a national icon? Was that our penance for the atrocities of the Algerian war of independence? Partly, yes. A British reader will struggle to understand why our reaction to the tragicomedy of Knysna was so violent, just as he will struggle to understand that the death throes of our immense and largely barren empire were the convulsions of a civil war, not the retching of a body trying to get rid of a virus. Zizou hadn't been penance, he had been hope, and so had Titi. And that hope was now shown in its true colours, which certainly weren't blue, white and red, unless it was accepted that our flag had been soiled and torn to shreds.

What exactly constitutes 'national identity', when what is meant by 'nation' is often unclear? Danes might say that it has to do with their language, which barely anyone speaks beyond their borders, and an atavistic detestation of anything Swedish. Britons will struggle to come up with an answer, preferring to define themselve as English, Scots, Welsh and Ulstermen, if not geordies, tykes or scousers. Spaniards will probably argue that they are a collection of nations in any case. France, however, is different from most European countries in that it was one of the very first to embrace the idea of nationhood as we now try to understand it, and could even be said to have invented it in its modern guise; and this, despite the remarkably heterogeneous nature of its population. The Massilia of the Greeks was no different from the Marseilles of today in that it funnelled immigrants from the whole of the Mediterranean basin long before anyone had thought of a word such as 'muticulturalism', which wouldn't have meant anything in the classical world anyway. In 1790, the golden year of the Revolution, when it really seemed that life – not just society, or the political system – could be reinvented, this concept, 'nation', became synonymous with France itself. But, as many foreign travellers remarked at the time, the *tricolore* was not the only flag displayed above the secular altars of the Republic; they noticed how the Union flag and of the Stars and Stripes featured in those manifestations of patriotism; this was a salute not just to the support of pre-eminent Englishmen and Americans such as Fox and Franklin, but to the essential brotherhood of man. There was, from its inception, an element of supranationality in the French idea of nationhood as defended by the constitutional monarchy, then by the Republic. 'Foreign' volunteers joined 'French' ones on the battlefields of Valmy and Jemappes, where one of their most brilliant officers was the future Maréchal de France Jacques Macdonald, whose Jacobite parents hailed from South Uist, in the Scottish Hebrides. Jean-Paul Marat, one of the chief ideologues of the Paris Commune of that era, was of Italian extraction, and had been born in the then-Prussian district of Neufchâtel. Jean-Jacques Rousseau, the idol of the sans-culottes, was Swiss, of course. Going back four generations in my own family, I find ancestors from Normandy, the Auvergne, Provence and Scotland, many of whom later scattered throughout the colonies (where, not so incidentally, they mixed with the natives to a degree unknown in any other imperial culture). In this I am a typical Frenchman. In other words, the notion of ethnic homogeneity has no place in any discussion about French identity, historically or otherwise – whatever Jean-Marie Le Pen might have to say about it. French football has in fact long turned its back on xenophobia and racism, without fuss or undue soul-searching, truthful to an idea of national identity which is genuinely inclusive and in which the fathers of the Republic could have found an echo of their own aspirations. In that, Knysna was a crime, a negation of what French football has stood for since the days of Raoul Diagne. It is a story that deserves to be told at this point, as it isn't that well known outside of France, and almost forgotten within. It is a story to which the South African debacle added a bitter postscript, tarnishing Henry's image beyond repair in the country of his birth.

Diagne played the first of his eighteen games for France on 15 February 1931, in a friendly against Czechoslovakia, a game the French lost 1-2 on a late penalty kick. That he had been picked when his twenty-first birthday was still eight months away was not a surprise to anyone. 'The Spider', as he was nicknamed (because of his remarkably long legs), was already considered one of his country's most reliable – and dangerous – full-backs. He would often swap positions with his left- or right-winger towards the end of tight games for his club Racing, when his physical presence (he was 6 feet 1 inch tall, a giant by the standards of that time) could create havoc in the opposition camp. In truth, the most remarkable thing about Diagne was that his presence among the eleven *Bleus* on that winter day was not remarked upon.

Because Diagne was black, the very first player of African origin to represent a then colonial power at international level. The lack of hostility he encountered from football crowds or the press might surprise students of French history, who will be aware of the emergence of far-right groups there in the late 1920s and early 1930s, when many war veterans, disgusted by the (very real) corruption of their elected representatives, yearned for a 'strong man' and looked up to Benito Mussolini as a kind of hero. But this should give us a clue to understanding what happened, or, more pointedly, what didn't happen then, and to what is happening now. No bananas were thrown on the pitch of the Stade de Colombes. No columnists lamented the dilution of good, sound French blood.

Prejudice is not quite the same thing as racism. One is based on unfamiliarity and ignorance, both of which co-existence and the passage of time can cure; the other on instinctive, irrational fear and irrevocable hatred. The France of that time was undoubtedly prejudiced. But racist? I don't think so.

Only three years before Diagne's first call-up, Jack Leslie, the London-born Plymouth Argyle inside-left, had been told he would play for England – that is, until the board of selectors realized that the handsome, swarthy youth's father was Jamaican. The invitation was swiftly withdrawn. England would have to wait half a century, until 1978, for a black man to wear the national jersey, and we all know how much was made of Viv Anderson's debut. By contrast, in 1986, *L'Équipe* came up with a remarkable statistic, one which is unique in Europe, I believe: 200 of the 600 players who had worn the French jersey since we played our very first international, a 3-3 draw against Belgium in 1904, had been of 'foreign' origin. Most of them hailed from the colonies or had fled persecution: Spanish Republicans, Italian anti-fascists, Austrian and German Jews. French football never took players at face value.

This is why the almost universal opprobrium it suffered in the wake of the infamous 'quotas' affair hurt so many, and so much. Indeed, France's indifference to the national or ethnic origins of its representatives has been one of the major reasons why it has risen so high from inauspicious beginnings. I look at the team that lost, so narrowly, a World Cup quarter-final 1-3 against holders Italy in 1938. Diagne is there. So is Ben Bouali, an Algerian; Darui, from Luxembourg, who was voted 'French goalkeeper of the century' in 1999; Héctor Cazenave, the naturalized Uruguayan defender; 'Fred' Aston, Red Star's twinkle-toed winger, whose father was English; Di Lorto, the son of Italian immigrants; Kowalczyk, the Pole; Povolny, born in Germany; Jordan, the Austrian refugee; Zatelli, another Italian, whose family had settled in North Africa and who would lead Olympique de Marseille to the League–Cup Double in 1972. Twenty years later, at the 1958 World Cup, in which France, in terms of the quality of its football, was only bettered by a magnificent Brazil, comprised three Poles, two Italians, one Ukrainian, one Spaniard and two North Africans, one of whom, Just Fontaine (born in Marrakech), still holds the record of the most goals (thirteen) scored in one single final phase of that competition: all foreigners, or men of foreign origin – that's the way 'communautarists' would describe them, anyway, because for us, they were French – the living, playing proof that 'Frenchness' doesn't equate with the stereotype of *berets*, *blanquette* and *baguettes*. Like Platini, Fernandez, Tigana, Thuram, Vieira and, today, Alou Diarra or Samir Nasri. Like Thierry Henry, our greatest-ever goalscorer.

The dream of a 'rainbow nation' that was born in the Stade de France in 1998 is not as hollow as the cynics would make it today. What should never be forgotten is that, had it not been for the remarkable way in which French football learnt, so early, to open itself to players of all origins, that dream would never have been dreamt. Until very recently, Ligue 1 was the only major championship in the world in which two of the country's top six clubs, Bordeaux and PSG, were managed by black men, Jean Tigana, born in Mali, and Antoine Kombouaré, a Kanak from New Caledonia. Like every other former imperial power, France is groping for a new sense of national identity. And in this, football is leading the way, in 2012 as in 1931, when a tall black man walked onto the pitch and sang the 'Marseillaise'.

That story, by the way, has an extraordinary ending. Raoul Diagne became the manager of Senegal after his father's country gained independence and, on 18 April 1963, his team beat a French amateur eleven in the final of the 'Games of Friendship'. He lived long enough to see the Teranga Lions emulate this feat on a far bigger stage, at the 2002 World Cup, before passing away at the age of ninety-two, in France. To the Senegalese, he is the 'grandfather' of their football. To me, he is also a Frenchman who took pride in representing my country, which was also his. Which is ours. Did the strikers of Knysna commit an act of betrayal? Yes – and one of its victims was Raoul Diagne.

One name has hardly been mentioned in these last few pages, that of Thierry Henry, and that is precisely why he will never be forgiven for what he did and, especially, what he didn't do when the foolishness of others gave him the chance to become a true hero. A few words from him would have swayed the indecisive; the team he had served magnificently for nearly thirteen years was crying out for a figure of authority such as the former French captain, a Vieira, a Deschamps, a Blanc, even a Zidane, who could seize the rebels by the collar and make them aware of the consequences that their shameful behaviour would have on their own careers – as it was clear that they had lost any sense, if only temporarily, of the duties attached to representing their country.

But Henry remained invisible and silent throughout. The FFF chairman Jean-Pierre Escalettes saw him sitting at the back of the 'bus of shame', as if he had been a mere passenger there, and felt an urge to walk up to him – but checked himself, fearing (or so he said) that it would make captain Patrice Évra 'look like a prick'. 'I wasn't good,' the septuagenerian confessed four months later, 'I was powerless.' It wasn't until the plane carrying the shamed team landed at Le Bourget airport that we finally heard Henry's voice, when he, very much like Ribéry had done before him, arranged to be interviewed on French national television on 25 June, in this case by the former PSG chairman Michel Denisot, now one of the best-known presenters on the Canal+ network. Once again, Thierry missed a beat, opening his defence by talking about the 'inventions' of 'people', speaking about France's debacle as if it had been nothing more than the consequence of a series of poor results, blown out of all proportion by the media. Despite the gentleness of the questioning, his answers sounded both banal and aggressive, as if he couldn't quite understand why he, the doyen of *Les Bleus*, could be associated with the greatest scandal in their entire history. There were flashes of frustration: 'I could have been the big brother [of this team], but . . . I wasn't any more. I felt as if I'd been set aside.' But by whom, by what? 'I wasn't spoken to as before. Everybody has their own reasons. And I don't want to go into details.' The details, of course, were precisely what people – the French people, not the 'people' Thierry felt had been after him for a long time – wanted to hear about. 'I felt I'd been set aside,' he reiterated, 'and [when that happens], a man's pride takes a knock.'

Henry sounded even less convincing when he tried to deny that there had been 'clans' within the French camp. 'Affinities', yes, as always. When Denisot teased him – gently – about the relationship between Gourcuff and Ribéry, he immediately looked for the exit door: 'I didn't see everything. When you go to your room to sleep . . .' Then, fixing Denisot with a far from friendly glare, he added: 'I didn't see any fight. I didn't see anyone applying pressure on anyone else.' Gourcuff became 'Yo', with a familiarity I couldn't help but feel was forced. And when the episode of the team bus was finally broached, Thierry said, again: 'I didn't see anyone applying pressure on anybody else.' Cut, back to the studio – and the PR exercise had turned into another disaster. I have yet to meet anyone who hadn't been shocked by Henry's desperately awkward performance. He sounded as if he had weighed his options until he had decided that he ought to do something. But for whom? Himself, and himself alone?

On the eve of this far-from-convincing exercise, Thierry had paid a grotesque visit to the Élysée palace to meet President Sarkozy, who had been so 'concerned' with the happenings in South Africa that he had taken time off from a summit with Russian Prime Minister Vladimir Putin in Moscow to let it be known that the French head of state wasn't amused. The footballer was whisked to the Champs-Élysées in a presidential car that picked him up on the tarmac of Le Bourget airport, after he had called De Gaulle's successor from South Africa, or so we were told. Remarkable: a ball-kicker could get the keeper of France's nuclear arsenal on the phone, just like that. Was it Henry (or his advisers) who thought it might be a good idea? Was it Sarkozy, the PR-obsessed politician, who felt he had to welcome France's star footballer in his office to keep 'in phase' with his disenchanted electorate? Over a hundred delegates from various NGOs who were supposed to meet the president at the time (11.00, 24 June) were shown the door in order to accommodate the former French captain and were requested to make do with the Secretary of State for Foreign Affairs instead. Quite understandably, to quote Richard Thompson, they 'took their business elsewhere'. What was said between Henry and Sarkozy never surfaced, despite the publicity given to their crisis talks. No cameras were allowed. No transcript of what must have been a fascinating conversation was passed on to the press. A parliamentary commission was put together for the sole purpose of holding an inquest on France's disgraceful failure at the World Cup. On it went, ridiculously so. Truly, France had had a breakdown.

*

I hadn't gone to the World Cup, hoping that I might get some rest from the longest-drawn-out season I had ever known. What happened is that, being one of the very few points of contact the British media had with the French left in London, I spent most of the second half of June trying to answer the same questions – what had *really* happened? And why? But no one could possibly know what had *really* happened, as Malouda agreed when we met in London, seven *France Football* readers in tow, five months after the Knysna implosion. There had to be as many real stories as there were participants in the whole sorry, *Rashomon*-like affair, save for the fact that the protagonists were not just three, but a whole squad, the French technical staff, the FA officials . . . we might as well add hundreds of journalists, and millions of fans who were watching the pantomime unfold live on their TV screens. The Chelsea winger had managed to come out of the whole shameful business, if not smelling of roses, at least not making you want to pinch your nose, something that couldn't be said of Franck Ribéry, for example. As soon as he had left South Africa – and perhaps even before that – Florent had put himself through a stringent *examen de conscience*, and found himself at fault on every count. He never sought to justify what he had done, least of all to himself; he repented publicly, answered all the questions that were put to him (including by his own mother, who was scandalized by her son's behaviour) with a willingness, candour and sincerity that contrasted with Henry's strangely defensive stance. As a result, when Laurent Blanc inherited Raymond Domenech's position, Malouda was seen, and rightfully so, as a leader-in-waiting, a man of moral rectitude who could be trusted to help rebuild the national team. Thierry? Thierry was crucified. Here is an excerpt of the editorial that French magazine *So Foot* opened its October 2010 edition with. Knysna hadn't been forgotten, or forgiven.

After a pathetic ending to his career in blue (the hand of Judas, the bus of shame, the teacher's pet visit to 'Sarko'), Thierry Henry thought he could acquire a new virginity by exiling himself in New York. For him, the nights on the tiles with Tony Parker and Spike Lee and a choice place in that 'football history' that is so dear to him – like Best, Cruyff or Pelé before him, he was about to deflower the Americans. For the time being, it's a 'fiasco'. Worse than that! He buys himself a three-storey penthouse in the heart of SoHo and, bing!, here's the motherfucking nouveau riche, bling-bling, rotten and spoiled, who'd do better running on the field, etc., etc. For a small flat costing seven billion CFA francs, not more than that. That's for sure, Titi is in the media eye. The cost of an over-marketed career? Could Henry, the footballer-politician, calculating and cynical, be the victim of a deceitful curse? He now lives in the same block where the late Heath Ledger lived.

So Foot, in case you wondered, is not a fanzine published by the Thierry Henry hate club, but a glossy magazine that outsells all other football monthlies in France. The nasty, vicious tone of this assault on the country's most prolific striker had much to do with this publication's idiosyncratic approach to football writing, a sort of new-wave gonzoism that cherishes 'mavericks' and shoots on sight whoever is suspected of courting the establishment. But this piece also showed, in its very excess, how Henry's stock had fallen like BP's shares on Wall Street after the *Deepwater Horizon* oil spill. Thierry had become as easy to hate as he had been hard to love. The purpose of *So Foot* was not so much to provoke and shock than to be in tune with the vengeful mood of its readership. By forcing the trait in so outrageous a fashion, they positioned themselves as 'opinion leaders' – when, in fact, the medium had followed the mass.

Far more balanced writers who had kept their counsel until then, to protect the national team as well as the memories they cherished of a superb footballer, felt that a tipping point had been reached, and that they couldn't defend the indefensible any longer. What's more, Thierry had alienated many of those who wished him well by retreating ever further in his cocoon, refusing to talk to anyone but the sycophants of his 'closed circle', and making no effort to conceal his disdain for the caravan of beasts of burden that followed his every move. '*People*', as he called them, making that sound as if they were some form of pond life. The excessive, even hysterical tenor of Henry's lynching in the French media (and among 'ordinary' fans) makes no sense unless it is understood that, by cutting himself from the crowd as he did, Thierry fed the resentment of many, and not just in the press box. A number of perfectly reasonable commentators who, for years, had reminded themselves of the respect he was owed for his achievements on the field felt that they had been released from their duty to speak fairly of him. Tongues had been wagging in the background for a long time; now a chorus of damning voices erupted, enacting a catharsis that wasn't necessarily edifying when you took a closer look at it, but which was nonetheless understandable.

In the immediate aftermath of the World Cup fiasco, on 29 June 2010, my own paper, *France Football*, published a photographic montage of Henry's face projected onto a shattered mirror. This, it implied, was Thierry's true image. Trusted colleagues of mine, some of whom had known him since he had been fast-tracked into the French youth teams, now spoke of an 'insufferable man', who 'had it coming to him' and had antagonized nearly everybody by his two-faced behaviour. 'He talks to you about another player,' one of them told me, 'and he rubbishes him – too slow, too thick, etc. Then you switch the tape on, he says that the same guy is world-class. Once you leave the room, you think to yourself, "What has he said that I can believe?"' There was an awful circularity about this. Thierry had learnt early, too early without a doubt, that he could trust almost no one in the game. Since then – since others had tried to sell his pound of flesh to Real Madrid – he had denied himself the capacity to open up to others. It was a mechanism of self-defence that was perhaps the only way he could find to extricate himself from a 'game' he knew very little about at the time, except that he loved kicking a ball and was very good at talking about it; in which he deserved understanding and sympathy, as he had been the victim of a manipulation, not its instigator. But, as he matured, and success came to him, on a scale he could only have dreamt of, the tables turned; he wielded enough power now to do away with such artiness, just as he should have been intelligent and perceptive enough to realize that you don't really *choose* your friends; you have to gamble, be prepared to be stung at times – and be rewarded too. That this weighed on him I do not doubt for a second: Thierry Henry must have lived in a very lonely place for a very long time, constantly watching his back when he should have looked at what was in front of him. The adulation of the Arsenal fans meant all the more for him; it was easier to accept, and not just because it fed his self-esteem to a degree that would make any head spin. It was a faceless adulation. Seen from the pitch, as Lee Dixon once said when recalling a (very rare) goal he scored in front of the North Bank, the crowd is not a collection of individuals, each of them as different as a drop of water is from another one – what you perceive is just the wholeness of an ocean, from which you can't discern any constituent part. You just throw yourself into it, and it is a feeling close to ecstasy. Imagine being Thierry Henry, and living this every day of your working life.

In South Africa, however, this ocean was just a remote blue spot, lapping in memory only. When finally called upon to do what he could do best – and he could still do a lot, far more than what his critics asserted – in the fifty-fifth minute of a game France had already lost, Thierry tried everything to shake off the mood of powerlessness that had engulfed what remained of his team, which was very little. French supporters cheered South African goals on 22 June – to the extent that French radio station RMC, to this day, still plays its commentator's Jean Résséguié description of Florent Malouda's late, insignificant strike as a reminder of the depths we had sunk to. France lost 2-1 when only a win by a substantial margin would have given them a chance of stealing past Mexico and Uruguay for a place in the last sixteen. Alou Diarra – who had learnt that he had been chosen as captain from his agent, not from Domenech – passed on the armband to Thierry with less than ten minutes to play. Some way to celebrate your 123rd cap. One hundred and twenty-three caps: nineteen fewer than Lilian Thuram, the French record-holder, but enough to secure Thierry's place in the all-time top fifty of international players, where most spots had been claimed by players of lesser football nations anyway. On the field, including on that day, Henry hadn't failed his country.

Off it, it had been a different matter altogether. His fast-diminishing conga of supporters had an explanation at the ready: 'His head is somewhere else,' and had been since Raymond Domenech had told him that he would only take part in the fourth World Cup of his career if he accepted being demoted to the bench. Thierry also knew that the lack of first-team action with Barcelona had affected his physical fitness, something that was bound to have a more discernible effect on a player who had long relied on his 'explosiveness' more than on his technique to slip away from defenders. He had never been a 'dressing-room player', in the sense that taking on the role of mentor for a group didn't come naturally to him, as it comes far more easily to ageing defenders in any case (Arsenal fans might think of the impact Martin Keown never ceased to have despite being sidelined in his last couple of seasons at Highbury, for example). Henry, however, could be generous in his dealings with individuals. He tried to offer help to some of the younger members of the French team for a while, just as he had taken David Trezeguet under his wing when the Franco-Argentinian had found himself estranged in Monaco, and just as he had welcomed Robert Pirès – his elder by almost four years – in London in the months that followed his transfer to Arsenal. This is what Patrice Évra, another child of Les Ulis, had to say shortly before the World Cup, words laced with the kind of raw emotion that was to cost him so dear soon afterwards:

Titi is the guy I share a room with, someone who tells me a lot about himself, and to whom I tell a lot about myself as well. We're more like brothers. We tell each other what we think. If we have to have a 'clash', we have it. It's about frankness, always, and I like it. We grew up in the same street, but we didn't know each other when we were kids. We met in Italy, when he was at Juve and I was struggling in small clubs. We saw each other in Milan, and he told me: 'Ah – so you're the guy from Les Ulis that people keep talking to me about?' And we never left each other since. When I was at Monaco, still a relative unknown, he invited me to watch a game in London. I slept in his home, for the first time. I'd been really surprised by the way he welcomed me. I didn't think that a player of his calibre could be so friendly with me, with my wife . . . Titi is not someone who opens up easily to others. I don't know how we got close – but, there you are, he's my friend.

Thierry too had benefited from the protection and encouragement of a 'big brother' in the early stages of his career, literally so, as it was his own, Willy, who had made sure everything was fine for the little one. He knew as well as anyone that, should he assume this role, he could have a profound impact on a group of players that was in desperate need of a figure of benign authority. He was the last of the world champions, for goodness sake. He was the last chance, perhaps, that France had of regaining the *esprit de corps* that had led them to three World and European finals in eight years. But he felt humiliated by the deal he had struck with Domenech shortly before the 2010 tournament, and the persona of a benevolent, non-playing role model didn't match the sense he had of his own worth. Had he overcome this blow to his pride, Henry could have exited international football in the fashion his achievements deserved, and, perhaps, silenced those who doubted that he could ever be considered a true 'great' of the game. Players still listened to him. All he had to do was to walk out of a bus. But he stayed put, seemingly unconcerned. He remained true to the policy he had adopted two months beforehand: do what's asked of you, no more than that, shut up, and let them self-destruct if that's what they want to do. You'll have nothing to do with this mess any more, you won't be responsible for it. Except, of course, that was precisely the way to ensure that he would be found guilty by everyone but himself.

Postscript

Unmasked, unhinged, beautiful.

A CHILD AGAIN

The closing line of the previous chapter would have made an abrupt end to this book, but I had originally intended to keep it at that. I hoped it would convey how much I had struggled to reconcile myself with the picture I had painted of Thierry Henry, the selfless egotist, the insufferable charmer, a walking oxymoron in shorts. So why not end with what amounted to a question mark? To say I was satisfied with that would be wrong. In fact, I got so entangled in the pros and cons of adding the positive postscript that Thierry's achievements deserved that I was tempted to rewrite the whole narrative of the Knysna episode. Henry would appear in a more favourable light, and his behaviour in South Africa would not seem to cancel all that happened before – most of it glorious. His belated success in Major League Soccer appeared inconsequential in light of what had preceded his arrival in New York. Whichever way you looked at it, Thierry's life as a top-class athlete had ended on a catastrophic note in South Africa. His fifteen goals and five assists for the New York Red Bulls in 2011* could be treated as a footnote; at best, as the proof that he still cared enough about his profession to do his utmost in a mediocre competition. The last, bitter act had been played already.

---

* The first of these goals, scored against San Jose Earthquakes on 16 April 2011 (3-0), ended a 690-minute personal drought in MLS which had prompted pointed criticism from the club's fans and the American media. Thierry had an even more productive season in 2012, scoring nine in nine matches for the Red Bulls, including his first hat-trick for the New York-based team in a 5-2 win over Montreal Impact on 31 March 2012.

Except that, thank God, we were wrong to think it had been. Henry had been training with Arsenal from November 2011 onwards, keeping himself in shape during the MLS off-season and seizing the opportunity to spend time with the daughter he had missed so much. Many other players – including David Beckham – had enjoyed Arsène Wenger's hospitality at the London Colney training centre before, without being seriously linked with the club. Therefore, not too much should be seen in Thierry's reacquaintance with his former playground. Soon, however, rumours were filtering from Arsenal's base. Wenger had told close friends how impressed he had been with Thierry in training, by his dedication, which wasn't a surprise, but also by his fitness and his sharpness in front of goal, which was, given his age – thirty-four and counting – and how long it had been since he had taken part in a proper competitive game. What's more, the strikers who would normally have provided back-up for the on-fire Robin van Persie, that is Marouane Chamakh and Park-Choo-Young, had provided close to nothing since the beginning of the season and were not showing signs of improvement. On 6 January 2012, following weeks of speculation, Arsenal announced that their record goalscorer had rejoined them on a short-term loan that would expire on 17 February, on the resumption of the American season. 'I am not coming here to be a hero or prove anything,' Henry said. 'I am just coming here to help. People have to understand that. I'll be on the bench most of the time – if I can make the bench, that is.' As Theo Walcott had inherited the famous number fourteen shirt, Thierry was allocated the number twelve, which he had been associated with throughout his career with the French national team.

Questions were asked about the true motives behind that decision. Was it a commercial coup, a PR stunt, a means to placate the disgruntled supporters who had sung 'Sign him up! Sign him up!' when Henry's statue had been unveiled at the Emirates in December? Could it be a genuine attempt to rekindle the flame of old, at a time when Arsenal were going through another of their now customary blips? The team was lying fifth in the League table, having recovered from a dreadful start to the campaign, but still looked brittle and short on inspiration, over-reliant on their Dutch captain and mysteriously prone to injuries of all kinds. Three days before Thierry's return had been officially confirmed, having opened the scoring, they had conceded two goals in the last five minutes at Fulham to register their sixth defeat in twenty League matches. But we soon had an answer to all these questions, and it was Thierry himself who gave it on 9 January, on the first truly unforgettable night in the Emirates' brief history, the night on which the new stadium became Henry's garden, just like Highbury had been.

It was 'only' Leeds United, a big name, but a Championship team. It was 'only' the third round of the FA Cup. But it will live longer in the memory of all those who were there than the previous season's 2-1 victory over Barcelona in the Champions League which, until then, had been the sole occasion on which the arena had been brimming with a fervour reminiscent of the old stadium. Thierry played in six other games over the course of his brief swansong and distinguished himself in most of them, scoring a crucial winner at Sunderland, fighting like no other of his teammates seemed to be prepared to when they were swamped 4-0 by Milan at the San Siro on 15 February, his very last appearance for the Gunners. Two goals* in a mere 160 minutes on the pitch: that was as many as Chamakh and Park had scored together in their combined twenty-five appearances; in other words, more than a vindication: a triumph. Thierry looked heavier-set and had lost his lethal power to accelerate over the first five yards – and keep up his speed over the next fifty. He had 'muscled up', was the way one of Wenger's assistants put it to me, but the killer had lost none of his instinct, the finisher none of his technical brilliance.

Brought onto the field in the sixty-eighth minute, with Leeds defending stubbornly if causing little threat of their own, Thierry ambled along nicely enough, playing within himself, careful in possession, but economical in his movement. Then came the defining moment, not

---

* The FA's 'dubious goal committee' probably took one of its most muddle-headed decisions, and certainly the most unpopular, when, very late after the event, it chalked off Thierry's 'goal' in the 7-1 atomization of Blackburn on 4 February 2012 and attributed it to Scott Dann instead, when all the Rovers central defender had done was to help into his own net a shot that was hitting the target. Thierry's final record, the right word, therefore stands at 228 goals in 376 games for Arsenal, and not 229.

just of that match, but of his Arsenal career, of his life as a footballer. Leeds had conceded a couple of corners but were soaking up the pressure with relative ease. The young Catalan left-back Ignaci Miquel took a quick throw-in fifteen yards away from the left-side corner flag, exchanged passes with Henry before finding an advanced Alex Song in the middle of the pitch, a piledriver away from Andrew Lonergan's goal. But Song has never been the piledriving type. He spotted Thierry in space on the left wing; Thierry, who instantly sensed the run was on, peeled off his marker and raced into the box, forgotten by the Leeds defence. The Cameroonian's pass was exquisite, as was Henry's first touch with his right foot. In one movement, he pushed the ball forward, balanced himself and found the opposite corner of the net. It was not a Henry goal – it was *the* Henry goal, perfect in its execution as it was in its timing.

The noise level had risen around the stadium from the moment Thierry had received the ball, and I'll never forget this instant crescendo, which exploded into a *ffff* when he placed it unerringly in the sweet spot of the net, as he must have done thousands of times before in training. He owned that goal. He owned us. Glory of glories, we owned him. What a player. What a story. Writing your own is the privilege of truly exceptional sportsmen. Ian Botham had done it by taking a wicket with his very first ball on his return to Test cricket in August 1986, some of my English colleagues said then, but I disagreed. Thierry's goal demonstrated the same capacity to shape collective events into a personal destiny, true, but had a dimension which is essentially alien to cricket, where a game's pattern is determined by a succession of duels and where, crucially, celebration is a postscript to the event, not an inseparable part of it.

Henry ran to the bench and embraced Wenger; Wojcech Szczesny ran from his goal to embrace his striker; I jumped off my seat to embrace whoever was sitting next to me, a scene repeated all around the ground, even in the corporate boxes, where David Beckham was beaming. Thierry beat his chest, his fist hitting the cannon crest sewn onto his shirt, screaming, abandoning himself to joy as we had never seen him do before. It was a fan's goal, and he was the fan. In an instant, all was forgotten, all was remembered. Henry, the man who had won everything he could win, who had nothing left to prove to anyone, including his father and himself, had achieved the ultimate fantasy, to score the winning goal for the team he loved when no one thought he could be called upon, that too much time had passed, and passed him by. Call it redemption if you want; to us, Arsenal men and women, it was truth restored. All the masks Thierry had been wearing in the pursuit of success had been discarded. We smiled the same smile, at last, completely.

Twenty days later, Emmanuel Petit entered the Arsenal dressing-room after their 3-2 win over Aston Villa in the FA Cup fourth round. Most of the younger players had left already. Thierry, who had played only a few minutes, hadn't showered yet. Grass was still stuck to his boots, sweat clung to his body. An hour and a half after the final whistle, Arsenal's greatest striker was reliving the evening's game, hanging on to his every memory of it. He didn't want to go anywhere else, ever. Manu was shocked that the last man present would be his old teammate and told me so – twice: 'Who do they think they are?' he asked, speaking of Henry's departed team-mates. Perhaps they were too young, too rich, too soon, to understand what could make Thierry Henry savour the last drop in his glass as he did. The wheel had turned full circle. He was a child again. He was a man, no longer lonely at the top.

Acknowledgements

My thanks first go to all those who were actors in, or witnesses of, Henry's progress from his first steps as a footballer to the very top of the game, and who agreed to share their memories of the player and the man with me. This book owes them – ex-players, managers, coaches, colleagues – a great debt that I can't repay. But it owes even more to those who were constant supporters during the three years it took to write, starting with Natasha Martin and Jon Butler at Macmillan, and my friend Jonathan Harris. I shan't forget their kindness and their patience with me. Jonathan Wilson of *The Blizzard* and Paul Simpson of *Champions* generously allowed me to use excerpts of texts I wrote for their publications.

Thierry Henry himself, who was aware of my project and its unauthorized nature from the start, made no attempt to interfere with it or impair my research; not all public figures would have done the same. I'm grateful to him for that, as I am grateful to him, as all Arsenal fans are, for giving us so much joy over the years. It is that joy which should and will be remembered.